Women in World History

MERRY CHRISTMAS 2019

TO

DOROTHY

With Love from

David
xx

Women in World History

1450 to the Present

Bonnie G. Smith

BLOOMSBURY ACADEMIC
LONDON • NEW YORK • OXFORD • NEW DELHI • SYDNEY

BLOOMSBURY ACADEMIC
Bloomsbury Publishing Plc
50 Bedford Square, London, WC1B 3DP, UK
1385 Broadway, New York, NY 10018, USA

BLOOMSBURY, BLOOMSBURY ACADEMIC and the Diana logo are trademarks of
Bloomsbury Publishing Plc

First published in Great Britain 2020

Cover design by Adriana Brioso
Cover images: (top) Militia women, Mongolia, 1969 © Universal History
Archive/UIG; (bottom) National Women's Conference in Houston, USA, 1977
© Bettmann. (via Getty Images)

A catalogue record for this book is available from the British Library.

A catalog record for this book is available from the Library of Congress.

ISBN: HB: 978-1-47427-292-6
PB: 978-1-47427-293-3
ePDF: 978-1-47427-295-7
eBook: 978-1-47427-294-0

Typeset by Newgen KnowledgeWorks Pvt. Ltd., Chennai, India
Printed and bound in India

To find out more about our authors and books visit www.bloomsbury.com
and sign up for our newsletters.

CONTENTS

List of Figures vi

Introduction 1

1 Productive and Reproductive Lives, c. 1450–1600 11

2 Early Modern Structures of Power 37

3 Imagining Their World, 1450–1700 61

4 Productive Life across a Connected Globe, 1500–1750 85

5 Populations, Ideas, and the Industrious Revolution, 1600–1800 111

6 Revolts, Revolutions, and the Rise of New States, 1650–1830 135

7 Industrialization and Work in a Global Society, 1800–1914 159

8 The Lure of Modernity, 1830–1914 185

9 Expanding Empires, Resisting Empires, 1870–1914 209

10 Global Warfare, 1914–45 235

11 Creating New Nations, Decolonizing Women 259

12 Women's Globalization in a High-Tech Age 285

Acknowledgments 309
Index 311

FIGURES

1.1 Women celebrating in Mughal Court 17

1.2 Aztec education of boys and girls 19

1.3 African woman in childbirth, c. 1600 31

2.1 Hurrem/Roxelana 44

2.2 Devi Revered by Brahma, Vishnu, Shiva (1710) 53

3.1 Birth of Muhammad, in his mother's arms and visited by Meccans, c. 570–632 69

3.2 Japanese woman composing a song, c. 1700 77

4.1 Wife of a Native American chief and their daughter, 1590, John White 90

4.2 Queen Nzinga, using her servant as a chair, c. 1626 102

4.3 Our Lady of Guadalupe by a sixteenth-century artist 105

5.1 Two Chinese women at work weaving silk textile 116

5.2 Lady Mary Wortley Montagu, 18th century 126

6.1 Market women head for Versailles to capture the king and royal family, October 1789 144

6.2 Manuela Saenz, 1971 153

7.1 Spinning machine powered either by water or steam, c. 1825 162

7.2 Woman, carrying child, pounding corn in Cape Province, South Africa, c. 1900 168

7.3 Mines in Scotland, 1848 179

8.1 Drawing of Harriet Tubman as soldier and spy 193

8.2 Japanese empress Haruko c. 1890 197

9.1 Indian ayah, Maria de Sousa, c. 1870 211

9.2 "The Conquest of Africa," 1900 Georges-Antoine Rochegrosse 221

9.3 Dahomey Amazons, women warriors, c. 1897 229

10.1 Women attendants of Marcus Garvey marching up 7th Avenue in New York, 1924 241

10.2 Frida Kalho, "Me Twice," 1939 (as Spanish/Mexican woman and as Amerindian) 247

10.3 Soviet women in the Second World War 254

11.1 French military operation in 1955 in Algeria 265

11.2 Eritrean People's Liberation Front Muslim woman soldier with Russian-made Kalashnikov AK-47 rifle 269

11.3 A model at the Fashion House, 1955 Moscow 272

12.1 Telephone workers in Kowloon, Hong Kong, 1990 293

12.2 Wangari Maathai and the Green Belt Movement founded in 1977 296

Introduction

This book brings the history of the world's women into a single story, unfolding over the past five centuries. It tells of celebrated Chinese women writers of the seventeenth century and equally celebrated Chinese film stars of the 1930s; of Indian princesses and their humble illiterate country women who taught themselves to read and write. Russian empresses in early modern times appear alongside the later Soviet women fighter pilots of the 1940s; Native American women chiefs and black and white US political activists assert their power. The book is also a mosaic of women weavers, healers, slaves, bosses, assassins, artists, sex workers, mothers, protestors, and heads of modern governments. It would take a multivolume study to capture the richness of women's past. This book is just the tiniest sliver of all they produced and experienced over the past 500 years.

Still, the history taught in school makes it appear as if there is an entirely male past of warfare, "exploration," industrial development, and innovation, followed by more warfare. The names of soldiers, generals, politicians, martyrs, scoundrels, workers, tyrants, businessmen, writers, philosophers, astronauts, activists, and geniuses—all of them men—are those we are taught to remember. We usually know their lives in detail, including the names of their children and even their pets (if they had either). Dates, wise sayings, battles, proclamations and policies, misdeeds, reading, and favorite music fill pages of their biographies and even pages of textbooks to enliven them. Men in history are usually full-blown characters: off the top of my head I know that General George Patton in the Second World War was an eccentric and took to discipline badly. Jahangir, emperor of India, abused drugs and alcohol, while Aztec leader Monteczuma was dignified in the extreme despite the bloodthirsty nature of Aztec rule. Is our knowledge of prominent female figures as detailed or as provocative?

The stories in this book will feature an engaging and unusual cast of historical characters—unusual because they are women and girls. We know so little about important and even unimportant women in world history, yet some are more than memorable. For example, the African warrior queen

Nzinga, who kept a large harem as did most rulers (though hers were men), stood up to the Portuguese and made alliances with several regional and international leaders to maintain her own state's power. She was actually a conqueror of neighboring tribes. The armed women who guarded many a harem continued to be protectors and warriors down through history until they had become the all-woman security forces for Libyan leader Moamar Qadafi in the twenty-first century. The fact is that there have always been women warriors, raising a number of questions, one of them being why we don't hear about them. Is it that male warriors are more important than women warriors are or that we simply don't know how to include women in standard accounts of history? Qadafi's all-female guards have become titillating rather than historic figures, swiftly forgotten.

There is even more to question in our standard history, however. For example, behind the effort of warriors is a massive support network, providing weapons, food, and other supplies. This supporting cast of women is crucial not only in backing armies but in reproducing new life to replace warriors who have been killed or disabled. Such needs have been constant for centuries if not millennia, and never more so than in the period covered by this book when conquest of many types took place and when loss of life in combat was a menace to community well-being and even its existence. Yet, the history of warfare suggests that only beginning in the twentieth century was warfare total—that is, employing the effort and skill of men and women alike. The dilemma is why the organization of this support network rarely makes the history books, especially the important fact that women were hard at the work of provisioning in the days before government sponsored medical, dining, and laundry services. Centuries ago among some Native American people women had a major say in determining whether their men would go to war. The justification was that they would have the burdensome work of supplying armies and tending the wounds of those warriors. Why, we can ask, do we not generally know that during the Atlantic slave trade African women slaves held by African authorities were less often sold to slavers than men were so that they could produce the supplies that fed African armies and that were sold to those same slavers along with humans.

The many other absences of women in ordinary history books suggest that we have long experienced the "gendering" of history. What does this mean? The first meaning is that history claims to be about everyone. For example, a statement about the scarcity of food in the First World War (1914–18) or in the Soviet Union in the 1980s might read that people stood for hours in line to get basic foodstuffs. In fact, it was mostly women who stood in line. More frequently, it was said of the outbreak of the same First World War that crowds in front of government buildings cheered the declaration of war. Images in fact usually show massive crowds of men. Or, only the candidates who could pass the exams got civil service jobs. In fact, women were not allowed to take the tests. To call any country in the world a democracy before 1893 presumes that such a universal statement is true when in fact only men—mostly white--could vote in elections. As Simone de Beauvoir put it, men are the universal, women are the [excluded] other. Their exclusion is taken as obvious and normal and goes without saying.

Isn't gender a substitute term for women? How can history be "gendered" if women aren't even present in most accounts of the past? Today the idea is that gender applies to both men and women, to masculinity and femininity. The pair are related to one another in that they are seen as opposites but opposites whose difference creates a hierarchy: one term (usually "masculinity") has power while the other (usually "femininity") doesn't. So history is gendered when men's power appears in women's absence from accounts. Only men count in history, making it gendered.

Some Views of Women in History

Some writers pay attention to women's voices as they reveal their opinions, cares, and concerns in everyday life throughout the past. Svetlana Alexievich, who won the Nobel Prize for Literature in 2015, did just this when she captured the everyday speech of people across eastern Europe. Far from having little of interest or importance to say, their conversations ran the gamut of topics. The cost of sausages, the rulers they liked and those they hated, their longing for this leader or that and their reasons for making such political judgments. For her, women on the street were "a chorus, a choir." They were involved: Just from talking to them, she discovered how ordinary citizens had dug through debris at Chernobyl where a nuclear power plant had exploded in Ukraine in 1986 with disastrous consequences. Before the fall of communism in 1989, they sat around their kitchen tables talking about what books they were reading. Ordinary people went to the ballet and discussed those performances. In the postcommunist world there was no time for reading books; they had to make money and buy things.

For long people believed that "biology is destiny," especially when it came to women. Because they alone physically could give birth to children and nourish them from their bodies, it was their destiny to do so and, it followed, to continue providing food through tending farms for their families for the rest of their lives. They, as women, were supposed to clothe the people to whom they gave birth and, additionally, everyone else in the family. In many cases they were to secure further bodily protection by providing housing, as Native American and Mongol women did, for example. It fell to women to take care of the sick or wounded bodies of their families and also to school the young to know how to accomplish adult tasks. The list of "womanly" tasks lengthened but these tasks were seen as "natural" instead of being part of history.

In her 1949 book, *The Second Sex*, French philosopher Simone de Beauvoir challenged the idea of an essential, biological destiny for women. One is not born a woman, she claimed, one is made into one. In addition to women's biology not determining their destiny, for some modern thinkers there is no single path to becoming a woman nor is there a single fate determined for those born female biologically as they mature to adulthood. The history we read supports the message of Beauvoir's philosophy and that of more recent feminists. It shows that women's lives in the past have been vastly different from one another, ranging from serving as goddesses to working as peasants and royal warriors. Some were chosen to be sacred human sacrifices while others were sex workers. They were performers, doctors, miners, and inventors. So when reading any history one may question whether the author does think that biology is destiny and whether those serving as agents of history—that is, kings, traders, servants, peasants— believed that or not. In other words history shows women leading such diverse lives—lives in some cases parallel and even identical to those led by men—that the force of biology in determining women's or men's life course is thrown into question. They forged identities in history, even though ideas *about* their biological nature affected that history.

Getting to Know Historical Terms and Concepts

Women's history, like many subjects including our standard histories of wars and politics, has some specialized terms that it can be helpful to understand. In the case of women's history, some of these terms may serve as background to a general understanding of subject matter, even when terms such as "patriarchy" and "agency" are not addressed specifically or used at length in the history of women's lives. Still they are worth keeping in mind when reading about women's past. There are historical questions that women ask about the past, such as whether and how life changed or did not change over time. You the reader can use examples from different centuries to judge how reproduction and sexuality had changed by the 2000s from the 1600s. You might want to know about women's agency or how the intertwining of race or religion affected social and political conditions in a process called intersectionality. Some of these general terms follow, while more specific terms and proper names appear in a glossary at the end of most chapters. Because this is a history, we'll begin with the ideas of continuity and change over time. We start here because readers often wonder "was it always like this"?

Continuity and Change over Time. This book is different from the few others that recount the history of the world's women in the context of "gender" history. For one thing, it follows change over time, proceeding to tell the story from "once upon a time" in the first chapter to how the story ended and how things are now in the final chapter. Some books look at family in one chapter, work in another, and sexuality in another, for example. This book puts sexuality, family, work (for example) in the same chapter and then shows how they all change at once over time or stay the same with some changing. Besides showing change over time, the idea is to show how work, sexuality, family, politics, and other topics all intersect with one another in any given historical period. We know today that work and family are said to be difficult for women to manage simultaneously. We aim to show how women experienced the different aspects of their lives and the ways in which this clusters of qualities of life varied from region to region and changed over time. That is, by exploring the politics of sexuality and the workings of the economy as they were transformed from one period of time to another, we can consider whether issues impacted on one another—the economy on sexuality, for example, or war on family life. It might be found that such interactions showed continuity rather than mutually changing.

Change and continuity are historical categories but they are also feminist, civil rights, and economic issues. We live in a world where politics centers on improvement and the belief in progress. History often charts that progress, looking for the world to get better. Often in women's history we ask whether life got better or worse for women when any change occurred. Historians sometimes see, let's say, the Middle Ages as a "golden age" for women while others call them "the bad old days." In the past people were also concerned about whether things were improving; women rioted when, for example, the price of bread rose more than they felt it should. When living conditions appeared to be deteriorating, as during wars, and prices soared, continuity seemed to be fractured, causing activism or anti-Semitism, or anti-foreign sentiment or racism.

Patriarchy. Let's continue with the very old term "patriarchy." It dates back centuries as indicating the power of fathers or in Latin "patria potestas." It also began as a key term when women's history came to the fore with the women's movement of the late 1960s and 1970s. Feminists saw patriarchy still as a powerful force in their lives. When women's history first started to be offered as a history course, one question was why men had been so dominant to the point that women couldn't even open a bank account or get a home loan on their own. Looking back to the time this book begins (c. 1450), men often had the right to kill their wives and children, but their domination was simultaneously more subtle. Ancient Confucian priorities in behavior, operational in much of East Asia, laid out a hierarchy of obedience and respect, with the father and then the oldest son ranking highest in esteem. As a result, they were obeyed and honored. In the Mughal Empire, which controlled much of South Asia until the nineteenth century, the name of the mother of the emperor was not considered important enough to be noted or for anyone to know. In France, a woman could not inherit the royal throne, while the law code passed by the celebrated emperor Napoleon stripped married women of their right to property, giving wages, land, and other holdings entirely to their husbands. In this case the "power of the father" or patriarchy radiated from the fact that women had no financial resources, even if they had paying jobs. In the pages ahead, we will see some of the legal conditions that still allow men to murder members of their families.

Women Worthies and Women's Voices. Which women do we want to study, given that we can't study everything? It used to be that queenly women or women "worthies" got much of the biographical attention. In part, as mentioned, that is because there were written records of their lives that could help an accurate history to be written. Moreover, there were oral histories of their time as rulers and consorts. Women saints or notorious women occasionally appeared in histories as well. Now all that has changed because of the multiplication of government, industrial, and journalistic records. The spread of public education has also allowed more women to keep diaries, even the poorest women as we will see in such published diaries and memoirs as that of escaped US slave Harriet Ann Jacobs (pseud. Linda Brent 1813–1897) or of Brazilian slum-dweller Carolina Maria de Jesus (1914–1977). Many millions of ordinary women over the past centuries have protested living standards, invasions, arrests, genocide, and oppressive policies. They have worked long hours, been used to test drugs, including birth control pills, and unknown to most people invented processes and procedures—all this suggesting that we need to look at the substantial mass of women in world history, not only the privileged few.

Still, some admired writers believe that in focusing on women's lives and deeds we are merely duplicating the worst features of history generally: whipping up people's emotions over warfare and bloodshed, making many flawed and even criminal people larger-than-life characters and even heroes, and assuming that people are fully rational in enacting their deeds. Trying to make women as important as men is fruitless, some maintain. So is following male chronology. In telling a good story, often history makes happy or satisfying endings.

Instead, women's history should be critique—that is, operate as oppositional to all that goes on in men's history. This does not mean simply creating an opposite cast of heroines. Rather it means telling a story that unpacks the unstated power of men, is perhaps directly critical of what men have written, and teases out its gendered and flawed nature instead of writing about women. The pages ahead featuring women suggest that women's history is an indirect critique on its own, all the while bringing a different cast of characters who will provide first-hand evidence of the problems with men's history as we know it.

Agency. Given all that women have accomplished in the past and given the lives they have led, building up new generations, shall we say that women are historical agents? A historical agent is one who makes change happen or keeps community life going. An agent might learn to read and write so that she can be a better worshipper or spiritual person; she might worship or undertake spiritual activism so that she can protect her community from hurricanes, droughts, or famines. Women in royal families often helped raise their sons to be rulers or in some empires they completely developed his skills and a network of supporters to help him come to power and keep control of the government. Women's agency is therefore seen to come in many forms, from doing everyday tasks to writing poetry to storing up corn to sell to assassinating an opponent. Many women may come together to be agents of resounding change such as the women who at several points in eighteenth-century Peru either in their own groups or alongside men rose up against Spanish rule. Feminist parades early in the twentieth century and women's marches across the globe in the 2010s similarly show mass agency. Women's control of their fertility over the past century is also seen as a result of action they took to exert that control—and thus a result of their agency. Their acts of violence would also be seen as something they determined to undertake.

Some question the idea of agency, and readers of the book may ask whether the many undertakings of women across the globe and over the centuries are actually produced by freely acting agents. The argument against this is that they have been thrown as individuals into a world of social, economic, and political ways of being that determine their life course. They are less free agents than they are performers of social customs, traditions of protesting, and adherents to community rules about child-rearing, norms of heterosexuality (or homosexuality) rather than being authentic or original thinkers.

In fact, one idea is that in modern times power or agency flows through people, they operate within grids of power, not coming either from the government or from any tyrant but as part of a social and life condition in which power is distributed through every living being who enacts it. In this regard, as mentioned earlier, we enact power as we obey myriad rules and customs that are part of our inner constitution. This inner regulatory power flows through—in and out—of everyone in the form of religion, family life, sexual identity, status, race, and gender. This way of thinking weakens arguments of agency—whether women's or that of anyone else. One moves with the currents of power, say toward feminism, sexual liberation, or women's economic participation. Agency, according to this way of thinking, is somewhat naïve. It reflects a contemporary and misguided way of thinking that sees people as having control of all their actions—and thus their agency. Whether women have agency or whether they are following a script of rules and regulations is an issue to consider as you read about women's history in the pages ahead. You the reader may decide for yourself.

Intersectionality. Divisions that led to defining male and female tasks in society as distinct and different still exist. Women and men also were different in social and economic status in society. Over the course of millennia, even their physical stature and overall well-being diverged according to physical evidence found by archeologists. These findings show that women's skeletons from earliest times were the same size as men's. Then closer to our own time, women's size diminished in comparison with men's, suggesting that over the course of centuries they were receiving less food and nourishment. From this and written evidence, we see that women themselves experienced gender discrimination with severe consequences as well as class and caste divisions and difference growing from whether they were slave or free people. Women's gender is and has been intertwined with other categories of differentiation and power (status, class, race, religion, free and unfree, for example). The intertwined nature of categories is called intersectionality—that is, the intersection of categories of difference. The facts of intersectionality—that is, multiple, interacting differences—will appear across the chapters of this book in many groups of women's lives and in individual experience.

Modern and Modernity. The chapters ahead also show women participating in trends and movements associated with modernity: global commerce, industrial production, rising literacy and education, political reform, human and civil rights, sexual reform, control of fertility, and the feminist quest for equal rights. Modernity is a complicated concept, but it is important to the history of the world's women because women were often seen as being backward. We will see them being thought of as backward in abundance. The term backward also came to be associated with people beyond the West—that is, local people who had been colonized including Amerindians or those who were not so endowed with technology as others. Sometimes, people who worshipped in a way different from Christians were said to be backward. Across the last century up until today, Europeans and US officials and citizens have justified the control of distant peoples with the accusation that they do not treat women equally and are backward. The ongoing war in Afghanistan that began in the twenty-first century centered in the press on the oppression of Aghani women by men—a sign of Afghani savagery and lack of modern values. Almost a century earlier, the British and French explained not awarding colonial peoples more rights as caused by the backward state in which they kept women. For that reason, men and women in colonized countries turned to upgrading women's education and other institutions in order to appear modern. Racial others are also treated as backward or not modern. Even though we might see modernity as based on technological development, in fact, claims of being modern has more usually been a propaganda tool justifying oppression of others. The effects have been gendered by using women as evidence of backwardness.

However, the question remains: what is modern and what is backward? It is odd that nations outside Europe and the United States called other men's treatment of women "backward." Many women in the Middle East in the nineteenth century had more rights than women in the United States and Europe did. They could own property whereas Western women couldn't, for example. Or is modernity about technology? We'll see a woman in Bengal writing about the use of solar power in 1905; meanwhile the practice of plastic surgery happened earlier in India far earlier than it did in other areas of the world. Some say that accusing whole cultures of being backward or not modern is pure propaganda and does not involve reality. We'll see how manipulating images of women was used to advertise or deny modernity.

Sexuality resonates throughout women's and gender history these days and appears across this history of women. The term is used to describe an individual's identity based on the sexual feelings she has toward others. Identities across history have been variously described as straight/heterosexual/cis, gay/lesbian/homosexual, bisexual, and, often conflated with one's gender identity, queer. These complex and still contested categories began to arise as such only in the mid-nineteenth century and continue to evolve to this day. Before that sexuality was connected with practices such as sodomy, while gender identity was similarly connected to practices such as transvestism. Sexual practices were scrutinized because of the need to ensure both social order and the replenishment of the population in times of famine, plague, and deadly warfare. Kings and queens, though free to have relationships with people to whom they were actually attracted, were obligated to have sex with an official partner of the opposite sex in order to procreate the dynasty. In fact, it is suggested that so long as one produced a new generation of children a more complicated sexuality was allowed at many levels of society. Officially heteronormativity was necessary if hardly total.

Across time, sexuality became less regulated and more open, many historians claim, until reaching the freedom of our own day. Ahead we will explore some aspects of early sexuality in comparison with that over the past century. One argument presented these days is that sexuality in fact became more pressured in modern times because most people had to announce their sexuality. Increasingly from the late twentieth century to the present, people have had to declare their sexuality and talk more about sexuality. In other words, recent so-called uninhibited talk about sex is part of the flow of power in which one is obligated to talk about sex. It is not freedom but a manifestation of the necessity to reveal, tell all to census takers, pollsters, officials, schoolmates, and a range of other institutions not to mention one's friends and even to complete strangers in therapy groups, for example.

Violence and Militarization. Another theme is the violence and militarization everywhere present in women's lives and in society as a whole across the centuries covered in this book. We hardly think of women being militarized, but our opening paragraphs give a sense of the ever-present wartime status of much of the world, culminating in military parades, battlefield tourism, statues to generals and ordinary soldiers of "great wars," and the announced need for "security," which is hardly new. We will see women called upon to replenish the population to secure the future. Around this less-remarked-upon postwar duty of women, history itself unfolds along the chronology of violent wars, revolutions, assassinations, genocide, and uprisings. These mark the passage of time in the history as we have been urged, if not forced to learn even in our earliest history lessons.

A less obvious militarization is the construction of urban and other space around militarization. Louis XIV of France built good roads for troops in the seventeenth century. Over the past century, grand highways allowed tanks and other large weaponry to destroy villages and the livelihoods connected to them as society was militarized. Homes were smashed and the environment of which women are often leading protectors suffered. Vast dams and other irrigation projects work to the same end as do shopping malls and other large-scale development undertakings—all of them needing "security" to keep them safe from interlopers and in today's terminology "terrorists." Many find militarization a constant force over the centuries and one that affects women's everyday lives. As food is ripped from them and their children to support armies—governmental or militias or bandits— even food needs to be protected and securitized. These forces have shaped women's lives.

Women's Past and Women's Present. We try to bring the history of women's lives up to the present, as in the case of militarization. The idea is, to repeat, that we are born into culture, that is, a set of beliefs, practices, values, thoughts, music, and artistic forms of expression that themselves have a history. So we are born into history and our ideas and values develop alongside the ongoing march of history. This deep culture forms the horizons of our being. We have trouble imagining the world beyond. It is this evolving yet historic culture that we perform as we go about following rules and norms in our everyday lives. Our present-day being, that is, the life of each of us, is surrounded by the past in its many forms.

Our parents may tell us their history or that of our grandparents or even great grandparents. It is an early orientation into the bigger world around us. What skills did they use, what bravery did they show, and what were the odds they had to overcome are all helpful for us to know whether we are aware of that or not. History shows us how people have maneuvered through life, whether grand or ordinary. It is like the house we first inhabit. We may take it for granted but we have to learn how it works and what the rules are. Then we learn that there is an outside world and that it too has rules, arising in the past but forming and ruling us in our present. Where did all of those rules we perform come from and what do they mean? Is it possible to change such enduring regulations? Does the context in which we were born regulate men and women differently? History can help in understanding our present lives by showing how women have lived through past conditions, modified rules and conditions, or contested the world they inherited.

Now that we know some of the terms of history and how they are used and the questions they raise, let's forge ahead.

1

Productive and Reproductive Lives, c. 1450–1600

What was it like to be a woman in any single part of the globe at the dawn of the modern world? How did she develop an identity in these heavily agricultural societies? As one example, a baby girl is born in central Mexico in the early 1500s. The midwife attending that birth surrounds the newborn with spinning and weaving equipment and perhaps a female garment. She utters the words, "Only inside the house was she to dwell, only inside the house was her home; it would not be necessary for her to go anywhere else. And that is to say that her duty was [preparing] drink and food. She was to prepare beverages, to make food, to grind maize, to spin, and to weave."[1] Eventually the infant receives a new, auspicious birthdate that will also shape her development. With that date and the incantation of duties and the eventual use of her household tools, this infant will become a woman. A cursory look at her genitals gives but a superficial marker, for as French thinker Simone de Beauvoir put it, "One is not born a woman but rather becomes a woman." In the case of this central Mexican infant, operating domestic instruments, wearing correct clothing, and adhering to community rules as announced by the midwife will establish her as a gendered human.

Given an existence produced by and even bound to a community, how did women live and experience themselves in a time when individual, family, and community formed an almost inseparable cluster? How did that experience change as the world's inhabitants became increasingly more connected and more urbanized? Whether in the Aztec Empire in southernmost North America or in the Ming Empire of China in the late fifteenth century two main duties dominated the lives of most women no matter how distant from one another. They were to give birth to the next generation of humans and to provide the goods needed for themselves and their families to survive. These were baseline functions that we might see as biologically determined but that were actually staged in a powerful, community setting.

Women participated in the day-to-day activities of a community of other humans, sometimes consisting of a neighborhood in a city but mostly in a tiny village or small town surrounded by fields, farms, and woods. They were thus partially products of community life, being formed not as individuals but as a fragment of a community. Among nomadic peoples, women's community was mobile, causing them to travel with portable housing and goods though nonetheless operating in line with their community. Women at the very top of an established social ladder might see a wider world, moving with a royal court from palace to palace and coming in contact with city and countryside alike. Alternatively, secluded in special quarters of wealthy homes or in convents, they might move outside infrequently. Feasts, holidays, and initiation rituals drew many into the broader community, although others regularly socialized at wells for water, at rivers for laundering, or at markets where they supplied their households or took produce to sell. Conditions for enslaved women could differ from any of these, and it was sometimes the case that the difference between slave and free individuals was more important than the difference between men and women. Vast numbers of women were enslaved worldwide in these early modern centuries.

Around the duties of giving birth and providing sustenance, women's lives were as varied from one region to another as they are today. Some would say that these diverse and multifaceted cultures differed from one another more than those of the present. They followed distinct sets of social, religious, and political rules around the notion of correct or healthy behavior that were not yet shared by societies thousands of miles distant from one another as is often the case today. For long it was believed that women could have no history because they were so tied to the uniform rhythms of their bodies. In contrast, men were uniquely free from bodily restraints and complications, including those of menstruation, pregnancy, menopause, and old age, and thus differed from one another and performed as unique individuals. Men were usually more attuned to the expansive world of important events; women to the world of their individual bodies.

Still, societies in fact drew a range of distinctions between male and female centuries ago and saw men's bodies as also important, albeit filled with exceptions to any strict male-female division. Humans fashioned a range of gendered roles and gendered tasks and saw these ideas of gendered behavior as fundamental to good order. Gods and goddesses had gendered roles as well, while aspects of nature were similarly gendered. Humans claimed, however, that these variously constructed roles were divinely-given or "natural" or foundational in some other sense. In 1500, gender operated as a differentiating idea of opposites or complementarity—a binary some call it. Gender paired power with powerlessness, cleanliness with pollution, superiority with inferiority, and so on. In their female embodiment, girls and women lived out these distinctions, definitions, expectations, and rules by adhering to them, by disobeying or modifying them, and by creatively turning them to their advantage when possible.

Women's Bodies

Humans some 500 years ago had a shorter life expectancy than people enjoy today, but the lifespan looks especially short when infant deaths are taken into account. Because the years from birth to late adolescence were perilous and the death rate of children under five enormous, the average lifespan was around forty. However, for those who reached the age of ten, life expectancy grew to between fifty-five and seventy, depending on the region of the world. Today the average, without subtracting child mortality, is generally into the seventies and eighties, again depending on region. Besides the decline of child mortality thanks to vaccines preventing deadly childhood diseases and to improved sanitary conditions, another change is the improvement in maternal mortality, again due to improved medical knowledge and technology. Five hundred years ago the idea of death in childbirth haunted the experience of many women.

Enmeshed in the reproductive expectation according to which women gave birth to the next generation of workers, tax and tribute payers, and soldiers lay rituals and rhythms of the female body. Girls reached menarche, or the onset of puberty including menstruation, at between fourteen and sixteen years of age at this time, somewhat later than in Roman times a millennium and a half earlier and again, differentiated by region. Communities marked this development in particular with a range of observances. For example, in Africa cohorts of girls or teens went through initiations together and formed an important unit of the society—an age-grade that constituted a life-shaping cohort and provided a group identity until they died. They also participated in body piercing, tattooing, and scarification, all of these giving them a chance to develop bravery in the face of pain as part of their womanhood. Initiations could also include religious confirmation as part of Christian ceremonies, while reaching puberty could also indicate the right time for a girl to leave her parents for the household of her husband's family as in South Asia. Even before that, a girl of eight or ten might leave her parents to enter the home of her future husband, moving an identity from one family to another as part of femaleness.

The greatest test for girls and young women in Africa and a few other parts of the world was the ritual of genital cutting, in which the clitoris alone or the clitoris and parts or all of the labia were excised, most often as the centerpiece of a collective ceremony of similarly aged girls or young women. Some girls had their genitals cut while eight or nine years old whereas others were not ritually cut until in their late teens or twenties. The latter group could be sexually active and even become pregnant, but the fetus would be aborted or the newborn killed. Practiced since ancient times, the ritual announced womanly sexual maturity and child-bearing but it also embedded that stage of life in community ritual not in an individual self. Among the various ideas behind genital cutting were that it prevented the birth of deformed babies or monsters or that it permitted better pregnancies and childbirth overall to benefit the family and community. Some believed that excision was a spiritual condition connecting generations past with those in the future. Although an intensely personal, bodily experience to modern eyes, genital cutting as a group ritual mobilized forces beyond an individual self—the community or region or even the kingdom. The intimate condition and sexuality of women's bodies were integrated into a greater social body. The act of excision showed the power of communities or states to form any individual girl or woman and her sexuality according to longstanding norms.

Community structures and belief systems thus revolved around ensuring the reproduction of families and society more generally, and achieving this goal required women's group participation. The development of bodies and gender were in part a social production making for stability in a very uncertain world. Reproductive activities involved pregnancy and childbirth but additionally included feeding, clothing, and sheltering children—usually in the context of the wider family, clan, or community. Reproduction also entailed shaping children into workers and responsible adults—then as now hardly an easy task. Additionally, some control of fertility was necessary so that there would not be too many children. Too many children would lead to starvation when there were more mouths than the harvest could feed; too few people meant not enough hands to staff agriculture and animal husbandry, with the same consequences. There were thus many traditions and practices that aimed to make the number of people in a community coincide with the collective resources, especially because economic subsistence—not plenty—was the norm. Subsistence was a concern in part because of the warrior mentality that destroyed crops and lives in a flash. The balance was also maintained because women often died in childbirth during their fertile years. Demographers attribute late onset of puberty to famine conditions, poor nutrition, and other causes. The same is true of menopause, again coming earlier than today and for the same reasons.

In this abbreviated span of bodily fertility and given the perils to infants and the threat to mothers' lives, societies saw the importance of ensuring that women reproduced in an orderly way and one that brought just the right number of replacements to the population and labor. To that end, the arrival of puberty for both boys and girls was announced with an array of ceremonies that included markings on the body. Boys and girls alike were often tattooed and scarred on reaching adolescence, in addition to any genital procedures, widely indicating that they were now approved for sexual intercourse and parenthood. Across the globe, male death in warfare was common, leading some societies to encourage an individual man to have more than one wife to make up for those adult men who died before fathering a replacement number of children. In some regions boys and girls were allowed to engage in sexual relations at an early age and only commit to marriage once the fertility of both partners was ensured by a successful pregnancy. Communities used many means of ensuring conformity to sexual and reproductive rules; the lives of individuals unfolded within the context of such commands, both enforced by elders and even by their own age group.

Reproductive systems varied across civilizations, but they were still scripted by custom, law, and community and family needs. In the Aztec militaristic society the reproductive work of women was part of gender complementarity wherein women's struggle in childbirth was parallel to men's struggle in battle. In China a newborn girl was put on the floor, while a newborn boy was placed on the table, showing hierarchy, while at the same time they came to be seen as part of a complementary yin and yang system of different qualities that needed to be balanced to produce harmony not just in an individual but in society overall. In China and other societies these harmonies were connected not to medicine as we know it today but to cosmic forces, including the appearance of the planets, stars, sun and moon, and other astrological signs. From the moment of conception and birth, gendered traditions, cultural norms, and the arrangement of the heavens regulated the production of men and women alike.

Where necessary, contraception, abortion, and infanticide were practiced; women themselves had medical knowledge and knew healing practices. Across the globe they used an array of abortifacients from ergot to rue and nutmeg. Reproductive systems varied by region, social strata, and religious affiliation: some societies employed infanticide of girls almost exclusively to control population, valuing them less where dowries were customary, for example. The idea was that girls needing dowries took resources out of the family. In South Asia, girls were valued less because at an early age they moved into the home of a boy to whom they were engaged, so the expense of raising them was not compensated. In hard times infants of either sex might be abandoned and left to die; elsewhere children were sold into slavery to preserve others in the family.

Sexuality and Sexual Identity

Sexual life proceeded according to local and regional customs that included slave and other sex workers—both male and female—such as concubines and courtesans. Unlike in Europe, in advanced regions such as China and Japan, sex workers were highly skilled in the arts because of their training in music, poetry, and dance. Both kingdoms were becoming more urbanized and literate in the early modern period; because of thriving commerce Chinese and Japanese urban people moved around more. Officials were often highly educated, so to entertain these more cosmopolitan clients, courtesans learned to converse and to provide amusing pastimes in addition to offering sexual relations. In Japan, the "floating world" of pleasure houses became legendary in art and poetry and grew in popularity because a rising middle class of merchants, officials, and professionals patronized the talented women who lived in these spots. The Japanese geisha became well known for her wide-ranging allure and often walked into public with a host of attendants. Concubines in wealthy families and royal courts also received training in singing, calligraphy, and other displays of talent. Like male slaves who rose to high positions among imperial officials, a trained intelligence was crucial to achieving influence. However, the process by which young girls (and sometimes boys) were seized from their families, often beaten into submission through rape and other abuse (and in the case of boys castrated) in order to enter a monarchical or upper-class household, remained a violent one across the Eurasian world. The world of the sex worker/slave was most often precarious and even cruel.

In this commercializing and mobile society, men and boys became eunuchs as a way of advancement that complicated gender identities. Notably, Ming China's rapid population growth and increasing number of young men competing for government jobs through the tough examination system literally blocked tens of thousands from obtaining even the lowest positions in the bureaucracy. Parents castrated their sons and young men castrated themselves to get ahead, as eunuchs gained a place in imperial officialdom. This trend came to confuse normative social and governmental order in China in terms of competence and sexuality, while in other states such as the Ottoman Empire there was less competition or rigidly distinct classes. Such practices weakened Confucian ideas of deference and the importance of correct behavior in a social and political order based on the gendered training of elites.

Early modern people participated in same-sex relationships, again seeming to weaken clear heterosexual reproductive markings. South Asian women in the royal courts are shown in paintings having same sex relationships with servants. Erotic poetry expressed desire, passion, and pleasure, with the royal or noble woman seen as meriting the pleasure and the women servants or slaves providing it. Images showed techniques for women to excite others sexually, while such ancient classic sex manuals as the Kama Sutra gave instructions in both heterosexual and same-sex erotic relationships. In Chinese, Japanese, and South Asian books, erotic images themselves were enjoyed by couples as stimulation for sexual play and intercourse. The custom by which a wealthy older man took a young male lover often constituted a rite of passage to adult masculinity in some societies. This practice was especially common among ruling circles where a young servant or slave might serve as the object of desire and affection. In fact, it was considered disruptive of social and political arrangements for an inferior to penetrate a superior. Sexuality had its customs and rules, many of them lessons in hierarchy, and not only applicable to heterosexuality.

Those rules were hardly uniform across the globe. Sexuality and sexual identity were almost as varied as they are today. In Aztec society, clothing for men and women was standardized and heterosexually regulated, while dressing as a member of the opposite sex was punishable by death. Yet

FIGURE 1.1 *Women celebrating in Mughal Court. Royal and upper-class women congregated for sociability and relaxation with servants ready at hand with food and drink. Gossip and rivalries were said to develop. Sometimes such scenes depicted dancing, musical performance, and same-sex intimacies, with servants offering sexual stimulation to their mistresses. Courtesy of Historical Picture Archive Getty Images.*

depictions of other Central American peoples show men dressed as women and vice versa. North American indigenous peoples accepted trans identities and even honored them in some situations. Ritual sexual intercourse as in Tibetan *tantrism* and phallic rites were central to public life in some cultures, while sexuality and sexual identity that crossed customary heterosexual borders often appeared as holy.

Women's inferiority to men both in power and social prestige was also widely accepted and connected to sexuality. Those who were penetrated—boys and women—were inferiors in relation to those who penetrated. Leaders in many cultures spoke more about that inferiority and simultaneously emphasized the superiority of men—ideas that were reinforced in belief systems and philosophies forged in what is called the Axial Age, that is, the period from the eighth to the third century BCE when a cluster of *Buddhism*; *Zorastrianism*; and *Confucian*, *Greek*, and other systems of thought took hold. In many of these, the sexed female body was a polluted entity, needing rituals of exclusion and purification to make it less dangerous or even lethal. The male warrior body also followed purifying procedures before going into battle; many such procedures concerned sexuality and included complete abstinence.

Gender and the Structure of Community and Family Life

In this context, people generally formed permanent heterosexual couples for reproducing the next generation. However, these couples did not form around the idea of "love" or the "intimacy" of a self-contained and self-sustaining couple. Rather marriage aimed to produce laborers. Then, upon establishing a partnership, the couple was inserted into a larger household. That household would include multiple generations, perhaps cousins of every level of closeness, and servants and slaves even from many corners of the world. From the household all of these individuals gained their identity, instead of gaining it from their relationship with a single heterosexual partner. In short what today we would call the conjugal couple living on its own, cocooned in its very own, separate nest generally did not exist. From the very top of the society to the bottom people survived or exerted power as part of an extended group or household. Marriage and the sexual relations that proceeded from it were about household formation, reproducing the labor force, ensuring well-being, and following rules from which identity flowed.

Households interacted with the communities they composed in order to ensure survival. Community structures monitored the correct reproduction of families and survival of society more generally. Obeying community norms, reproductive activities involved traditions of pregnancy and childbirth but additionally included providing sustenance and shelter for the household's multiple generations. Children, trained as workers and rule-bound adults, followed the same norms—in order to make the transition to community life. Children were segregated by gender to learn skills and appropriate gender discipline; they additionally might be exchanged in late childhood or early adolescence to acquire skills and correct behavior from

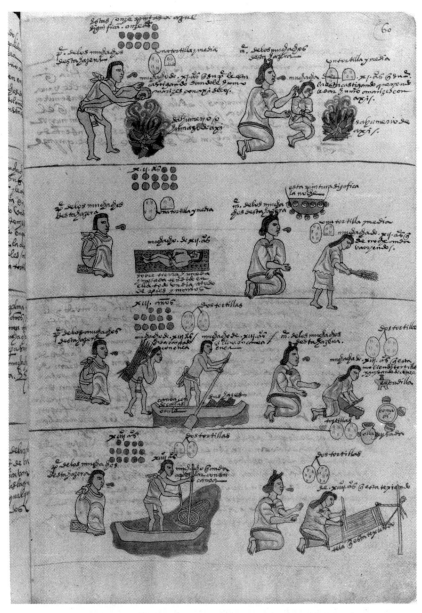

FIGURE 1.2 *Aztec education of boys and girls. Parallel, if different, education of girls and boys trained them in adult ways from infancy. Women's and girls' weaving and preparation of tortillas was crucial to the feeding and clothing of the population. Prosperous as Aztec society was, skills ensured survival. Such depictions also documented and helped create social order. Courtesy of Ann Ronan Pictures Getty Images.*

living in a different family. It is not that parents might not come to love their children but that was not the central undertaking of a household.

Still, some social control of fertility was necessary so that there would not be an excess of children—either in the family or the community. Too many children would lead to starvation when there were more mouths than the harvest could feed; too few people meant not enough hands to staff agriculture and animal husbandry, with the same consequences. There were thus many traditions and practices that aimed to make the number of people in a community coincide with its collective resources. In European societies youth cohorts sprang up to monitor the sexuality of their comrades. In other societies, strict segregation and seclusion of women kept the sexes from procreating before the time that would keep population and subsistence in balance. Where economic subsistence—not abundance—was the norm it was especially important that there not be too many births.

In this period, a warrior mentality and constant warfare served to meet subsistence and ideological, religious, and political needs. The resulting destruction of crops, livestock, and workers could threaten food security in a flash. Because fighters generally did not have regular provisioning by the state or by military leadership, they lived off the sometimes scant provisions of local people. Additionally, the balance of food to population was simultaneously maintained and threatened because women often died in childbirth during their fertile years. However, because of male loss of life in high-ranking, warrior families, elite men in particular might have multiple partners, concubines, or wives to safeguard the family line, which was key to power and status.

In many societies, harmonious, usually hierarchical order in the household was a top priority given these factors that threatened well-being. Not only did it insure controlled reproduction, especially of male children, the secure ordering of gender, age, and status in the household also signified order in the kingdom or state as a whole. Athenian men had considered the household and its inhabitants as grossly inferior and not worth interacting with except for reproducing children. In contrast, other cultures including many of those in the Western Hemisphere had a more complementary view of gender in the household even if they saw men as superior. In many societies both sexes were seen as useful and were hoped for when pregnancies occurred. The family was a little kingdom in terms of its need for order and its service as a model of order. All along the line, from the state to the individual, the maintenance of heterosexuality was a necessity.

People valued the contributions of both masculinity and femininity to maintaining social order, seeing both of them as essential to achieving balance and harmony in the family and in the universe. "To live among us without a wife," one Iroquois reported in the early 1600s, "is to live without help, without a home, to be always wandering."[2] Household rituals in China included women in ancestor worship, for example, albeit from a lesser position in the ritual. In fact, although men conducted the major rites, women performed the essential tasks of maintaining family shrines, preparing for family rituals, and ensuring daily observances. Worship of ancestors provided ritual depth to the family, perpetuating gender, age, and status hierarchy by differentiating levels of ritual observance according to gender, age, and other markers of status.

Women assumed many functions as head of the family should the man be too preoccupied with his official or scholarly duties. Family governance was largely male according to doctrine but in a multifaceted reality it could be loose when it came to actual gender behavior. Women were usually in charge of a set of tasks deemed "female" or in cases of seclusion the tasks that took place in the women's or inner quarters. Because households were multigenerational, female hierarchy also existed, generally determined according to seniority among people in the household as well as in villages and towns. The wife of the head of the household held a position of command among those younger or with less prestige.

Other living arrangements developed around the precarious nature of men's lives in some societies or around the production of wealth. In West Africa, Muslim men could have as many as four wives if they could support them. According to religious principles, a man should not enter into a polygamous relationship without the financial or other means. As mentioned, such an arrangement benefitted societies in which men's lives were precarious due to war and enslavement. Where men's deadly occupations prevailed, a man with several wives could not only help repopulate the community but also guarantee a safe level of food and population security. Multiple wives also protected the continuity in family lineage and property where death in childbirth was not uncommon. In some African cases a husband went to live with his wife's family, again making for stability since men's lives were unstable. In the African case, the presence of additional wives could work to the benefit of the head wife: she could organize, direct, and profit from the agricultural work of those who were secondary wives from lower-status families. Such a situation could also be productive if the additional wife brought with her a dowry in land or animals whose benefit could accrue to the head wife. Not just the head wife but a man could also benefit from the productivity of his wives.

A somewhat similar situation existed among the Mandans of the northwestern region of what would become the United States. There, men's lower life expectancy resulted from hunting and warfare. They thus moved in with their wife's family of women to ensure the security of the clan. Children were raised by an extended network of female relatives, who also built the massive housing for the family. Family sociability often took place on the roofs of these women's round houses, between thirty and forty feet in diameter, when the family gathered for celebrations and feasting or simply for conversation and sociability. Iroquois women may have been more productive because they worked as a community, joining their forces to farm a single field as a group and then moving on to the next.

Teamwork characterized their labor, while overall, community solidarity, correct education of the young, and collective policing helped guarantee social order.

Marriage

Economic concerns and community values shaped marriages in most regions of the world, while political goals were usually primary in arranging marriages at the very top ranks of society. Women at all levels of society brought property of various sorts to their unions. These "dowries" could include animals, pieces of land, cash, and personal property such as clothing, linens, quantities of textiles that they prepared themselves, and other household goods meant to support family life, including the provisioning of children. In many cases the wife was seen as responsible for the support of herself and her children; it was not the father's responsibility. Men also made similarly varied contributions to the bride's family—bride price, this was called in some places. Bride price can be seen as a way of compensating a family for raising a daughter to be an adult skilled in agriculture, food preparation, and the production of textiles—at the very least. Both her reproductive and productive labor would be lost to her family of origin. Bride price stretched the capacity of some families to provide it.

Where societies achieved prosperity, wealth raised the stakes in transactions leading to marriages. By the beginning of this period, the demands from Chinese aristocratic families for contributions as a prerequisite for marriage with one of their children were significant. Because many cultures stressed the lesser position of women and their inferiority, social commentators sometimes feared that women bringing large dowries to a marriage might feel themselves more important than they should, even lording it over spouses and in-laws. A large dowry could upset the natural order of things when it came to gender and the smooth functioning of families. Rising commerce that benefited China, for example, created wealth outside the relatively small aristocratic circle. These newly rich families so valued a relationship with those blessed with an impressive lineage that they paid even greater sums than before (just as US wealthy families in the nineteenth and twentieth centuries paid handsomely to marry their children into aristocratic British families). Both Chinese emperors and their officials worried about the practice, citing the ways in which daughters-in-law in aristocratic families claimed superiority over members of the family into which they had married, upsetting both the gender order and status by age. Still, later in this millennium, there remained problems with dowries, specifically that in-laws would mistreat a young woman whose dowry they suddenly judged as insufficient in order to raise additional funds, goods, or land from her parents. Such behaviors may seem to be personal matters without social and political consequences for society as a whole, but officials came to see rising dowry demands as destabilizing of both hierarchy in a family and the wider political and social order. Individualism was a curse not a blessing.

Awareness of the centrality of a marriage as an economic, political, and social partnership and one with major repercussions for entire communities makes the use of professional marriage brokers and other skilled intermediaries understandable. In the fifteenth and early sixteenth centuries, the Aztecs of middle America organized marriages at the highest political and military levels with great care, using matchmakers and negotiators to reach a final agreement. Lower down on the social scale, parents might undertake arrangements, though in some cases grown children might have a say. In societies like the Maya, in close proximity to the Aztecs, parents arranged marriages when their children were still young, giving them little choice in the matter. Among Hindus in South Asia, some parents arranged marriages among infant children and if not then, more generally they married their girls before they began to menstruate. The idea was that such a practice would eliminate the possibility that the wife's impurity would corrupt the unity of the couple. The husband's prior sexual encounters had no bearing on purity. Additionally, most girls had no say in any marital arrangement; men, who in some cases were far older than the teenage girl or especially one 8 years old, could have a say, especially if they were in their thirties, forties, or even older. Such dictated or parentally-negotiated arrangements were yet another way to maintain familial and community stability when life in general had so many uncertainties, especially the uncertainty of war and peace. Men's command and control of women made for the appearance of order and stability.

Competition for recognition and control of a wife's wealth may have led to property being handed down in this controlled way. Hindu prescriptions asserted that women should not own property except for their jewelry and possibly hard money. Other cultures had similar proscriptions against women's ownership of property, but as in the case of medieval India and other regions, in fact women sometimes gave land and other property to temples, suggesting that in fact they had resources. When law or tradition allowed, women guarded their dowries for their own needs, for those of their children, for charitable donations, or for the greater good of the family. Women in the Middle East were known for their endowments of charitable institutions from their own assets. Still different was property ownership among the Incas and other indigenous people of the Western Hemisphere. Women in the many ethnic groups along the Andes of South America often inherited property from their mothers and passed it down to their daughters according to matrilineal traditions.

Problems arose with widowhood when women could come into their own as property owners and as more autonomous beings. In some societies such as the Mongols (see below), a widow remained with her husband's family and married a brother or other close relative, thus keeping property in the husband's extended family or patriline. In contrast, some societies frowned upon widow remarriage of any kind, with India being the most severe: South Asians valued widows who immolated themselves. Although seen as sacred and ennobling of the family, widow suicide also kept property in the husband's patriline, whereas in China, where a widow's chastity was prized and remarriage discouraged, the widow returned to her birth family, taking her property with her. As with widow immolation, Chinese widows aspired to the admiration they received for not remarrying and were often memorialized for remaining chaste.

By contrast, in European societies, widows became empowered when they took over a husband's workshop, printing establishment, or other business enterprise and became fully autonomous. They could handle this transition to ownership because they had usually worked in a variety of capacities to help the craft or other business flourish. Because much of Europe dispossessed women of their property on marriage and allowed them a substantial portion of their own and husband's property only on his death, widows were among the most privileged and influential women— commoner and noblewoman alike—in European communities.

In the Byzantine Empire women could thrive, despite its being a prosperous center of the Christian religion and imperial rule. Women were allowed to keep and enhance their property during marriage and aristocratic women in particular became rich through engaging in business and taking part in politics. They could inherit property, pass it to heirs, and sell it on their own. They became nuns but they also became scholars, as the opportunity for learning was greater here than in most other European states, perhaps due to the fluidity caused by migration through the kingdom. The most sterling, if early example is Anna Comnena (1083–1153) who wrote the *Alexiad*—the history of her father Alexios I, the Byzantine emperor's reign. Anna Comnena was raised in a literary tradition but also in that of administration and science. After serving as head of a hospital and as a physician, she participated in an unsuccessful attempt to seize the throne from her younger brother. Defeated, she passed the rest of her life as a nun, studying and writing more than a dozen books. Women's traditional medical knowledge or their professional expertise, which they passed down through familial and community networks, functioned as an asset on which they could draw.

In terms of health, however, nothing halted the Black Death, a pandemic which arrived in the fourteenth century and spread across Eurasia, killing from a third to a half of the population. Women felt the impact of the catastrophe is specific ways beyond the loss of family and other close community members. In some places their work lives, including their pay, were slightly improved because of the labor shortage that plagues and famines left behind. At the time of the plague, however, Christian preachers and politicians attributed the disaster to women's sexual sins and lust, while among commentators in Cairo the too frequent appearance of women in public had whipped up men's passions and thus brought on the deadly affliction. Women in some cases sought to deflect these accusations by increasing their pious behavior in atonement. Gender was enlisted to designate those innocent in the spread of the plague—men—and those guilty—women. As in other disasters, gender reinforced and restored hierarchy that extreme social distress had weakened; misogynistic attitudes persisted into the next century.

Relatedly, women's seclusion and veiling were normalized during these events and thereafter, especially in aristocratic and very wealthy households across Eurasia and Africa. Seclusion meant the virtually complete shutting off of women from society generally but especially from the presence of men and boys except those in their immediate family. Writings on the topic had multiplied and became more assertive over the centuries into early modern times. Chinese texts came to indicate that women should veil themselves when they left the inner quarters. Other aspects of seclusion entailed women's completely enveloping themselves in textiles, with only small slits to enable vision. Seclusion intended to preserve the legitimacy of the family line—that is, to ensure that the head of the household was the actual father of the child. This meant that entire sections of households including palaces were cordoned off for women's use and entry exclusively. By the eleventh century, Chinese thinker Sima Guang hardened rules for the separation of male and female spheres, ruling that seclusion begin at an early age: "When a boy is ten years old, he should be educated by a teacher and live in the outer quarters. When a girl is ten years old, she should not leave the household. Women should not cross the threshold into the streets even when they see their brothers."[3]

In royal and noble households across Eurasia and Africa seclusion offered career or status opportunities for women. The existence of separate sections of households for women came to entail elaborate household staffs of medical, scribal, legal, and other highly trained female service personnel. As for the women who were secluded, it was said in these years that such was God's will or that seclusion protected women from men's lust. Another rationale was that strict privacy in exclusive quarters preserved women's modesty and innocence, especially shielding women from the nastiness of the outside world. In some cases, seclusion was a kind of sanctification of women, spiritualizing them and making them holier than those in the turbulent public. Seclusion also indicated men's power to keep women's human interactions confined to the smallest portion of the wider human race and focused exclusively on the commanding male head of the household and his heirs. Diverse spatial regimes were obviously in play, however, especially among working people in their everyday lives. Most women of necessity moved outside the home at times and even earned their living in the public sphere.

Eunuchs often ensured that seclusion was not violated, thus being engaged in monitoring the heterosexual regime. Eunuchs' castration took many forms: it could entail complete excision of male sexual organs—penis and testicles; or it could involve simple destruction of the testicles' ability to produce semen. In this latter case, castrated men could actually engage in sexual acts though these would not result in pregnancy. Specially selected eunuchs also monitored the sexual activities of rulers to ensure that they conformed to ritual and social norms and medical notions of sexual health, all of this varying from society to society. In some societies, they were sexual partners to monarchs. In addition to performing this range of roles connected to sexuality, eunuchs also did menial work, served as attendants to monarchs, became scribes and trusted advisors, or even rose to command in the military.

Work in Everyday Life

In addition to reproducing life women were active in supporting it and fulfilling governmental requirements for tribute and taxation. They worked in silk, wool, linen, and cotton textiles, in a variety of crafts, and generally in agriculture. Medical and legal work fell to women as well, and they were especially recognized for their work in healing. Accounting, finance, and behind-the scenes management of businesses in urban areas also made use of their skills. Although farm families—the vast majority of the population—generally were self-sufficient in providing all the goods they needed to subsist, urban people were not. Those in the higher ranks employed women in personal service that ran a range from household management to bodily assistance such as beautician and masseuse to wet-nursing and childcare. Women even served in military and policing forces in many regions of the early modern world.

All of these undertakings demanded skill and know-how broadly connected to a range of technologies. Their activity and the knowledge connected to it were at the heart of gendered systems of labor, which varied from region to region, making gender an unstable and hardly uniform category. Parents taught children productive skills, especially in agriculture, but children were also sent out as apprentices in neighboring or even distant households to learn craft and other intricate skills, including medical and artistic ones. Women who could read, write, and calculate might even have an edge in some marriage markets, as parents sought out skilled partners who would match or complement the skills of a son or fill the needs of the family business. Training girls in any of these undertakings fell to women in a household.

The sexual division of labor was always flexible and arbitrary. Among some nomadic peoples, for example, women rode horses and might fight as men did while in other cultures masculinity might be exclusively connected to care and use of large animals especially readying them for military ventures. Women's major role in West African agriculture but also in farming across the continent gave those societies their special character, with slave women excelling in farming that fed the slave men conscripted into early modern armies. These farmers made the continent as a whole into a well-stocked and flourishing source of nourishment by cultivating millet, sorghum, a range of melons and yams, beans, groundnuts (peanuts), coffee, eggplant, and dozens more plants. Beyond their horticultural skill and with the cooperation of men who often built some of the infrastructure for irrigation and drainage, they also put effort into gathering the wild herbs, fruits, and the leaves of certain bushes and trees to make food more flavorful, adding those to the fish, molluscs, or reptiles found in the environment.

Among the Mandans of North America, who practiced settled agriculture, women planted corn, squashes, and other vegetables in river basins, tilled the soil with tools made from animal bones, and harvested crops. They also preserved ears of corn and dried slices of squash and meat for the winter, housing some of it in the large buildings that they constructed of reeds, grasses, and mud, which then dried to hardness. Native American women dug deep pits able to store tens of thousands of ears of corn. When droughts came and crops failed, local women returned to gathering the many wild fruits and herbs from far and wide as their main source of food.

As the Mandans prospered, other Native American peoples came to their settlements to obtain food and other supplies. In times of general scarcity, Mandans might have nothing to offer. This led to violent invasions, in preparation for which women took the lead. Beyond building their houses, they dug six wide trenches six feet deep around their towns, in some cases adding new trenches as their towns expanded. In addition, they built fortifications and other protected buildings to keep out unfriendly interlopers. Although these often allowed the Mandans to continue to thrive, growing trade and interactions among Native Americans and eventually with Europeans could not block out contagious diseases nor defend against those warriors who came to have guns and horses. Still, strong, competent, and resourceful women as elsewhere across the globe were key to survival.

Chinese women, likewise, were constantly at work providing the goods needed to maintain life and earning bits of money, sometimes to pay taxes and tribute. One especially important task that caught the attention of poets across the centuries was tea-picking, perhaps because it was done by girls and young women. Some wrote of the girlish laughter and others of their gay bodily movements. Young women did this job, however, out of serious need: often to make tribute payments to the imperial government. Meanwhile the government needed the tribute to finance its expenses and to keep the general population healthy: Chinese health improved when the boiling water in which tea steeped killed water-born germs. The tribute in tea was so important that government officials oversaw the work. Young women were distressed if there were problems with the harvest because the consequences of a shortfall in tribute payments to them and their families could be severe. Here is a poem that catches the contradictions in these tea-pickers' lot:

> The Fenghuang Peak is sweetened with spring dew;
> The girls in blue skirts have nimble fingers.
> Passing over the streams and crossing the clouds, they go to pick tea;
> At noon they return home with baskets still half empty.
> The express edict for "tribute tea" has come down from the capital;
> Regardless of the fact that the cold weather has delayed the sprouting
>   of tea.
> After curing, grains of tea appear like seeds of lotus;
> Who understands? More bitter than lotus seeds are their hearts.[4]

In some societies, men were coming to direct and participate more fully in agricultural production. Historians estimate that beyond growing crops, women spent hours each day processing produce so that it could be edible: five hours is one estimate of the amount of time it took African women to strip away stalks and outer shell of millet to reach the germ and then grind the germ and sieve it into flour, followed by crafting the cakes and cooking them. The process was also especially arduous because of the heavy mortars used to smash the germ. Similarly long and fatiguing work was involved in regions where wheat or rice needed extensive processing to become an edible component of daily meals. Women in ethnic groups that migrated took their agricultural know-how and products with them: when the Mande people moved southward and westward from the Niger River to the coast in the twelfth century, they introduced the production of rice to women in their new home and all the technologies involved in it. The technologies for processing of produce, cooking it, and other preparations were those usually devised by women—again a generally unacknowledged accomplishment that women's history has helped bring to light especially in the case of the highly skilled African women farmers and slaves.

Beyond food production, women participated in a range of artisanal and other skilled employment in medieval Mesoamerica, serving as scribes, for example. In China, with the increasing separation of the sexes, women had artisanal and specialized jobs such as lawyers ministering to the "inner quarters" where women and children were secluded. Mayan women, however, worked in artisanal jobs alongside men, sharing space with them in contrast to practices of seclusion in force elsewhere. Despite ideological and legal restrictions on women's activities and access to space, many in the Chinese upper and middle classes read, raised their children to advance in society, participated in their husband's activities, and managed finances. Moreover, Chinese women during these centuries were initiating the spinning and weaving of cotton, which became lucrative for the family economy, contributing to the rising prosperity that the empire experienced.

In other areas there were also clear gender divisions in craft work: in northern Nigeria men did all the wood carving, much of it religious in nature, while women did the dyeing and weaving of textiles. Much of the dyeing was connected to fertility in the region: indigo dye was said to generate fertility and was thus monopolized by women, while men were kept at a distance from the dyeing pots. In other parts of Nigeria, however, men did weaving and women carved vessels. In China, women had come to be the major spinners of silk thread and wove vast quantities of cloth to pay taxes for the household. Yet some Chinese men were weavers outside the home, for example, in large state-run workshops. Across Native American society in Mesoamerica and South America, women were also the primary weavers of the fine cotton textiles that clothed rulers in the region. These textiles were similarly sold or used to fill tribute obligations. The intricate patterns, fine texture, colorful dyes, and overall liveliness of cloth in the Western Hemisphere amazed later colonizers because none of these could be found in European textile production.

As in Eurasia so in the Americas, where the elite classes wore the most exquisite textiles. In the Andes, these fine textiles might also include textiles of feathers woven on special looms—looms too large, some say, for women to have produced these elite materials. Still, women did weave luxury goods from rabbit fur and the finest cottons alike. The women artisans who wove these textiles were highly valued in Aztec and Mayan societies but not in the Incan Empire nor in far-off Malaysia, once again proving that gender hierarchy exists in various forms and that there is little of biological determinism in work roles. The complementarity of functions as a social value was nonetheless strong. Both household and state workers wove the most intricate fabrics, but in some cultures households mostly focused on ordinary textiles both for home use and for the state. Governments used ordinary textiles to clothe the military in an age of continuing warfare that destroyed both warriors and their garments.

Beyond textiles, women were often the skilled brewers in many societies, including the British Isles and Africa, again a craft emanating from their agricultural activities of growing hops and beer's other ingredients. In Incan and across Andean societies generally, elite women similarly dominated the craft. Among the less elite brewers, running an inn was a natural offshoot, and Chinese women often helped their innkeeper husbands. As well as being potters to provide containers for the crops they grew and the ingredients they processed, Native American and women elsewhere wove baskets, a still different container for holding food. Many of these baskets were so tightly woven that they could hold liquids. The craft of dyeing also fell to Amerindian women because it was mostly done with herbal plants they had grown, though among the indigenous people of present-day Mexico both men and women worked with the cochineal bug that made a vivid red dye. Again, though men in China gradually came to work in textiles, women kept hold of the specialty of batik design on these textiles. The gender plasticity of artisanal work in some societies or in some crafts coexisted with strict gender divisions of labor in others.

It becomes clear that artisanal work was most often small scale and domestic unlike the vast scale of industrial production that would come later. Goods taken to market were often simply those in excess of what the family needed for its own use. Still, in some instances, women's craft production led to the formation of guilds or solidarity groups that insured their well-being as craftspeople. Some organized craftswomen were also organized market women, and this combination of production and marketing gave them a powerful position. African potters constitute a case in point: on the West Coast of Africa the coordination of production and marketing made these women influential and their position almost unassailable by men who would eagerly have replaced them in order to become wealthy in their own right. European women also formed guilds to ensure solidarity as their craft position was often under siege by men who believed that women's work should be neither well remunerated nor secure.

In another occupation, midwives had special knowledge and experience in the birthing of children and in some societies were much revered. As in the case of Mexican Amerindians, they also aimed for procedures around the birth to follow cultural traditions apart, in today's view, from the medical aspects of parturition. Among both Aztecs and Incas, where warrior values prevailed, midwives were seen as guiding the battlefield struggle of childbirth and providing the newborn with appropriately gendered paraphernalia—a spindle for an infant girl and a sword for a boy. Like craftswomen, they too had associations, where ritual knowledge was organized and disseminated and where they built occupational solidarity.

Among many societies in the Western Hemisphere, production was intertwined with religion. Inca rulers, whose empire was growing in the fifteenth century, demanded that conquered communities establish special buildings—the House of Chosen Women—and grounds where a select group of beautiful young women would be confined to weave and prepare special foods for priests, priestesses, and the rulers. Later, some few of these girls and women went to the Incan capital to become wives to the Inca or to other high officials or imperial heroes. One major qualification of those not married off was complete abstinence from sex. Anyone breaking this rule would be buried alive with her paramour. Other girls about ten to twelve years of age and the most beautiful in their communities were taken to the capital and groomed for several years to be sacrificed to ensure the gods' favor. To be chosen was an enormous honor not just for the girl but for her family and wider kin network.

In Mesoamerica women's work ran beyond the usual textiles and food-based activities. They were scribes and teachers, and like African women they oversaw the operation of thriving markets. Similarly African and Southeast Asian women were marketeers beyond the region, engaging in long-distance trade and financial transactions including moneylending. One

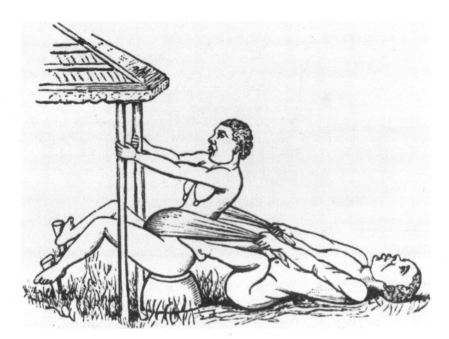

FIGURE 1.3 *African woman in childbirth, c. 1600. Birthing practices differed around world. This candid image provides one version, with two people participating in forcing the birth. In other instances, women went off by themselves or were surrounded by neighbors or attended by a midwife, who might not do better than a woman on her own. Courtesy of Hulton Archive Getty Images.*

suggested rationale behind such activity was that men were so busy training and serving as warriors that essential functions of trade fell to women. Ma Huan who recorded the routes of the great Chinese fleets in the early fifteenth century noted of Siam in 1433 the "custom that all affairs—all trading transactions great and small are managed by their wives." Two and a half centuries later a traveler again saw that "The money-changers are here [Siam/Thailand] most women as at Tonkin [Vietnam]."[5]

Slavery as a system of productive, reproductive, and sex work existed everywhere at the end of medieval times and all races, religions, and ethnicities were subject to enslavement. Women slaves were taken captive when their communities were overrun by victorious troops. Pirates raided coastlines in the seas around China and along the Indian Ocean and Mediterranean coastlines. There was also general raiding to pick up women slaves to sell to wealthy clients: for example, horsemen raided across southern Russia to gain women for *Mughal*, *Ottoman*, and Central Asian households. Africans picked up women to enslave as agricultural workers because of their legendary know-how, though they also took them across the Sahara to sell in North Africa as sex and domestic workers. Slavery was thus widespread, filling the labor and reproductive needs in uncertain times, and making for a vigorous local and regional trade in humans.

Here too, there was no definitive division of labor along with many varieties of unfreedom. In Africa, fourteenth-century Moroccan traveler Ibn Battuta noticed women slaves working alongside men in copper mines. As in Africa, generally most of the Saharan trade in slaves consisted of women, valued because they could farm, spin and weave raw materials into cloth, and simultaneously produce children from whom their owners could profit in multiple ways. However, in some societies there were apparently few actual women slaves but many women who were by custom tied to a household or who otherwise lived in states of dependence. Unfree labor was a complex phenomenon, as in times of famine parents would sell children and husbands sell wives. Women in Native American society involved themselves with their husbands in trading slaves, while as captives during wartime they were integrated against their will into the victorious tribe. Slavery would become even more complicated and dire with the imminent coming of the Atlantic slave trade.

Solidarity and the World of Ritual

Community rituals bound people together in both their reproductive and productive lives and positioned the individual as but an element in a larger scenario. In Aztec society women undertook some essential tasks such as weaving as part of a group. They would stroll together while working. Laundering in streams or at river banks also brought sociability and bonding for women in many parts of the globe. Other community building tasks included agricultural and food processing ones that were often done collectively: harvesting, preserving, and storing corn, for example, or haying. Women built housing together, not to mention the fortifications that they also are known to have built. Some of this housing such as Mongol *yurts* or *gers* was temporary, causing women also to pack it up. They also wove and felted the sturdy cloth walls of these circular dwellings. In many places ceremonies following the birth of children or childbirth itself was another community event that could include family members, a wider audience of kin, or unrelated observers from the neighborhood or village. Childbirth at the topmost ranks of society included high officials as witnesses to this politically significant event.

Women also controlled important festivals. In China, for example, the needle-threading festival took place on the seventh day of the seventh month (it was also called the double seven festival) and there they demonstrated their skill in dimly lighted rooms. The festival was based on the myth of two separated lovers, one the daughter of a goddess and the other a common herder. The festival, focused on women's domestic skills, came to be akin to Western Valentine's day for its reference to lovers finding one another. Women, however, provided the fruits, hibiscus water, and other ceremonial needs for the festival. In Europe, charivaris were a kind of counter-festival marking the world turned upside down, especially in matters of sex. They occurred when a woman married a younger man or a very old man married a girl. Pots and pans clanged outside the offenders' home, obscene remarks and gestures were hurled, and the couple might be made to ride backward on a donkey amidst jeering neighbors. At Carnival, which observed the coming of Lent for Christians, people drank or dressed excessively, sporting a phallus for a nose, for example, or donning clothing of members of the opposite sex. They might try to look high and mighty to mock aristocrats or clergymen. Unlike the threading needle festival, women did not necessarily control such observances but the rituals nonetheless could target them or fortify gender rules.

Pilgrimages to shrines—both distant and nearby—took place in groups. In the Ottoman Empire shrines were common, dotting the landscape and offering the possibility of frequent brief trips where they might seek out a holy person's blessing of a child or of good health or healing. Japanese women regularly visited the significant and more minor holy places, while women across Europe and the Ottoman Empire similarly acknowledged relics, icons, and sites where miracles had occurred or which holy people had sanctified with their presence. For Muslims, trips to Mecca as part of religious obligation could be life-transforming events for women and men alike. Women voyaged to Mecca, however, in all-women groups, accompanied by a male relative. In the region they could also worship the tombs of the Prophet's family—both immediate and extended. Adherents to mystical Islam—or Sufism—often had opportunities to go on retreats in special hostels for meditation.

Hindu women in South Asia could empower themselves and their family through their ritual suicide on the death of their husbands. Known as "fire-eaters," widows could pledge to kill themselves through self-cremation. Widows even in their early teens who had made such a commitment fasted and purged themselves of all earthly desires and then processed through their community and entered the flames before their family and other onlookers. The ritual sacrifice was holy, a sign of devotion and sanctification, and ennobling for the sati's family and all who looked upon her death. Onlookers collected ashes or any remains, for these too the community considered sanctified.

Conclusion

In 1500, women's lives consisted of several common experiences, the first being that most bore children and had an obligatory relationship in nurturing them. They all faced the possibility of dying in childbirth or having their children die; both maternal and infant mortality was high. Second, most women did the productive work of farming and participating in or overseeing the preparation of food. Third, most dealt in the creation of textiles: growing cotton and flax; securing and processing animal fibers or skin or tending mulberries; spinning threads; and weaving textiles. Even noblewomen usually took work with textiles, including embroidery, as their domain. Fourth, most women lived in societies shaped in differing degrees by the idea—varying from region to region—that men were in one way or another superior, though without any reason attached to this superiority. They simply were the dominant god, force of nature, or leader of a community or family.

That said, across the globe variety reigned among women. From enslaved women to empresses and high priestesses, women's lives differed profoundly in terms of the types of violence and coercion they faced and in their economic circumstances. Although most women followed social rules for their behavior, societies differed in the value assigned to those roles. Women in the Western Hemisphere enjoyed greater complementarity with men; their daily tasks were valued and their power over many community decisions held. Across Eurasia in contrast they lived under strong patriarchal rule that emphasized hierarchy in the power of kings, noblemen and male officials, fathers, and elder brothers over women. Like everything else, the structures of power women and men faced were themselves complicated, with room for maneuvering and with sites that women might dominate.

Glossary

Buddhism	A religion that developed in Central and Eastern Asia and that centered on the belief in the essential suffering in life. Concentration and the erasure of desire through wisdom could alleviate this suffering.
Confucianism	Emphasizes the importance of correct behavior and the fulfillment of obligations in all aspects of life.
Greek philosophy	Thought that emphasizes the love of wisdom and scrutiny of accepted beliefs.
Mughals	A dynasty ruling parts of Central and South Asia from the early sixteenth century to 1857.
Ottomans	An Islamic dynasty ruling at its height the Middle East, North Africa, and parts of Europe from the fourteenth century until the 1920s.

Tantrism   From the word "weaving." A set of practices among some Hindus and Buddhists, including meditation and sexual and other rituals.

Yurt (also called a ger)   A felted, round and portable dwelling of Mongols and other nomadic people.

Zoroastrianism   A set of religious beliefs centered on the universal conflict between the good forces of light and evil forces of dark.

Notes

1 Quoted in Lisa Sousa, *The Woman Who Turned into a Jaguar and Other Narratives of Native Women in Archives of Colonial Mexico* (Stanford, CA: Stanford University Press, 2017), 32.
2 Quoted in Judith K. Brown, "Economic Organization and the Position of Women among the Iroquois," *Ethnohistory* 17:3–4 (Summer–Fall 1970): 153.
3 Quoted in Robin R. Wang, ed., *Images of Women in Chinese Thought and Culture: Writings from the Pre-Qin Period through the Song Dynasty* (Indianapolis, IN: Hackett, 2003), 416. Translation by Ping Yao.
4 Susan Mann and Yu-Yin Cheng, eds., *Under Confucian Eyes: Writings on Gender in Chinese History* (Berkeley: University of California Press, 2001), 235. Translated by Weijing Lu.
5 Anthony Reid, *Southeast Asia in the Age of Commerce, 1450–1680: The Lands Below the Winds* (New Haven, CT: Yale University Press, 1988), 164.

Further Reading

Chatterjee, Indrani, and Richard Eaton, eds. *Slavery and South Asian History.* Bloomington: Indiana University Press, 2006.

Fenn, Elizabeth A. *Encounters at the Heart of the World: A History of the Mandan People.* New York: Hill and Wang, 2014.

Furth, Charlotte. *A Flourishing Yin: Gender in China's Medical History, 960–1665.* Berkeley: University of California Press, 1999.

Gutiérrez, Ramón A. *When Jesus Came, the Corn Mothers Went Away: Marriage, Sexuality, and Power in New Mexico, 1500–1846.* Stanford, CA: Stanford University Press, 1991.

Kellogg, Susan. *Weaving the Past; A History of Latin America's Indigenous Women from the Pre-Hispanic Period to the Present.* New York: Oxford University Press, 2005.

Powers, Karen Vieira. *Women in the Crucible of Conquest: The Gendered Genesis of Spanish American Society, 1500–1600.* Albuquerque: University of New Mexico Press, 2005.

Sarkar, Tanika. *Rebels, Wives, Saints: Designing Selves and Nations in Colonial Times.* London: Seagull Books, 2009.

Smith, Bonnie G., ed. *Gender History: Critical Readings*, vols. 1 and 2. London: Bloomsbury, 2018.

Sousa, Lisa. *The Woman Who Turned into a Jaguar and Other Narratives of Native Women in Archives of Colonial Mexico*. Stanford, CA: Stanford University Press, 2017.

Wiesner-Hanks, Merry. *Women and Gender in Early Modern Europe*. 3rd edn. Cambridge: Cambridge University Press, 2008.

2

Early Modern Structures
of Power

Bugis-born slave To Ayo began her grown-up life as partner to the king of Jambi in seventeenth-century Southeast Asia. Becoming his wife, To Ayo reached a pinnacle of female success in those days, until, that is, the king took two more wives, both of them from noble families in Macassar. They ganged up on To Ayo, calling her "the Bugis whore." Still, operating in the complex web of royal political power, she held her own as the most prominent woman in the kingdom. Then a differently gendered power formation took shape: after their husband's death, the three wives banded together to rule the kingdom as a team and to accumulate wealth because of running its trade. Though male-dominated, royal arrangements allowed some women to reach the height of wealth and influence in their societies.

States were broadly diversified in terms of size and variety. In general, large states, including kingdoms and empires, were dynastic. That is, they were headed by a central family or clan that would transfer power from generation to generation and that might keep control for centuries. A complex royal cast of characters was part of early modern structures of power; power centers such as castles housed the family and officials—many of them both close and distant relatives. Some of these ruling households expanded because of the rising centrality of efficient states to social and political stability. Nomadic clans existed alongside these increasingly powerful dynasties. A few extensive empires such as the *Ming* in China or the Ottomans in North Africa, the Middle East, and southeastern Europe involved complicated and large political structures, but there were also many smaller principalities like Jambi, urban regimes that were connected to the agricultural labor of the surrounding areas, and chieftaincies that were set in the midst of an agricultural heartland. Gender figured importantly no matter what the size. Royal power made demands on women that they bear children or manage complex households but it also gave elite and even not-so-elite women opportunity.

As in the case of To Ayo, living in a small kingdom, regulations and precepts found in Islam or Confucianism or other belief systems also shaped the state. Religious and ritual leaders were influential because they exercised control over sexuality, marriage, and still other institutions setting rules for behavior. Thus, both elite and ordinary people passed their everyday existence surrounded by multiple forms of power. These included an array of religious instructions but also guidelines appearing in mythology and long-held proverbs, stories, and customs. Laws regulating kingdoms were themselves a product of all of these as well as a result of royal command.

In every system of power, women seized opportunity or created it, even as others were trapped in inequity and the suffering brought on by events such as famines, kidnapping, domestic violence, and warfare. Because structures of power in those days centered on the family, women were in fact central to its operation. Not only could some like To Ayo come to be a ruler and wealthy in her own right, systems of power rested on employing women of the royal family to uphold codes and preserve sanctity. For example, in many states segregation of the sexes in royal households made not only for organizational complexity but also for an aura of power and purity to develop around rulership, including its household. The protection of women's space from outside intruders and influences was a major undertaking, often employing hundreds and even thousands of workers. Although in some instances eunuchs stood guard over harems and other confined spaces for women, trained troops of less advantaged women often protected secluded areas—some of them massive. In the Southeast Asian kingdom of Aceh, one that had a succession of queens, 3,000 armed women were sentinels around royal buildings. In kingdoms of Muslim India, there too women might be armed protectors of royal zenanas. These protected spaces of a household were sites of female skill, training, commitment, and general activity. In other words, women played varied roles in the institutions of monarchy, empire, princelings, duchies (ruled by dukes), chieftaincies, or large landed estates given by monarchs to military heroes or adventurers to rule on their own terms.

The Gender of Rulership

Since early times, rulership has involved maintaining control over other humans and in many cases bending them to a ruler's will, desires, ambitions, and financial demands. Rulers generally depend on the intellectual and physical skill of others to supplement their own command, thus the need for selecting wise advisors or people of fighting prowess to be part of an intimate circle. So much of early modern rulership depended on physically engaging in combat or at least showing oneself on the battlefield, that rulership was coded as male. This does not mean that women never entered the battlefield: to the contrary, hundreds of women gained their reputation as expert fighters and incredibly brave and skilled military leaders. In 1548, Queen Suriyothai, also of Southeast Asia, was killed in a Thai war with Burma. Her husband's elephant having collapsed, Suriyothai positioned her own elephant so as to protect him from danger. The Burmese king killed her even as her husband made a successful return to battle. Thanks to her he eventually ruled into the late 1560s.

The ruler of large empires or kingdoms held the central position—and usually one of magnificence and drama—amidst a large cast of characters who were most often related. Genealogy in those days was crucial and determined the standing of members surrounding the ruler. In the early South Asian Mughal Empire the mother of the emperor stood at the place of honor, exercising prerogatives and receiving deference. Should the mother be deceased, aunts of the emperor took that precedence, with the oldest aunt having the most power in terms of household ritual. She organized public feasts and would receive regular, ceremonial visits from her nephew. The older generation of women even outranked the ruler's wife or wives. However, in other societies, power might be distributed differently among women and men alike, but most often among family or clan members.

Systems of marriage and reproduction were important to rulership, and these systems also varied from place to place. A state's strength, wealth, and territorial security might depend on a strategic marriage as did the longevity of the regime in the reproduction of the next generations of rulers. In the fifteenth century, strategists in the rising Ottoman Empire in Anatolia (Asia Minor) took the goal of imperial expansion into account when arranging marriages. Early sultans allied themselves with rivals by choosing wives from these competing families or even from those that had been defeated. The sultan in the next generation would then be the product of such a union; he benefited from an alliance that might bring the territory of his mother into the empire that he inherited. Because men could have four legal wives under Islamic law, wives were responsible for raising a son to be a potential leader and for gaining him acclaim so that he would become that ruler as opposed to the sons of other wives. As a sultan's son was sent to administer various centers of the growing empire, his mother left the sultan's quarters to help groom her son for power, all the while knowing that there would be intense and even murderous rivalry among competing sons and their households. Her responsibility was to build networks of support for his ascendancy and if possible to protect him from harm. The reproductive duties of these women were thus of real consequence, lasting into their children's adulthood and beyond. Should her son become sultan, his mother would then head the imperial household; should he fail, he most likely would be strangled or otherwise murdered.

Other marriages involved the direct transfer of significant territory to which the bride was heir, usually when there was no male to inherit it. In such a case the new queen often benefitted from the magnificence of her dowry, as was the case with several European queens from the Middle

Ages and thereafter. Isabella of Castile (1451–1504) merged the enormous kingdom she governed with that of Ferdinand of Aragon; the union laid the foundations for modern Spain. The Habsburg Empire—a powerhouse in early modern and modern history—grew to its massive size through this continuing practice of such astute marriages. The dowries in land brought by women helped it encompass for a time in the sixteenth century much of Central Europe, the Low Countries, parts of Italy, and the Iberian Peninsula,

Still, there was enormous variation. Among the *Incas*, who settled in Cuzco in present-day Peru c. 1000 CE, the duties of the chief Inca interwove religious and political rule, with the Inca considered a god and his wife, the Coya, a goddess whose burial displayed her high, sacred status. Usually a relative—even a sister—of the Inca, the Coya ruled over the large royal establishment, worked to determine issues of succession, and presided over the main ceremonies to the moon. Like many royal consorts, she was crucial to the successful maintenance of royal power and, in the case of Coya, could even be venerated, especially after her death. She was nonetheless an inferior to the Inca, though still of very high rank, and the extreme veneration she received carried with it an implicit commemoration of that inferiority. When the Inca himself went to war, however, she administered the empire and with her vote could break ties arising within the Incan council. Moreover the Coya stood at the head of the women of the empire in their complementary roles to those of men—roles that were not denigrated as being inferior. The people of the empire gave her—as they did the Inca—tribute to fund her household and undertakings.

Still other gendered power arrangements existed. Across North America, where there was great individuality among the several hundred language groups, women generally received more respect and authority in Amerindian communities. Because of their relationship to agriculture by which they processed food and often grew it too, they controlled the disposition of land among some woodlands peoples. Many of these chieftaincies were matrilineal (descent through the mother) and some were matrilocal (spouses, children, and other relatives were based in the mother's home), in some cases stemming from the fact that women themselves built the houses for their kin. Among the Iroquois, control of food and houses resulted in their authority to eject men from the kinship circle and even to make decisions about going to war. They claimed this right to decide on undertaking war because the women would be the ones provisioning the warriors. Among the Iroquois, they also determined who would serve as chief and when chiefs had proven themselves sufficiently unworthy of the office to be dismissed and replaced. In fact, among some groups such as the Iroquois it could be said that women tipped the balance of gender power in their favor.

Many Amerindian groups in North America as well as societies around the world specifically made room for transgendered people. From an early age, someone who preferred the traditional tasks of the other sex was allowed to perform as that sex. The name attached to this sexual identity was berdache; the berdache could dress and behave as the chosen sex and have relationships as he or she wished. In Indonesian and other cultures transgendered people were considered sacred because of their ability to move back and forth among sexual identities. Some of these dressed in what today would be called queer costume—that is, costume that was neither male nor female. Cross-dressing existed in theatrical performances as well in many parts of Eurasia. Moments in the calendar of festivals when the world was "turned upside down" involved men and women switching dress, roles, and social spaces. Such times both eradicated gender demarcations and underscored them. As such playing with gender was part of the structure of gender power, blurring, mocking, or upending it for a time.

Where men held power as a matter of course, as was the usual situation across the globe, legendary male rulers such as Monteczuma of the Aztec Empire, Suleyman of the Ottoman Empire, and Babur of the Mughal Empire came to prominence in the early sixteenth century. Their masculinity itself became celebrated as it was defined in terms of military prowess and leadership. In all three cases, the rulers were constantly at war, with the booty of warfare important both financially and religiously. In victory, Monteczuma had the heavy responsibility of performing blood sacrifices of captive soldiers as offerings to keep the cosmos functioning. Living individuals from the defeated enemy were ritually killed, their hearts cut out while they were still alive.

Before this system unfolded, however, Aztec society in central Mexico believed in the shared responsibility of male and female in keeping the universe harmonious; with a powerful goddess interacting with a male god, women had a more expansive public role. The wife of the head of state was seen as a complementary authority, receiving tribute like the Coya of the Incan Empire. Gradually Aztec men interpreted women's role as purely domestic; they should be removed from participation in public life or decision-making. Once there had been important priests and priestesses to represent that duality and priestesses often prepared the victims to be sacrificed, but later leading men presided alone over the human sacrifices made in the name of a single male god. Nonetheless, across Aztec societies, there were remnants of complementarity as women's birthing of children remained analogous in the population's eyes to the valor and sacrifice of the warrior on the battlefield.

Also a conquest-based state, the Ottoman emperors mobilized ghazis or warriors to advance their holdings or defeat non-Muslims; victorious ghazis gained the spoils of war as soldiers would do for many more centuries. Selim I (1470–1520) captured important middle eastern territory, including Egypt. His son Suleyman the Magnificent (1494–1566) expanded the empire even more and undertook major battles against Christians and, like his father, against Shia Muslims (see p. 43 below). Akbar, the grandson of Mughal founder Babur, enhanced his masculinity by instituting a large, closed off harem whose occupants went nameless even if mothers of royalty—a change from the time of his grandfather. Households of 5,000 or more women swelled the masculinity of many African rulers, showing sole rulership not just over men but over thousands of women.

Despite the exoticization of harems that would come later from the pens of Western writers, such harems were places of rule, finance, bureaucratic organization, the pursuit of agriculture and other productive wealth, reproduction, education, and sexuality. In other words, the innermost workings of government were often accomplished there, again with differences among governing households. In the reign of Zahiruddin Muhammad Babur (1483–1530), founder of the Mughal Empire in South Asia, his household was often on the move as he set out to conquer, defend various holdings, recapture, and otherwise remain both nomadic and settled in the location of his empire. Some women in the household moved with him; others did not; still others were sent as diplomats to create relationships across clans and noble families; yet additional women negotiated the finer terms of those relationships. In Babur's case, as in others, the harem was a complex institution, having little of the secluded, highly sexualized nature often seen in it by would-be colonizers and travelers searching for exoticism.

As for the sexuality of the royal household, it demonstrates through the writings and paintings of royalty and nobility an example of the complex relationship among military and other men and among women. In his youth, Mughal Emperor Babur was married to Sultan-Ahmad Mirza's daughter Ayisha Sultan Begim with whom he has to be forced to have sex, so little is he attracted to her. His diary openly presents his lack of sexual feeling toward her. In contrast, at about the same time Henry VIII of England first enters an arranged marriage and then is so driven by his emotions that he marries and then divorces or executes a series of wives as his passions get the better of him. Like the samurai (warriors) of Japan in this period, many Islamic warriors of the Central Asian tradition (Mughal, Safavid, and Ottoman) freely engaged their emotions in same-sex affairs of varying degrees of intimacy. In the long run, male sexuality, especially for royalty and the upper classes, was panoramic, covering a breadth of possible experiences.

Queens, Consorts, Regents, and Advisors

Despite a male dominated power structure in most places, women exercised varied authority at the top of the ruling pyramid. Even as male privilege seemed to increase across the globe, women's relationship to power was flexible. The royal household was usually extensive in the early modern period, containing the monarch's family, a large number of kin, and networks of advisors. The dynastic state was not separate from the family and all its relations. In fact, a dynastic state in which power passed down through generations operated in the clutches of family rituals, customs, and struggles, though differing from region to region. The state also included the functionaries who made it operational, as well as a large staff of soldiers who guarded it. Slaves populated the royal household, serving in any number of positions: advisors, scribes, educators, domestic workers, concubines, and many other posts. To sum up, the royal household—whether secluded or not—was at once a site of government, reproduction of the dynasty, finance, social welfare, and education. All those participating in the monarchy gained their lessons here and passed their lives connected to the household.

Hurrem Sultan (c. 1502–1558) was the legendary wife of Ottoman Sultan Suleyman I. She was legendary because around this time Ottoman sultans changed their sexual and reproductive strategies. They stopped marrying women from other royal or noble families and relied on concubines—that is, sexual partners, either slave or free, whom they did not officially marry—to produce heirs to the throne. The idea was that there were no families of any worth comparable to that of the Ottomans. Marrying with a rival family only fostered ambition and encouraged the rival to build a competing alliance of supporters who might challenge the ruler. Suleyman broke the tradition of having a large number of sexual partners by sending away other concubines, marrying the slave Hurrem, and relying on her advice and information. Especially when he was away on military campaigns, her reports on the scene in Istanbul shaped his understanding of political needs and guided his policies. In the tradition of the Ottomans and other Muslim women especially in the upper class, Hurrem actively endowed many charitable institutions such as the soup kitchen in Jerusalem described in terms she set down. It served meals to 500 needy people a day and was still functioning into the eighteenth century.

Women also ruled in their own right. State-building was the order of the day in early modern times, and singular women such as the Southeast Asian queens and including Queen Isabella of Spain and Elizabeth of England took actions that centered on creating wealth, using that wealth to build state power and fighting capacity, and overseeing the consolidation of a governing apparatus. Isabella's marriage to King Ferdinand of Aragon showed the potential for royal consolidation of their two territories; the devoted Catholic king and queen spearheaded the move toward a strong centralized government funded by overseas expansion across the Atlantic. Consolidation also included driving out the Muslims (Moors) who had taken over the peninsula in the eighth century and maintained a stronghold there even as their power diminished. By 1494, Isabella and Ferdinand had revitalized Catholicism and used it to provide spiritual and cultural unity across the once separate kingdoms. The task became somewhat easier with the slow trickle, which eventually became a flood, of wealth from the new world. Using this wealth, they bought sophisticated weapons, including ships that could house cannons—all of this in the service of unification and centralization. Isabella's Catholic faith was a centerpiece of this consolidation.

FIGURE 2.1 *Hurrem/Roxelana. Hurrem, also known as Roxelana, was initially a concubine in the Ottoman royal household. Exceptionally she became the wife of Suleyman the Magnificent, breaking the tradition that sultans did not marry. Hurrem's life skills allowed her to become so trusted that she carried out policies when Suleyman was away on the battlefield. Courtesy of Heritage Getty Images.*

Elizabeth of England (r. 1558–1603) brought her fractured people together after decades of Catholics and Protestants killing one another in the name of religion. In 1588, Elizabeth's ships drove off the Armada of Philip II of Spain, who aimed to conquer and convert England to Catholicism. After that triumph, Elizabeth focused on building commerce, sponsoring pirates to seize Spanish treasure ships, and advancing England's entry into the New World. Elizabeth wisely used captured wealth to build state and national power. She also fought off contenders to the throne and thus continued to lay the groundwork for institutional stability in the kingdom. In the process, she also became a model for women.

Nur Jahan (1577–1645) was one consort among many in the women's quarters of Mughal emperor Jahangir, but an incredibly powerful one, as her contemporaries acknowledged. She came close to rulership when Jahangir picked her out as a favorite. In one sense the Mughal Empire was more developed than Spain had been when Isabella ruled and far more mature than the kingdom run by Elizabeth. Yet Sultan Jahangir was an opium addict and alcoholic; his favorite consort, Nur Jahan took the reins of power early in the seventeenth century and made the very most of them. She worked behind the scenes through trusted courtiers because women were not supposed to deal publicly with men. From this more or less unobtrusive position, she fostered economic development by encouraging foreign trade, sponsoring crafts, and experimenting in creating new products with her household retainers and staff. Nur Jahan made sure that tariffs were collected on foreign trade and generally aimed to build up the treasury in order to expand the Mughal reputation through buildings and good works. Her goal was to consolidate its prosperity.

In societies where men kept large retinues of women, many of them were similarly crucial advisors, both on an ad hoc basis and as part of tradition of women serving as counselors. In one African king's large household with thousands of women in addition to male retainers, the women held a variety of jobs. At one end of the spectrum, they managed the king's properties, oversaw agriculture, or collected or kept records of taxes and tribute. At the other, they were basic household staff or simple agricultural workers. The large households of women in Africa grew as different locales or important families in the kingdom or in adjacent kingdoms sent their women as a way of building a relationship with the monarchical center—the center of power. The mother to the king in many West African kingdoms played an important part not just in the household but in advisement to the ruler. The queen mother knew the history of the kingdom as recounted orally; this knowledge included the history of feuds and alliances. Her networks of information and her assessment of a current diplomatic or other situation were also valued ingredients in determining royal policy.

In the Ottoman Empire, during its early centuries, when a woman of the harem gave birth to a son, she no longer had intimate relations with the sultan, unlike the case of Hurrem/Roxelana later in the Ottoman Empire. This did not mean that she became a nobody; rather she became a serious political actor, grooming her son for power and building networks of support for him. Similarly, in parts of Africa queen mothers were king-makers and co-rulers. In troubled times, a queen mother could hold a kingdom together, work to keep her family in power, or guard its assets. During the religious wars of the sixteenth century, French queen Catherine de Medicis (1519–1589) worked to maintain royal unity by serving as regent for her sons and marrying her daughter Margaret to the Protestant king Henry of Navarre. At the same time as she tried to bring the two sides to negotiate, she also seemed to be behind massacres of Protestants at her own daughter's wedding. Her attempt to build a unified state in this manner failed as outright battles over religion plagued France for decades.

Used to forge and strengthen political alliances, women were traded in marriages with rulers and nobility. As shown, the fifteenth-century marriage of Isabella of Castille and Ferdinand of Aragon was the foundation of Spain as a modern state, as the two major provinces were joined by the union. The joining of realms, as in this case, was hardly unusual because it built state power if the marital alliance was nurtured and if elites would agree to the new arrangement of power. Preoccupation of rulers and elite men with military actions often left decisions about alliances and the selection of specific mates to consorts and wives. In many cases, royal women determined both—who would marry whom and how the process of conceiving and giving birth to the next generation would proceed. Consorts of rulers had the responsibility for becoming knowledgeable enough to make such selections and diplomatically astute enough to see them through. Leading wives might select concubines.

In times of imperial expansion, intermarriage of conquerors and the conquered, especially of high rank, was one facilitating institution for ensuring a lasting peace. Mughal Emperor Akbar had some 300 wives, many of them because of their political and familial connections. Akbar, who continued his grandfather Babur's conquest of South Asia, also used marriage to cement his conquests, citing a wife's connection to the conquered territory as pivotal to integrating it into the empire. Akbar, a Muslim, married *Hindu* princesses, and thus blended peoples and cultures in his very household and family. Foreign princesses were central to the construction of an empire's diversity, signaling the inclusion of varying religions, ethnicities, territories, languages, bloodlines, and cultures representative of both the extended ruling family and its many subjects. Marriage was a powerful force for integration.

Another strategy of empires was to create an aura of sanctity around themselves and especially around the ruler. This sanctification had consequences for all levels of society, for instance, in the belief that the ruler's touch could cure various diseases. The cosmic importance of the Aztec ruler was his connection to the heavens and to the divine order; as male rulers came to claim precedence over the women co-priestess of ceremonies, their sanctity and power rose. European monarchs similarly partook of the belief in their connection to the spiritual as noted in the theory of the divine right of kings. The Catholic Church lodged the monarch in the hierarchy of creation just below saints, angels, the pope, and other recognized divine beings. Some kings were even canonized. In the Mughal realm, whereas Babur had initially been one of many chiefs struggling for control of territory with the help of male and female relatives, the official accounts of his grandson Akbar's life featured a story of his divine birth with little in the way of human sexual activity involved.

The result for women was their devaluation in the power structure of the monarchy. Whereas under Babur, a woman's clan and pedigree fortified the regime in lore and in the court, under Akbar only a few decades later, Akbar's mother was not even named in accounts of his birth. Moreover, while Babur's entourage included male and female family members and other allies, under Akbar, women passed their days in living quarters separate from those of men and from public business. Women of the highest rank were suddenly "veiled" and secluded, their participation in activities given virtually no notice or credence and access to them highly restricted. In Akbar's newly constructed royal palace, rings of guards that included both eunuchs and women preserved the "sanctity" of the women's quarters. In fact, Akbar insisted on the spiritual nature of his "family" of wives and many concubines, aligning it with that of the Prophet Muhammad and of his own divinity.

In many places, royal women managed funds, while noble men pursued military matters such as peacekeeping and expansion. In Tunisia, for example, where shifting interregional politics made for instability, noble women physically moved royal treasuries from the central compound to distant safe places when conflict threatened. Others served as go-betweens, guides, translators, and advisors during this era of increasing movement and imperial growth. In the fur trading country of North America, Native American groups regularly allied young women with English and French traders in a relationship that was recognized as crucial to imperial economic and political development. Native American women knew how to make the moccasins so necessary to the outsiders and to produce the pemmican that sustained the traders on long trips. In this way they served those seeking to build their power. More central politically in this era of ongoing combat around the world, they negotiated peace among rival ethnic groups as did women of high status on the other side of the globe. However, as women performed all these daily tasks—high and low—royal and noble men's spiritual, even holy, aura was shining brighter.

In the gendered arrangement of dynastic political power, reproductive capacity was crucial. The mother of the sultan came to have immense power in the harem, organizing, directing, arranging, negotiating. She might conspire with others to have rivals to her son executed; she also oversaw the hierarchy of concubines and maneuvered within it. As power was expressed in sexuality, it allowed male and even in some cultures female rulers numerous sexual partners instead of just one, adding to the complexity of royalty. Akbar's 300 wives were a testament to his all-encompassing power, of which sexuality was a major part; even in seclusion and unseen, the simple idea of these women's existence magnified his mysterious authority. While radiating sexual privilege, Akbar regaled audiences with his abstemiousness both in terms of sex and food. This was hardly the case with a contemporary of Akbar, Margaret of Valois, the daughter of Catherine de Medici and Henry II of France. She had so many lovers and was so known for her flagrant promiscuity that her husband, another King Henry, had no trouble getting his marriage to her annulled. In such cases, having multiple sexual partners was part of royal privilege, but in other royal households—some in Africa, for example—the multiple wives did not necessarily have a sexual relationship with the monarch as they were simply domestics or women with technical skills or agricultural workers. Moreover, in a royal harem there were still rules governing sexuality such as the already mentioned decree that once an Ottoman sultan's sexual partner gave birth to a son, she was removed from the pool of sexually available women. In China, although the emperor had many partners, his sexual intercourse with any one of the women was timed by palace eunuchs as a matter of royal health.

Because marriages across classes were generally arranged and managed, liaisons based entirely on personal affection were usually extramarital. Love—high and low—was considered disorderly, so that confining it to concubinage was an attempt to fend off chaos. A sultan or other ruler might have an official wife and at the same time have steady, even faithful relations of love and friendship with a specific concubine or other woman. Rulers often had children with these "favorites," treating them with affection and possibly even preferring them to those he had fathered as part of his royal responsibility. Although adultery was considered a serious crime in many cultures, even a crime punishable by death, such was generally not the case with the monarch. Bevies of women indicated his or her prowess, dominant status, and privileged body in addition to supporting extensive alliances both with noble families and other monarchs. In these situations, the women involved with a male monarch were not necessarily powerful, though they might temporarily receive gifts and special treatment. Their position was fragile, dependent on the king's favor and yet in some cases open for them also to have nonmarital sex.

Sexuality among members of the same sex was also part of the rituals of power in some societies, amounting at times to a rejection of heterosexual relations with consorts. Zahiruddin Muhammad Babur (1483–1530), Central Asian warrior and founder of the Mughal Empire, kept a diary from 1499 to 1519. Known as *The Baburnama*, it speaks of warfare, food, geography and nature, and politics. This driven conqueror was simultaneously a connoisseur of fruits and of beautiful countryside. His diary also presents a picture of his feelings, including those springing from his first marriage and from a crush on a boy from his military base. The boy arouses so many emotions that he uses poetry in talking about him. The powerful Shah Abbas of Persia/Iran (1571–1629) is also depicted as having his most touching moments with a boy in the royal household and as entering coffee houses where "curly-locked" and attractive boys could be found.

Somewhat uniquely, Babur's prose and poetry express these intense sentiments and also an open detachment in the heterosexual relationship with his wife. He opens with an account of Sultan-Ahmad Mirza's daughter Ayisha Sultan Begim, who becomes his wife in 1500. His family drives him to have sexual relations with her, but he admits to being bashful and ultimately losing any affection at all toward her. He notes the power of his royal mother who every month or six weeks forced him "with all the severity of a quartermaster" to have sex with his wife. Standing in the way is his growing attraction for a market boy—Baburi: "*I made myself miserable over him*," he admits. Being unmoved by desire and the poetry of love until that time, he turns to passionate longing that he begins to express in poetry: "*May no one be so distraught and devastated by love as I . . . .*" Still he remains bashful and can barely interact civilly when Baburi appears. "I almost went to pieces," he writes. in his memoir:

> *I am embarrassed every time I see my beloved. My companions are looking at me, but my gaze is elsewhere.* In the throes of love, in the foment of youth and madness, I wandered bareheaded and barefoot around the lanes and streets . . . oblivious to self and others. *When I fell in love I became mad and crazed. I knew not this to be part of loving beauties.* Sometimes I went out alone like a madman to the hills and wilderness, sometimes I roamed through the orchards and lanes of town, neither walking nor sitting within my own volition, restless in going and staying. *I have no strength to go, no power to stay. You have snared us in this state, my heart.*[1]

Apart from their involvement in the intricacies of royal and upper-class heterosexuality, women were responsible for carrying out diplomacy and negotiating deals, even those of the utmost importance. In the mid-sixteenth century, the Portuguese merchant Fernão Mendes Pinto (1509–1583) described the arrival of a high-level woman ambassador in Southeast Asia. An adventurer, briefly a Jesuit, and observer of the customs of countries where he traded, Mendes Pinto also recorded events, including diplomatic negotiations and preparations for war. In particular he became aware of the position of women in Southeast Asia, which he often noted. Their activities were not hard to find, as they controlled trade networks and were often engaged in a variety of important economic transactions, even from their position as energetic rulers of their kingdoms.

One day when he is arranging trade in the Bantam market, "a woman by the name of *Nhay Pombaya* arrived there, on an embassy from the king of Demak, emperor of all the islands of Java, Kangean, Bali, Madura, and all the other islands in this archipelago. She was a widow, nearly sixty years old, whom he had sent to deliver a message on his behalf to the *Tagaril*, King of Sunda . . . to the effect that within a period of a month and a half he was to meet with him in person in the city of Japara, where he was then preparing to go to war against the kingdom of Pasuruan." At this point the king, hearing of her arrival, goes to the port personally to welcome her and then to accompany her "with great pomp" to pass her visit in the royal palace alongside the queen. "[H]e moved to another apartment far from there, since that was the highest honor he could pay her."

Pinto proceeds to explain the "ancient custom" of using women as high-ranking diplomats: It is, he says, a "very ancient" and kingly custom "for matters of great importance requiring peace and harmony to be handled through women. This is true not only of private messages that the lords send their vassals in this particular instance, but also of public and general affairs that some kings handle with each other through their embassies. The reason they give for this is that the female sex, owing to its gentle nature, has been endowed by God with more affability and authority, as well as other qualities that make them worthy of great respect than men, who are blunt and therefore less likely to meet with favor by the parties to whom they are sent.

> However, they say that the woman who is chosen by these kings for the kind of mission I am talking about must have certain qualities that they deem necessary in order for her to accomplish her mission satisfactorily. They say that she must not be single because an unmarried woman who leaves her home will lose the very essence of her being, for it is said that though a woman is loved by everyone for her beauty, at the same time it may also be more of a cause for dissension where peacemaking is required, than for bringing matters to a successful conclusion where peace and harmony are sought . . . .
>
> The *Nhay Pombaya* who brought the message to the king of Sunda left the city of Bantam immediately after the conclusion of her mission. Not long afterwards the king completed his preparations and departed with an armada . . . fully equipped with food and munitions.[2]

The arbitrary operations of gender, with tasks assigned to either men or women, characterized the highest levels of power.

The Rule of Religion and Tradition

Varieties of religious structures also affected the lives of women, awarding them power or demanding their submission. For millennia, women had played a major role as shamans, witches, and those under the spell of spirit possession. As intercessors with the forces of nature or humans whose occult secrets allowed them to reach the heavens, shamans worked on healing, foretelling, divining, and articulating wisdom. Both men and women were shamans. It was often believed, however, that women had special powers as shamans, so that among certain groups in North Asia—one place where shamanism flourished—male shamans often dressed in women's clothing to reap female power. Shamanism as a practice was a display of women's skills and knowledge that often grated on the male establishment's control of world religions such as Buddhism, Judaism, Christianity, and Islam.

In spirit possession, women interpreted forces that had seized hold of them while in trances. When a spirit took control of their consciousness, the medium—that is, the person so seized—then passed on the communication from that spirit or other non-earthly being. Spirits or ghosts provided messages from ancestors, but as with shamanism it took training to be gripped by the spirit or in the case of shamanism to access special knowledge. Women's abilities in relating to the unseen forces driving the phenomena of the seen world—including weather, sexuality, health, and well-being—gave them prestige and often economic well-being.

Alongside shamans, local people in Mesoamerica followed their belief in coordinate male and female gods and goddesses when performing their daily activities, observing the regulations stemming from these divine beings. The male gods in the long run had more power but there was no devaluation of women or their regular demonization. Important goddesses among the divine pantheon regulated and influenced sexuality, especially for the wealthy who might be prone to excess with multiple partners. Goddess of sexuality Tlazolteotl and goddess of sexual discord and excess Xochiquetzal are associated with excrement, personal disorder, and bodily disease. Sexual stages in the life cycle were important moments for accessing goddesses and the unseen world—as in sacrifices and divining—to be purified.

Most of the world's people also lived guided by broad, usually strict and highly gendered rules for behavior. Such rules derived from religions or general moral principles seen as organizing the cosmos. Gathered up into systems such as Confucianism and the Laws of Manu, these ideals for the conduct of everyday life were especially enforced by men because such ideals championed male dominance. For example, a collection of over 2,000 precepts called the Laws of Manu was developed in South Asia more than 3,000 years ago. Said to be handed down by the creator of humanity—one of the Manus—they were written down c. 150 BCE and expressed the hierarchical traditions of South Asian society. Many of these precepts concerned women's nature and inclinations; others gave instructions on how to treat women in order to ensure social harmony. These precepts are often considered important today as a set of laws or guide to life. One can see the gender politics in these guidelines for male and female relations.

55.   Women must be honoured and adorned by their fathers, brothers, husbands, and brothers-in-law, who desire (their own) welfare.

56.   Where women are honoured, there the gods are pleased; but where they are not honoured, no sacred rite yields rewards.

57.   Where the female relations live in grief, the family soon wholly perishes; but that family where they are not unhappy ever prospers.

58.   The houses on which female relations, not being duly honored, pronounce a curse, perish completely, as if destroyed by magic.

59.   Hence men who seek (their own) welfare, should always honor women on holidays and festivals with (gifts of) ornaments, clothes, and (dainty) food.

60.   In that family, where the husband is pleased with his wife and the wife with her husband, happiness will assuredly be lasting.

Chapter IX, 1–25

1.   I will now propound the eternal laws for a husband and his wife who keep to the path of duty, whether they be united or separated.

2.   Day and night woman must be kept in dependence by the males (of) their (families), and, if they attach themselves to sensual enjoyments, they must be kept under one's control.

3.   Her father protects (her) in childhood, her husband protects (her) in youth, and her sons protect (her) in old age; a woman is never fit for independence.

4.   Reprehensible is the father who gives not (his daughter in marriage) at the proper time; reprehensible is the husband who approaches not (his wife in due season), and reprehensible is the son who does not protect his mother after her husband has died.

5.   Women must particularly be guarded against evil inclinations, however trifling (they may appear); for, if they are not guarded, they will bring sorrow on two families.

6.   Considering that the highest duty of all castes, even weak husbands (must) strive to guard their wives.

7.   He who carefully guards his wife, preserves (the purity of) his offspring, virtuous conduct, his family, himself, and his (means of acquiring) merit.

8.   The husband, after conception by his wife, becomes an embryo and is born again of her; for that is the wifehood of a wife, that he is born again by her.

9.   As the male is to whom a wife cleaves, even so is the son whom she brings forth; let him therefore carefully guard his wife, in order to keep his offspring pure.

10.   No man can completely guard women by force; but they can be guarded by the employment of the (following) expedients:

11. Let the (husband) employ his (wife) in the collection and expenditure of his wealth, in keeping (everything) clean, in (the fulfillment of) religious duties, in the preparation of his food, and in looking after the household utensils.

12. Women, confined in the house under trustworthy and obedient servants, are not (well) guarded; but those who of their own accord keep guard over themselves, are well guarded.[3]

Household practice was religious practice among Hindus in South Asia and constituted a structure of power in the family. Parents gave their daughters in marriage as children or just before they entered puberty. As she reached puberty, say at age fourteen, or even earlier, the marriage was consummated with a ceremony. At that young age, a girl's life of constant, uncomplaining, devoted household service began, and this devoted practice was called *dharma*. As part of living out her *karma*, she undertook to fulfill the needs of the preceding generation of in-laws and to bear children, whose needs she also cared for. Her needs, whether in terms of food or other life necessities, had the lowest priority according to religious traditions. Moreover, it was crucial that she remain unable to read, write, or calculate; otherwise she would fall into sin. Should she become literate her husband

FIGURE 2.2 *Devi Revered by Brahma, Vishnu, Shiva (1710). Devi or Mahadevi is an all-encompassing goddess from whom other goddesses spring. As all-encompassing, she can be kind and gentle or ferocious in her protective force. Brahma the creator, Vishnu the protector, and Shiva the Destroyer all revere her for without this female principle—the Mother—they cannot exercise their divinity—a counter to negative views of women. Courtesy of Heritage Getty Images*

would die or she herself would become an adulteress, so the teachings of holy men went, regulating women's being.

Similarly, the ancient philosopher Confucius had proposed in his *Analects* principles for daily life that affected the conduct of women and the regulation of gender. Ban Zhao (45–116 CE), a famous Chinese woman author, was born into a family of writers. Young, literate, and scholarly, she finished a history of the Han dynasty that her brother had begun and became court historian. Then she turned to writing about women, whose correct behavior, according to Confucius and other thinkers, was crucial to harmony in the family and society. Ban Zhao maintained that the book was in fact a guide for her daughters because she herself had been nervous and unsure of familial and social rules on her marriage at age fourteen. Based on Confucian thought, *Lessons for Women* continued to be read down through the centuries and was repeated by authors in early modern times. Her thought that women needed to be educated as much as men did also remained current for more than a millennium.

These three ancient customs epitomize woman's ordinary way of life and the teachings of the traditional ceremonial rites and regulations. Let a woman modestly yield to others; let her respect others; let her put others first, herself last. Should she do something good, let her not mention it; should she do something bad let her not deny it. Let her bear disgrace; let her even endure when others speak or do evil to her. Always let her seem to tremble and to fear. When a woman follows such maxims as these then she may be said to humble herself before others.

Let a woman retire late to bed, but rise early to duties; let her not dread tasks by day or by night. Let her not refuse to perform domestic duties whether easy or difficult. That which must be done, let her finish completely, tidily, and systematically. When a woman follows such rules as these, then she may be said to be industrious.

Let a woman be correct in manner and upright in character in order to serve her husband. Let her live in purity and quietness of spirit, and attend to her own affairs. Let her love not gossip and silly laughter. Let her cleanse and purify and arrange in order the wine and the food for the offerings to the ancestors. When a woman observes such principles as these, then she may be said to continue ancestral worship.

No woman who observes these three fundamentals of life has ever had a bad reputation or has fallen into disgrace. If a woman fail to observe them, how can her name be honored; how can she but bring disgrace upon herself?[4]

Most belief systems and cultures had goddesses as well as gods except for the Mediterranean religions of Judaism, Christianity, and Islam; the tales of goddesses provided examples of noble behavior for women and became inspirational models. For example, among women raised in certain branches of Hindu culture, the goddess Radha is the principle consort of the Lord Krishna. She embodies a perfect kind of love, not just wifely but spiritual in its conjoining of thoughts and feeling. The image of Radha guided behavior, while fortifying women emotionally. Depictions of Krishna romping with the *gopinis* or women cowherds gave women a sense of possible joy and pleasure to accompany them in their daily lives of relentless hard work and suffering. Beautiful Christian statues of the holy figure of Mary as she, though not a goddess, gave glimpses of loveliness to those who deprived themselves of food and comfort to sustain the lives of their children. East Asian women also appealed to Guanyin, goddess of mercy to spare them or their children some of the excessive pain of life.

Political thought was often intertwined with religious and moral precepts, constructing an ideology undergirding social hierarchy and correct behavior. These precepts targeted feminine and masculine roles in order to keep a strict gender order as the basis of social and political stability. Correct behavior in the family and the outside world was essential as formulated in Islamic, Christian, and Confucian thought to name a few. In general, these precepts advocated women's inferior position in society, which was expressed in obedient behavior to men, including at times to orders from their sons. However, Confucian thought additionally promoted a hierarchy of males to one another according to generations and to birth order among male siblings. Oldest sons were doted on and legally advantaged among cultural groups across the globe, sometimes to the complete impoverishment of daughters.

Christian, Jewish, and Islamic belief systems from the Middle East then spread to Europe, Africa, and other parts of the world with their ideas of women's polluted and more sinful nature. This essential sinfulness was based in the original sinfulness of Eve found in these "people of the book"— that is, those where truths were found in the Torah, the Bible, or the Holy Qu'ran. Christianity and Islam also advocated a warrior ethos against "infidels," who should be slaughtered. In undertaking crusades and jihads, men waged holy wars and gained glory from them, along with the wealth that they might steal from defeated people. For this holy combat or struggle, family resources were directed from women in the family to the sanctified military men. From the family to the wider society, religion and moral tenets composed structures of power that produced rules for and images of women as inferior humans.

A male hierarchy consisting of a pope as head of the Catholic Church and many levels of a male clergy dominated Christianity, which in 1500 flourished across Europe and in some parts of the Middle East. Although in theory both male and female souls could be saved through belief in a male deity and his son Jesus, and although the sexes could equally be sinners, the principle of clerical celibacy suggested that sexual contact with women was sinful. To put it another way, it was far superior for men not to be involved with women. Female celibacy was also mandated, but shunning women was in fact the height of holiness. Despite the number of women who had martyred themselves in the early days of Christianity, the sanctity of men and especially their proximity as disciples to Jesus was the foundation of Christianity as it unfolded over the centuries. Moreover, there was this evaluation of women in the Catholic Bible: "No wickedness comes anywhere near the wickedness of a woman" (Ecclesiastes 25:19). Evidence of women's experience as followers was discounted as not being meaningful. Nonetheless in early modern times, women were faithful, especially as devotion to Jesus's mother Mary increasingly became a regular part of Church doctrine and ritual. The male domination of Christianity and the virtually nonexistent role allowed women as Christian leaders remained a powerful part of Catholicism.

Islam began in the early seventh century when the angel Gabriel first spoke to the Prophet Muhammad (570–632) with the words of God. Thereafter God spoke to Muhammad, handing down the spiritual tenets of Islam and those for the conduct of everyday life. Unlike Judaism and Christianity, many of whose features Islam integrated, Islam did not say that Eve alone was responsible for disobeying God's precepts; instead, together Adam and Eve failed in their obedience. Muhammad's family was full of strong women, especially his first wife Khadija, who supported his ministry financially and emotionally, and the last of his twelve wives Aisha, a woman he reportedly married when she was still a child and who compiled his preachings and sayings. Muhammad's daughter Fatima nursed the Prophet through his last illness and joined these two as models of support for later generations of women. From all these women he drew strength, particularly in debate and discussion.

The Qu'ran is a transcription of the words Allah spoke to the Prophet Muhammad in the early seventh century CE. The Qu'ran provides some precepts about women, which were later expanded by religious teachers. In particular, Islam made female infanticide a crime and allowed women to inherit property. Both of these ideas were far in advance of laws in other regions of the world at the time, but it also contained precepts about women that appeared long-standing ideas in other religions and cultural traditions. On the one hand, the Qu'ran says, "Whoso doeth good works, whether male or female, and he or she is a believer, such will enter paradise." Simultaneously, the Qu'ran maintains that "Men are in charge of women, because Allah hath made one of them to excel the other."[5] There are many linguistic versions of the Qu'ran, and the quotation below is yet another, giving still further instructions on the behavior of women:

And say to the believing women
That they should lower
Their gaze and guard

Their modesty: that they
Should not display their
Beauty and ornaments except
What [must ordinarily] appear
Thereof: that they should
Draw their veils over
Their bosoms and not display
Their beauty except
To their husbands, their fathers,
Their husband's fathers, their sons,
Their husbands' sons,
Their brothers or their brothers' sons,
Or their sisters' sons.[6]

Amidst these utterances, the women in Muhammad's family and their descendants played a large part in the flowering of Islam and in its dissensions. After the death of his merchant wife Khadija, his first convert, Aisha assisted him and after his death she became a major figure in the defense and spread of the religion. Aisha, however, was seen as the "wandering wife" who had sexually betrayed her husband. Those who defended her and gained her exoneration became one major group of Muslims—the Sunnis. She handed down the words of Muhammad and helped organize pitched battles to maintain the Sunni interpretation of Islam—most notably the Battle of the Camel in 650, which she observed from her perch on this commanding animal. In opposition, Fatima's husband Ali, a nephew of Muhammad, and their sons were taken as the most legitimate heirs of the Prophet and because of direct descent were seen as a competing group called Shias/Shiites. Under Fatimid rule, they dominated many regions in the Middle East and became the sworn enemies of the Sunnis.

As interpreters of Islam, a few but important Sunni women wielded influence, gaining legitimacy because of their closeness to Aisha and other especially revered spiritual leaders over the centuries. Thus, the complexities of Islamic life continued, with women as prophetesses and religious teachers of girls and other women and with many poorer and working women hardly able to keep themselves in seclusion but instead working in markets and on farms. Moreover, even among the strict Shias, in the twelfth century Arwa and Asma served as queens in Yemen, while in the eleventh century Sitt al-Mulk ruled the Fatimid kingdom when her brother went mad. Thus Islamic teachings and traditions were also part of early modern structures of power, even though Islam had a less consolidated officialdom than did Christianity. Down through time, the interpretation of those traditions did not appear to serve women overall but at the same time women believed in the benefits Islam did offer, honored its values, and conducted their lives according to its principles and regulations.

Conclusion

Men dominated the structures of power—secular, political, and religious—in the early modern period. They generally served as the supreme authority in almost every realm of human life, despite women having a coordinate or complementary realm of influence in such empires as the Incan. Although monarchs fortified their leadership with brawny, adept military men, they also operated in an environment filled with underlings—women, common servants, dwarfs, eunuchs, and holy people. In most cases their existence was to emanate from a ruler's own being and serve to enhance and make possible his sovereignty. Even a consort's existence had this servile aura to it. Yet time and again royal, elite, and even commoner women acted in powerful ways, exercising their will and displaying their ability to shape policy. They gave birth to heirs and often exerted power as queen mothers and regents, but they also wielded influence through determining marriage choices, creating diplomatic alliances, and deciding issues of war and peace.

Religions and systems of established doctrines such as Confucianism also formed a mental and political container in which people lived their lives. Those systems, in force across Eurasia, generally supported a strict hierarchy of male superiority and female inferiority, despite the crucial role women played in giving and sustaining life and despite the crucial assistance they often provided. Among peoples in the Western Hemisphere and Africa, there was greater complementarity between the sexes and greater value attributed to women than among Confucians, Buddhists, Christians, Jews, Muslims, and others. While many goddesses and holy women in these creeds bolstered the positive side of women's spiritual life, other aspects of these doctrines emphasized women's polluted, whorish, even demonic nature. Still, women participated in these powerful systems, integrating beliefs and obedient behavior into their daily activities. Many thrived despite the degrading characterizations attributed to them and some even invaded the world of intellectual, artistic, and spiritual accomplishment that men claimed as their own. Fluidity and change, in fact, characterized the rules of gender and the roles that men and women assumed within the structures of power.

Glossary

Hindu   A polytheistic religious practice that developed mostly in South Asia.

Inca   A name for the ruler of a large South American highland empire that stretched several thousand miles along the west of the continent until conquest by the Spanish in mid-sixteenth century. Also the conventional name given the empire as a whole.

Karma   One's destiny as determined by actions or behavior in previous existences.

Ming   A Chinese dynasty (1368–1644) known for its lively trade, urban life, and arts.

Notes

1 Wheeler M. Thackston, trans. and ed., *The Baburnama: Memoirs of Babur, Prince and Emperor* (New York: Smithsonian Institution/Oxford University Press, 1996), 112–13.
2 Source: Fernão Mendes Pinto, *The Travels of Mendes Pinto*, Rebecca D. Catz ed. and trans. (Chicago: University of Chicago Press, 1989), 382–4.
3 *The Laws of Manu*, trans. Georg Bühler (Oxford: Clarendon Press, 1886; repr., New York: Dover, 1969). The Bühler translation is available in many editions and on numerous websites, for example, Fordham Modern History Sourcebook: Modern India Sourcebook http://legacy.fordham.edu/halsall/india/manu-full.asp. The version presented is excerpted from Bühler version on the Fordham website.
4 Nancy Lee Swann, trans, *Pan Chao: Foremost Woman Scholar of China* (New York: Century Co., 1932), 82–4. There are many web versions: http://acc6.its.brooklyn.cuny.edu/~phalsall/texts/banzhao.html.
5 The Holy Qu'ran quoted in Linda T. Darling, "Islam," in *Oxford Encyclopedia of Women in World History*, Bonnie G. Smith ed. 4 vols. (New York: Oxford University Press, 2008), 2:625.
6 The Holy Qu'ran, 24:32 as quoted in *Women in World History: Volume 1 – Readings from Prehistory to 1500*, Sarah Shaver Hughes and Brady Hughes eds. (New York: M. E. Sharpe, 1995), 1:152–3.

Further Reading

Andaya, Barbara Watson. *The Flaming Womb: Repositioning Women in Early Modern Southeast Asia*. Honolulu: University of Hawai'i Press, 2006.
Clendinnen, Inga. *Aztecs: An Interpretation*. Cambridge: Cambridge University Press, 1991.
Graubart, Karen. *With Our Labor and Sweat: Indigenous Women and the Formation of Colonial Society in Peru, 1550–1700*. Stanford, CA: Stanford University Press, 2007.
Kallender, Amy Aisen. *Women, Gender, and the Palace Households in Ottoman Tunisia*. Austin: University of Texas Press, 2013.
Lal, Ruby. *Domesticity and Power in the Early Mughal World*. New York: Cambridge University Press, 2005.
Lal, Ruby. *Empress: The Astonishing Reign of Nur Jahan*. New York: W. W. Norton, 2018.
Peirce, Leslie. *The Imperial Harem: Women and Sovereignty in the Ottoman Empire*. New York: Oxford University Press, 1993.

Peirce, Leslie. *Empress of the East: How a European Slave Girl Became Queen of the Ottoman Empire*. New York: Knopf, 2017.

Spellberg, Denise. *Politics, Gender, and the Islamic Past: The Legacy of 'A'isha bint Abi Bakr*. New York: Columbia University Press, 1994.

Tedlock, Barbara. *The Woman in the Shaman's Body: Reclaiming the Feminine in Religion and Medicine*. New York: Bantam, 2005.

Thackston, Wheeler M. trans. and ed., *The Baburnama: Memoirs of Babur, Prince and Emperor*. New York: Smithsonian Institution/Oxford University Press, 1996.

3

Imagining Their World, 1450–1700

One of the most inventive woman storytellers in world literature appears in the *Arabian Nights* or *One Thousand and One Nights*—a collection of small tales told by Scheherazade over the course of many nights to her husband Shahryar. King Shahryar has experienced betrayal by his wife and has her killed. Thereafter, he trusts no woman to the point that he murders each successive wife after their first night together so that she cannot betray him sexually as his first wife had done. Put together over the centuries from West, South, and Central Asian lore, the tales are told by Scheherazade, who has volunteered to marry the king and to try putting an end to the slaughter of young virgins. She does so by presenting one of the intriguing or magical, or comic or erotic stories in her repertoire each night, but stopping at a crucial spot in the tale before morning. The king so desperately wants to hear the end that he lets her live for the finale until the next night, when she finishes that story, starts another, and then breaks off at a suspense-filled moment. Through storytelling, Sheherazade puts an end to the murder of women.

The *One Thousand and One Nights* took shape somewhere in the ninth century and continued to amass further tales of Scheherazade that were ultimately written across the centuries. They were probably told as clusters or even large groups of women spun thread or sewed or potted. They might also have emerged in cafes and been invented by different authors. They were mostly, however, put in the frame of women's storytelling. Although women were less powerful than men in most societies even given diversity of life experiences, stories of heroic women rippled through culture, often motivating and uniting them. Myths of goddesses were similarly empowering to many, while tales of women in the family of the Prophet Muhammad or Sundiata, founder of the Malian kingdom in Africa, were inspirational across the centuries. Because women had memorized and recounted religious and other tales to their children, they had staying power and lived on in the world of imagination. Women had access to these older tales, including that of Scheherazade, through the oral tradition along whose networks the poetry and prose of heroism or wickedness reached them by ear. In later centuries they arrived through reading, exactly as upper-class French women received them in the early eighteenth century when they were first translated from Asian languages into European ones.

Gradually during the centuries before 1500, women's literacy rose in China and Japan, especially among elite women and women in cities and then soared. Literacy eventually advanced elsewhere across the globe as urbanization increased. Cities brought people and ideas in closer contact, stimulating conversations and writing. Frequently women sought out reading skills to have access to religious texts such as the Qu'ran and the Bible independently of other people's interpretations, while in some cases they explicitly looked for texts by women. They also became poets, novelists, and authors of diaries and memoirs themselves, creating, elaborating on, and also perpetuating both new and old narratives of women's power, courage, and sentiments. Fictional accounts captivated them: *The Tale of Genji*, composed by Lady Murasaki in c. 1000, is a prime example of an enduring work that later Japanese women authors dreamed of, emulated, and modified to fit their own style.

Others created to bring honor to their families, as people across several kingdoms celebrated their women writers' and artists' reputations. The family often served as a workshop in the literary and visual arts; there numerous women found opportunities to learn techniques and ultimately create masterpieces on their own. In some places creative skill could improve a young woman's chances of making a good marriage or increasingly, teach. Courtesans were often adept in the arts, using their well-developed skills to engage their clients. In so doing they helped promote erudition and culture. Simultaneously, men imagined and represented women in their own literary works in ways that were occasionally empowering but more often confining, even slanderous. They not uncommonly reacted to women's intellect, craft, and artistry with scorn; in some cases their misogyny goaded women to vigorous response. In these centuries and down to our own times a "querelle des femmes"—that is, a quarrel or hot debate over whether women's creativity had any value and more generally whether women themselves had any worth at all—has continued, always sparking women's creativity in refuting such claims.

Women's writing moved in multiple ways to shape society and fill their complex lives. They engaged with spirituality and the natural world in writing, visual arts, and music. Chinese society placed the most importance on such accomplishments, so much so in fact that women there produced thousands of books and many works in the visual arts during the early modern period. Even as children, some hungered to learn to write and paint or to devote their lives to religion. All of this occurred even though in many prosperous societies such as those of South Asia the main religious and philosophical principles deemed that women should have no cultural accomplishments, reading skills, or any knowledge whatsoever, unless it was directly related to their spiritual lives. Contradicting it all, the story of Scheherazade, which it is believed to have emerged in its earliest form in South Asia, provided inspiration: she kept herself alive by night after night telling compelling stories, timing her performance to build suspense, and thereby taming the murderous emotions of her husband.

Goddesses, Devotions, and Opportunity in the World of Faith

People globally lived in a world thick with religious beliefs, festivals, and commemoration; often belief systems served as an explanation for the happenings in everyday life and grand events, including the creation of the universe. Goddesses were often seen as creators of the entire cosmos or of the earth itself—Mother Goddesses—in which case a male might appear as the complementary god of the heavens or the sky. Where both female and male entities existed as such powerful forces, their union often produced lesser gods and goddesses—that is, a subset of the divine who then produced humans. Or the founding deities produced individual humans, usually heroic ones. In any of these cases, the reproductive role of women sometimes held center stage as bringing the whole of existence into being. Pueblo Amerindians handed down across the generations the story of Thought Woman (Tsichtinako) who sent the first women—two sisters—from beneath the ground to the surface of the earth, telling them it was time for them to emerge with their baskets.

> "In them you will find pollen and sacred corn meal. When you reach the top, you will wait for the sun to come up and that direction will be called [east]. With the pollen and sacred corn meal you will pray to the Sun . . . . They now prayed to the Sun . . . and sang the creation song. Their eyes hurt for they were not accustomed to the strong light. For the first time they ask Tsichtinako why they were on earth and why they were created." She tells them that they were made by father Uchtsiti, the creator of the world and all else. The reason for their emergence is that his creation is not complete until they, with their sacred corn and their prayers, come to rule the earth in all directions.[1]

The story of Thought Woman and the Two Sisters, repeated over the generations, reminded people of women's generative and sacred powers. All the while suggesting spirituality, other belief systems provided a panoply of comforting, terrifying, and inspiring lower-level goddesses, who were nonetheless mighty, with equally specific tasks and capabilities. South Asian religious belief offered the goddess Kali, who was horrible in her reported deeds and in graphic depictions of her actions. Summoned in times of danger, Kali appears to defeat enemies with the utmost violence, symbolized in the skulls that adorn her body and the blood that surrounded her. Women in Greek and Roman mythology were similarly goddesses of war or connected with the post-death underworld of Hades. As such they were violent but just as often they served as protectors and providers of wisdom. Agricultural goddesses like Ceres ensured and brought forth harvests. There were also thousands of household gods across the globe, whom women were responsible for speaking to and commemorating regularly. They especially repeated their stories, perhaps embellishing or otherwise modifying them along the way.

Gods and goddesses thus metamorphosed over time in popular beliefs, as people—perhaps women—transformed their images and attributes. A striking example of such a metamorphosis comes in the transformation of the Buddhist *bodhisattva* of compassion, Avalokitesvara, from being a South Asian male or sexless figure—that is, one who transcends or goes beyond gender—to being the goddess of mercy Guanyin in China, Japan, Korea, and Vietnam. From the medieval period on, this transformation unfolded, even as the faithful across Asia followed the deeds of the bodhisattva in the sutras or Buddhist scriptures, which promised that the bodhisattva would answer prayers. Avalokitesvara or Guanyin heard the voices of ordinary people. For the faithful in East Asia, Guanyin was and remains vital in their lives. Women charted miracles, encouraged charitable deeds, asked for other benevolent acts of Guanyin, and built shrines and cloisters to her. Among her popular images as seen in statues and wall-paintings was the Guanyin who answered requests for a child or Guanyin who championed mothers.

Guanyin, like other goddesses and nature spirits, appeared in a variety of folkloric forms adapted to specific locales. The Taras were additional female celestial beings in some forms of Buddhism. Endowed with special energy that might be tapped through meditation, the Taras were protectors. In Buddhism, all are equal, but in Tibetan Buddhism, men have a superior position, according to some of the Sutras—that is Buddha's announced teachings—while women are said to be part of a Tantra way representing Buddha's secret instructions. In Tibetan representations the Taras are widespread, as are their temples. Their temples were especially known for their importance as centers for meditation. The acquisition of enlightenment—or awakeness—as the goal of Buddhist practice can also diminish the force of gender.[2]

In Vietnam, the goddess Lieu Hanh was described in lore variously as a daughter of an emperor, an inn keeper, a market woman, a prostitute, or the child of a god. Women developed festivals to celebrate her, while a huge market operated to commemorate her deeds—often described as miracles punishing male sexual predators. In the eighteenth century the renowned author Doan Thi Diem (1705–1748) wrote an influential collection of women's lives, including an account of the Princess or Mother (common titles awarded these cult figures) Lieu Hanh that placed her in the company of wives or long-suffering women. Doan Thi Diem herself was educated and refused marriage until she found an intellectually suitable mate. For her Lieu Hanh was a heavenly figure who arrived on earth because she had not been observant enough as a member of the *Jade Emperor*'s court. Having become learned on earth, she returned to the court and acquitted herself well. Lieu Hanh descends to earth once again, this time as a powerful deity not to be trifled with even by learned men, as she crushes the enemies of good village people and soars above both the military and educated male scholars. Her incredible deeds on behalf of the Vietnamese people and her advancement of learning make her someone to be worshipped as a deity. Her movement across time and space also aroused the special worship of women traveling as merchants and entertainers as well as market women.

Buddhism, despite its distrust of women, had its share of teachings and popular vignettes in which women were teachers of truths or somehow implicated in revealing the truth. The Buddha's enlightenment begins when he rejects the pleasures of the flesh as embodied in the lovely women his father has provided to keep him from becoming an ascetic. At the same time, it is through women that the Buddha goes down the path to enlightenment, as he sees them for what they are: in exhaustion after pleasures they are cadaverous, ugly, and suppurating bodily fluids. His Vietnamese adherents picked up the worship of Lieu Hanh, giving different versions of her life and her place in the celestial pantheon. In the *Daoist Zen Flesh Zen Bones* a monk is chastised for carrying a woman's image around with him, thus being distracted from following "the Way."

Divine Goddess of the West Xi Wangmu, whose worship was strongest in medieval times, is the Daoist protector of passion and immortality. Women adhered to practices connected to her cult including meditation and sometimes deprivation of food. For her adherents and for those in religions such as Christianity extreme fasting allowed for transcendence as it signaled a release from bodily needs. The Divine Goddess of the West had an overarching power, as she governed mortality and also served as a guide—a Daoist teacher. She and her entourage of beautiful young women were talented beyond compare:

> The Queen Mother rode an imperial carriage of purple Cloud ... as a belt pendant she had a diamond numinous seal. On her clothing, fashioned of multicolored damask with a yellow background, the patterns and variegated colors were bright and fresh. The radiance of metal made a shimmering gleam. At her waist was a double-bladed sword for dividing phosphors, and knotted flying clouds made a great cord. On top of her head was a great floriate chignon ... She stepped forth on squared-off, phoenix-patterned shoes, soled with rose-gem. Her age might have been

around twenty. Her celestial appearance eclipsed and put in the shade all others. Her numinous complexion was unique in the world.

The Daoist Queen Mother of the West was like no ordinary housewife, ruled by Confucian precepts and obedient to husband and sons. Instead, women performers, poets, nuns, and other special women were those who paid most attention to her cult. For long, she stood above all other goddesses because of her overwhelming power, beauty, and riches.

Nature was also alive with meaning for women, leading them to worship and attend to the needs of goddesses of the moon, corn, water, specific animals, and other protectors of the environment. Women performed ceremonies appeasing, invoking, honoring, and seeking help from all of these deities. Some served as priestesses and high priestesses to the gods and goddesses connected to life and to nature and were bound in their loyalty to regular devotion and often to perpetual celibacy. Shamans also participated in rituals accessing the natural and spiritual worlds to bring about healing. Sometimes using hallucinatory drugs, they might change shape or even become animals. Many shamans were women and concerned themselves with reproduction and female illnesses; as mentioned earlier, male shamans often dressed as women in order to make contact with women's symbols and healing powers, especially as they were manifest in nature.

Despite these powerful shamans and goddesses, cultural leaders gradually came to emphasize male gods. The author Chandrav(b)arti (c. 1550–1600), who lived in what is present-day Bangladesh, challenged this dominance in her version of the *Ramayana*, a massive ancient tale of the god Rama. Chandravarti was born into a poor family, her father earning only a small income as a street poet and entertainer. From him and the world of popular culture in which she lived she learned the classics, including the *Ramayana* epic. In the standard telling, Rama stars as the god struggling to free his consort Sita from the grasp of an evil-doer king and his sister, whose advances Rama has spurned. Rama makes alliances and fights heroic battles to regain Sita. Chandravarti in contrast retells the epic in her unfinished version as the story of Sita, the wife who adheres to *dharma* or her responsibility and suffers for it. Chandravarti eliminates the endless descriptions of warfare in favor of describing Sita's faithfulness in the face of constant attempts by kings and others to undermine her loyalty. Sita even features as the main narrator of the tale. Critics down to the present have mocked Chandravarti's unusual retelling, but she would not be alone in challenging men's divine dominance as they are celebrated in popular traditions. Tens of thousands of women also found in Sita the model of the obedient and faithful wife and someone to emulate through their own obedience and devotion to a husband, no matter what situations might arise.

Women's imagining of the world through religious devotions were complex, differing from region to region and among families. Worship of ancestors dominated some cultures, with households marking important ancestral moments with offerings of food and goods or with sacrifice of animals. Household and individual prayers marked other observances, while speechifying and reading from commemorative writing dominated still other ceremonies. In many societies, women carried the main responsibility for such observances and for the preparation of the dead for their voyage to the afterlife. In China's ancestor cults, rites were carried out by men in the family but all the preparations and daily observances to the dead were the responsibility of women. In some places women of an important family or household were themselves killed as part of burial ceremonies. Women envisioned departed relatives as connecting generations and providing social glue transcending time. Without the proper, continuous attention, they became wandering ghosts who could bring about retaliatory events.

Women, like men, went on sacred journeys to especially holy spots, but in many instances they had to imagine themselves as impure beings. Muslim women could not participate in prayers, enter a shrine, go on the Hajj, or visit cemeteries during menstruation; afterward, only a purifying bath allowed them to resume their religious observances. Jewish women, likewise, were to see themselves as impure in their bodies and refrain from religious obligations while menstruating and, as in the case of Muslims, participate in a ritual bath to cleanse their impurities. Despite notable women's interpretations of hadith and of other religious writings, charitable women's contributions to society, and the many holy women in these "religions of the book" (Judaism, Christianity, and Islam), women were generally to imagine themselves as disqualified from intellectual work and leadership because of menstruation. "A woman who learns [how to] write is like a snake given poison to drink," went one distortion of the Prophet's ideas.[3] In the world of religion and myth, there was much to encourage and much to discourage women's imaginings.

Opportunity in the World of Faith

During this time that is often called early modern, many changes arose in the world of religion, and these infiltrated women's interpretation of life and often transformed it. These included the rising power of priests and their enforcement of regulations applying to women. Among the Aztecs of Mexico, for example, rulers subtly transformed the formerly coordinate or parallel power and responsibility of the priest and priestess into a system in which the high priest was clearly dominant. Increasingly, epidemics and famines became the fault of women, according to explanations of male religious authorities. Yet, even where male domination in religious institutions developed, fluidity in roles and power remained possible for women both to envision and to exercise.

Other important religious changes reached deep into beliefs about gender and challenged ideas about human nature. Before the sixteenth century, religion was a realm where there was expressive and leadership opportunity despite most religions being male dominated. Women were nuns in Buddhism and Catholicism, while Sufism, an especially mystical form of Islam, held that the soul was feminine. Women also remained shamans, witches, and healers whose connections with the spiritual and natural world were powerful and acknowledged as such. People often went to those known as witches for resolution to physical, spiritual, and everyday problems. However, some religions came simultaneously to proscribe women's activities, often seeing them as polluted and capable of doing greater evil than men could. Beautiful young girls were prime sacrifices among the Incas, while women served as especially honored priestesses in other cultures.

The rise of the Sikh religion offered a form of worship that stressed the equality of women and the role of women adherents, beginning with the relatives of Guru Nanak (1469–1539) who first handed down the precepts of the new religion. Guru Nanak's mother and sister were his special supporters, but others followed because of the stress on gender equality. In addition to gender equality, Sikhism objected to the division of people by caste. The second Guru Angad, a disciple of Guru Nanak, followed his leader's idea for setting up "langar"—a practice that provided food for all, no matter what the caste, on terms of equality. His wife Mata Khivi (1506–1582) was central to making langar a reality and became one among the many Sikh women celebrated for their charity and devotion. Another, Punjab-born Mai Bhago, was trained by her father in military skills of archery and swordsmanship, gained fame as the warrior who protected the Tenth Sikh Guru from the forces of the Mughal Empire, enhancing the tradition of women's military prowess among the Sikhs.

From its founding in the sixth century, Islam, as we have seen, provided a range of inspirational religious figures, and the relatives of the Prophet Muhammad served as models: Khadija his first wife; Aisha, his last; Fatima, his daughter. In the early institutionalization of Christianity, Mary the mother of Jesus played only a small role in Catholic Church beliefs but she received more devotion in Islam. However, over the centuries the celebration of Mary's life and people's devotion to her increased in Catholicism. Religious orders committed their worship to her, making their rituals into requests that she intercede with her son for their spiritual welfare. Special prayers and novenas to Mary were central to the forgiveness of sin. The chapels devoted to her and statues of her, alone or with the infant Jesus, grew in number. People also implored specific women saints for protection and guidance in the face of trials.

Religious change inspired women and gave them voice, even a sense of freedom. In particular, they helped develop doctrines endorsing a personal and direct experience of God. In the first centuries of the Islamic faith, women saints were major contributors to the development of Sufism, which emphasized full devotion to God in the context of Islam. This devotion had little to do with achieving paradise, according to one of these, the woman

FIGURE 3.1 *Birth of Muhammad, in his mother's arms and visited by Meccans, c. 570–632. Artists depicted the Prophet Muhammad's birth, focusing on his mother, Aminah bint Wahb, holding the infant and a crowd of Meccans in awe on viewing him. The faces of mother and son are covered, conforming to the Islamic idea that one should not imitate the creations of Allah—that is, animate beings including both humans and animals. Courtesy of PHAS/UIG Getty Images.*

Sufi saint Rabi'ah al-'Adawiyya al-Qaysiyya (713–801), who brought to Sufism one of its principle articles of faith: love of God that virtually obliterated the self—sometimes called a self-forgetting love. Women across the centuries were attracted to Sufism, perhaps because a central belief held that the soul is female and also that daily relationships have no comparison to that with God, which should be all-encompassing. In contrast, non-Sufi Islam directed human relations as well as spiritual ones. Those who had completely immersed themselves in God lost their physical bodies and thus their sexuality. Once that had happened, particularly adept women who had obliterated such everyday aspects of being could associate freely with equally accomplished men because they no longer possessed physicality.

Women took up the memorialization of saints from across the spectrum of religions. Women saints represented aspects of the divine in their lives, although some were seen as the living presence or incarnation of the divine itself. These saints represented relationships to God—not those to clergy or select members of the upper class—that women seemed to crave in their religious devotion. The Bhakti movement had begun before the early modern era in South Asia, challenging the privileging of high caste control of religious thought and customs. Instead of focusing on ritual practices that few could afford, Bhakti worship stressed ordinary people's direct, emotional connection to the gods. Bhakti men actually wrote in the voice of a woman to emphasize their lowliness and suffering. Some women wrote of their perseverance in the face of trials: the allegorical Bhakti poem of a woman devoting time at her spinning wheel in pursuit of her family's well-being is one such example.

The most famous of the actual women Bhakti poets was Mirabai (1498–1557), now a Bhakti saint for whom there are shrines and sacred memorials and a number of films of her life. She was born at the end of the fifteenth century to the ruling family of Meerta, India, and at a young age was married into another princely family. A member of her new marital family attempted to poison her because of what was seen as her excessive religious fervor and her disgraceful attention to outcasts and ascetics. As a result, she escaped the family to live among the poor and disreputable as part of her commitment to simplicity and to the exclusive worship of the god Krishna. Her poetry mixed devotion to Krishna with a folkloric form, repeating words and thoughts like an incantation.

I'm colored with the color of dusk, oh *rana*,
    colored with the color of my Lord.
Drumming out the rhythm on the drums, I danced,
    dancing in the rhythms of the saints,
        colored in the color of my Lord.
They thought me mad for the Maddening One,
    raw for my dear dark love,
        colored with the color of my Lord.
The *rana* sent me a poison cup,
    I didn't look, I drank it up,
        colored with the color of my Lord.
The clever Lifter is the Lord of Mira
    Life after life he's true—
        Colored with the color of my Lord

Mirabai's poem emphasizes her steadfast devotion, even to the point of drinking poison—an element of the verse echoing her own alleged experience of being poisoned by the *rana* or male family member—perhaps the very man whom she had married. Critics point to the ways in which Mirabai's emphasis on steadfastness and strength compares to the Bhakti poetry of men who tried to imitate a woman's voice through stressing female weakness.

Sufi Muslim men and women alike wrote love poetry emphasizing the beauty of the beloved. Love poetry, however, was usually seen as a male genre not suitable for women. Those who used it were somehow failing in their female role as steadfast wives living in private and immune to cravings to write—especially about love. Those who ventured into such writing could explain their rapt devotion to a beloved and their extreme expressions of love as worship of God's creation. Love or lust poetry only articulated love of the divine—the true Beloved—for many of these authors.

To have time away from the daily activities of the home and from parenting and other family relations that essentially took the entirety of a woman's, many joined holy orders. Religions—from Buddhism to Christianity—had long offered such opportunities for participation in the divine on a full-time basis. Initially, Buddha had scorned the idea of women as monks or bhikkhunis, but he soon put his standing on the line by letting them participate in spreading Buddhist teachings and caring for sufferers in their communities. Given the general misogyny of most religions, the appearance of women's religious orders that accompanied the flourishing of world religions showed the fluidity that also existed. Most religions claimed that souls were equal even as they claimed that men were holier or closer to the divine by their very sexual identity. Even Buddhists generally believed that in attaining enlightenment a woman changed into a man or higher being.

Christian nuns also sought escape from household life in order to devote themselves to full-time study and worship. Beyond the world of spouses, children, and the arduous duties necessary to keep them alive, convents offered the opportunity to become literate and to work in educational, healing, spiritual, and charity work. Buddhist nuns took up the latter goal, while entire religious orders such as the Ursulines devoted themselves to running schools in distant lands, including those in the Western Hemisphere. Like the French nun Marie de l'Incarnation who went to Canada, other orders went to Native American villages to live, convert, and educate local people. Still others aimed to educate themselves and even become highly learned.

Turmoil in the World of Faith

Two developments across the globe began the process of raising women's writings and other creative activities to the levels found in other parts of the world, most notably the accomplishments in China, Japan, and South Asia. The first of these was humanism—that is, the concern with the human condition as found both in ancient Latin and Greek thought and in grammar, rhetoric, history, and poetry. It is not "humane"—that is, concerned with the treatment of others—so much as concerned with the humanities. Theology was suddenly of less interest as was its understanding of the working of the universe, which is not to say that people did not address it. Women in Italy—a major and early center of humanist activity both in literature and the arts—turned to ancient learning, becoming expert in classical languages and literature. They translated the classics and wrote tracts in praise of relatives or public figures in Latin. Others from the upper classes and nobility became renowned for the patronage of humanistic artists and writers. Vittoria Colonna (1490–1547) produced celebrated poetry about her family—especially her unfaithful husband whom she loved passionately—and urged reform of the Catholic church.

The second development that awakened Western women's intellectual activism was the Protestant Reformation of the sixteenth century that split Christianity into Protestant and Catholic branches. Martin Luther (1483–1546) was a German Catholic monk who in 1517 accused the Catholic Church of corruption and disregard for the true word of God. According to him, instead of reading the Bible people believed they had to follow priests who themselves were sinners. For him, the Bible was the only true authority. In Europe, Protestantism stressed the individual's relationship to God and rejected the hierarchy of priests, bishops, cardinals, and the Pope as necessary intermediaries for the faithful. These clerics, according to reformers, did not make a relationship to the divine possible. Instead, Martin Luther maintained that people had only to read the Bible to gain a close heavenly relationship. More than that, he preached that God made two sexes to procreate and that the clergy's celibacy went against the divine plan. The "Protestant Reformation" had much that appealed to women, even as it denounced most of the sanctity surrounding holy women such as Mary and other martyrs and saints. In claiming that the human universe had fewer sacraments and intrusions by the hand of God, he opened the way for studying natural laws instead of seeing every hurricane or death as the result of divine intervention.

The "Protestant" breakaway from Catholicism began as a practice that appealed to many and empowered them. The idea of a direct relationship with God via scripture encouraged women to learn to read and boosted confidence in their own abilities. Simultaneously, however, in writing and speaking about marriage and women's general behavior, Luther had other thoughts that subtracted from that empowerment. He wrote and spoke about his new ideas often and widely in sermons and in writings for princes and followers from the nobility. One "lecture" refers to the story of Adam and Eve as written about in the book of *Genesis* in the Bible: "Moreover this designation [woman] carries with it a wonderful and pleasing description of marriage, in which, as the jurist says, the wife shines by reason of her husband's rays. Whatever the husband has, this the wife has and possesses in its entirety." he lectured. "The result is that the husband differs from the wife in no respect than in sex; otherwise the woman is altogether a man." Luther then proceeded to mix equality with inequality as stemming from the Bible and the divine origins of humans: "Whatever the man has in the home and is, this the woman has and is; she differs only in sex . . . she is a woman by origin, because the wife came from the man and not the man from the woman . . . for this reason she is called a woman, or, if we were able to say so in Latin, a 'she man.' "

Luther's fame brought many to his home after he himself married a former nun Katharina von Bora (1499–1552) and began a family. The collection of his conversations with these visitors and followers as they recorded them is named his "table talk." In these conversations he addressed many topics, including the role of women in the family and in the wider world: "The wife governs the household—preserving without damage, however, the husband's right and jurisdiction." However, he was clear about whether women should have a major say in public affairs: "The dominion of women from the beginning of the world has never produced any good; as one is accustomed to saying: 'Women's rule seldom comes to a good end.' When God installed Adam as lord over all creatures, everything was still in good order and proper, and everything was governed in the best way. But when the wife came along and wanted to put her hand too in the simmering broth and be clever, everything fell apart and became wildly disordered."[4]

Still, women became ardent followers, not just learning to read but daring to preach. As Protestantism evolved, different subgroups or sects arose, some of them promoting more radical kinds of equality that fanned out from the idea that all people could have a direct connection with God. Anabaptists took experimentation into the realm of sexuality. Quakers encouraged women to preach and engage in religious activism. Women became some of the most ardent Protestants, flocking to the many different forms that it took and turning to the sciences and the study of behavior as determined by human not sacred law. Some Catholic women redoubled their efforts, joining foreign missions and demonstrating intensity of belief in their religious practices. Eventually these Christian missionaries would arrive in other parts of the world where they met up with longstanding stories that galvanized women and informed their everyday thoughts. When women worked, someone might tell stories of beautiful princesses, evil witches, ghosts, and monsters. They heard legends such as that of the warrior Mulan or the Trung sisters who went into battle to save Vietnam from Chinese invaders. "The Ballad of Mulan" was one version of the tale of an obedient daughter-turned-woman-warrior Mulan from sometime around the fifth century CE by an unknown author in northern China. Since women were known to ride horses, Mulan's search for a horse despite her being a homebody and her escape from home to ride for twelve years is not entirely far-fetched.

> But last night I read the battle-roll;
> The Kehan [emperor] has ordered a great levy of men.
> The battle-roll was written in twelve books,
> And in each book stood my father's name.
> My father's sons are not grown men,
> And of all my brothers, none is older than I.
> Oh let me go to the market to buy saddle and horse,
> And ride with the soldiers to take my father's place.

The story of her breaking gender rules by fighting invaders shows her putting family and also emperor first. After she does her civic duty in helping the emperor's forces achieve victory, she then follows the rules of daughterly duty and asks to be sent back to her family:

> Oh, Mulan asks not to be made
> A Counselor at the Kehan's court;
> She only begs for a camel that can march
> A thousand leagues a day,
> To take her back to her home.

Told and retold, Mulan's essentially Chinese virtues had real staying power in both the Chinese and world's imagination right down to the present.[5]

Equally, the legend of Sundiata, founder of the Mali kingdom passed down through generations, showing a different kind of activism by a number of women in Sundiata's orbit, including his family. Sundiata is born disabled to the king Maghan Kon Fatta and Sogolon Kedjou, a woman brought to the king because of a prophecy that, ugly as she is, she will give birth to a great hero. The problem is that the king already has a wife, Sassouma Béréte, who has given the king a son and heir. As she plots against Sundiata using witches and other magical forces, Sandiata's sister contracts a bad marriage so that she can learn of additional plots against her brother. Meanwhile, his mother Sogolon has all the while been dutiful, and it is because of her fidelity that Sundiata gains full use of his body and conquers the forces against him, indicating that "the child is worth no more than the mother is worth."[6] The narrative of women's power and the force of faithful motherhood passed down through the oral tradition. The story gained additional purchase because it showed both the intertwining of older spiritual beliefs and Islam: when Sundiata finally conquers his kingdom, he does so fully clothed in Muslim garb.

Women and the Arts

Women of many stations in life expressed themselves in the arts, often in relationship to their status as women. Across cultures, they drew on the heritage of earlier authors and artists. The *Tale of Genji*, composed in the tenth century by Murasaki Shikibu (c. 973–1014), described the life that noble and royal women experienced as residents of the Japanese court. Lady Murasaki was a pioneer, writing the first novel in Japanese and in fact one of the first ever written. Because it described women's longing for a prince who romanced them and then took them for granted, the work constituted a kind of dream world of complicated fantasies. By the early modern period many a Japanese imitator had produced similar tales, including those of women who appeared as ghosts or who sought after the ghost of a dead lover. An innovator, Murasaki chose to differ from educated men who flaunted their knowledge of the more prestigious Chinese language by writing in her native tongue. The story of the "shining prince" Genji, like the later retelling of the *Ramayana*, wove into a single tale the emotional suffering of the many noble women whom Genji loved and left. It also, however, told of Genji's downfall.

Franco-Italian author Christine de Pisan (1364–1430) from the other end of Eurasia focused one of her works differently in her poem celebrating Joan of Arc (1412–1431). In this celebration of Joan, Christine recounts the sad situation of French king Charles VII, challenged by the English and hardly in command of his kingdom. Taking up arms, Joan fought off the English, helping Charles achieve his rule. Even though an author, Christine knew the need for female valor: widowed at a young age and losing her father shortly thereafter, she took up her pen and supported her children and mother. At the time women's authorship was rare, while women themselves were little appreciated. Christine's poetic tribute to Joan's rescue of Charles VII highlighted women's talent—in this case military talent—and the debt that men owed them, as the theme of this saintly valor resonated across time.

> And you, Charles, now the king of France,
> The seventh king of that great name,
> Who earlier suffered such mischance;
> You thought the future held more shame.
> But by God's grace, now look how Joan
> Has raised your fame on high, oh see!
> Your enemies before you bow –
> This is a welcome novelty!- –

Future Western women in the arts signposted Christine de Pisan's role in keeping women's positive reputation thriving.

In China where women's writing flourished, courtesans often displayed learning and skill in the arts or in culture more generally. Like Christine, some of them might have been trained in learning from a young age. The

Ming Empire (1368–1644) became increasingly urban, prosperous, and sophisticated, with an overall appreciation for the arts among its elites. At the same time, courtesans in this society came from a poorer social background but were instructed in brothels from a young age to please the instructed male clientele. Many became celebrated. On the one hand, achievement in the arts hid the sex work connected to being a courtesan; on the other, the courtesans initially surpassed in learning many elite women, who were embedded in family life. The idea was to engage patrons who had rarely chosen their wives, either for their intellectual accomplishments or for potential intimacy, but instead for connections and similar economic or political backgrounds. China had thriving cities because of its booming commerce in textiles, porcelain, iron wares, and commodities—all of these well-crafted products and many considered works of art themselves. Thus, trained young women, even young teenagers, would provide men with a choice of sexual and cultural companion, which the marriage system did not generally allow. Whereas marital values centered on duty and obedience and male/female separation, relationships with girls and women outside of marriage emphasized sexual, emotional, and cultural intimacy.

In China and Japan, then, accomplishment in poetry, music, drawing, and calligraphy were central to attracting clients and thus earning a living. In both societies where learning was prized and even required to hold high government positions, men were often accomplished in the arts themselves or had a real engagement with them. An instructed appreciation of the beauties of nature across the seasons and for mountains, rock formations, and streams were also central to a valued person's identity. Thus, ambitious courtesans used their artistic skills to attract would-be clients by suggesting the future happiness intellectually, socially, artistically, and sexually that the man might garner from a relationship. Famed Chinese courtesan poet, Jing Pianpian (1578–1620), produced many admired poems that were wide-ranging in their mood.

> Every day fancy carriages arrive,
> Intimate words with upper class friends.
> But no one here is from Suzhou
> And I miss those Suzhou soft sounds.
> Together we feast deep into the night.
> After I've softly tuned the lute
> We sit and tie a lover's knot,
> Inviting the moon into the room.

Other verse alluded to the insecurities of the courtesan with clients she might have hoped to keep. The process of aging, about which she also wrote, further expressed the precarious nature of her life because she was so dependent on securing a partner who would support her through the years.

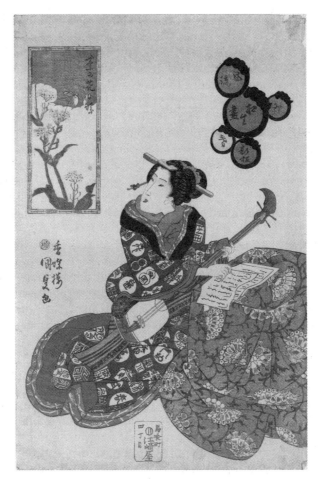

FIGURE 3.2 *Japanese woman composing a song, c. 1700. This Japanese woman looks at a picture of nature as she composes a song on her stringed instrument. Most likely located in a thriving city, she may feel nostalgic for nature in a place with a lively street life. Above all, she represents urban women's accomplishments in the arts and letters. Courtesy of Buyenlarge Getty Images.*

In fact, Jing Pianpian did marry, but when her husband was caught up in scandal, she committed suicide.[7]

By 1600, married women had taken up the brush in greater numbers to engage in poetry and other forms of writing. Their motivation was varied, but official endorsement of their intellectual activities centered on the value of women's learning to the strength of the state. A highly literate cadre of elites ran the Ming Empire and these officials had all won their government positions through success in a kingdom-wide examination based on knowledge of the classics. Because classics such as Confucius's Analects were about correct behavior in the family and in the kingdom, a grounding in these works enabled the smooth functioning of society. Mothers, it was determined at the time—and with increasing conviction—could begin the process of excelling in the practice of those standards by being educated in them. They themselves needed to study, and women took up the task in earnest.

In societies like China where cultural expertise was valued, some educated families began seeking out similarly accomplished wives for their sons, and parents slowly began to educate their daughters and even to enjoy conversing with them at a high level. Well-educated Wu Deyin, who lived in the mid-seventeenth century, so fancied becoming an erudite adult scholar that she changed into boy's clothing whenever her father's cultured friends visited. A few others similarly imagined themselves as reaching the heights of learning, even as they married.

Paired according to cultural compatibility, couples then experienced the beauties of nature or their skills as calligraphers together and even developed their own talents in tandem with one another. If a man were married to a practically oriented as opposed to an aesthetically or intellectually oriented woman, he might bring an accomplished concubine into the household. In times of need, such couples sometimes sold their paintings or widowed women used their talents, especially painting and calligraphy, to raise funds in the bustling art markets. In fact, the sixteenth-century artist Yu Shih, known as Miss Yu, and her husband earned their living across their married life by marketing their works.

Courtesans' painting focused on orchids and they themselves were sometimes described in those terms: "I found her again like a fragrant orchid flower growing in a secluded valley," one customer wrote of the courtesan Tung Pai.[8] Sexual symbolism appeared in the willows and orchids women employed in their paintings. In contrast Artemesia Gentileschi (1593–1652/3), an Italian artist born into an artistic family, learned her métier from her father Orazio and produced daring scenes. She painted within this context and in collaboration with her father, unlike the courtesans of East Asia. Her image of Judith beheading Holofernes shows a determined widow (Judith) and her maid straining to accomplish the blood-filled beheading. Similarly, Susanna and the Elders, painted when Gentileschi was seventeen, stages the notable men of the community as lecherous sexual harassers and Susanna as their most unwilling prey. Gentileschi herself was raped and then tortured for the truth, but despite this disgrace she continued to have clients across Europe. Her work explicitly took on the subject of men's sexual assault of women and substituted violent or offensive scenes for the Chinese pattern of depicting the beauty of nature, even though it might symbolize erotic feelings.

Women continued the work of dealing with historical topics as Gentileschi did. Gul-Badan Begum (1523–1603), whose names means "rose body," was the daughter of Babur, founder of the Mughal Empire, sister of his successor Humayun, and aunt of Humayun's son and future emperor the great Akbar. It was Akbar who called on members of the court to gather documents and write histories of it. While Gul-Badan's *History of Humayun: Humayun Nama* was to cover Humayun's reign, in fact the history contained less of the standard genealogical "lives of great men and their successors" than usual. Instead, it presented an insider look at everyday life of people in women's private circles and also in the Mughal court generally, including the everyday life of people in it and the interactions of royal women and men. In the 1570s and early 1580s, Gul-Badan Begum, then in her fifties, led a pilgrimage of royal women on the Hajj—a trip both sacred and filled with day-to-day struggles including shipwrecks.

Although she did not include the *Hajj* in her writings that we know of, her history of Humayun reveals the role of women in ensuring the future of the monarchy. By her accounts, they made major interventions in the process of matchmaking and assuring the next generation of royal babies: "My lady, who was Maham Begam [widow of Babur], had a great longing and desire to see a son of Humayun. Wherever there was a good-looking and nice girl, she used to bring her into his service. Maywa-jan, a daughter of Khadang, the chamberlain, was in my employ. The day (after) the death of his Majesty [Babur], my lady said: 'Humayun, Maywa-jan is not bad. Why do you not take her into your service?' So, at her word, Humayun married and took her that very night."

The women of the royal court, however, did not let the situation resolve itself and instead took daily interest in the dealings of the monarch and his relatives, and the conduct of women in the royal household: "Three days later Bega Begam came from Kabul. She became in the family way. In due time she had a daughter, whom they named Aquiqa. Maywa-jan said to Lady Maham Begam, 'I am in the family way, too.' Then my lady got ready two sets of weapons, and said: 'Whichever of you bears a son, I will give him good arms.' Then she packed up the arms, and got ready gold and silver walnuts. She procured also the (special) arms of a Mughal commander, and was very happy, and kept saying: 'Perhaps one of them will have a son.' She kept watch till Bega Begam's Aquiqa was born. Then she kept an eye on Maywa-jan. Ten months went by. The eleventh also passed. Maywa-jan said: 'My maternal aunt was in Mirza Ulugh Beg's [Babur's uncle] haram. She had a son in the twelfth month; perhaps I am like her.' So they sewed tents and filled pillows [preparing for the baby]. But in the end everyone knew she was a fraud."[9] In such instances—false and other pregnancies or liaisons or betrayals—royal women, especially the most senior ones, were the keepers of good order, including proper sexual and reproductive conduct. In the case of Akbar's aunt and other literate women, these events found their historians. They show an often neglected side of the complexities of power.

Quarrels over Women's Worth

Whether women were worth anything was a constant topic of writing, stemming in many cases from religious opinions and long-standing cultural writings showing women as less valuable than men. Early writers had engaged in what seemed to be a constant attack on women's intellect, morality, and overall merit. Christine de Pisan, for example, some two decades before praising Joan of Arc, had commemorated the faithful and heroic deeds of women in ancient times, some of them martyrs in the cause of their faith. She also pointed to women's virtuous conduct in order to fend off the mean-spirited attacks on their character in the celebrated book of its day, *Romance of the Rose*. Directly referring to the author of this misogynistic outburst, she produced an imaginary "City of Ladies" and populated it with numerous worthy women. She challenged the idea that women were worthless simply because they were women.

By the century after Christine de Pisan, young women in Ming China began a different kind of campaign against traditional beliefs in their inferiority. During the Ming regime (1368–1644) the influence of elite official experts in the classics and thus in correct behavior began to decline. Bandits ran rampant especially in the provinces around the capital Beijing but descending southward into the commercial heartland of the empire. Commerce itself stirred up greed and desire for higher positions if not more wealth. Eunuchs entered the imperial regime, many of them with far less schooling in Confucian values and commitment to traditional social order. Early in the 1500s, the emperor himself was far more engaged in horsemanship, physical prowess, and the enjoyment of good times than in strict attention to wise government. Men's character seemed to slip away from the correct behavior that had helped ensure social order for centuries.

In this tumultuous situation of male criminality and neglect of duty, teens and young women began showing themselves to be committed to virtuous behavior. Beyond almost anyone's standards at the time, these young women began committing suicide on the death of a fiancé often by hanging or starving themselves to death. The goal was to demonstrate their fidelity, and they did so to such an extent that suicide or other extreme acts performed by these young women merged together to form a so-called faithful maiden cult. Widows also aimed for a scrupulous chastity instead of forming new partnerships; some even tried to replace a husband condemned to death for acts against the government. "I am willing to have my head chopped off in the market in exchange for my husband's life," one wrote.[10] Such acts became a stern rebuke to men for their disorderly lives and a claim to women's worth because of their ability to follow the traditional rules underlying social harmony.

Mihri Hatun (c. 1460–1515) was an unmarried poet in the Ottoman Empire, who also wrote in the context of the general dismissal of women's intellect. The idea at the time was that a married woman could not produce good poetry, but Mihri gained attention for her virginity. Those who anthologized her were at pains to explain why her brilliance should be recognized. Essentially, they came up with the justification that she was masculine in her intellect because unmarried. She, however, took their words and turned them around. "You say women have little understanding and that you do not listen to them for that reason. Yet Mihri, who prays for you [and wishes you well], explains—and clever and mature people confirm it: a talented woman is better than a thousand untalented men, a woman of understanding is better than a thousand stupid men."[11] Mihri Hatun referred to what generally has been called the "querelle des femmes" or the debate over women. Here are two translations of her defense against misogyny:

Since they say women lack reason
All their words should be excused.

An efficient woman is much better than
A thousand inefficient men.[12]

Women's rulership added to the quarrel over women. Anne Bradstreet (1613–1672) arrived in the Massachusetts Bay Colony in 1630, where she became a leading figure and wife of the colony's governor. She too was a poet—in fact, the first published North American colonial poet in her 1650 volume of verse. Although praised for her domestic virtues, Bradstreet was an advocate for women's capacities and a critic of men's attitudes toward women. She wrote a century after the Scottish religious leader John Knox had stated that women rulers "defiled, polluted, and profaned the throne of God," but his attitudes were still held by many men. Her poem "In Honour of That High and Mighty Princess Queen Elizabeth of Happy Memory" praises the late Queen Elizabeth (1533–1603) whose reign inspired admiration because of her skill in statecraft, her ability to defeat enemies, and her determination to launch England on a prosperous path.

Now say, have women worth? Or have they none?
Or had they some, but with our Queen is't gone?
Nay masculines, you have thus taxed us long,
But she, though dead, will vindicate our wrong.
Let such as say our sex is void of reason
Know 'tis a slander now but once was treason.
But happy England which had such a queen;
Yea happy, happy, had those days still been.[13]

The seventeenth century saw an array of authors similarly honoring women—high-born and more ordinary—against what they saw as vicious slander.

Conclusion

China and Japan had long traditions of women writing, reading, and painting, encouraging generations in the early modern period to do the same. Their poetry, like that of theoretically secluded and illiterate Ottoman women, connected women to one another as it was read aloud or circulated among the middle- and upper-classes via letters. In the sixteenth century, the Protestant Reformation in Europe followed in advancing women's desire to read, write, and even preach on that continent. Although women still eagerly sought places in Catholic nunneries, Protestants found it appealing that one could pray on one's own and, especially, read holy scripture as legitimate forms of religious belief. Christian women's development of their religious capacity struck a blow at one governing structure—the Catholic Church. Perhaps for this reason, women's literacy and writing began to thrive more than ever before across Europe. Luther had some less flattering things to say about women like most men of his time worldwide, but nonetheless the promise of independence and individual agency led both wealthy and poor women to support the cause— sometimes with their lives. Queens and elite women sponsored the Protestant cause, even as the Reformation brought about religious strife.

Still, across other parts of the globe the panoply of goddesses—absent from Judaism, Islam, and Christianity—provided perhaps a richer and continuing source of inspiration. Goddesses and strong women such as Sundiata's mother were models of behavior and often their deeds expressed feminine strength, provoking constant devotions or imitation by millions of women. The telling and retelling of centuries-old fables infused women's lives. In ethical systems, even the Buddha credited women in the progress of his Enlightenment. By the early modern period, however, poets and other writers were defending real women, writing histories of their actual good works. These emphasized bravery and strength of character. In addition to helping women bond with one another, poetic production—exchanged in the wider world—also challenged the domination that men exercised over their confinement—wrongly so, many of these authors believed. Some men are known to have encouraged their wives and daughters to write or paint and mentored other women beyond the family. There was also growing interaction—often hidden from view—among literary and other learned women as they came to promote one another's talent.

Glossary

Bodhisattva   A person who has devoted his or her Buddhist practice to benefit humanity.

Daoism   A Chinese philosophical school emphasizing naturalness, humility, balance, and harmony in one's everyday practices and overall being.

| Hajj | The religious pilgrimage to the holy site Mecca that Muslims should make at least once in their lives if they can afford it. The hajj is one of the five pillars of the Islamic faith. |
| Jade Emperor | The ruler of heaven and of the lesser gods who inhabited it. |

Notes

1 See Matthew W. Stirling, *Origin Myth of Acoma and Other Records* (Washington, DC: Smithsonian Institution, 1942), 3–5 for the entire story.
2 See Glenn H. Mullin with Jeff J. Watt, *Female Buddhas: Women of Enlightenment in Tibetan Mystical Art* (Santa Fe, NM: Clear Light, 2002), 17 and passim.
3 Quoted in Julia Clancy-Smith, "Exemplary Women and Sacred Journeys: Women in Judaism, Christianity, and Islam from Late Antiquity to the Eve of Modernity," in *Women's History in Global Perspective*, Bonnie G. Smith, ed. (Urbana: University of Illinois Press, 2004), 1:127.
4 Quoted in Susan C. Karant-Nunn and Merry Wiesner-Hanks, eds., *Luther on Women: A Sourcebook* (Cambridge: Cambridge University Press, 2003), 121, 123, citing Jaroslave Pelikan, ed. *Luther's Works*, 55 vols. (Concordia Publishing Company, Muhlenberg Press, Fortress Press, and Augsburg Publishing Company, 1955–1968): "Lectures on Genesis," Vol. 1. p. 137; "Table Talk I," no. 1046, p. 528.
5 Unknown author, *The Temple and Other Poems*, Arthur Waley, trans. (New York: Alfred A. Knopf, 1923) in *Images of Women in Chinese Thought and Culture: Writings from the Pre-Qin Period through the Song Dynasty*, Robin Wang, trans. (Indianapolis, IN: Hackett, 2003), 251–2.
6 D. T. Niane, *Sundiata: An Epic of Old Mali* (Hong Kong: Longman African Classics, 1992), 22.
7 In Paul Ropp, "Love, Literacy, and Laments: Themes of Women Writers in Late Imperial China," *Women's History Review* 2:1 (1993): 113–15.
8 Quoted in Marsha Weidner, ed., *Flowering in the Shadows: Women in the History of Chinese and Japanese Painting* (Honolulu: University of Hawaii Press, 1990), 91.
9 Gul-Badan Begum, *The History of Humayun* (New Delhi: Munshiram Manoharlal Publishers, 2001), 112–13. Translation by Annette Beveridge, 1902.
10 Weijing Lu, *True to Her Word: The Faithful Maiden Cult in Late Imperial China* (Stanford, CA: Stanford University Press, 2008), 45.
11 Quoted in Suraiya Faroqhi, *Subjects of the Sultan: Culture and Daily Life in the Ottoman Empire*, Martin Bott, trans. (London: I. B. Tauris, 2000), 122.
12 D. Havlioğlu, "On the Margins and between the Lines: Ottoman Women Poets from the Fifteenth to the Twentieth-Century." *Turkish Historical Review* 1 (2010): 43.
13 Excerpted from Sandra M. Gilbert and Susan Gubar, comps., *The Norton Anthology of Literature by Women: The Tradition in English* (New York: Norton, 1985), 66.

Further Reading

Cahill, Suzanne E. *Transcendence & Divine Passion: The Queen Mother of the West in Medieval China*. Stanford, CA: Stanford University Press. 1993.

Dror, Olga. *Cult, Culture, and Authority: Princess Lieu Hanh in Vietnamese History*. Honolulu: University of Hawaii Press, 2007.

Havlioğlu, Didem. "On the Margins and between the Lines: Ottoman Women Poets from the Fifteenth to the Twentieth-Century." *Turkish Historical Review* 1 (2010): 25–54.

Idema, Wilt L., and Beata Grant. *The Red Brush: Women Writers of Imperial China*. Cambridge: Harvard University Press, 2004.

Ko, Dorothy. *Teachers of the Inner Chambers: Women and Culture in Seventeenth Century China*: Stanford, CA: Stanford University Press, 1994.

Lu, Weijing. *True to Her Word: The Faithful Maiden Cult in Ming China*. Stanford, CA: Stanford University Press, 2008.

Mullin, Glenn H. with Jeff Wyatt. *Female Buddhas: Women of Enlightenment in Tibetan Mystical Art*. Santa Fe, NM: Clear Light, 2002.

Tharu, Susie, and K. Lalita, eds. *Women Writing in India: 600 BC to the Early 20th Century*. London: Pandora Press, 1991.

Weidner, Marsha, ed. *Flowering in the Shadows: Women in the History of Chinese and Japanese Painting*. Honolulu: University of Hawaii Press, 1990.

Young, Serinity. *Courtesans and Tantric Consorts: Sexualities in Buddhist Narrative, Ritual, & Iconography*. London: Routledge, 2004.

4

Productive Life across a Connected Globe, 1500–1750

In the fifteenth century, Iberian sailors began extending their sailing routes along the north and west coasts of Africa, searching for gold in which Africa was rich and doing small amounts of trade in commodities, including slaves, that could be sold back home. In 1441, for example, Portuguese sailors captured a stray West African male and then spotted a "Mooress" or African woman. Fearing conflict with a nearby group of local men, they debated her capture. The ship captain maintained that "if they scorned that encounter, it might make their foes pluck up courage against them. And now you see how the word of a captain prevaileth among men used to obey; for, following his will, they seized the Mooress."[1] Besides these random seizures of humans to sell, the Iberians built fortresses along the African coasts to house soldiers and the families they developed by partnering with well-connected African women. In 1492, a team of Spanish ships commanded by Christopher Columbus, aided by favorable winds, crossed the Atlantic to the Caribbean. In 1498, Vasco da Gama sailing under the Portuguese flag rounded the southern tip of Africa to reach the rich markets of South Asia. By the seventeenth century, Britain, the Netherlands, France, Denmark, and other kingdoms had joined in the oceanic hunt for riches, including human beings to enslave. In Eurasia, the Russians reached the Pacific Ocean and the Chinese fought their way west across the Asian continent to conquer millions of square miles. The world's peoples were now connected in new ways, including oceanic ones, especially once Spanish ships returned from circumnavigating the globe in 1521. Oceanic connections—both Atlantic and Pacific networks—linked Western and Eastern Hemispheres and in so doing brought about profound change.

Local Amerindian women and men alike felt the devastating effects of the developing Atlantic empires of Spain and Portugal; these contacts were followed by the expansion of Britain, France, and the Netherlands.

Europeans brought with them deadly diseases such as smallpox and measles that weakened productivity in both North and South America as well as eroded the political strength of local communities. The European invasion broke down health care systems, increasing mortality. Asian peoples also felt the incursions of empire builders, notably the Mughal and *Qing* regimes in India and China, respectively. Hybrid societies developed, with conquerors imposing their values—though not thoroughly—and fathering children with local women. Invaders also recognized the need to adapt. Their adaptation included this partnering with the women of local elites, who then became a vanguard of integration and also a force for stability amidst the chaos that conquest often brought. These women instructed the conquerors in local ways and used them to help restore order. Indigenous women themselves usually experienced the violence of conquest as well as working to stop it. This violence included enslavement, rape, the death of spouses and children, and new levels of forced labor. In the end, survivors had partially to adopt conquerors' ways of life, intermarrying with them, and bearing them children; others living away from scenes of battle maintained their community traditions because they might have reduced connections with the invaders. For many women, however, Iberian triumph in the Western Hemisphere entailed a grim end to parallel systems of respect and authority that they once enjoyed. European patriarchal values were more extreme than those among local peoples of the Western Hemisphere, while European men themselves valued women far less than Amerindians had.

The new empires of early modern times ultimately involved life changes on all sides: for the conquerors, who were leaving their homes and culture, and for local people, whose safety and way of life were threatened. In addition to the violence that empire entailed in the early modern period, there also resulted the mixing of people—voluntary or not—and the intersection of cultures—voluntary or not. In the end, empires in early modern times and the widespread connections they entailed transformed the daily lives and cultures of people across the globe, bringing benefits such as new foodstuffs and ultimately immunities for those who survived the many diseases. These connections, however, often discarded and devalued everyday practices of local peoples while it disrespected the lives of the conquered—especially those of women.

Beginnings

From the mid-fifteenth into the sixteenth century ambitious rulers and adventurers moved out of their home base to conquer communities inhabited by people mostly foreign to them. They thus built empires, whose main characteristics are conquest of and dominion over peoples by others arriving from beyond their own homelands to exercise this control. In 1453, the

Ottomans—Turkic people initially from the other side of Asia—captured Constantinople, the capital of the Byzantine Empire and proceeded to conquer Egypt and then much of the Middle East and North Africa. At about the same time, the Aztecs in present-day Mexico and the Incas along the Andes in South America established two Amerindian empires, though adventurers from Spain took them over in the 1520s and 1530s, respectively, marking major steps in the development of Spain's overseas empire. In 1526, Central Asian leader Babur moved into the northern section of the South Asian peninsula and established the Mughal Empire. The process of empire building was an ancient one but also one that has continued almost to our own day.

Across the globe, the approach to new territories entailed making alliances to help in conquest, seizing wealth, and enabling trade. The alliances would-be conquerors made were often with the enemies of the target community—as in the case of Spain's employment of local ethnic groups in its conquest of the Aztecs and Incas. In these instances women stepped in as go-betweens and diplomats, either informal or formal ones to arrange support from enemies of the Aztecs (present-day Mexico) or the Quechua ethnic group ruling across the Andes. Communities along coastal regions initially saw great opportunity for trade with Iberian newcomers. Interlopers' desires for colorful or warm clothing and resources kept family productivity high—for example, to meet the demand for cotton textiles from South Asia that European women snapped up. These easily cleaned, comfortable clothing had earlier appealed to people in the Pacific and Indian Ocean world. Because other newcomers often wanted furs to help their consumers endure harsh winters, Native Americans and indigenous peoples across Asia provided treated skins and additionally sold foodstuffs and other exotic products for sale in the home country even as imperial expansion was taking place. These were most often crafted by women; so the benefits that women in distant lands offered pulled conquerors toward them.

Local peoples crucially provisioned long-distance traders in addition to teaching them new commercial skills that were customary in an unfamiliar region. In the case of the Atlantic world, those settling in North America were dependent, not dominant for many decades despite expressions of their own power. Essentially, down into the nineteenth century, Native American women and men kept white interlopers from starving or freezing during harsh winters. Conquerors also hungered for wealth and the array of goods that dazzled them. They would and did do virtually anything to obtain them. The rise of empires from the sixteenth century on constituted a vast, often violent school in newly globalizing ways of consumer life for millions of people. Women and men alike received schooling in the relationship and would continue to do so well into the twentieth century. For as long as empire and globalization continued, foreign peoples and their resources incited desires, greed, violence, and murder.

The Economy and Violence of Empire-Building

Empire-building around the world was an exercise in violent masculinity. It generally entailed conquest by armies of swordsmen and armed adventurers—both employing increasingly powerful weapons, especially guns. The Mughals of India, the *Manchus* who conquered China, and the Ottomans of the Middle East used imperial armies with a variety of weapons to expand the territories under their control, riding teams of horses, camels, and elephants while slaughtering people in the way of their progress. These conquerors had diverse views of their mission, but the one rationale common among most of them was simply the seizure of territory, precious metals and other treasure, and harnessing the labor of conquered people including sex and reproductive labor. There were also commercial empires where the goal was establishing a firm foothold in regions controlled by traders from the home region—many of them women—or even by other long-distance traders, for example along the Indian Ocean and West African coasts. Usually would-be conquerors saw their own way of life as superior, whether in terms of religion, social and cultural customs, or simply in terms of having an overall better ethnic or racial identity. Empire meant taking people with skills in crafts or agriculture into custody to support the supposedly superior conqueror. In other words, the quest stemmed simultaneously from the conquerors' inferior economic position—even poverty as in the case of the Iberians—and lack of skill except perhaps in violence. Empire was about a complex domination, tempered by the need to bow to local peoples' knowledge and their access to resources such as food, furs, minerals, and other supplies. Conquered and conquering people's lives were entangled in multiple ways, many of them through sex and gendered encounters.

Some women directly participated in the conquest. Queen Isabella of Spain (1451–1504) and, decades later, Elizabeth of England (1533–1603) supported adventurers and their expeditions either financially or with a royal endorsement or charter, largely in hopes of building the treasuries of their kingdoms. A century and a half after Elizabeth, Catherine the Great of Russia (1729–1796) also expanded her imperial borders, annexing Crimea and regions farther to the east. Other women reportedly fought with invading forces. Ines Suarez (1507–1580) left Spain for South America around 1537 to search for her husband, but learning of his death she partnered with the conquistador Pedro de Validivia. She came to the aid of his soldiers in battle and, most famously, put down an uprising in Chile in 1541 by personally beheading Indian hostages and tossing their heads over fortress walls of Santiago. By legend, the sight of their comrades' bloody, severed heads frightened the resisting troops into surrender. Catalina de Eranso and Maria de Estrada also appear in the military lore of Spanish conquest, while women's military role in the struggle for empire appeared in many societies across the globe.

From another perspective, women were those who kept invaders alive because they themselves could profit from relationships with the violent newcomers. In the North American continent, even in the late seventeenth century, Native Americans in all but the extreme eastern shores kept political and economic control of vast regions. To the north, the first interlopers merely amounted to armed traders from whom local people could profit, even as they waged war against neighboring ethnic groups. For decades Europeans were keenly aware of Native American strength and their own lack of it, often using women's knowledge to compensate for what they lacked. French and British traders had no "empire" in the Great Lakes or other interior regions but rather were dependent on their relationships with Native Americans who controlled access to highly marketable products such as furs and who also had the food and other supplies that these traders would often desperately need. The many Native American clan groups based their political power on marrying daughters into other groups, including Europeans, which led to greater harmony instead of friction or even warfare. Women negotiated these cross-clan alliances as well as those with traders.

In a similar way, women made trade among the French and *Anishinabe* in this region function, and thus established their clan's reputation as successful, wealthy, and powerful. Women cleaned the furs for sale and also grew and processed corn, beans, and other foodstuffs not just for their own consumption but to sell to Europeans. They repaired canoes used by the foreigners and also made them items of clothing such as moccasins and pouches. Important for both sides, by this time Anishinabe women were not just marrying into other clans but with the French themselves. These alliances drew the French into Native American society, and they especially gave Anishinabe women greater access to trade and important information. Their productivity, trade networks, and political alliances were central to Anishinabe well-being and control of the Great Lakes region—and even beyond, to western lands—into the eighteenth century. Only later did Europeans turn trade into domination.

Further to the west, along the Missouri River, Native American women produced the tens of thousands of bushels of corn on which European traders and explorers depended for their survival even into the early nineteenth century. This was Native Americans' most important and most frequently traded item. Not only did Mandan women, as seen earlier, farm the corn, they dried it, removed kernels from the cobs, and stored the food for sale. Other Native American people specialized in hides: women clothed their own people with these hides after they had prepared and fashioned the hides into garments; then they sold clothing made from hides to travelers. The European adventurers were often desperate for the basic necessities of life and were thus at the mercy of these women provisioners all along their route. White invaders also sought Native American women slaves for

FIGURE 4.1 *Wife of a Native American chief and their daughter, 1590, John White. Croatan Indian chief Manteo served as intermediary enabling John White to depict everyday life of a Native American woman in the sixteenth century. The chief's wife has tattooed arms and a carrier made from a gourd. Today scholars wonder how her daughter came to have the doll, which looks European. Courtesy of Henry Guttmann Getty Images.*

sex, and male tribal leaders in negotiations for hatchets, guns, and other metal objects obliged the whites with a brisk trade in women that they had captured in warfare and in horses that the travelers also needed.

Native American men provided their wives to white adventurers and traders for sex as well. The idea behind this custom was that through sexual intercourse any power the whites had in their being would pass to the wife, who then would transfer it to her husband during intercourse, which should follow soon after a sexual encounter with the whites. Whites heard of this custom and reportedly determined to enlist in trading and exploring teams in order to have access to sex as well. Not understanding local practices and wedded to their own definitions of morality, they came to believe that Native American women were wanton and oversexed. This belief then inspired the purchase of women and girl slaves from traders in conquering tribes. Women slaves, like free Native American women, usually had the wide range of skills and knowledge that would keep men from perishing as they traversed unknown territory and faced unknown conditions. Despite the indispensable help, the men usually come across in histories as unique individuals possessing almost superhuman capacities as they crossed oceans and continents unassisted—a complete perversion of the truth. Gender power was created in such "great man" tales of masculine prowess and heroism, which at the time were actually slight. Invading men survived in large part because of women's productive, geographic, healing, and other capacities.

Empire opened opportunities in many parts of the world. As Ottoman forces swept across North Africa, capturing most of the region except Morocco, women based in conquered areas found benefits in the situation. With Ottoman conquest came Ottoman institutions such as the coffee house or café. Local women opened and tended them for long-distance travelers and for urban dwellers along the North African coast of the Mediterranean. Sailors, merchants, and ordinary professional or working people frequented them, hearing the latest news or story, all to women's profit. In North African cities, where many elite women of all faiths often led sex-segregated lives, Jewish and Muslim women also worked as sellers in bazaars where women were the sole merchants and customers. As population grew, they were also brokers for the brisk maritime trade that took place; tempest-tossed sailors and passengers or street vendors where residences were distant employed central markets' specialized women healers.

Attacking Northwest Africa to set up forts and commercial centers where they could, the Portuguese were known for their brutality against women, especially sexual assault. Even Portuguese travelers and soldiers admitted that the Muslims were far less violent with hostages or conquered women, separating them from both men hostages and from their own military men. As they moved down the west coast of Africa, the Portuguese sought out commercial opportunity and gradually built a trade in slaves with African rulers and traders. They established a colony on Sao Tomé and populated it with thousands of convicts, white families, and Jewish children kidnapped and forced to become Catholics. Life on Sao Tomé, though off the coast of the malaria-filled inland, still killed off sailors and settlers, encouraging the intermarriage with African women who had more natural immunities. As one Portuguese pilot noted: "It sometimes happens that, when the wife of a merchant dies, he takes a Negress, and this is an accepted practice, as the Negro population is both intelligent and rich . . . Children born of these unions are of a dark complexion and are called Mulattoes."[2]

As first the Portuguese and then the Dutch moved around the southern and eastern coasts of Africa, they continued making inroads by establishing ever more trading footholds in the late fifteenth through seventeenth centuries. Sailors and traders on their own wanted slaves to work for them on the site and also to provide them with information. The Dutch often partnered with women whom they had captured while killing the men, who usually served as warriors defending their turf. The women would then give birth to additional slave-workers. The Portuguese had a still different strategy along the eastern coast of Africa where matrilineal communities dominated. They would promise parcels of conquered lands to daughters who partnered with Portuguese men, with power over the land belonging to the mixed couple and their children. This arrangement cemented a cross-cultural relationship that was beneficial to both sides by expanding access to cultures, economies, and political power.

Women in Indian Ocean ports, like Native American women on trade routes and near markets, could also benefit from interlopers. Successive Dutch traders in Southeast Asia in the middle of the seventeenth century, for example, took Osoet Pegua as a temporary wife because of her experience, connections, and power built on commercial networks. With the sponsorship of the royal family, she controlled both import and export commerce with the Dutch and her own people, providing the former with porcelain and copper among other things and the latter with rice. Such alliances soon drew the attention of Portuguese royal officials, who wanted more strictly Portuguese marriages and offspring. In the mid-1540s, they devised a program for orphans to be sent to Portuguese bases in South and Southeast Asia to be partnered with Portuguese traders and sailors. To sweeten the marriage, the program provided dowries for the orphaned young women, chosen because they were from respectable families. The dowries consisted of good-paying posts for the man who would marry them or at times an award of land or even an annuity of some kind. The young women, however, were the ones who often balked, for the prospective husbands were generally aged or infirm because of their struggles on the sea or with other traders. They might also be disreputable traders or soldiers, run down by their time in the inhospitable tropics. The young orphans hoped for better.

Women's Bodies to the Rescue after Devastating Loss of Life

Asserting imperial superiority included killing supposedly inferior peoples, raping women as a rite of conquest, and enslaving survivors in stupefying numbers. Massive slaughter was a sign to all inhabitants of where power lay and was thus part and parcel of domination. In the mid-seventeenth century, Manchu soldiers from the northern borders of China finally cinched their conquest of China's ruling Ming dynasty. After decades of whittling away at Ming power and taking control of the government, they kept roaming streets and entering buildings of Chinese towns they had captured to find new victims. Those who escaped death did so by securing often bizarre hiding places or by moving from street to street and even from house to house as the troops moved through killing men and raping women or taking them as sexual slaves. Spanish conquests in the Western Hemisphere and Manchu victories in China both took decades of lethal violence to accomplish. Local women's sexuality and reproductive potential were important to the conquerors, who invaded without sexual partners, in part to replenish the supply of laborers after murdering others. Those among the conquered lacking immunities died from diseases foreign to their communities, and they too needed to be replaced, but in other instances soldiers simply satisfied sexual desires and only incidentally hoped to rebuild their own ethnic stock.

As these military men progressed, they developed various sorts of intimate relations with surviving local women. Often these relationships were simply part of military violence and took the form of rape, as mentioned. Murder could follow the rape, again as part of asserting the male domination central to empire. In the case of the Spanish and Portuguese, the military leaders and even ordinary invaders entered somewhat longer-lasting marriages with women in their region. High-ranking European men benefitted from the resources in land and workers that planned alliances with wealthy or noble local women belonging to prestigious families of North America, the Caribbean, and South America. Dowries from elite families made European men wealthy beyond anything they had known, providing them with the labor of dozens and even hundreds of Indian slaves an Incan or Aztec princess or high noblewoman might own. Across the social scale, conquerors benefitted from women's knowledge, networks, wealth, and survival skills, while their sexuality produced new generations of human wealth even as these conquerors were killing off inhabitants at a rapid pace. The women tried to acculturate the conquerors, sometimes successfully and at other times not.

The situation was even more complicated, however. Elite local women found their circumstances dramatically changed in such relationships. Once part of elaborate systems of planned alliances, a royal woman partnering with an imperial conqueror could bring some protection for a princess's status, but not for long. For example, Francisco Pizarro, Spanish conqueror of the Inca, married Quispe Sisa, daughter of the Incan ruler, after she had been baptized with the new name of Inés Huaylas Yupanqui. When Pizarro was under attack, Quispe Sisa sent for troops from her mother. Their daughter Francesca married her uncle Hernando Pizarro. Similarly, Hernando Cortes, conqueror of the Aztecs with the help of their enemies from surrounding territory, had children with his local translator and diplomat Malinche and with Aztec princess Tecuichpotzin, among other partners, who additionally included a Spanish wife. Complementarity of power not being a value in European society, Gonzales Pizarro, brother of Francisco, simply raped the Incan Coya—the most important woman in that empire and someone who was a goddess to the Incan people. At the lower levels of imperial society, European men easily abandoned women and children once they had secured their riches, or, because violence was a value in achieving empire, they often beat women with whom they had partnered and even those they had deserted to find additional sources of wealth. Beating up women in a variety of scenarios went along with imperial expansion.

Iberian sexual beliefs and traditional customs were far different from those among the original societies in the Western Hemisphere where sex was seen as pleasurable and a natural act. In addition, virginity was often less prized among many groups in the Americas; rather, sexual inexperience, it was often believed, constituted a drawback to entering a long-lasting relationship. Catholic Europeans, however, learned from their local priests that sex was filthy and only acceptable within marriage for the sake of producing children. Those who remained celibate were of a higher order than those who did not. Thus, local women who engaged in sex with the invaders were newly cast by the invaders in the role of whore or prostitute or sinful woman; eventually, most conquered women fell into that category in the Iberian imagination. They could not accept difference in sexual customs, although they welcomed the receptivity of those same women to sexual intimacy whether married or not. Local women over the centuries adapted to this new, Catholic norm, many taking seriously the European idea that sex for anything but childbearing was sinful. A woman's most important task came to involve tightly monitoring her sexuality, whether single or married. If the former, safeguarding her virginity should be a main preoccupation while if a wife, remaining faithful to her husband was the most important value in her life.

The Europeans also worked hard to eradicate polygamous relationships, insisting that those they dealt with and conquered get rid of concubines and additional wives. Priests and other Christian clergy tried—in many cases unsuccessfully—to get high-ranking local men to become monogamous. Similarly, Catholic priests in common with the military told high-ranking women such as the African Queen Nzinga of Ndongo to dismiss all their male concubines in order to be confirmed—and thus deal as monogamous Catholics with Portuguese and Spanish administrators. Meanwhile, Iberian men who had left their families in Spain appear to have had no hesitations about stocking their households in the new world with sexual partners, including their women slaves. Clergy stationed outside the metropole—whether in the Western Hemisphere or the Philippines or Asian trading enclaves—had both short- and long-term sexual relationships, fathering children and working to advance their careers.

In fact, commentators on masculinity claimed that Iberian men and eventually all men engaged in conquering foreign lands needed very active sexual lives with multiple partners. Additionally, they were said to have had too many other things to worry about and so their own sexual restraint fell by the wayside. The Spaniard Francisco de Aguirre, a conqueror of Chile, recounted that he had fathered some fifty children with local women, despite having a wife in Spain.[3] Iberian merchants traveling the world on business often did so accompanied by a bevy of sexual partners, most of them newly purchased slaves. These European voyagers' aggressive sexuality caused so much turmoil that officials published edicts that forbade unmarried women from boarding ships, but to little effect.

The Imperial Slave Trade

While slavery existed worldwide, the slave system introduced by Europeans into the Western Hemisphere is generally seen as the cruelest and most devastating to human life. As a result of almost ninety percent mortality among the Native American population, the Spanish and Portuguese empires increasingly depended on slave labor from West Africa and the Indian Ocean coast. Iberians had first begun picking up individuals, including women and children, to sell into Europe. The trade, which the Dutch, English, and French, among others, took up somewhat later, became highly gendered. African men were preferred because the Europeans associated them with prowess in metallurgy and agriculture. To some extent this was true, given that some men did the building of heavy agricultural infrastructure such as foundations for irrigation systems. They were also wanted for mining, though travelers to Africa noted that women slaves did mining alongside men. It may have been the case that males were those African leaders would sell, and they gained a higher price than those from Indian Ocean regions. In Africa, women were too valuable as the prime agriculturalists in the area for rulers to part with.

Women's agricultural labor along the West Coast of Africa brought great wealth to African rulers because of rising sales of food to slavers not to mention the sale of captured slaves. The food-rich continent produced yams, cereal grains, okra, pumpkins, rice, bananas, melons, groundnuts, hibiscus, and a range of other crops. These goods stocked the ships of European slavers crossing the Atlantic and provisioned other Europeans stopping in southern Africa, often ill and starved for nourishment. Arab traders in East Africa also relied on African women's know-how. Because women were the main cultivators of food and also the main tradespeople, they knew what agricultural goods were available and what goods brought by the Europeans could be sold to Africans. That is, they often controlled both food production and trade. Additionally, their knowledge of prices made them good bargainers. Thus, local women played a crucial part in the slave trade and in the accumulation of African, European, and their own wealth.

African women's trading networks led to the growing establishment of Afro-European families centered on "marriage" with European men. In the seventeenth and eighteenth centuries, Europeans set up some sixty fortified stations along the Gold Coast alone. West African women among the Ga, who lived in the coastal area where the Atlantic slave trading flourished, had many kin and trade networks. These families were distinct from those Africans who might be sold into the trade, and the daughters partnered with European men in what were known as *cassare* marriages—a serious but temporary alliance. For the men, an African wife's networks facilitated the procurement of slaves and the selling of goods the Europeans wanted to exchange to pay for the human cargo. Like Koko Osu early in the eighteenth century or Severine Brock in the nineteenth century who each partnered with a Danish official, these women did not always live with their spouses but rather kept within their African family compound, which was one source of their power. Occasionally, the African woman and the European man co-habited in a European-style house, their children attending Christian schools and living an Afro-European life. Educating her children in European ways, an African woman reaped the benefits and security of having anchors in and knowledge of both worlds. Men's diaries and other accounts reveal that many of them gained not just economically, sexually, and politically, but emotionally as well. Other men, however, simply had sex with enslaved and other women available along the African coast.

African women taken for slavery across the Atlantic brought their agricultural talents with them, enriching the biodiversity of the Western Hemisphere but eventually stripping Africa of its population and upsetting its societies. It has been shown that African slaves were taken for their know-how and brains rather than simply for their brawn. This was especially true in the case of women, as many would-be plantation owners had little knowledge of agriculture not to mention mining and metallurgy. Simultaneously, the Portuguese picked up many Asian young girls from Indian Ocean coastal areas to profit from their virginity. These captives, once certified as virgins, fetched a good price in the Manila slave markets in the Philippines and were then taken to be resold in New Spain (Mexico).

Women slaves became increasingly important because of depopulation resulting from disease and warfare in a globalizing world. Given the high mortality of local people under attack, women were sought to reproduce the population as well as produce for it. Cross-border, landed seizure of slaves from competing groups was thus important in Asia and Africa for local well-being. In many cases in both Asia and Africa, religious and secular law offered protection and even advantages to enslaved women and those living free under colonialism. Conversion to Islam could lead to the freedom of the slave convert, for example. Along with people, products moved, bringing inventiveness and adaptation. The circulation of unknown goods across the globe caused many people's lives to change, making people more energetic and life healthier for those not enslaved. Women were often important for integrating new, nourishing products into their family and across society more broadly. Despite the hazards, free women began to travel more extensively to find opportunity in a globalized world.

The extraordinary wealth and other benefits African slaves brought to their masters and to the Western Hemisphere and even to the world, did not guarantee that their lives would be free from suffering, pain, and torture. To the contrary, pain and torture were all but guaranteed; short, arduous, and brutal lives were likely for most caught up in Atlantic slavery. The suffering was varied and multiple, beginning with the dangers of sugar production that entailed dangerously high fires and boiling liquids. Alternatively, a town like Bridgetown in Barbados had a cage where runaway slaves were held after capture. Hanging and other forms of execution awaited many of them, but before that, women's, like men's, bodies bore the marks of whippings, and other beatings. An advertisement for "Jane," a runaway slave who escaped to that city, described the many scars on her body: branding on one of her breasts, an extensive scar on her back and other scars perhaps from a whip or from an African initiation ritual. Such advertisements provide additional insight into the condition of women's bodies and their owners' intimate knowledge of those bodies.

Some few women in the new world became free, even to the point of owning slaves themselves. They achieved their freedom in several ways: one way was to earn money on their own, taking in laundry or doing odd jobs on the side or when owners were away. Some were rented out at a fixed return to the owner, with any extra going to the slave. They then, though rarely and often with difficulty, bought their freedom. Another way was through marriage to a free black man who then purchased the wife's emancipation. On her death in 1791, Rachael Pringle Polgren, a freed black businesswoman in Barbados, emancipated several but not all her women slaves in her will. White slave owners occasionally did something similar: on his death in 1799, George Washington freed his slaves, though he could not free the slaves who were the property of his wife Martha as they passed down to her descendants by law. That said, from 1796 on, the Washingtons had relentlessly sought to capture their escaped slave Oney "Ona" Judge. Chino slaves from Asia were more likely to be freed from bondage in Mexico than were Africans, in part because they blended in with Native Americans, who by law were not to be enslaved. Additionally, Africans were seen as more robust and thus not in need of freedom.

White women also owned African and other slaves in the Western Hemisphere, as they did across the globe. Whereas generally European law codes prohibited married women from owning property, exceptions were often made when it came to slaves, which they might own in their own right. In addition, once widowed, they regained the same possibility for ownership that they had before marriage and that men regularly enjoyed. These women could buy and sell slaves, inherit them, or pass enslaved people on to the next generation. More than that, the widow or single woman could determine who would be kept in the family after her death and who would be sold— an enormously powerful position in a slave-holding society. White women often rented out their slaves for sex especially in port cities where sailors arrived after arduous oceanic voyages. They also rented their slaves out for wet-nursing, cooking, and a range of other chores and might give slaves special training so that they yielded even more funds for the white family.

Around the world, the use of wet nurses across the globe was common, especially among royal, wealthy, and working women. Some women had problems producing milk, and in those days there were few alternatives beyond finding a reliable wet nurse who had had children of her own and was still lactating. Once European women settlers joined male invaders, they found wet nurses among the local free and slave populations—both Amerindians and Africans alike. Yet, much as they used them, humoral theory made them wary and suspicious. The common belief was that a nursing child imbibed the bodily characteristics of the nurse. According to humoral theory, the bodily and personality characteristics among the races differed wildly because each group of people had a different set of humors. So that a European baby nursed by an Amerindian woman would become Amerindian in habits, outlook on life, and adult behavior. Still, wealthy husbands often demanded that their wives give the nursing of a newborn over to a wet nurse so that sexual relations could resume, which by tradition should not occur during nursing.

The Culture of Conquest

Conquerors across time have announced their superiority in one field of endeavor or another. By the early modern period, that superiority was overwhelmingly centered in religion among Ottoman and European conquerors. Ottomans sought conquest on behalf of Sunni Islam—a religion to which they had converted centuries earlier—while Iberians ventured forth on behalf of their Catholic faith. Priests sailed in almost all voyages with the goal of bringing heathens to the word of the Catholic god. Conversion was at the heart of the priestly quest for domination however much gold and glory were also at the forefront of adventurers' minds. However, the rise of the Atlantic slave trade worked a gradual change in the rationale for conquest. Whereas many initially saw African women as stately, other descriptions of black women came to focus on their breasts and animality—an animality that also came to justify enslavement.

Women in Spanish- and Portuguese-controlled territories faced a severe and permanent transformation in their status. Iberians brought in a new level of male command, enforced in politics, economics, and social relations. Moreover, male domination became especially pronounced in religion where the array of goddesses were stomped out in favor of a single omnipotent male god. Women's roles in traditional religious observances also declined, while those continuing to hold their beliefs were hauled before the Catholic Church's religious courts, there to be humiliated, tortured, and even executed. Despite the comparative infrequency of executions, the threat of persecution was always present in sermons and in the general atmosphere where priests held prominent positions in imperial life. To the extent possible, Iberian officials including the clergy made their territories in Latin America and the Caribbean religious police-states. In this new configuration, local men lost some of their religious authority but hardly as much as women lost; they lost both their religious standing and the inspiration they derived from their traditional goddesses. Torn from the religious forces in the culture of their African habitat, transported women slaves lost virtually everything. Both African and American Indian women, however, would uniquely create hybrid beliefs born of both traditional ways and the religions imposed by the conquerors.

Across the globe, additional conquest was taking place when, in the early 1600s, groups from outside Ming China's northern borders entered the empire and made inroads on imperial rule. While Ming officials called these invaders "bandits," the Manchus, an ethnic group living on the northern boundaries of China, gradually crossed the frontiers of Ming China and through conquest brought many Ming administrators, soldiers, and civilians to their side. In 1644 they finally overthrew the dynasty itself, capturing citizens and enslaving or ransoming them. To cement the conquest (as Europeans were doing), the Manchus had Han (the name of indigenous Chinese) military officials marry Manchu women. There was more change to come in this takeover.

Like the Iberians, the Manchus were conquering far wealthier people. At cities and villages in this most prosperous part of the world, the Manchu soldiers went house to house, barn to barn, and storage area to storage area especially to loot. They further made money by enslaving women and selling them, with some women committing suicide to avoid these consequences. After that the conquerors, here as elsewhere, set out to leave their mark on the culture. Their attempts affected men and women, including their distinctive markers of masculinity and femininity. For men, resistance was a disaster; for women the results of the attempt to instill new cultural norms were mixed.

Attacking a conquered group's notions of masculinity was a strategy of rule. The Manchus issued a range of directives for male behavior. Among the decrees of the new "Qing" dynasty, as the Manchus called it, was the order that all men had to shave their heads, only growing a queue or pigtail at the back of the skull. At first the edict only applied to soldiers, leading to desertion by significant numbers of them. This change in the grooming of men was a big blow to the idea of piety toward one's parents: a man's hair represented his filial relationship to them. The Qing showed that the gender order, including masculinity, was under restructuring with the new regime. Then the edict was applied to all—military and civilian men alike— that they shave their heads, growing at the back "a coin-sized rat's tail [a queue]." They were given three days to do so, with death as the penalty for not obeying the order. Soon, "the men had shaved their heads shiny clean." There were exceptions. Some hid out, hoping to see the edict changed, but as the edict remained in force and everyone seemed to obey it, even young rebels complied and shaved their heads. Except for one: "Old Master Sheng, who'd been in charge of the imperial hunting park, lived not far from my family. But we saw only his butler, carrying a net cap [a summer cap] and sobbing as he walked back toward Master Sheng's home. We asked him why, and he said, 'The old master of my household was unwilling to shave his head . . . But today, having heard that everyone—big and small—in the whole capital city had shaven, he had no recourse but to shave as well. I saw him there crying, heartbroken . . . And later when I saw him shaven, indeed, he looked very ugly. I can't help but shedding tears too.'"[4]

Everyday Life in a World of Imperial Conquest

Even as the Manchus enforced the adoption of the shaved forehead and the queue for men, they attacked women's everyday practices. Oddly, they reaffirmed the constriction of women's feet for Han (ethnically Chinese) women: the phenomenon of foot-binding took everyday attention and caused everyday pain. The bound foot signified multiple levels of power: the mother who bound the foot over the daughter or the male who sought out a bride with tiny feet over the female, to name just two. Women among the Han elite experienced the most painful, constricting form of binding, while women in the laboring classes—rural agricultural or urban market and craft workers—had far looser binding. Many women, however, took pride in the accomplishment of small feet. The reduction of foot size was achieved over years of their dedication to the task and its pain; moreover, these tiny feet were clad in richly decorated shoes they had produced themselves.

Manchu women at the top of the hierarchy were completely free from this excruciating and crippling pain in its extreme form, although they used a kind of small raised sandal imitating a bound foot on which they placed their larger foot. Only the smaller shoe appeared at the hem of their robes.

At first, Qing officials had ordered that Han women unbind their feet, an attempt that was so completely resisted that the officials dropped the order. Like genital cutting, foot-binding was not just a matter of sociability among girls and women but represented an entire culture for them—one with other consequences. Specifically, the marriage market was invested in bound feet, as men were said to fancy tiny feet above all else. They even wrote poetry to the "lotus" foot, despite the fact that it was often infected or had oozing sores. Given its centrality, women embellished and poeticized over foot-binding, often unleashing their creative powers to embrace their culture.

Backing down on this issue, the Qing attacked other native customs with more success. For instance, the practice of widow suicide rippled across Chinese society as a way for women to prove their virtue and bring honor to their families. Women committed suicide frequently and often publicly during the Manchu takeover, making it look like massive resistance to the Manchu Empire. The Qing called the practice barbaric—actually they hated its anti-Qing message—and declared that the regime was going to civilize all of China differently. It honored chastity instead of suicide and in the name of additional civilizing squelched the customs of minority women by mandating more modest clothing, greater restraint between the sexes in public, and an end to *matrifocal* living arrangements for couples. The Iberians conquered in the name of a gendered Catholic civilization, the Manchus civilized in terms of a quasi-Confucian "upgrade" to gender.

Women dealt with and mounted resistance of other sorts to the demands of "civilizers." Nzinga Mbande (1582–1663) became queen of Mbundu people in central Africa after her brother the king committed suicide (or was poisoned) in 1626. Before that, she served as his negotiator with the Portuguese over the trade in slaves and guns as the Ndongo kingdom faced the power of the invaders. In the first of those meetings, the Portuguese leader had taken the only chair—and an elaborate one at that—in the room. Recognizing the tactic of making everyone else sit on the floor as an acknowledgment of Portuguese superiority, Nzinga had one of her servants become a chair by getting down on all fours. The queen then sat on her back. As queen, she was constantly attacked by the Portuguese, who kept her on the defensive as they whittled away at her kingdom. Hers was a small but so noteworthy an act that it was immortalized in legend and in drawings.

Meanwhile, Nzinga herself undertook conquest and like all notables and rulers in the region took and traded in slaves. Yet she made and broke alliances, losing and then expanding her power regionally as she faced continuing struggles with the Portuguese. She converted to Catholicism to gain Portuguese favor, it was said, but she also kept to the religious practices of her people. When in need of their support, she would bring out the bones of her brother as important relics and consult traditional priests. One of them told her that to become "a vassal of the Portuguese was to lose freedom and become a slave." In the name of her brother, who, like many monarchs, became sacred on his death, she had fourteen girls sacrificed on

During their long wars of invasion, the Portuguese met a formidable adversary in Queen Nzinga of Matamba

FIGURE 4.2 *Queen Nzinga, using her servant as a chair, c. 1626. This drawing has become iconic as a display of resistance to European power and a sign that Africans respected their own values and hardly cringed before these invaders. In her behavior, Nzinga demonstrated the majesty of African rulers—female and male. Courtesy of Fotosearch Getty Images.*

his grave.[5] She also waged outright war against enemies with the help of the Dutch and other African powers. Although many a plot targeted her, the Portuguese never succeeded in killing Nzinga, as they hoped. Instead, she began the Angolan pattern of constant informal warfare against these European imperialists—a pattern that finally eliminated Portuguese control in the region only late in the twentieth century.

Despite resorting to warfare, Nzinga showed diplomatic savvy in many instances and in daily life relied on it all the more as she advanced in age. While converting to Catholicism, she maintained the traditional religious practices of her people. Nzinga constantly renewed or adapted alliances, calling out those who did not follow through on their commitments. Perhaps as she became less nimble militarily, her instincts for a fair deal seemed more alive than ever. The Portuguese captured Nzinga's sister and refused to release her, while Nzinga refused to release the Portuguese official she held prisoner as long as her sister remained captive. Nzinga sent successive dispatches of hundreds of slaves that the Portuguese assured her would bring her sister's release. The Portuguese broke their part of the bargain time after time. In 1655, she wrote to the Governor-General of Angola once more, intertwining praise for the Portuguese king and his officials with an account of all the slaves she had sent as part of a deal to get her sister's release. That said, she refused new demands for slaves: "I have given the slaves Your Honor must know of to past governors and envoys, to say nothing of my gifts to secretaries and servants from your noble house and to many settlers whose treachery I still endure to this day." She professed to being agreeable to filling his request for 130 additional slaves "a hundred of whom I will send as soon as my sister reaches Ambaca. I will keep your envoy hostage until I can see with my own eyes my sister arriving." It was not, she said, that she herself mistrusted the governor. "I believe this delegation is a very honest one." Rather, her own advisors and local nobility would object "because they remember the deceits of the past."[6]

The Portuguese constantly pointed out to local people that Nzinga was a woman and thus could not be a legitimate ruler. The idea was to undermine her and turn supporters against her. At every turn, Queen Nzinga fought back with action when diplomacy didn't work. On the battle field she was a ferocious fighter and one skilled with weapons. As a leader she had no qualms about killing her relatives, advisors, slaves, and sacrificial victims. It was the way of monarchy in almost all if not all parts of the world in these days of global trade and conquest.

Everyday religion was as complicated as was resistance in a world imperiled by empire builders. Iberian conquerors of the Western Hemisphere, the Philippines, and various small outposts around the Indian Ocean world had an announced mission to expand the Christian religion and thus save its subjects from sin and burning in hell in the afterlife. After the birth of Protestantism, the task became more difficult and meant persuading local people to become Catholics instead of practicing another religion. Conversion was uneven, as it usually resulted in the merging of Catholic beliefs and rituals with those of local people. Spanish religious authorities scrutinized people's lives and everyday behavior; neighbors who lost a child or had a relative become gravely ill might accuse someone around them of witchcraft to explain the tragedy.

Both Amerindians and African slaves in Spanish America were objects of suspicion not just because they were different but because they used traditional charms or potions to cure people of their illnesses or to help them attract lovers. In 1624, the slave Paula de Eguiluz was tried for witchcraft. It was reported that she had killed a child by sucking on her navel; at the same time she had used other skills to devise of potion to help cure her master's illness. Still Paula de Eguiluz knew the Lord's Prayer and Ten Commandments, went regularly to Sunday mass, and faithfully made her confession. The inquisitors in this first hearing condemned her to 200 lashes and ordered her to perform charitable work. In her third hearing, she fully confessed to being in league with the devil and a witch even as she continued to frame the use of her African healing knowledge as a Christian act. By that time she had been convicted and ordered to be sent to government officials for execution.

As shown in many similar incidents, methods to ensure orthodox belief and practices of the Catholic faith were often brutal. Outcomes were mixed wherever the Inquisition was at work; it was a tool of the church to ensure correct Catholic practice and belief and to check that converted Jews and Muslims had not been secretly following their religions. Indigenous and enslaved African women as well as men were, as in the case of Paula de Eguiluz, tortured, killed, and otherwise punished for deviations from this faith that they were supposed to adopt. Moreover, the Church demanded that local people follow a sexual path seen in Catholic doctrine. Specifically, in most cultures, Catholicism decreed that the sacrament of marriage was a union between two people that did not allow for the polygamy that many cultures practiced. The change in religious belief aroused resistance in the form of syncretism—that is, the fusion of beliefs and practices—as well as dissimulation or the pretense of following an official doctrine such as Catholicism. Women were guilty of both.

At the same time, many local women and men as well as imported African slaves across the Spanish empire adopted Catholicism. Other women and men merged traditional practices with those from distant lands, as empire began to bring cultures closer together, even though distant from one another. In 1531, the Aztec Cuauhtlatoatzin, whose baptismal name was Juan Diego, had five visions of the Virgin Mary on a sacred Aztec spot of the corn goddess, near Mexico City. As a result of one of her miracles, an imprint of her form was left on Juan Diego's cape. That imprint revealed Mary to be an Aztec woman wearing a robe with Aztec designs and symbols. Moreover, the placement of the designs mirrored the Aztec heavens, calling the Aztecs to merge themselves with Catholicism. The cult of this "dark virgin"—Our Lady of Guadalupe was brown-skinned—grew over the centuries, as Juan Diego's visions prompted the building of a church and many shrines, and as her story was written down in Spanish and in Nahuatl. The Dark Virgin replaced some of the suppressed goddesses, as women in particular took up devotion to her as a symbol of motherhood—her impending motherhood visible in her appearance to Juan Diego. Beyond that, her revelation to an impoverished local person uplifted the poor and further enhanced her worship in New Spain (Mexico); many of the local poor were now awarded as laborers by Spanish monarchs to the conquistadors.

Still further adaptation came. Chino slave Caterina de San Juan (c. 1606–1688) was abducted as a child from India, sold as a virginal slave in Manila, and then freed from bondage in Mexico. She became admired for her good, even miraculous deeds and Catholic devotion; into the present day she is seen as a national but also polyethnic symbol. In other parts of the world similar mergers occurred: the Japanese integrated the Chinese goddess Guanyin with the cult of the Virgin by depicting Guanyin in the

FIGURE 4.3 *Our Lady of Guadalupe by a sixteenth-century artist. Painted by a local craftsman, the Virgin of Guadalupe has the long, straight black hair of native people and darker skin than do European images of Mary. Aztec designs in the image were also appealing, but local people approached the shrine on their knees because of their traditional belief that gods could inhabit depictions. Courtesy of Leemage/Corbis Getty Images.*

style of Mary. In fact, the cult of Mary became popular across the globe, mostly joined to the established traditions and beliefs of local people.

Spanish Catholics—many of them women and their families—gradually set up dozens and eventually hundreds of convents and monasteries for women across the vast transoceanic empire. Mexico City had a large number of them, and in fact cities hosted virtually all the convents in order to gain Christian adherents but also to benefit the nuns and to maximize the number of people they could help. Nuns had an array of tasks including philanthropy, education, meditation, prayer, and general ministering to others. Some orders were strictly cloistered, engaging in no outreach other than prayer, reflection, and spiritual activity. They also undertook fund-raising and work to support themselves.

Nunneries in the colonial world resembled those back in the metropole in terms of class. Women from wealthy families had more privileges in that they entered well-endowed orders with many lower-class nuns who did most of the work. Women from the poorest families then did domestic work, gardening, cooking, and other menial jobs from which the wealthier sisters were exempt. The class structure in the empire was more complicated in that it also included the racial definitions that had taken shape across New Spain and the other colonized regions of Spanish America. Mulatto and *mestiza* women almost automatically fell into the lower-status ranks in any convent. No matter what their background, some nuns in the Spanish world came to advance not just spiritual and material well-being but intellectual and cultural development as well.

Across the Western Hemisphere, colonized women, including slaves, continued to use legal systems and religious values to their benefit whenever possible. In Lima, between 1760 and 1820, they brought almost twice as many suits as men did, appealing to both secular and ecclesiastical courts when they had grievances. Problems with abusive spouses and masters were primary among their complaints, though aggrieved women also disputed the confiscation of their property and their children. In 1783, the slave Manuela petitioned that she be sold by the convent that owned her to the master of her husband. Her reasoning involved the importance of leading a properly married life in the same location as her spouse. The courts agreed, but the convent did not execute the sale of Manuela. She pleaded again: despite the high status of the convent the court now more emphatically ordered the sale of Manuela and the reunion of the spouses.

Four years later in Lima, Maria del Carmen Ollague, a free black, petitioned the court to order her husband—a slave—to stop abusing her and to return her certificate of manumission, which he had confiscated. Alternatively, she asked that she be sent to a convent, though she preferred rebuilding a calm domestic life. Despite the fact that the household contained slaves, he forced her to do all sorts of menial labor, beyond that of a normal wife, and even had her chained up in a bakery to work there. She went on to describe that her husband "think[ing] himself a man" often ordered her to go to the tavern. Should it take more time to get served or should she say a few words to a friend, he would lock her out of the house, exposing her to thieves or other "evil people." When he finally let her in, "it is just to kick, punch, and bite me."[7] With at least some confidence in the colonial system, Maria Ollegue looked to the power of the Spanish courts to hear her petition and adjudicate it fairly. Such was her only way out of a bodily problem situated in race and gender.

Conclusion

The birth of new empires and the expansion of older ones in these years generally affected most conquered people's lives for the worse. Iberian empire-builders were usually poor in comparison to those they attacked, raping, enslaving, robbing, and usually behaving in uncivilized ways while ultimately claiming to be more civilized than those they conquered. Because invaders were desperate for wealth but unaware of other people's customs, women partnering with them could help them develop networks and learn trading and other customs that would advance their goals of gaining wealth. Some conquerors also married into their new lands' leading families, both in order to be acculturated and to have access to the women's wealth. Reproduction across ethnic lines made for complex identities and new complications in the distribution of power. Within these hybrid scenarios, some women prospered.

Because conquest in the Atlantic world was so destructive, women's responsibility both to reproduce humans and to produce crops was a heavy one. The transatlantic slave trade developed slowly until reaching a peak in the eighteenth century. The number of women sold was lower than that of men, in part because African owners of women slaves needed their agricultural skills to grow food to sell to slave ships. Gradually some colonists and traders developed a contradictory assessment of African women: a traveler in the 1640 called one African woman "of the greatest beauty and majesty together: that ever I saw in one woman." She carried herself "with far greater Majesty and gracefulness" than Queen Anne herself. Simultaneously, this same author employed a language of black women's monstrosity developed that in effect erased their humanity. When in the fields, black women's breasts "hang down below their Navels, so that when they stoop at their common work of weeding, they hang almost to the ground, that at a distance you would think they had six legs."[8] Gender difference was often transformed, even heightened, in this early age of brutal conquest in the Atlantic World. Racial and ethnic difference thrived in signaling superiority and inferiority. Still, across the globe, women created forms of resistance, accommodation, and acculturation at the time and those ways of interacting would be transformed still further in the next centuries of imperial expansion.

Glossary

Anishinabe	People local to the northeastern North American continent composed of many sub-groups such as the Otawa and Potawatami, often called woodlands people.
Manchus	A steppe people from Manchuria who overthrew the Ming dynasty in 1644.

Matrifocal	A household or society in which women head the group.
Mestiza	A woman of Spanish and Amerindian heritage.
Qing	The name of the dynasty founded by the Machus in China in 1644 and overthrown in 1911–12.

Notes

1 For the entire account see Gomes Eanes de Azurara, *The Chronicle of the Discovery and Conquest of Guinea*, Charles Raymond Beazley and Edgar Prestage, trans. (London: Hakluyt Society, 1899), 40–3. Also available on Project Gutenberg, https://www.gutenberg.org/files/35738/35738-h/35738-h.htm

2 Quoted in C. R. Boxer, *Women in Iberian Expansion Overseas, 1415–1815* (New York: Oxford University Press, 1975), 17.

3 This account is based on C. R. Boxer, *Women in Iberian Expansion*, 108–10.

4 Yao Wenxi (from a prominent Chinese family), "Daily Jottings from the End of the Ming" manuscript, in *Voices from the Ming-Qing Cataclysm: China in Tigers' Jaws*, Lynn A. Struve, ed. and trans. (New Haven, CT: Yale University Press, 1993), 64–5.

5 The quote and account are from Linda M. Heywood, *Njinga of Angola: Africa's Warrior Queen* (Cambridge: Harvard University Press, 2017), 84.

6 Letter of Queen Ana Nzinga to the Governor General of Angola, December 13, 1655 in Kathryn Joy McKnight and Leon J. Garofalo, eds. *Afro-Latino Voices Shorter Edition: Translations of Early Modern Ibero-Atlantic Narratives* (Indianapolis, IN: Hackett, 2015), 33.

7 Both cases appear in Maribel Arrelucea Barrantes, "Slavery, Writing, and Female Resistance: Black Women Litigants in Lima's Tribunals of the 1780s," Joseph P. Sanchez et al., trans. in *Afro-Latino Voices (Shorter Edition): Translations of Early Modern Ibero-Atlantic Narratives*, Kathryn Joy McKnight and Leo J. Garofalo, eds. (Indianapolis, IN: Hackett, 2015), 187–91.

8 Richard Ligon, quoted in Jennifer L. Morgan, " 'Some Could Suckle over Their Shoulder': Male Travelers, Female Bodies, and the Gendering of Racial Ideology, I500-I770," *William and Mary Quarterly*, 3d Series, 54:1 (January I997): 167–8.

Further Reading

Dunbar, Erica Armstrong. *Never Caught: The Washingtons' Relentless Pursuit of their Runaway Slave Ona Judge*. New York: Atria, 2017.

Fenn, Elizabeth. *Encounters at the Heart of the World: A History of the Mandan People*. New York: Hill and Wang, 2015.

Fuentes, Marisa J. *Dispossessed Lives: Enslaved Women, Violence and the Archive*. Philadelphia: University of Pennsylvania Press, 2016.

Heywood, Linda M. *Queen Njinga of Angola: Africa's Warrior Queen*. Cambridge: Harvard University Press, 2017.

Ipsen, Pernille. *Daughters of the Trade: Atlantic Slavers and Interracial Marriage on the Gold Coast*. Philadelphia: University of Pennsylvania Press, 2015.

Ko, Dorothy. *Cinderella's Sisters: A Revisionist History of Footbinding*. Berkeley: University of California Press, 2005.

McKnight, Kathryn Joy, and Leon J. Garofalo. *Afro-Latino Voices Shorter Edition: Translations of Early Modern Ibero-Atlantic Narratives*. Indianapolis, IN: Hackett, 2015.

Poska, Allyson M. *Gendered Crossings: Women and Migration in the Spanish Empire*. Albuquerque: University of New Mexico Press, 2016.

Powers, Linda Vieira. *Women in the Crucible of Conquest: The Gendered Genesis of Spanish American Society, 1500–1600*. Albuquerque: University of New Mexico Press, 2005.

Rodriguez, Jeanette. *Our Lady of Guadalupe: Faith and Empowerment among Mexican-American Women*. Austin: University of Texas Press, 1994.

Socolow, Susan Migden. *The Women of Colonial Latin America*. 2nd edn. New York: Cambridge University Press, 2014.

Sousa, Lisa. *The Woman Who Turned into a Janguar and Other Narratives of Native Women in the Archives of Colonial Mexico*. Stanford, CA: Stanford University Press, 2017.

Struve, Lynn A. *Voices from the Ming-Qing Cataclysm: China in Tigers' Jaws*. New Haven, CT: Yale University Press, 1993.

5

Populations, Ideas, and the Industrious Revolution, 1600–1800

Quantities of colorful cottons, lavish embroidery, and painted fabrics of many kinds circled the globe after 1600 because of the newly created worldwide marketplace. Large parts of the world suffered from a "little ice age" in the seventeenth century, and scarcity alongside lower temperatures added to the pressures not only to seek protective cover provided by furs in cold climates but also to obtain produce and other goods that were plentiful in sunnier regions. The circulation of microorganisms and healthful products across the globe helped increase world population a century later outside of places devastated by disease and slavery. Exceptionally, the number of people in Africa by the end of the early modern period had actually declined due to both external and internal trade in humans; moreover, the constant warfare on the African continent to secure people to sell led to the destruction of villages and agriculture. In contrast, after the violence of the Manchu takeover in 1644, China entered another era of incredible expansion and prosperity. The sum of these changes occurred alongside ongoing imperial activity worldwide and revolutions in leadership, with change being uneven from one region to another and even from one community to another.

People—women foremost among them—reacted to the need to support a rising population and to the availability of goods from across the globe with growing industriousness. In some regions of the world, people worked harder because of the massive destruction caused by steady warfare in the seventeenth century and into the eighteenth. They got more work done not just because of rising population but also because they needed to repair constant military devastation. They also wanted the diverse or better products that were entering their own markets from foreign ones. In addition, governments demanded more taxes or tribute from subjects to support state-building and the military nature of the expansion itself. Taxes rose or were more efficiently collected to pay for new roads, ships, harbors, weapons, and the officials to monitor these activities. Whether weeding in fields, weaving at home, making umbrellas, or inventing new techniques or foodstuffs such as varieties of cheeses, women were at the forefront of growing economic activity.

Thinking about new goods and desiring prosperity also encouraged some women, along with men, to engage in writing, studying science, translating books, and working in the arts even as they raised children. The world was becoming more mobile; households dealt with a flow of unknown goods, and ideas entered communities and families from around the world—all of these providing food for women's thought. Not only did women have the old standbys—the writings of Confucius and Ban Zhao, oral histories of Sundiata, or lessons from the Qu'ran and the Bible—they themselves were reflecting on governance, household conduct, and values in a globalizing world. Science occupied the minds of some, while others took to philosophy and social reform. Still other women translated a range of ancient or foreign works; and many proposed evaluations of the condition of women's lives more generally. Some called this era a time of "Enlightenment," but a number of women did this new thinking as if it were all part of their daily responsibility to examine the course of events and even participate in politics.

Creating an Industrious Revolution

By the 1700s people across the globe were simply working harder and producing more than ever before—a phenomenon labeled the industrious revolution. This industrious revolution based mostly on hard work, changes in agriculture, and acceleration in commerce is distinguished from the Industrial Revolution that arose in good part from the substitution of mechanical power for human energy. The causes of the industrious revolution were even more complex: for almost the entire seventeenth century, Chinese society experienced devastating warfare, first from the Manchus hammering away at villages and towns in order to gain control. Once they had taken over the Chinese government, the Manchu/Chinese military set out to conquer regions to the south and west, eventually seizing more than a million square miles. Japan and Korea experienced similar conflicts and attempts at conquest, all of this destroying farms, villages, and the people of entire communities. It took massive amounts of work to bring empires back to prosperity and to make up for all that had been lost: Qing China was a perfect example of restoring one's manufacturing, trade, and agricultural might and even advancing it, in part by stressing the need for women to work.

Much of the world faced a similar situation: the European continent experienced the Thirty Years' War (1618–48), the English Revolution and civil wars (1640–88/9), and the military expansion of France and other ambitious monarchies. For most of the sixteenth and into the seventeenth century, the Mughals were on the march into South Asia as were the Russians into central and eastern Asia. The seventeenth century saw additional devastation as more Europeans slaughtered their way across the Western Hemisphere to gain colonies and as local peoples fought back. The Atlantic slave trade grew; Africans undertook warfare against other Africans to capture neighboring communities to use as laborers and soldiers and to sell. Given the seventeenth century's never-ending round of revolutions and wars of religion, conquest, and empire, there was much to repair and restore not to mention making up for the military men removed from productive work.

Alongside devastation and the struggle to correct its effects, new agricultural processes were put into place, as ultimately population growth led many into towns and cities and as travel yielded opportunities. New rice planting techniques in some places, new irrigation systems in another, and novel forms of fertilizer all freed up workers; farms often took less skilled attention and children could be substituted. Practices such as crop rotation moved from one part of the world to another, increasing productivity. The discovery that some crops acted as fertilizers similarly boosted production because fields would not have to lie fallow until their fertility was restored. Some innovations simply meant that fewer workers were needed on average to produce normal amounts of goods or food, sending the unneeded workers, including women, into other productive sectors of the economy.

Commerce was one place where many women thrived, often controlling markets large and small and traveling to pursue their business interests. In Spanish Latin America, women of the more prosperous classes owned liquor stores, paper stores, and establishments that sold other artisanal goods as well as variety stores, though they might have agents run them. In Argentina, by the end of the eighteenth century, a cluster of women had commissioned seventeen shiploads of commercial items such as fabrics to sell. They also exported goods including an array of raw materials such as many kinds of animal skins. Wealthy Ottoman women invested in housing projects and real estate, as commerce continued to make city life attractive to those no longer needed in rural households.

Glückel of Hameln (1646–1724) was one of these prosperous merchants; she traveled the urban landscape but also experienced the ups and downs of commerce. Glückel was married at age fourteen to Hayyim Hamel from a commercially active Jewish family like hers. Embarking on business with her husband at the end of the disastrous Thirty Years' War, she bore twelve living children to whose individual schooling in business she devoted energy as well as to the overall prosperity of the family's commerce. Many of the adult children went into other businesses, even as she set up a stocking factory in Hamburg and continued the family's trade in gems after her husband died in 1689. While her husband was alive and thereafter, she kept the books for their enterprises, hired agents, traveled extensively to commercial fairs, and kept abreast of economic conditions across Europe.

Success in business did not come easily to her offspring or herself, and she was often forced to intervene, as in the case of her son Loeb. As she wrote, "[M]y son Loeb, I told you, was still a lad and knew nothing of business. And his father-in-law, far from keeping a steady eye on him, let him run like a loose sheep." Glückel was proud of her son's very large store in Berlin, stocked with a vast array of goods. However, he was negligent and decidedly a bad steward of his business. "The help, men and women, stole right and left. Other worthless folk, such as are to be found in Berlin and thereabouts, made up to him, and while they went through the motions of bargaining stole from under his eyes."

Things were even worse than this, as Glückel—and perhaps many mothers in similar situations—soon found out. Her son Loeb loaned large sums to other Jews in Poland. Unawares, she and others in the family, in turn, loaned money to him with the idea that his was a thriving business. Then she went to one of the large, commercial fairs in Germany, where merchants from many parts of the continent gathered to sell their goods and do other transactions. Merchants from Amsterdam confronted her with the promissory notes of her son. She was shocked until Loeb said he would send her the funds for repayment. In the meantime, she paid his debts and returned home, where she had every expectation that the funds would be waiting for her. There was nothing from him, except a series of letters full of excuses. How disturbing this must have been for a woman who was a careful and hardworking merchant!

"What was I to do? . . . Two weeks later, a good friend came to me and said, 'I cannot keep it from you, I must tell you that your son Loeb . . . is heavily plunged in debt.' Such and more my good friend told me, and my soul nearly died within me, and I fainted on the spot."

"I now began to talk with him. 'They are saying,' I said, 'thus and so of you. Bethink yourself of God and of your good and honest father, that you bring us not to shame.'" By that time, Loeb owed his mother a hefty sum, which she regained by taking some of his excess merchandise off his hands. "[R]egardless of everything, I only sought to help my children,"[1] she concluded. Her earnest pursuit of family well-being was not necessarily unusual in Jewish society, for many striving men in those days might choose to study religious texts and allow their wives to support the family. Her memoir charts the rationale behind her business decisions and the many successes she achieved. Yet, the unlucky, if successful Glückel some years after her husband's death remarried a wealthy banker in hopes of securing her future only to find that he too was deeply in debt. His bankruptcy brought her financial ruin.

Women in Africa were likewise active and successful in these busy days of commerce. Lutheran clergyman, Wilhelm Muller, served the employees of a Danish trading company based in the West African region that is present-day Ghana. Like other travelers to West Africa and extending as far east as Indonesia, he found markets there full of life, run by committed women with hardly a man in sight. Dotting African towns, he wrote, were the markets "in which they sell their wares every day. Apart from the peasants who bring palm wine and sugar-cane to market every day, there are no men who stand in public markets to trade, but only women." Among these, some brought large bowls of chopped tobacco and pipes with bowls "the size of a fist." Other women had poultry and eggs, while still others had different kinds of oil.

"Besides the aforementioned trade in livestock," he continued, "the Fetu people conduct great trade in salt, which they know how to boil in their country themselves, for they fill large earthenware pots with the stagnant water which is brought inland when the salty sea overflows and which then settles there. They place the pots on a large fire, let the water become hot and boil it till the brine has completely dried up and turned into salt. Then they tip the salt out in the sun and stir frequently, till it is dry, fine and good. Fetu salt is so strong and white that it is not inferior to the best European salt in taste or colour."

Referring to more extensive trade networks, Reverend Muller, noted that the women traded salt both in their local market but then transported additional quantities of it great distances to the interior. In addition, they were astute in their conservation of commodities and forthright in their sales pitches: "The Fetu tradeswomen devote great energy to selling the goods they have carried to market before the day is over, so that nothing is left over for the following day, or is spoilt, or must be consumed by themselves. Consequently, one hears women vying with one another to attract passers-by with persuasive words, and they do not willingly let these passers-by out of their hands until they have bought something."[2]

There was commerce of many types during the industrious revolution, as the kinds and number of goods multiplied because of globalization, frequently leading officials to find commerce destabilizing. Disorienting to male traders from Europe, women from Southeast Asia often had control not just of markets but of extended trading networks, including local, regional, and international ones. Reorienting their gender beliefs in order to trade with women was difficult for some. In contrast, Chinese women's production of rice on farms and weaving of textiles—especially silk fabric—to pay taxes were comforting signs to observant officials of social and political stability. By the mid-eighteenth century, however, women had moved on to produce tea, mats, and a range of other products that were more lucrative on the market. As important, men had taken over weaving, leaving women the less remunerative jobs of tending mulberry trees and silkworms, which caused some to branch out. Industriously, they turned to still different tasks that would make them money in China's thriving commercial centers. Women's commercial activities in public were seen by the government as disruptive in comparison to more isolated and hidden work at home.

A somewhat similar situation existed in Europe, where governments tried to control trade in order to stabilize society by keeping artisans employed in their traditional jobs. Those jobs involved making the same textiles year after year or the same shoes or the same hats. Importing textiles from Asian family workshops that involved the skills of women changed all that. Now foreign commerce upset that steady and cozy European productive world. Artisans there physically assaulted women wearing colorful cotton dresses imported from India and China, even though men also picked up made-to-order, brightly printed "banyans" or bathrobes. The governments of France and Britain outlawed imported cottons, but women consumers bought smuggled ones. Daring dressmakers then flaunted the restrictions, making new kinds of washable clothing that undermined the heavy brocade styles set by women at court. Next, queens and aristocratic women took to Indian cottons, while the king's mistresses chose brightly flowered Chinese silks. Industriousness in the field of commerce sparked change.

FIGURE 5.1 *Two Chinese women at work weaving silk textile. Part of the industrious revolution, these two women operate a complex weaving machine, showing their skill and their contribution to making early modern society hum with activity. While people globally snapped up Chinese textiles, Chinese women in turn learned to use such exotic imports as pumpkins. Courtesy of Corbis Getty Images.*

In the British colonies of North America, Scottish-born Elizabeth Murray (1726–1785) set up a thriving business in Boston selling quality British goods, including those on sale from other parts of the world. Active, loving business, Murray traveled to London to find just the right items for trade and made her husbands—she had three of them—sign prenuptial agreements securing her control of her businesses and her property. In British law, a woman's property became her husband's on marriage and all her earnings during the marriage became his as well. Murray would have none of it, perhaps gaining in confidence as she traveled internationally, but her successes led her on a disruptive path. She advocated that women become more enterprising, sent young women to found their own commercial spots, and offered courses from her store in the most up-to-date embroidery stitches and designs.

In some places, women lower down on the social scale were the ones selling in streets and smaller markets. In Latin America, for example, poorer Indian women, mulattas, and Africans had stands selling fruit, vegetables, cacao, and sometimes cured meat such as ham. They were also the ones who went door to door in towns lacking a central market with their produce. Similar itinerant sales women in the cities of the Ottoman Empire took their goods to urban neighborhoods, where women could enjoy "curbside" service when they had neither time nor inclination to leave their quarters. In fact, women's commercial industriousness was global: reportedly in the Ottoman-controlled Balkans, when farm women got wind of travelers in the area, they would put down their work, mix flour, liquids, and flavors together, and bake breads and cakes to sell along the route.

Women Investors and Producers

Seventeenth- and eighteenth-century elite women in Cairo, Egypt, were also ambitious and became wealthy through trade and investments in manufacturing in this age of industriousness. Unlike European women (including those living in North and South America), they could own and manage their own property. An advantageous way of doing this was to endow what today might be called a charitable trust (waqf) but from which they and family members could draw funds almost in perpetuity even as they did good deeds. As independent investors and managers of trusts, they owned large workshops, apartment buildings, and warehouses—the latter profitable because of the growth in commercial goods passing through the region. Members of the sultan's harem and high-ranking women in Istanbul similarly made a range of investments, especially in real estate that flourished because of trade and migration. In Ottoman convents, nuns also made extensive loans not just among themselves but to the public at large.

While they invested and otherwise created wealth, women in Europe learned to integrate Indian cottons into everyday life, creating wall hangings, tablecloths and bed linens, and new kinds of underwear. To gain these, they contributed to the industrious revolution with increased inventiveness and productivity at home of goods for the market. They were growers of hemp, carders of wool, spinners of thread, and often weavers—all of this done in the home or on the farm. Women in China integrated sweet potatoes, pumpkin, beans, peas, and other foods from distant lands into their cuisine, just as the African woman farmer added to her botanical repertoire, expanding dietary variety. In Japan and elsewhere, women were demanding consumers of textiles and other global products that became increasingly available because of improvements in water transportation, including not just ships but the construction of harbors, canals, and adjacent roads. Thanks to infrastructure improvements and globalization, women across Africa bought Indonesian batik, painted cottons or, for special occasions, only the finest of silks. Those in the Pacific wanted goods from China, and prosperous settlers in Latin America also craved textiles from various cultures though rarely inferior products from Europe. Exquisite imported textiles, precious stones, and porcelain manifested family wealth and distinction.

The appearance of so many new products ramped up activity as people struggled and worked harder to obtain these goods, but the growing state apparatus and its need for expensive weaponry also came into play. Qing officials penned pamphlets encouraging Chinese women to work, especially to work at textiles in the late seventeenth and eighteenth centuries. Government directives divided women's labor according to economic and social standing, the poor being encouraged to produce silk or cotton thread and weave hats from straw. A woman of middling prosperity could produce finer cotton garments and venture into silk. The textiles created and the type of work done—producing mulberries, preparing raw cotton, spinning thread, and weaving—might vary according to locale too. There was less variation among the highest social strata of women, whose work was to focus on producing silkworms, silk thread, and even the silk textile itself. Work in silk indicated the highest degree of cleanliness and purity. The Chinese empress led in performing such tasks to the point of conducting the symbolic ceremony honoring the empress Lei Zu, goddess of silk production and reputedly the inventor of silk textiles in ancient times. Women from the most refined households also undertook embroidery, the most desirable embellishment of textiles and a product that was in high demand. Delicately embroidered fabrics enjoyed a worldwide market. From all walks of life, Chinese women like women elsewhere kept busy.

Social stability and government income were both at stake. "Where a woman works diligently, her family will surely rise; where a woman is lazy, her family is certain to fall," one local Chinese official wrote in this era.[3] By this time, male artisans were making inroads on some of the work provisioning families and creating textiles with which to pay taxes that women had once done. Anxieties arose on several fronts, the first being that newly idle women could cause social disorder and upset not just their own families but both local communities and the empire as a whole. Second,

China had no fixed social categories, so there was concern that families would fall into severe poverty, should women slack off from provisioning the household and making goods with which to pay taxes—the latter of primary concern. Finally, a hardworking woman symbolized overall good values that could resonate within her family and across the community. Chinese opinion-makers publicized that there was much riding on women's productivity, as the constantly refreshed supply of encouraging texts and images of busy women show.

Some inventions caused women's work to shift by allowing children to take over tasks. A good example is a rice harvesting machine developed in Japan during these years. This machine, like a large comb, moved along the paddies squeezing rice from the stalks—a job when done by hand needed the strength of an adult woman whereas the rice harvesting machine could be manipulated by a child. Women were then freed up for increased weaving and spinning. As urbanization boomed and as people traveled more for commerce and for carrying out official duties, animal and human waste became publicly available manure in the public space and women scooped it up and sold it. Changes in fertilizer from twigs and other debris to human and animal waste from cities not only opened up land that had supplied twigs to farm land but also changed some women's job of collecting them to an even wider variety of more fruitful work, for example, producing new goods or farming additional land.

Even as officials broadcast the uplifting economic and moral effects of women's productive work, the tasks themselves were hardly so refined, as seen in China's households. One poem describes "Mountains of Wu caterpillars with their snowlike cocoons,/ The silk-spinning wheel rumbles behind the brushwood door./ The young wife at the wheel, her disheveled hair flying,/ For two months she toils, her elbows bare. Mornings forgetting to wash and comb, nights without sleep."[4] Productivity was not, in this poet's mind, a genteel or even womanly undertaking. Chinese women also peddled water wheels, dredged up mud from rivers and then carried the mud to rice fields as fertilizer. When it became known that gold had been found in Korea, some women packed up their entire family to seek their fortunes, whether in mining itself or in provisioning adventurous miners. In the same era of industriousness, elderly widows in the town of Foxton, England, gathered stones in the winter of 1772–3 from fields to repair the roads. Working in the cold, snow, and rain, as did the widows Gregory and Baxton, the widow Cowper picked up individual stones from muddy fields, put them in a large sack, hauled the sack to a cart, and deposited them until more sacksful had filled the cart. Eventually, she earned two pounds for the twenty-seven carts she filled, enough to keep her off the list of paupers.[5]

Wealthy women were also active in the grubby side of productive industriousness. Some adopted new techniques on their estates, while they then threw people off the land and into utter poverty, all in the name of efficiency. Not all that far from the widow Cowper, Elizabeth, Countess of Sutherland (1765–1839), orphaned at age one, inherited some 800,000 acres in Scotland. Marrying a massively wealthy financier at age twenty, she removed in one way or another hundreds of tenants from her estate and then proceeded to create unified acreage for raising sheep and farming on a large scale with the help of day laborers, who were cheaper than tenants and who had no claims to the land. Her methods were often ruthless, pushing some people to migrate across oceans in order to survive and leaving others to die in abject poverty nearby. Still, she was known as industrious for adhering to her own work ethic. As one who was immersed in industrious profit-making she chased out villagers with her own hands. New efficiency in agriculture was a force for increased productivity but also for immiseration of ordinary people.

Lower down on the social scale were women confined to their households because of social customs, who nonetheless needed to make money through industriousness. Among those in the more "respectable" classes, hidden away they worked making refined cottons, silks, and woolens and doing intricate embroidery—the latter an especially valued skill because it added color and complexity to apparel. Pirates captured women embroiderers from China, Japan, the Philippines, and the Coromandel cost of India to enslave, so enriching was this skill. Women's development of lace-making as a domestic occupation also arose and expanded during the age of industriousness. Nuns in convents used their expertise in needlework to support their religious orders, selling complicated secular wall hangings and intricately decorated textiles for religious use as garments for the clergy, adornments for churches, or decoration of religious statuary, especially of the Virgin Mary.

Social Complexity in an Urbanizing World

The era was one of striking mobility, both socially and geographically. Because of new job opportunities and new efficiencies on the land, locally people moved from rural areas to cities, especially in thriving empires such as China but also in more backward areas such as England where agricultural modernization occurred, including the modernization on the lands of the Countess of Sutherland. The mobility was both a cause and a result of industriousness and much of it connected to the circulation of global goods. Women in modest circumstances made the most of mobility too; for example, in Buenos Aires the widow Dona Maria Josefa Flores rented out rooms in her home to three men from Spain. Others started inns to bring in strangers traveling to participate in the expansion of commerce or cooked food to sell around mines and on the streets of growing cities.

Other mobility was forced, revolving around the ongoing global slave trade. Demand for sugar, tobacco, coffee, tea, and cotton drove the industrious people across the globe to work harder so that they might have those addictive consumer goods. The slave trade across the Atlantic world provided forced laborers to produce increasing amounts of those commodities. While business people demanded profits, consumers demanded commodities, many originating in the Atlantic world. Both demands to a large extent were products of the African slave system: specifically, the brawn and know-how of both male and female slaves and the reproductive capacity and unique agricultural and marketing skills of imported African women. African women were a major force in the development of industriousness, dredging up salt in coastal areas and around islands to preserve food for an urban population, growing and processing rice, cotton, sorghum, sugar cane and tobacco in the colonies to supply a thriving productive system, and tending the vast agricultural enterprises in Africa that provided commodities for slave ships going to the new world and food for slave armies.

Once the Atlantic slave trade began, Western African women were active in that trade, not only provisioning ships and resident European traders but also pulling larger amounts of global goods into their markets. The more foreign goods one accumulated to sell, the brisker the business. As across the commercial Indian Ocean world, it was common in all these areas for local women to take temporary husbands; between these partners exchange of knowledge and influence flowed. French-African or Danish-African families in West Africa for generations were composed of mixed-race couples and their offspring. Often children born of these unions had international connections too, becoming workers for the trading companies or for their local communities in organizing slave and other trade. Some traveled to the Caribbean or to European cities where their white families had properties or businesses. There was hardly a trader who wasn't aware of the wealth many of these women possessed and the international networks on which their trade thrived. Tight family ties across cultures also ensured that these African women and their offspring would not be themselves be caught up in the slave network and sold. Fathers sometimes even sent their talented daughters to Europe to be trained in math, languages, and business skills.

Betsy Heard (1759–after 1812) was one of the most powerful and legendary of successful Anglo-African business women. Trained in England, most likely Liverpool, she participated in her father's network and then took over his businesses. Ultimately, she owned ships, a major wharf, and warehouse from which she operated her thriving trade. As a trader, used to dealing with rivals and a large pool of clients, she became known for interpersonal prowess and even chosen (as in the case of Southeast Asian women) to negotiate between governments and trading companies. On the one hand, Heard was part of a cohort of successful African business women; on the other hand, among African women generally, she was extremely fortunate to escape the horrific middle passage experienced by millions of others.

Given multiple forms of global mixture—ethnicities, foodstuffs, and customs—not only did people have to rethink their lives, they also faced less predictability in society and sometimes faced a confusion of social identities even as new identities were being created. The old status identities became blurred as conquerors married local women, often of different ethnicities, races, and levels of social distinction. One way of charting identity was through mandating specific clothing for each segment of the population; these were called sumptuary laws. The variety of textiles had been increased by the circulation of fabrics globally and by the mixing of traditions. In the middle of the eighteenth century, Jorge Juan and Antonio de Ulloa, well-born Spanish scientists, made their discovery of platinum while on a French scientific trip to South America. They also observed the geography and local life in Central America and along the west coast of South America and in 1748 published an account called *Voyage to South America*. We remember that at the time, Spain had the most extensive and oldest transoceanic empire in the world, so that understanding its colonial system could provide lessons for would-be colonial powers such as France, the Netherlands, and Britain. Understanding gender dynamics in relation to status, race, and ethnicity—called intersectionality—was one important key. Thus, during their nine year stay abroad, they also noted complex social differences—in this case through the clothing of the women in the mining town of Quito. The racial, ethnic, and class distinctions in the population were a major characteristic of the Spanish colonies as they arose after the first invasions of the Western Hemisphere. The first people they identified were the upper classes, who were supposedly easiest to spot: "The dress of the ladies of the first rank [Spanish] consists of a petticoat . . . ," they wrote. "On the upper parts of their body they wear a shift, on that a loose jacket laced, and over all a kind of bays [a textile], but made into no form, being worn just as cut from the piece. Every part of their dress is, as it were, covered with lace; and those which they wear on days of ceremony, are always of the richest stuffs, with a profusion of ornaments. Their hair is generally made up in tresses, which they form into a kind of cross, on the nape of the neck; tying a rich ribband, called balaca, twice round their heads, and with the ends form a kind of rose at their temples. These roses are elegantly intermixed with diamonds and flowers. When they go to church, they sometimes wear a full petticoat; but the most usual dress on these occasions is the veil."

Wearing proper dress among the Spanish, mestizos (people of mixed Spanish and Indian blood), and Indians showed that one knew one's place in society. Instruction in these dress codes for the increasing number of foreign travelers, military, officials, and merchants taught such newcomers how to identify social classes, especially the tricky business of calculating the exact mixture of races and ethnicities in such people as the mestizo. "The Mestizo women affect to dress in the same manner as the Spanish, though they cannot equal them in the richness of their stuffs. The meaner sort go barefooted." Then they described the Amerindian: "Two kinds of dresses are worn by the Indian women; but both of them made in the same plain manner with those worn by the men: the whole consisting of a short petticoat, and a veil of American bays." However, even the Amerindians were subdivided:

> The dress of the lowest class of Indian women is in effect only a bag of the same make and stuff as the frocks of the men, and called anaco [large piece of textile going over the head to make a cape]. This they fasten on the shoulders with two large pins called tupu, or topo. The only particular in which it differs from the frock is, that it is something longer, reaching down to the calf of the leg, and fastened round the waist with a kind of girdle. Instead of a veil, they wear about their neck a piece of the same coarse stuff dyed black, and called Lliella; but their arms and legs are wholly naked. Such in the habit with which the lower class of Indian women are contented.

What a help this was to foreign merchants in networking or deciding on overtures for sales!

After describing the lowest class, they returned to the mestizo and Amerindians of the higher class:

> The caciquesses [wife of a chief or high official], or Indian women, who are married to the alcaldes majors [top municipal officer], governors, and others, are careful to distinguish themselves from the common people by their habits, which is a mixture of the two former, being a petticoat of bays adorned with ribbands; over this, instead of the anaco, they wear a kind of black manteaux, called acso. It is wholly open on one side, plaited from top to bottom, and generally fastened round the waist with a girdle. Instead of the scanty Lliella which the common Indian women wear hanging from the shoulders, these appear in one much fuller, and all over plaited, hanging down from the back part of their head almost to the bottom of the petticoat. This they fasten before with a large silver bodkin, called alto tupu, like those used in the anaco. Their head dress is a piece of fine linen curiously plaited, and the end hanging down behind: this they call colla, and is worn both for distinction and ornament, and to preserve them from the heat of the sun; and these ladies, that their superiority may not be called in question, never appear abroad without shoes. This dress, together with that universally worn by Indians, men and women, is the same with that used in the time of the Yncas, for the propriety of distinguishing the several classes. The Caciques at present use no other than that of the more wealthy Mestizos, namely, the cloak and hat; but the shoes are what chiefly distinguish them from the common Indians.[6]

It was all a great deal to learn and there were even more social classifications in this mobile society. There were still other racial and ethnic mixtures, but these were the ones among women that counted for European travelers and for officials and migrants moving to the Spanish empire in

South America. Sumptuary laws could become most effective whenever and wherever variety in textiles took hold. Colored charts showing examples of gendered, racial, and ethnically hybrid individuals also made hierarchies and forms of intersectionality more easily recognizable.

As mobility and the whirl of change threatened to disturb community stability, commentators in China reemphasized the importance of women's seclusion and attention to the household. As teachers of their children, they inculcated Confucian and other enduring principles of correct behavior found in the classics of Chinese culture. In the face of the wider world's lure and the transformations that globalization was bringing, it became more important than ever that women, for example, preserve the rootedness of the family in household space, as many Chinese believed.[7] Seclusion marked higher from lower status. Active women in a busy urban culture could hardly accommodate such restrictions, because the industrious revolution progressed with their participation. The same was true in Ottoman cities where women undertook all sorts of tasks in neighborhoods and even beyond them. In the long run, where segregation or seclusion was operational, elite women's distance from urban streets became a symbol of stability. Even then, however, their publishing and attendance at festivals, for example, diminished the effectiveness of seclusion as an actual standard of order and virtue.

Intellectual and Artistic Work

Religious thought and philosophy advanced among women writers as many of them considered the changing world around them. Sor (Sister) Juana de la Cruz (1651–1695), a nun in Mexico City, studied classical and religious texts assiduously, coming to write poetry, philosophy, and religious essays. Part of her life seemed to break away from the social and cultural structures that had shaped her childhood. Instead, she wrote of her unfeminine love of study and her turn to the religious life in order to keep from having to marry. An entire poem devoted to the working of her mind exalted the power of imagination and concentrated thought in her own life; its verses soared with allusions to the beauties of using one's intellect. Her situation came to reflect the contradictory attitudes toward women. Becoming well known and even celebrated for her devotion to learning, she was eventually reprimanded and forced to stop her studying.

Sor Juana de la Cruz was born to an unmarried *criollo* (creole) mother—that is, someone of Spanish descent in its colonies who might have a small amount of Amerindian blood. Studious from a very young age, she learned Latin, Greek, literature, and many other subjects. Explaining her studiousness, she remembered as a child having a "sweet tooth," but also avoiding cheese because "it turned people into dunces." She learned how to read and write by the time she was six as well as to execute womanly tasks such as embroidery and sewing. She astonished everyone with her memory of facts—these having been gained from books in her grandfather's study. After taking up Latin, she continued her life of constant study to quench her thirst for learning. At sixteen, she entered a convent and while there wrote not just poetry but essays built on her love of learning. Convents were the one place where women could survive outside a family setting.

In fact, a portrait of Sor Juana shows her surrounded by books. Then, "I entered a religious order because, although I was aware that that lifestyle had certain things . . . that were abhorrent to my character given my total rejection of marriage [but] it was the least objectionable and the most respectable one I could choose with regard to my desire to safeguard my salvation."[8] As she attracted attention for her accomplishments, leaders of the Catholic church, who had once marveled at her brilliant mind, became upset with her studious life, making her discard her books and repent her sinful ways. Sor Juana tried to explain herself to officials who represented the power of the Catholic Church back in Rome. It didn't work and she ended her studies as ordered, soon dying of the plague while tending its victims.

Globalization shook old certainties and exposed women to new phenomena. Women, like men, made breakthroughs in science and technology and strived to capture the workings of the natural world. Paintings more scientifically depicted the details of plants and animals as found in nature in part due to the growing interest in studying and talking about natural facts. Migration opened people's eyes to the natural diversity offered around the globe. Dutch botanist Maria Sibylla Merian (1647–1717) traveled in her region but also went to the Dutch colony of Surinam to study plants and insects. Uniquely, she portrayed both plants and insects in their stages of development and in their interactions with one another. Her detailed style was seen by some as representing Protestantism's implicit encouragement to study science.

Lady Mary Wortley Montagu, wife of the British ambassador to the Ottoman Empire, spent two years in Constantinople/Istanbul in 1716–17. While there, she observed women from the Ottoman harem and judged Ottoman women to be the freest in the world. They saw her corsets either as a form of chastity belt or as a punishment that European husbands used against their wives. Like many Europeans at the time of the Enlightenment and Scientific Revolution, she marveled at medical and other knowledge in foreign lands, especially the Ottoman habit of taking a bit of cowpox and inoculating their children with it to prevent the deadly smallpox disease. She recorded her observations, inoculated her own children, and wrote back to the royal court on the prevention of this lethal illness, as seen in her letter of April 1, 1717:

"A propos of distempers, I am going to tell you a thing, that will make you wish yourself here. The small-pox, so fatal, and so general amongst us, is here entirely harmless, by the invention of engrafting, which is the term they give it. There is a set of old women, who make it their business to perform the operation, every autumn, in the month of September, when the great heat is abated. People send to one another to know if any of their family has a mind to have the small-pox; they make parties for this purpose, and when they are met (commonly fifteen or sixteen together) the old woman comes with a nut-shell full of the matter of the best sort of small-pox, and asks what vein you please to have opened. She immediately rips open that you offer to her, with a large needle (which gives you no more pain than a common scratch) and puts into the vein as much matter as can lie upon the head of her needle, and after that, binds up the little wound with a hollow bit of shell, and in this manner opens four or five veins . . . The children or young patients play together all the rest of the day, and are in perfect health

FIGURE 5.2 *Lady Mary Wortley Montagu, 18th century. While her husband served as British ambassador to the powerful Ottoman Empire, Mary Montagu soaked up its benefits, adopting Ottoman medical practices such as inoculation against deadly smallpox and sending that beneficial knowledge back to Britain. She also admired and adopted the corset-free, streamlined dress of Ottoman women. Courtesy of Heritage Getty Images.*

to the eighth. Then the fever begins to seize them, and they keep their beds two days, very seldom three . . . There is no example of any one that has died in it, and you may believe I am well satisfied of the safety of this experiment, since I intend to try it on my dear little son. I am patriot enough to take the pains to bring this useful invention into fashion in England, and I should not fail to write to some of our doctors very particularly about it."[9]

Women in the middle and upper classes thrived on the life of research if their circumstances and personality allowed. In Europe alone, women came to teach the sciences in universities, for example, Laura Bassi in chemistry and Marie Agnesi in mathematics both at the University of Bologna. Emilie du Châtelet translated Isaac Newton's revolutionary work in physics, *Principia* (1687), from Latin into French. She was joined in her enthusiasm for science by Caroline Herschel, who, along with her brother William, studied astronomy and who herself found new stars. In applied medicine, renowned midwife Madame du Coudray made cloth models of pregnant women's reproductive organs and took them around France to upgrade midwives' medical knowledge. These two centuries were an age of extraordinary scientific discovery and application, in which women were happy to participate and in which they also excelled.

From China to Europe many such accomplished women had been trained in their family home by brothers or fathers or had followed a male family member in his profession, benefiting either from his patronage or influence in the intellectual world. Such was the situation of Agnesi, whose father had first held the chair in mathematics. Caroline Hershel was entirely ignorant of astronomy but once tutored by her brother and working alongside him, she came to make her own observations and discoveries. Emilie du Châtelet was already born into French high society, but she became the companion of celebrated writer Voltaire, who encouraged her accomplishments though he hardly did her work for her. Merian learned painting from her stepfather, while Ma Quan, an accomplished Chinese painter of insects and flowers, studied in her father's studio as did other Chinese women painters of nature.

Literacy grew even more during these years, often moving with empire and the acceleration of trade. In the seventeenth century, the nun Marie de l'Incarnation (1599–1671) serving among Native Americans in French North America composed a dictionary of their language. Marie had had many mystical experiences, leading her to the religious life among the Amerindians. In one such vision she saw the Virgin Mary and Jesus near a church in a strange place, which her religious advisors told her was the new world—specifically Canada. It was there, they believed, she was destined to go. Having struggled to arrange her voyage, Marie arrived full of fervor, learned several Amerindian languages, and opened the first Ursuline school for Amerindian and French girls to become literate. Her activities combined the mystical with the rational, religious fervor with training of the mind.

In the upper reaches of the Mughal Empire, religion, scholarly activity, and politics were also combined. Zebunissa (1638–1702), daughter of

Emperor Aurangzeb, received an extraordinary education in mathematics, the sciences, and literature, becoming expert in Arabic, Persian, and Urdu—classic languages of West, Central, and South Asia. Before that, by the age of seven she had learned to recite the entire Qu'ran. With all her accomplishments she was seen as full of erudition and wisdom and because of it became a crucial advisor to her father. Her Sufi faith in part guided by her aunt Jahanara, also a Sufi author, Zebunissa produced several books, some of poetry completely in the Sufi idiom by which love of the divine is expressed in the language of human love. "My veins are aflame with the molten rays of Thy beauty,/ Thy love is infused as marrow and life in my bones."[10] Despite the erudition and supposed politic acuity, Zebunissa landed in prison after she seemed to take the side of her brother in a coup against their father and spent the last two decades of her life there.

Well-to-do Chinese women in particular were encouraged to become literate in order to help their sons and daughters thrive. Because China was a society of mobility, well-educated children if male could pass the exams to rise in the bureaucracy with the sustained help of a literate mother. A mother who taught her daughter not only appropriate conduct and household skills but also reading and writing made that daughter more marriageable. In Japan's urban areas, women's literacy was high, almost 100 percent by some estimates. Another reason was the global spread of knowledge and the emphasis on science and reason fostered by a movement called the Enlightenment in Europe, which led women to explore science, teach in universities, and generally question all received authorities. Still, Japan and China had higher rates of literate women and by the eighteenth century had developed an avid cohort of women readers.

In other parts of the world, many wealthy women as opposed to those in the lower rungs of society were literate, but this was uneven across cultures. At the top of the political pyramid in the 1780s, French queen Marie Antoinette had difficulty spelling French words and writing grammatical sentences, though, as an Austrian, she was writing in a second language. Russian empress Catherine II promoted literacy by setting up schools for girls from good families and even chose a woman to oversee the production of the official Russian dictionary. Catherine herself read the work of philosophers from across Europe in the eighteenth century and corresponded with them.

As some empires such as the Ming of China fell into turmoil and as conditions were transformed around the world, gender roles often came under pressure. In the midst of economic expansion, elite Chinese women and those from merchant families like others across the globe, in theory, lived increasingly solitary lives, separated from spouses in particular. Men traveled more frequently to pursue careers as officials, to keep their commercial operations at a high pitch of activity, or to find jobs as manual laborers in thriving cities. Soldiers engaged in more distant wars. As oceanic travel grew, men across the globe signed on as sailors, navigators, cooks, doctors, and simple adventurers, leaving their partners to fend for themselves. Literacy and numeracy became important tools in women's and familial survival. The Manchu administration in contrast put special pressure on women's purity, with a 1646 law on rape maintaining that a woman's claim to rape was only believable if she died in the attack or if she struggled without interruption. Any let-up in resistance indicated compliance and thus condemned her to death. Writing, however, turned out to offer an outlet to challenge such on-going repression.

In the beginnings of the Qing Empire (1644–1911/12), Chinese women used their intellectual tools to preserve their families' reputations and livelihoods. Their poetry proliferated as they continued to excel as artists, poets, and authors, and their number continued to increase as did the numbers of intellectually active European women though hardly in the thousands as could be counted for Chinese women. For some, the idea of reputation, even glory, led them to write on a range of topics. Poetry flourished as both a private endeavor and as a shared enterprise. For the Chinese, women's accomplishments brought renown to their families, which was especially important in the turmoil of the mid-seventeenth century, when those who had worked for the Ming government or received patronage from it lost out when the Qing conquered China. At that point, women's poetry helped rebuild family fame and standing in uncertain times, but by the eighteenth century a great deal of poetry portrayed the erudite mother grooming her male children for examinations and her female children for a good marriage based on her knowledge of the classics that she would teach to the next generation of exam takers. Yet there was more to the poetry than this.

In the aftermath of the Qing takeover of China, women authors, armed with education, focused in their poetry on their experiences and accomplishments in foot-binding, for example, as they represented a world of female agency and connectedness—a connectedness that took them beyond the confines of the inner quarters to which they were relegated. Women's networks such as literary ones that went beyond any single household created new relationships, overcoming physical structures of isolation. Correct behavior in writing and in life would bring them eternal renown and familial recognition that might reestablish menfolk, who had lost their government positions or patronage. It also brought women renown beyond the walls of the inner quarters. In fact, some, such as Huang Yuanjie, became renowned teachers of women and girls, while others added mastery of classical pen and ink forms in calligraphy and drawing and used them to excel in the visual arts—again, practicing and displaying their skills beyond their confined domestic sphere.

Simultaneously, centers of Islamic, Christian, and other religious scholarship flourished. Muslim women were transmitters of the *hadith*—that is, accounts of the prophet Muhammad's words and actions; they also promoted Islamic schools and education along with being patrons of the building of such schools. As seen in the studies of Jahanara and her niece

Zebunissa religious texts dominated their concerns: Zebunissa reportedly had one of the largest libraries in the empire. In regions where men specifically disallowed women literacy in order to monopolize reading and writing for themselves, they nonetheless might encourage women to learn the Qu'ran or Biblical scriptures. Reciting such verses daily helped women's intellectual life flourish.

Writing the Reform of Women's Condition

In the early modern period, aspirations for equality, if not power, abounded, even to the point of a woman poet fantasizing about rising to be the right-hand "man" of the emperor. In many regions women were formally expressing discontent in their writing and also questioning conditions both in their own lives and among women more generally. In China, changing customs under the Qing since the mid-seventeenth century brought the issue to the fore, as it did in England, which underwent several regime changes in the seventeenth century. The protests first came indirectly.

In China, the writing of romantic poetry displayed this roundabout resistance. With marriages arranged, often at a young age and with no concern for the preferences of those directly involved—that is, the two young people pledged to be married—the turn toward expressing longing and love for a spouse undermined the system of parental control over these utilitarian and calculated lifetime unions of the next generation. In its turbulent early days, the Qing system placed its expectations on sturdy arranged marriages as the foundation of social and political stability. One wife of a failed examination candidate, however, celebrated their relationship in poetry to overcome the disappointment: "The dejected one cannot let go of his sorrow./ But the mums by the fence are open, let's toast them./ I'll pawn my gold hairpin to buy the wine." They would enjoy time with one another.

Defiance flourished in more outright forms right down through the end of the eighteenth century. Chinese poetry, depicting actual feelings, came to express both women's ambition and disappointment that there was no room for such emotions in the hierarchical structure of Chinese gender arrangements. Critique came to replace sentiments of romantic longing and emotional partnership with a spouse in other works. The prolific poet Wang Yun (1749–1819) produced biting commentaries on the inferior status of women in the world of culture. When it came to judging merit, she proclaimed, women's verse and other writing was automatically seen as inferior to that of a man.

I am full of ambition, want to soar up to Heaven,
But with Mulan and Chonghu I have nothing in common.
Jade Temple and the Gold Horse are not in my destiny;
I can only consign my aspirations to dreams.[11]

Wang made her points allusively but clearly when she expressed her lack of commonality with Mulan and Chonghu, two women who fought heroically dressed as men. She also indicated that because she was a woman she would never hold a prestigious post (Jade Temple and the Gold Horse). These were not to be had; her destiny as a woman—no matter how instructed and talented—was elsewhere in household seclusion.

In Europe, focused discussions of women's lack of rights and overall inferior situation blossomed from the seventeenth century on. Beginning in 1642, the English Revolution and the upheavals that followed, ultimately led to a settlement in which the Parliament installed King William (of the Netherlands) and Queen Mary of the British royal family as joint monarchs in 1688–9. Their accession was couched in restrictions set by Parliament. The so-called Glorious Revolution was followed by philosopher John Locke's treatises declaring that all people were born free and equal in a state of nature and that government was founded on the contract of all people—a contract that was broken should rulers become tyrannical and not observe those rights. Locke's insistence on the equality and rights of both men and women had repercussions at the time and would have them down to the present. The question that many women writers had—Mary Astell was one who questioned—came with Locke's insistence that despite this equality, men should head families. "If all men are born free, how is it that all women are born slaves," Astell asked. Her challenges related to the actual laws in force that eradicated women's equality and especially had eliminated rights over property.[12] Rendering them propertyless, the law made women dependent and inferior.

From the Glorious Revolution on, Locke's founding principles of "liberalism"—that is, the belief in natural rights, freedom, equality, rationality, and the right to rebel—became part of modern political theory. Thinkers debated ideas of freedom and equality as they applied to diverse groups of people including the propertyless, slaves, non-white ethnicities, and women, to name a few. Phillis Wheatley (1753–1784) took up these issues in terms of her religious faith. She was seven years old when she was taken from her West African home and purchased by John Wheatley of Boston. In their home, she learned to read and write and advanced to reading Greek and Latin and the classic works of Virgil and Homer. She wrote her first poems before she was a teenager and met important people, including George Washington, as a result. Her poems can be complicated and full of fancy language that was common in poetry at the time. Phillis Wheatley was freed on John Wheatley's death in 1778; however, she died in poverty in 1784 because she could not arrange for publication of further poems. At the time, the movement for the abolition of slavery was taking shape based on both religious and liberal ideas.

On Being Brought from Africa to America
'Twas mercy brought me from my Pagan land,

Taught my benighted soul to understand
That there's a God, that there's a Saviour too:
Once I redemption neither sought nor knew.
Some view our sable race with scornful eye,
"Their colour is a diabolic die."
Remember, Christians, Negro's, black as Cain,
May be refin'd, and join th' angelic train.[13]

Conclusion

Globalization inspired women and men to be more industrious and forced the millions of slaves to labor even to an early death in the name of profit and material wealth. The growing military needs of expansionist states and empires also demanded greater effort and a growing population. Slave women endured rape by their masters that would raise their numbers. The world's women did virtually every conceivable job in these centuries, and rapid transformations in agriculture added to the search for employment as people were driven from the land so that landlords, including the Countess of Sutherland, could drive down the costs of labor and drive up productivity. In a climate of globalization, most women—slave and free—also integrated the world's goods into their agricultural, artisanal, and domestic repertoires. As population increased over these centuries, local famines continued, but many places began to experience abundance. The abundance and growing population diversity saw women exploring these changes and turning to the sciences and education for answers. They also questioned their own inferior situation within the unequal structures of power that produced their living conditions. Questioning emanated from men too until, joined by women, uprisings erupted in many parts of the world.

Notes

1 *Glückel. The Memoirs of Glückel of Hameln.* Marvin Lowenthal, trans. (New York: Schocken Books, 1977 [1932]), 165–8. Web access: *Jewish Heritage Online Magazine:* http://www.jhom.com/personalities/gluckel/son_debt.htm.
2 "Wilhelm Joann Muller's Describtion of the Fetu Country, 1662–1669," in *German Sources for West African History, 1599–1669,* ed. and trans. Adam Jones (Wiesbaden: Franz Steiner Verlag, 1983), 243–4.
3 Quoted in Susan Mann, *Precious Records: Women in China's Long Eighteenth Century* (Stanford, CA: Stanford University Press, 1997), 164.
4 Yan Wosi, *Qingshi duo,* Zhang Yingchang, ed. 2 vols. (Beijing: Zhonghua shuju, 1983 [1869]), in Mann, *Precious Records,* 166. The poem dates approximately the last third of the seventeenth century. The author is Yan Wosi, a high government official.

5 Rowland Parker, *The Common Stream* (New York: Holt, Rhinehart, and Winston, 1975), 192.
6 Jorge Juan and Antonio de Ulloa, *Voyage to South America* (London: Lockyer Davis, 1772), I:261–7.
7 Ibid.
8 Sor Juana Inés de la Cruz (1691) "Answer by the poet to the most illustrious Sister Filotea de la Cruz," William Little, trans. Santa Fe College, copyright 2008. Santa Fe College http://dept.sfcollege.edu/hfl/hum2461/pdfs/sjicanswer.pdf. Accessed October 28, 2015. Also available Sor Juana de la Cruz, "The Reply to Sor Philothea," in Hilda L Smith and Berenice Carroll, eds. *Women's Political and Social Thought: An Anthology* (Bloomington: Indiana University Press, 2000), 92–9.
9 Lady Mary Wortley Montagu, *Letters of the Right Honourable Lady M--y W--y M--e: Written During her Travels in Europe, Asia and Africa...*, *vol. 1* (Aix: Anthony Henricy, 1796), 167–9; letter 36, to Mrs. S. C. from Adrianople, n.d. Widely available on the web, including http://legacy.fordham.edu/halsall/mod/montagu-smallpox.asp and Archive.org.
10 Zebunissa, *The Tears of Zebunnisa, Being Excerpts from the Divan-I-Makhfi* Trans. Paul Whalley (London: W. Thacker, 1913), 18.
11 Quoted in Paul Ropp, "Love, Literacy, and Laments: Themes of Women Writers in Late Imperial China," *Women's History Review*, 2:1 (1993), 118, 125.
12 Quoted in Susan Kingsley Kent, *Gender and Power in Britain, 1640–1990* (London: Routledge, 1999), 44.
13 Internet Archive, Project Gutenberg, and many other net sources such as http://www.poemhunter.com/poem/on-being-brought-from-africa-to-america.

Further Reading

Boyar, Ebru, and Kate Fleet, eds. *Ottoman Women in Public Space*. Leiden: Brill, 2016.
Cleary, Patricia. *Elizabeth Murray: A Woman's Pursuit of Independence in Eighteenth-Century America*. Amherst: University of Massachusetts Press, 2000.
Davis, Natalie Zemon. *Women on the Margins: Three Seventeenth-Century Lives*. Cambridge: Harvard University Press, 1997.
Everyday Life in Joseon-era Korea: Economy and Society. Michael D. Shin, ed. and trans., Edward Park, co-trans. Boston, MA: Brill, 2014.
Ferreira Furtado, Júnia. *Chica da Silva: A Brazilian Slave of the Eighteenth Century*. New York: Cambridge University Press, 2009.
Hafter, Daryl M., and Nina Kushner, eds. *Women and Work in Eighteenth-Century France*. Baton Rouge: Louisiana State University Press, 2015.
Mann, Susan. *Precious Records: Women in China's Long Eighteenth Century*. Stanford, CA: Stanford University Press, 1997.
Molony, Barbara, Janet Theiss, and Hyaeweol Choi. *Gender in Modern East Asia: China, Korea, Japan*. Boulder, CO: Westview, 2016.
Ropp, Paul S. "Love, Literacy, and Laments: Themes of Women Writers in Late Imperial China." *Women's History Review*, 2:1 (1993): 107–41.
Socolow, Susan Migden. *The Women of Colonial Latin America*, 2nd edn. New York: Cambridge University Press, 2014.

6

Revolts, Revolutions, and the Rise of New States, 1650–1830

Queen Nanny or Nanny (c. 1686–c. 1755) on the British-controlled island of Jamaica was a leader of a *maroon* community of escaped slaves. She herself had been born in West Africa, a member of the Asante ethnic group, but she was seized during a local conflict there and sold for transport to the prosperous sugar island. Escaping enslavement, Nanny then helped others flee their captivity and reach the maroon enclaves on the island. These escapees supported themselves by occasionally trading produce and crafts in local markets but more often by growing their own crops and raiding plantations. Maroon communities developed across the vast slave-holding regions of the Caribbean and South America; those in Jamaica could thrive because the island was relatively large. A healer and religious leader like Nanny could unify her community so that these escapees from the Atlantic slave system were able to sustain themselves at some remove from deadly plantation life. In fact, her community was so thriving and she so effective in stealing away slaves that the British tried to put the maroons down. Nanny is credited with developing guerilla war tactics that saved the Jamaican maroon settlements, which exist to this day, and with being the force behind treaties in 1738 and 1739 that guaranteed freedom to the local Amerindians and to escaped slaves in her and other maroon communities across Jamaica.

Queen Nanny's activism was just part of the overall resistance to tyranny, domination, and the lack of basic freedoms that swelled in the eighteenth century against both enslavement and empire. Because of the complexities of government and economic systems, people were motivated by developments that were often full of paradoxes. Activists protested imperial advances of many sorts even as others outside the imperial elite found opportunities to profit from growing global connections. As entrepreneurs, women—white and black—were slave owners, and traders in slaves. They trafficked in women worldwide or gained funds from the global market in textiles and other goods. Afro-European trader Betsy Heard was just one of these, legendary for her trading networks that crossed continents, her numerous trading ships, and political influence. These were business leaders against whom revolts were common, including those of *jihadis* in Africa against non-Muslim traffickers in slaves. No matter where expansion occurred, invasions by interlopers were destabilizing to community life and even lethal; much of the African continent suffered violence in the wars to obtain captives for the Atlantic, Indian Ocean, Mediterranean, and Red Sea trade. Africa thus had its own revolutions, relevant to the lives of women.

The Chinese were simultaneously consolidating their regime on the western borders, protecting against bandits along the eastern coast, and sometimes succumbing to tropical diseases when maintaining order in the south. Slaves across the Western Hemisphere escaped to form new communities and to resist, with revolts taking shape along lines of solidarity built on experience in slave armies in Africa. At the same time, pirates continued to disturb community life when gaining captives from the Chinese coast, the Balkans, around the Mediterranean, and in the Atlantic world even as uprisings such as Nanny's contributed to ideas of freedom. Yet, in some societies, such as Britain and its colonies, those in power came increasingly to explain mistreatment of their fellow human beings as either religiously ordained or as the just desserts of inferiors. Still other protestors opposed the work of those wanting to modernize state power and make it more efficient.

In a world of multifaceted revolts and ongoing global movements— the age of revolution, it has been called—women's participation was multifaceted too. Contests over land and struggles over state-building kept the use of women negotiators and guides alive, for example: Sacagawea (c. 1788–1812?) lent her survival skills and geographic knowledge to Lewis and Clark. In the Western Hemisphere new nations were born and old ones resisted incursions with the practical and intellectual help of women, including learning new foodways and the defensive techniques of guerilla warfare.

Most of the nation-building of this period, however, ultimately kept women from rights, participation, and freedom. Still, the many political struggles of these years bear the imprint of women, whether the goal was independence from empire, overthrowing monarchies, setting up new governmental entities, or preserving older types of rulership. In this plurality of political forms—chieftaincies, independent cities and their surroundings, extensive monarchical states and smaller ones, empires, and nations about to be born—they found ills to cure and opportunities to seize. Despite their best efforts and active participation, most of the major revolts and revolutions did not have positive outcomes for women. Nonetheless, revolutionary ideas and principles remained inspirational for future change.

Early Uprisings across the Spanish Empire

In the eighteenth century, Spanish officials developed new policies for more rational government and more efficient ways of raising money to support the growth of a large centralized state—one needing increasing funds to protect the empire. The colonies in North and South America were targeted as especially important in this money-raising venture. Officials demanded more textiles in tribute, often made by women; priests and high clergy making their rounds simply took food from the lavish meals they demanded instead of paying for it. Women's household budgets bore the costs of confiscated resources and rising taxation to fund the various aspects of empire; extra work of all sorts obviously fell on women's shoulders as well. Moreover, intrusions disturbed community life by attacking long-standing rituals and the customs followed by local leaders. The growing power of states was making itself felt in everyday life.

Across the Spanish occupation in the Western Hemisphere, women had participated in active resistance against the invaders—an activism that seemed sustained even into the eighteenth century—in support of local traditions and values. Especially in rural and religious movements, they expressed their discontent, forming units of all women fighters armed with machetes, knives, and even rocks and protesting injustices by imperial officials or overbearing behavior by priests and officials. Religious activists claimed that the Spanish were false gods or that the Spanish god was no longer active or even alive. In the former Incan lands, several Incan royal and noble women actively opposed the Spanish government in a concerted uprising that began in 1742. Following the prophet Juan Altahualpa who proclaimed himself the new grand Inca, they moved in an all-women battalion and gained notice for their commitment to freeing native peoples from their enslavement as the Spanish ratcheted up their claims on them.

This movement defeated, in 1780, another uprising of ethnic groups battling Spanish rule in the Andes broke out. Micaela Bastidas was the wife of Inca Tupac Ameru, who led a forceful rebellion against Spanish authorities in an attempt to restore the former Inca Empire and to liberate local people from the increased demands for labor and taxes. Part Inca, Bastidas was by reputation the operational manager and chief enforcer of loyalty to her husband's uprising against Spanish rule. In this role she was especially brutal. She threatened slackers, even her husband, whom she chastised for following losing strategies. She ensured that the troops were supplied with arms and food and that the soldiers were paid—concerns that Tupac Ameru seemed to forget. Alongside Bastidas, who mostly directed military activity, entire units of women soldiers took to the battle fields in several parts of the empire, building on traditions of active resistance. Spanish soldiers noticed them as well for their intense commitment to fighting and winning, calling them "supermasculine" and one fighter in particular "as bloody a butcher as her brother."[1] The rebellion was soon put down, and its leaders captured.

In 1781, the Spanish colonial government (in present-day Peru) had Micaela Bastidas dragged bound hand and foot to her execution, garroted, then hanged; finally they cut her body to pieces with her head posted on a pike for all to see. The execution and mutilation brought her leadership against colonial rule to a horrific end, while the movement itself had continued the long tradition of women's participation in anti-imperial and antislavery rebellion. By the time of Bastidas's execution women's revolutionary leadership against the Spanish had become notorious; it would grow in the nineteenth century. Then, as later, such leadership would increasingly be seen as problematic—a deformation of gender order, even though for centuries indigenous women had resisted Spanish demands not just in courts but as warriors.

Revolution in North America

European invaders into North America continued to assault the homelands of Native American communities and settle on them. Although Amerindians, including women, seized on opportunities for trade and kept many settlers alive by providing them with food, the invaders pushed westward, waging war against any who stood in their way. Both sides engaged in slaughter, but the Amerindians also took captives instead of killing everyone and either incorporated captured settlers into their communities or sold them into the trade in slaves. In the often tense world of Native American and white relations, Mary Musgrove (1700–1765), born Coosaponakeesa, stood out as an enterprising and effective diplomat even as she became wealthy and rose in status. With a white father, Musgrove operated among ethnic groups and different cultures, negotiating borders, conditions of trade, and exchanges of land.

Musgrove operated during tense times in the Atlantic world, with uprisings across Spanish Empire and the French and Indian war (1754–63) breaking out over contested borders to the west of the coastal Atlantic colonies in North America. The American Revolution (1776–83) resulted from heightened tensions among rulers and the ruled as well as among invaders and local peoples. This uprising against British rule aroused women's patriotism but hardly the kind of visible female leadership that Bastidas exercised nor her "star power." The Revolution had erupted in 1776 after the stage had been set when European settlers on the eastern shores of North America kept pushing to the west in the eighteenth century, upsetting Native American life. The French and British fought the global French and Indian war over control of many trading areas and rights to settlement, with the British emerging victorious; in contrast, their Native American allies suffered loss of crops, fighters, and civilians. Because the war was costly in terms of lives lost and immensely expensive, the British restricted westward settler expansion, fearing further alienation of Native Americans who had suffered so much during the war. To pay the war debt, the British decided the colonists should bear the financial responsibility for their own protection— past and present. From 1765 on, they imposed a range of taxes on legal papers and imported goods such as sugar and tea. Colonists determined to resist, writing protest documents and urging boycotts.

Women rallied with men to protest the restrictions and new taxes especially through the imposition of boycotts during which they stopped purchasing British goods or buying commodities imported in British ships or sold by British merchants. Foremost among these were the luscious textiles imported from India; such fabrics, as mentioned, were unparalleled in their design and color. The finest imported muslin was like gossamer—a delicacy that no Westerner knew how to achieve at the time. Determined colonial women, however, began committing themselves and their families to making and wearing sturdy homespun made of linen or wool. "As I am (as we say) a daughter of liberty," thirteen-year-old Anna Green Winslow noted in her diary in 1771) "I chuse to wear as much of our own manufactory as possible."[2] Women entered the realm of politics when they held spinning parties to make thread or other gatherings to weave or fashion garments of rougher, less colorful homespun. In 1773, when the British added a tax on tea, to which colonists like the homeland British themselves were addicted, colonial women boycotted that too, substituting coffee and a range of other beverages. Boycotts and homespun parties also built a sense of community— one based on colonists' standing together but independent from Britain.

Once fighting began, the British began to reassert their rule, confiscate weapons, and then occupy towns, cities, harbors, and routes for communication. Women became divided in their allegiance, with one group supporting independence and the other taking up the pro-British or Loyalist side. Women on both sides have left evidence of their fright and often of their bravery in the face of invading soldiers from the opposing side in the struggle. These soldiers commandeered housing and ordered women to feed and otherwise serve them. Women hid soldiers or others who were being hunted, while they also fed, clothed, and nursed trapped combatants, helping them survive and then move to another safe spot. Thus, women were the supporters of armies on both the colonists' and the British side; some today insist they should be considered part of the military. They created uniforms and flags and sent messages for the wounded, taking up what would later become the government's responsibility to supply, nourish, and heal the troops. Many women were forced to move as armies requisitioned their homes and their stores of food. The American colonies were full of lively, active women settlers and their descendants, who faced these tough life-and-death situations.

The poorest women followed their men in the army, often bringing their children with them. These so-called "camp-followers" were and even now are equated with prostitution perhaps because of their poverty but more likely because they lived among large groups of men. Yet the army could hardly have done without them in these days when resources for soldiers' well-being were lacking. The women cooked, mended, and did laundry for a spouse and for others in his unit as a way of earning their keep. There were many stories of women taking up arms to replace their partners who had been wounded or killed. Supporting Britain, loyalist women in the colonies were often expropriated of their properties and physically assaulted in what was both a war for independence and a civil war between those against and in favor of a relationship with Britain. Many of them became refugees, moving to Canada, wandering the globe, or migrating to Britain in hopes of some recompense for their losses as loyal subjects. Their fate was not a pleasant one, though women favoring independence but living in Loyalist areas faced the same kind of harassment, theft of property, and sexual or other abuse as did the Loyalists.

Mercy Otis Warren of Massachusetts wrote one of the first histories of the revolution and penned many a barb against slackers and those on the wrong side of it. Her sharp tongue made her enemies as well as drawing in admirers. The competence women showed generated interest in opening up educational opportunities for them and in bolstering their talents with instruction in practical subjects such as mathematics. In the aftermath of victory in 1783 and the creation of a US Constitution and new laws in 1789, women lost rights that they had had before the conflict, making many believe that independence marked a setback. Slaves who shouldered the revolutionary workload and endured deprivation also received no tangible results, as the Constitution enshrined their enslavement in its provisions. As state governments reduced the property qualifications for voting, white men lower down on the social ladder could participate in elections. Simultaneously, where women and blacks did have the vote such as in the state of New Jersey, male state assemblies passed new laws prohibiting them from exercising that right, first excluding blacks and then women. In almost every respect, the new United States was a setback for women, blacks, and slaves in terms of citizenship.

In the meantime, women began adopting a set of ideas and behaviors built around the idea of "republican motherhood." Under this rubric, white women's main goal as a member of the nation was to educate the next generation of citizens—a category that came to replace people's identity as subjects of a king. Because being a citizen involved participation rather than passive obedience, individuals now needed an education so that they might fulfill their duties as citizens in an informed way. Women saw themselves in need of instruction too: "If we mean to have heroes, statesmen, and philosophers," Abigail Adams wrote of the American nation, "we should have learned women."[3] In an age without an established system of schools, mothers needed to mold young hearts and minds with early lessons in civic responsibilities but also in a basic understanding of the family, community, and nation. An ideology of empowerment arose around white motherhood even as blacks and white women were denied the rights of active citizenship and for enslaved women denied any rights at all.

Alongside, this reconstruction of womanhood as essentially about motherhood came the reconstruction of white masculinity as centered on "armed virtue"—that is, the surrender of everyday individual concerns to those of nation. The nation in times of danger needed men to serve it as soldiers, protecting territory, property, and families. Whereas across European kingdoms, soldiering had formerly been the task of the lowest rungs of society, including serfs, commandeered, or even kidnapped by recruiting agents, soldiering in a modern nation was a mark of citizenship. The virtuous citizen protected the nation's liberty, and across the span of these new or reformed nations, liberty was almost always depicted as a woman. The nation of brothers, banded together as honorable and honored soldiers, would now protect liberty—that is, the bodies of weak and fragile women. This formulation along with the exclusion of women from the rights and dignity of full citizenship has led historians to see the nation-state of modern times as essentially gendered and built around a heterosexual pairing of physically vigorous men shielding with their power and privilege the frail woman, increasingly portrayed with children.

Still, many women emerged from the American Revolution with a sense of accomplishment. They had successfully mounted boycotts, run farms and businesses, supplied armies, nursed and protected the family, and kept community life intact while men were away at the battlefield or preoccupied with the politics of revolution. It possibly combined with other factors to prepare women for the sturdy feminist movement of the next century. Lucy Flucker Knox, whose husband Henry Knox was an officer in the revolution and later Secretary of War, handled family affairs in her husband's absence. She wrote that she had become "quite a woman of business." On his return from the front, she expected that he would no longer act as "commander in chief of your own house" but rather see that there was now "such a thing as equal command."[4] For the moment, however, the American Revolution was an event on behalf of white men, consolidating their privileges as both slave owners and as newcomers for whom freer access to Native American lands opened exciting possibilities. A large, cohesive state emerged to protect those privileges and expand opportunities for wealth and achievement.

The French Revolution

For years, French women had participated in the development of a spirit of debate, lawlessness, and even criticism of traditional monarchical power. Simple lawlessness arose as women flaunted governmental edicts saying that they should not wear imported cotton from India and China because it competed with French textiles. Men flaunted these laws too but it was remarkable how many women had their portraits painted in colorful flowered imports. At the top of the list was King Louis XV's celebrated mistress, Madame de Pompadour, whose lavishly embellished gown covered the most prominent part of the canvas. In wearing those imported fabrics some of them had become facilitators of debate about the nature of government and about the capabilities of the French monarchy, especially in comparison to what was seen as the wiser rule of the Chinese emperors, for example. Wealthy women held salons where conversation about new social and political ideas flourished. While some produced lively commentary in essays on everyday events, others wrote much discussed poetry and novels. Women were part of a gendered ferment flowing through France in the 1700s.

Many Enlightenment debates of the eighteenth century concerned the equality and capacity of women, most of them giving women more credit than they had reaped in the past but equivocating on whether women were equal to men. Some said yes; others, no. On the one hand, women were being driven out of their traditional crafts by men, but on the other they were gaining some ground as artists, dealers in new products coming from around the world, and inventers of new styles and commodities. Élisabeth Vigée Le Brun, for instance, was a favored portrait painter of Queen Marie Antoinette and of many in the upper classes. As we have seen, women taught in Italian and other universities and were medical educators and practitioners. In a Western world needing increased literacy and mathematical skills, they served as accountants for family firms or overseers of colonial businesses for absent male relatives.

There was a backlash; alongside women's activities there were those who hated seeing them operating in markets or tending boutiques. For some, simply referring to women could bring up associations of evil and corruption. Women's sexuality launched a host of wicked characterizations, and authors did not hesitate to sell books by invoking their perverse sexuality. In novels, nuns were presented as oversexed and corrupting of the innocent, for example. One woman whose life increasingly garnered horrific attacks was Queen Marie Antoinette, said to be a monster to her children, unfaithful to her husband, a debauched lesbian, and overall a debased human—a symbol of the immorality of monarchy. In fact, nurtured in debates over the decades of Enlightenment rethinking, the issue of gender was a major focus as well as a major weapon in the uprising that erupted in the spring of 1789 that became the French Revolution.

In the 1780s, famines broke out in the countryside and the monarchy went bankrupt due to corruption, its lavish lifestyle, and the huge costs of supporting the Americans' revolution against Britain. The king so desperately needed funds that he summoned representatives from across the nation in hopes that they would help him financially. The representatives brought the complaints of the people and a host of ideas about reforming government to the meeting in May, 1789. Amid their assembling the press depicted Queen Marie Antoinette and King Louis XVI sexually, she as a seducer of men, women, and children and he as a cuckolded husband. The monarchy was in this way gradually made less sacred and more disconnected from the divine right status as rulers attributed to kings. By the summer of 1789, many of the delegates had peeled away from the king's meeting, which privileged the nobility and high clergy of the Catholic Church, and declared themselves a national assembly. The event was one of the most transformative in history, for the delegates at this assembly rejected the status of subjects to a king and became through their actions and words a nation of citizens. They codified this transformation in the Declaration of the Rights of Man and of the Citizen in August 1789. It assured the right to citizenship, the ownership of property, free speech, and trial by jury, among others (the United States followed this declaration of rights by adding a Bill of Rights to the new Constitution).

Unlike in the American Revolution, women were on the front line of politics and remained so for several years, chipping away at monarchical and male power. In the fall of 1789, the market women of Paris marched to the center of kingly power—the palace at Versailles—and forced the king and queen to move to Paris where they could be watched over by the "people." The event was marked by the murder of the queen's best friend, whose head was carried by the triumphant crowd on a pike and whose genitals were displayed as well. Women continued to see the connections between gender and revolution. They achieved official statements and even legislation that diminished the power of the father in the family, made husband and wife more or less equal arbiters of family matters, made marriage a civil ceremony and divorce easy to acquire, and made male and female children equal recipients of their parents' estates on their death. In 1791, playwright and activist Olympe de Gouges (1748–1793) declared women's right to citizenship and demanded recognition for their duties to the nation as mothers. Inspired by ideas of reason and liberty, she produced a document proposing a list of rights for women as had been done for men in the Declaration of the Rights of Man of 1789 when the Revolution first began. The document needs to be seen in full to understand its relationship to later demands for just and equal citizenship around the world and down to the present day:

Mothers, daughters, sisters, female representatives of the nation ask to be constituted as a national assembly. Considering that ignorance, neglect, or contempt for the rights of woman are the sole causes of public misfortunes and governmental corruption, they have resolved to set forth in a solemn declaration the natural, inalienable, and sacred rights of woman . . .

1. Woman is born free and remains equal to man in rights. Social distinctions may be based only on common utility.

FIGURE 6.1 *Market women head for Versailles to capture the king and royal family, October 1789. The world's women made markets thrive and often developed group solidarity as they did so. In 1789, amid revolutionary uprising, the market women of Paris marched to the royal palace to push the revolution further by bringing the royal family back to Paris where the population could keep an eye on them. Courtesy of Hulton Archive Getty Images.*

2. The purpose of all political association is the preservation of the natural and imprescriptible rights of woman and man. These rights are liberty, property, security, and especially resistance to oppression.

3. The principle of all sovereignty rests essentially in the nation, which is but the reuniting of woman and man. No body and no individual may exercise authority which does not emanate expressly from the nation.

6. The law should be the expression of the general will. All citizenesses and citizens should take part, in person or by their representatives, in its formation. It must be the same for everyone. All citizenesses and citizens, being equal in its eyes, should be equally admissible to all public dignities, offices and employments, according to their ability, and with no other distinction than that of their virtues and talents.

7. No woman is exempted; she is indicted, arrested, and detained in the cases determined by the law. Women like men obey this rigorous law.

9. Any woman being declared guilty, all rigor is exercised by the law.

10. No one should be disturbed for his fundamental opinions; woman has the right to mount the scaffold, so she should have the right equally to mount the rostrum, provided that these manifestations do not trouble public order as established by law.

11. The free communication of thoughts and opinions is one of the most precious of the rights of woman, since this liberty assures the recognition of children by their fathers. Every citizeness may therefore say freely, I am the mother of your child; a barbarous prejudice [against unmarried women having children] should not force her to hide the truth.

12. The safeguard of the rights of woman and the citizeness requires public powers. These powers are instituted for the advantage of all and not for the private benefit of those to whom they are entrusted.

13. For maintenance of public authority and for expenses of administration, taxation of women and men is equal; she takes part in all forced labor service, in all painful tasks; she must therefore have the same proportion in the distribution of places, employments, offices, dignities, and in industry.

15. The mass of women, joining with men in paying taxes, have the right to hold accountable every public agent of the administration.

16. Any society in which the guarantee of rights is not assured or the separation of powers not settled has no constitution. The constitution is null and void if the majority of individuals composing the nation has not cooperated in its drafting."[5]

Many formal women's groups sprang up during the Revolution, some demanding a role in the army. Market women continued their vigorous interventions, joining crowds to beat up nuns and cheer on the execution of those seen as counterrevolutionary. They were active and brutally outspoken. Women opponents of revolution—especially those objecting to attacks on the Catholic Church and the monarchy—were equally bold in hiding those aristocrats and clergy the revolutionary police sought out for execution. They fervently supported the old regime based on deference to monarchy and clergy and loyalty to the Catholic order. Gendered language, concerns, and activism played a role in replacing the kingdom of subjects with a nation of citizens and opening up the idea that women might be citizens too. Such a transformation was the work of what came to be called the political "center" and "left"—based on seating in the new National Assembly. Anti-revolutionary women, however, took a position on the "right," favoring the Catholic religion and the monarchical and aristocratic rule of society.

War has often curtailed ideas of freedom and equality, especially when it comes to gender, even as it allows and even demands that women play a role. Beginning in 1792, other kingdoms sought to defeat the French revolutionaries and thereby keep revolutionary values from spreading. Prussia and Austria hoped to preserve the monarchical order in the face of calls for rights, causing leaders in France to become more radical in defending male citizens' newfound status. Revolutionaries had initially equated the authoritarianism of the king with the excessive power given to fathers and husbands in a family. They reduced the power of the father and in January 1793, executed the king. In 1793, the French Revolution moved back to a more authoritarian, male government: in the fall of that year the government executed the queen of France along with other prominent women, including Olympe de Gouges. The charge against de Gouges was that she was a "counter-revolutionary" who wanted to bring back the monarchy. Legislation was later passed banning women from appearing in public in groups; eventually they would be banned from attending political meetings at all.

The tide thus turned further with women's rights sharply curtailed and their status as independent adults diminished. Instead of a familial metaphor, revolutionaries had talked about the "brotherhood" of man and invoked the "fraternité" of all male citizens, turning that rhetoric into legal and explicit exclusion of women from the all-male fraternity of citizens with rights. Given the needs of war, however, the government demanded that the entire French nation participate in sacrifice, in contributing funds and human effort, and in earnest support for the wars. Matters became worse when Napoleon Bonaparte (1769–1821) took control of France at the turn of the century. He expressed an opinion that the most worthy woman was "the one who had the most children," and openly scorned politically or intellectually active ones. He endorsed the idea of republican motherhood, just as Americans had. More important, from the jumble of customary and regional laws, Napoleon created a unified code of laws for the nation—one that endures to this day and that influenced the reform of legal systems around the world. On the one hand, the Napoleonic Code, which went into effect in 1804, clarified rules for a wide range of economic transactions still mired in medieval custom and precisely defined political citizenship. On the other, the Code greatly privileged men in virtually every realm of life— political, economic, familial, and personal—and prevented women from acting as autonomous individuals in those same arenas.

Specifically, as citizens, women were passive, not active members of the French nation: they had no right to participate in politics nor could they bring suits against wrong-doers or be witnesses at trials. Their nationality followed that of their husband, losing their French citizenship should they marry a foreigner. Economically, they could not own a business in their own name nor work without their husband's permission. If they did work, their wages belonged to their husbands. On marriage, a woman's property, with some exceptions, became that of her husband. In marriage, a wife had to reside where her husband directed. If found guilty of adultery, she would be jailed; an adulterous man would not be punished unless he had brought his "concubine" to live in the marital home. The children of a marriage were the property of the husband. If the husband died, they would be in the custody of a family council, not their mother. In sum, the Napoleonic Code created women's poverty and their civil inferiority, even their non-existence except as living entities subject to their husbands and to the state's whims. Not having funds of their own even if wage earners, the Napoleonic Code virtually forced women to remain with their husbands. They had no options.

The explicit inferiority of women created in the Napoleonic Code eventually became a rallying cry for French women, but at the time its effects were immediately damaging, causing women to give up leadership positions in business and lose whatever economic power they might have had. Moreover, the fact that other countries saw the Code as a model affected the lives of women worldwide. Still French women spoke out, despite the threat of being arrested: "You can tell by the way it treats women," one put it, "that the Code was written by a man." The American Revolution seemed a tiny blip on the global scene, while the French Revolution, taking place in a powerful state, had the widest impact because it effected a social revolution—not just a political one. It sparked further uprisings of those aiming to build representative institutions and create nations of citizens, not subjects. However, as in the United States, the final contours of the new political system were of critical importance to women because their rights as citizens had not materialized. The "rights of man" or men had been expanded and guaranteed, while those of women were eradicated.

The Haitian Revolution

Stories of women's heroism in this age of revolution and gender discrimination circulated widely. As slave revolutions erupted in the Caribbean, Flore Bois Gaillard became legendary as a leader of revolutionary forces on St. Lucia. The island itself had extensive networks of underground tunnels and human-made caves, along with copious large holes for escape and hiding. Fortified installations also indicated the presence of maroon communities. As the British tried to capture the French island during the revolutionary upheavals, St. Lucian slaves and free blacks armed themselves to defend the freedom that the French had promised. Among these was reputed leader of the armed forces and former slave Flore Bois Gaillard, who also performed more "womanly" tasks of feeding and nursing along with spying. Revolution in the Caribbean resonates in the murky but forceful lives of such heroines.

Alongside the ferment of liberal ideas traveling the globe, news of uprisings and reforms sparked multifaceted activism across the Caribbean and a dramatic revolution in present-day Haiti, then known as San Domingue—a sugar-producing Caribbean island colony of France whose slaves made plantation owners fabulously wealthy. In one sense the uprising began when free blacks from Haiti traveled to France with the aim of convincing reformers to protect their natural rights to liberty and equality. Meanwhile, with news of revolutions in France and the United States circulating in the Atlantic world, slaves protested the horrific conditions in a variety of ways, with women reputedly poisoning the worst whites when possible, organizing support groups around *vodun*, participating in messaging across the island, and building their skills in the use of weapons. In 1791, a slave uprising erupted against owners and overseers on the plantations, supposedly when a slave woman killed a pig—a vodun sign for war. Sanite/Suzane Belair, in some accounts the one who slaughtered the pig, went on to serve as an important officer in Toussaint Louverture's liberation army. Free blacks soon joined the rebellion. Once the uprising began, some women such as Belair became soldiers in the field, using the skills that some had gained in African kingdoms such as Dahomey, where they held important military positions and fought alongside men.

The Haitian Revolution was a confusion of interests. Women profited from the fluid situation and the high death rate of men on all sides to find new partners to support them, moving easily—or so it seemed—from rebels to planters. They beefed up their agricultural and other activity to provision their allies on whatever side, as crops were also targeted to starve out the combatants. Their religious leadership of vodun was vigorous, providing signals to begin battles or targeting certain people or areas or interests. As troop strength diminished, they moved to the battlefield in greater number and undertook to spy and pass on crucial information. Markets became their equivalent of today's media; there they encouraged people to rally or warned them to protect and arm themselves. There was, however, a downside to this participation.

All sides targeted women as the uprising entered its second decade and even before. White women were vulnerable because they had owned slaves. Some partnered with the black leadership, though this move did not necessarily protect them from black rage nor from white revenge either. Blacks paid back white treatment of slave women by murdering those from slave-owning families and by raping them before torturing and murdering them. Former slave women, suspected of spying, soldiering, and leading assaults against whites were also murdered—whether they had participated in the uprising or remained loyal to their owners. The rebels ultimately defeated the French, although tropical diseases were an enormous, and actually a decisive help. Haitian independence was declared in 1804 and consolidated in the Constitution of 1805. This constitution created a "chief magistrate" and "emperor" and decreed in Article 14 that "the children of one and the same family, of whom the chief magistrate is the father," would not have complicated racial identities but be known simply as blacks, thus homogenizing complex distinctions set up by Europeans while hardening the power of the father as chief magistrate or emperor. Finally, Haitian citizenship was masculinized still more in Article 9: "No one is worthy of being a Haitian," Article Nine declared, "if he is not a good father, a good son, a good husband, and above all a good soldier."[6] Lessons from Haiti were powerful when it came to race, slavery, gender, and citizenship as revolutions continued across the Atlantic world. Principles of liberty and equality were inspiring to everyone, not just to whites while the power of men, as in France, was enshrined in the new laws.

Activism against and beyond the Centralizing State

Uprisings of many sorts continued across the globe, often sparked by famine conditions to which centralizing rulers seemed to turn a deaf ear. In league with husband Qi Lin, Wang Cong'er (1777–1798) led an unsuccessful, if menacing, revolt against the Manchu empire in 1797. The White Lotus was a Buddhist group that had existed for hundreds of years across China. Given poor conditions at the time, the uprising roused tens of thousands of followers, including women fighters. When Qi Lin was killed, Wang Cong'er was chosen to take his place, becoming known as the "deadliest of all the fighters." The Qing administration was plagued by corruption and disorganization by this time but ultimately came up with a plan to corner White Lotus forces by driving local peasants into fortresses and thus depriving Wang of the local fighters she enlisted as she moved across the countryside. The Qing plan worked and Wang, along with her women soldiers, committed suicide by throwing themselves off a cliff.

As empires consolidated and needed more funds, the attractions of older political and social forms such as chieftaincies remained vivid, challenging the move toward imperial and national modernization and consolidation. Settler Mary Jemison was twelve years old when captured by Native Americans living in the eastern North American colonies. The Seneca group of Indians chose her to replace one of their kin, killed by white settlers in an earlier battle. Jemison was integrated into the Seneca's society and learned their way of life, including marrying and having seven children with two successive partners. The bi-lingual Jemison interacted with whites in her home in upstate New York and eventually helped negotiate treaties and land sales more favorable to the Seneca than the newly independent United States initially offered. Even though Jemison missed her family and enjoyed interacting with whites, she never wanted to rejoin them, far preferring Native American values and their way of life.

While rising nation-states such as the United States and France seemed eager to redistribute all forms of power to men and to impoverish women, in other regions women chieftains exercised their prerogatives even as centralizing, reforming male power brokers made strides. In the latter case, the efforts of jihadi Muslim leaders in West Africa to oust lax Muslim rulers, those who had turned Christian, or who maintained traditional African beliefs and rituals often led to the reduction of women's central roles in the chieftaincies or ethnic groups. Gone were women's negotiations of marriages and alliances and the mythical place women held as community builders and even community founders. Where traditional chieftaincies continued, however, as in South Africa, and where nation-building and state formation based in large capital cities had not materialized, the privileges of men still felt a counterweight in those of women. The great Zulu leader Shaka reputedly gathered all power in his hands, but not entirely. Women related to male chieftains there often owned cattle—a testament to their exceptional status and privilege. They also performed major religious rites and additionally fought alongside men. Such activities were not the result of Shaka's influence but rather of the women's capacity. Mmanthatisi, Shaka's aunt (1765–1840), served as regent, while other women in his ambit also exercised power.

New Nations from Spanish Colonies

As the Qing Empire was saved from White Lotus rebels and others of its internal problems, a far more successful challenge to empire came early in the nineteenth century with further uprisings against the Spanish grip over its Atlantic world colonies, lasting into the 1820s. Tupac Ameru and Micaela Bastidas's rebellion in the 1780s—as one in a string of uprisings—was followed by revolutions across Spanish America, with indigenous women and men joining creoles to fight off the peninsulares—that is, the Spanish sent from Spain as privileged officials, merchants, and soldiers. Their additional goal was to create independent nations ruled by those born in the Americas. In early-nineteenth-century Mexico, male and female Amerindians, mestizos, and creoles constituted mass armies following the lead of two priests demanding an end to their poverty and high taxation. Some did so invoking the cause of the Dark Virgin—Our Lady of Guadelupe. The Spanish defeated these groups and executed their leaders in 1811 and 1815.

Almost immediately new armed uprisings broke out across the Spanish Empire, both in Mexico and Spanish South America, this time under the leadership of creole generals, not priests. Creole women joined the upper-class leadership, providing financial assistance and supporting their armies. They served as spies and couriers and sometimes housed top military officers. When the creoles saw that they could not win without the support of men and women from the lowest ranks, including slaves and indigenous peasants, commitments to free slaves and improve overall conditions drew in these people too and helped finally to achieve political freedom. That said, as in the French and English revolutions, debates over whether women should be allowed to pitch in because of their delicacy and intellectual inferiority flourished in the New World struggles against the Spanish. The male leadership's rhetoric did not stop them from forcing women to make hundreds of uniforms on command, to find and prepare vast quantities of food for soldiers, and to offer the soldiers shelter, medical services, and, in many cases, sex. Yet, among indigenous peoples, traditional values and rituals in which women had participated long before the arrival of the Spanish remained strong and continued to make them major participants.

Policarpa Salavarrieta (c. 1791–1817) was from a well-off Colombian family, but after the death of her parents and several siblings, she began participating in revolutionary activities to liberate the Spanish colonies. With forged papers, she got herself across the heavily guarded entryway to the *royalist* stronghold of Bogotà in 1817 and posed as a servant in a revolutionary household. From there, she entered royalist circles by selling her skills as a seamstress to wealthy pro-Spanish households. As such, she heard gossip about military maneuvers, identities of the royalist leadership, and reports from spies. She worked to recruit soldiers from the royalist side to revolutionary forces until in the autumn of that year she was discovered and executed. Policarpa's way of pursuing her revolutionary cause—private and unannounced rather than open, public activism—was a common one for women, not just in this struggle but in many more to come.

Simón Bolívar, born in Caracas in present-day Venezuela, quickly became the chief of forces in the north of South America, communicating with supporters and other leaders to the south. Like other revolutionaries, he used gender imagery to surround the act of revolution and to cover up the activism of women in the struggle to free the colonies from Spain. In one of his public letters, he sees Spain as the mother giving birth and protecting her infant colony. However, at some point the mother became cruel and evil, denatured as was imputed to Marie Antoinette in France and imposing her will in a destructive way. She—Spain—aims to keep her male children dependent and to block their rise to maturity. In fact, Bolívar sees the Native American cultures as likewise monstrous, with the educated white creole men as the rational force that will restore order and values.[7] The ideal is for virile men to rescue and safeguard the old, children, and especially women; such is the goal of the revolutionary enterprise. Once achieved, Bolívar proceeded to take from his hero, Napoleon a sense of urgency to enact the elimination of women from citizenship. In the new language of independence, we see the gendering of the modern nation as the work of free white men only who serve as defenders of liberty's, that is, woman's fragility. Slaves by their very nature are not citizens either, and part of male protection of women is the racist aim supposedly to protect them from non-white men. Even as the Spanish king was overthrown, the political line of Bolívar rehabilitated the father in the family by degrading the mother or stepmother—not the father—as someone who strives to block the mature independence of her sons.

The language of gender and the family continued to infuse the revolution against Spain, spinning out Bolívar's use of family roles to make the main figures of the independence movement and new nations male. As many women fought valiantly in pitched battles, they received praise for their Amazonian level of fighting, but in the final telling of the independence story these women turned into devoted patriots with all their female fragilities and vulnerabilities. They needed protection as did the well-publicized rape victims—nuns, widows, and young virgins—who were equally helpless. The retelling of women's participation in the Latin American independence movement shows the opinion-making leaders' ambivalence toward women fighters and those who heroically sewed, nursed, spied: they were, in the first reality, amazons; then in the movement's aftermath they became pathetic victims of Spanish brutality, especially rape. The need of protection for the nation's weak women and their children became a founding principle of the modern, independent nation.

Still, women from every social group participated. Manuela Saenz (1797–1856) was an illegitimate child sent to be educated away from her family in a convent. To keep her from trouble, her father had her married to a wealthy English doctor who took her to live in Lima, Peru. By that time, the revolt against Spain was well under way and Saenz moved in to play many of the different roles assumed by revolutionary women. She supported her lover General Bolívar, who was not just a military leader but a visionary committed to making a United States of South America just like the United States of America. Saenz tirelessly gathered supplies, passed on information about Spanish troop movements, and, helping her in her role as a spy, hosted civilian leaders and soldiers alike in her home in Lima. She ensured Bolívar's escape from assassins more than once and additionally saw to it that others escaped capture; the former feat gave her the popular title "the Liberator of the Liberator." For this and many other accomplishments, she was momentarily seen as a heroine of the South American struggle against Spain. For all that, she died in poverty, because, to influential critics, her position as Bolívar's mistress and her relentless activism made her suspect. No longer creating the "moral" domestic life that Bolivar saw as the goal for all women, she was out of her place and even in later critics' eyes a public woman—that is, a whore.

The Post-Revolutionary Ferment

Feminist authors, abolitionists, artists, and theorists were energetic in promoting the cause of freedom, equality, and opportunity emerging from the theories and activism of the years of revolution. They were often at the forefront of efforts to end oppression, though just as often they did not directly benefit from political independence in their regions. An astute observer of political and social life, British author Mary Wollstonecraft

FIGURE 6.2 *Manuela Saenz, 1971. Saenz was among the many women of different classes, ethnicities, and races who participated in the early-nineteenth-century struggles for liberation from Spanish rule in the New World. Saenz was not a battlefield figure but a protector of Bolívar, a spy, a provisioner of fighters, and a transmitter of information. Courtesy of Harvey Meston Getty Images.*

(1759–1797) had rushed to observe the French Revolution. From watching the events, she wrote in support of the "rights of man" and then proceeded to extrapolate from that book lessons about the rights of women. In *A Vindication of the Rights of Woman* (1792) she explained women's use of cunning and concern for personal appearance as behaviors born of their weakness and lack of instruction. Women received no education to prepare them for adulthood and the law weakened them by stripping them of property and rights. Wollstonecraft knew from her own experience of women's vulnerability: her brother had inherited the family resources, and the small amount given to his sisters he took for himself too, leaving them penniless and at the mercy of men. One sister married a man who beat her and from whom Mary had to rescue her, while Mary herself was abandoned by the father of their child.

From Wollstonecraft's perspective, the development of character and rationality should be the aim of girls' upbringing. Not only would it allow women to raise children to be rational and virtuous citizens, it would enable them to have a companionate relationship with a husband. As it stood, women were simply objects of lust—and they actually made themselves up and behaved immaturely in order to serve this end. Moreover, the entire system of stripping women of their wages and wealth as well as their rights, raised questions about women's relationship to the evolving nation that additionally refused to provide women with an education and moral resources. From her perspective, "women have no country" as governments left them enslaved to men's desires and greed.

In fact, the revolutionary period saw an increase in awareness of vulnerabilities and differences among women. In 1801 Mirza Abu Talib Khan published "Vindication of the Liberties of the Asiatic Women," clearly referencing the late Mary Wollstonecraft's work. An author who occasionally worked as a civil servant for the British, Abu Talib Khan traveled to Britain at the end of the eighteenth century, where he mingled with high society. Some challenged him with reports of women's ill-treatment in South Asia. At the time, the British East India Company was accelerating its inroads on the power of the Mughals and the new South Asian states springing up from Mughal decline. The hope was to make up for the loss of its North American colonies and justifications for expansion multiplied, among them condemnation of Indians' alleged abuse of women. Even as he was being observed and feted by the cream of English and Anglo-Irish society, however, Abu Talib Khan was watching them, including the imperialists' treatment of their own women. Before returning home in 1802, he published a rebuttal to all the criticisms he had heard of the situation of women in Asia—in part gaining confidence from the talk about rights, reform, and revolution current in his day. He proposed that in fact women in Europe had far fewer rights than did women in Asia, who had complete control over family funds whereas European women were left utterly without resources of their own no matter how wealthy the family or how hard-working the woman herself. In contrast to Britain, South Asian women had ultimate command over household staff, and, in case of divorce, girls went with the mother and boys with the father rather than women losing all parental rights. Despite the facts, the imperial powers' new justification for denying independence to colonies and (both then and in our own times) for invading entire countries grew in strength: that is, takeover would halt the abuse of women in Asia and the Middle East despite the unequal pay, lack of political power, and violence against women in Western countries. Across Europe and Asia, the situation of women at the time was seen by instructed women themselves as far more favorable for those outside the West.[8]

The tenor of debate about women's rights, their place in society, and the building of their capacities shows movement toward a new insularity in heterosexual relationships, one evolving in tandem with the emphasis on individual rights. Wollstonecraft, like critic Jean-Jacques Rousseau, focused on the conjugal couple, not the extended household as the basis of society. Rousseau, as his ideas made their way into the Napoleonic Code and its offspring in other countries, believed that that couple should operate to the benefit of the new and active male citizen. His partner should be educated to provide for his needs in an emotionally supportive way. He wrote of the character "Sophie's" motherhood and wifely service not her intellectual companionship. While acknowledging women's maternal responsibilities, Wollstonecraft added the dimension of education for the task of being an instructed mate, whose companionship would last longer than the youthful lust of her husband.

In China, authors similarly aroused a complex pro-woman enthusiasm among some parents when it came to education of their daughters and to valuing women's writings. Building on the powerful tradition of women's literary achievements, in 1831, a learned Chinese woman, Wanyan Yun Zhu, published *Precious Record from the Maidens' Chambers*, a history of Chinese women's writing that included the poetry of women from different social strata. The anthology especially featured those who had led virtuous lives in their family while writing, thus eliminating the works of those earlier, accomplished courtesans. Wanyan Yun Zhu privileged women's place in the household, seeing it as domestic, albeit with a far wider compass for the definition of that domesticity. Many of them saw that domestic role as an educational one, however, as the needs of society became ever more complex, involving growing commerce, increased urbanization, and ever more dependent on wide knowledge not just of classics but of current affairs.

Inclinations to write about women were not uniform across the globe, however. Nor were all states revamping themselves to cement men's control of the public sphere. Women continued to hold positions of power where states were not necessarily reorienting themselves around centralized command, a large professional bureaucracy, and standing armies. Within clans and ruling families in South Africa, for example, during these same revolutionary decades women in royal families or clans with long-standing claims to regional domination could still exercise leadership. Down to the end of the nineteenth century, some enjoyed warrior status. Additionally, rulers continued to choose women to serve as armed guards, often with an array of shields and weaponry.

Conclusion

Haitian women saw the effects of their revolution in the abolition of slavery, while the Haitian Revolution itself dealt a heavy blow to the slave plantation system as a whole if only by showing that slaves could be freed. The end of slavery in the world of Atlantic plantations would take place over the next decades even as slavery in Africa continued, though not for the purpose of stocking trans-Atlantic plantations with laborers. Few other women benefited at the time from the revolutionary uprisings, however. From the French Revolution they gained the right by law to relatively equal inheritance. Some white women in the American Revolution took charge of businesses and farms, building their confidence and self-esteem as they did. Some of these wrote about the importance of women's education to help instill civic skills in the coming generations of citizens. Activist French and Latin American women who survived the turmoil and bloodshed of the revolutionary years likewise gained in political wisdom, some of them adding their voices to the new politics of nationhood. A poet like the slave Phillis Wheatley spread her literary wings in the immediate aftermath of the revolution and could express hope, and though not experiencing revolution, Chinese women kept up their prodigious literacy.

For the most part, however, women lost out in the immediate revolutionary settlements even as they had been fully present in the struggles. Their multifaceted contributions had been crucial to success, but the postrevolutionary constitutions and codes of laws ignored those contributions. Instead, they gave power to men that they had lacked before and in many cases took power from women. In most places, noble women lost status, if they didn't lose their lives; business women lost the right to own property in their own name; working women lost the right to their wages, because property was given over to men in the codes of laws that appeared in important new regimes. Women from households on the wrong side of revolutions usually lost everything, including family members, their homes, and their property. Some slave women in North and South America gained freedom but often fell victim to harsh new conditions, while slavery actually expanded in Africa itself. It was the firm articulation of men's privilege and women's inferiority and legal impoverishment that would make the revolutionary period in fact the basis for women's modernity. Individuals saw how much they had lost both in contrast to what men had obtained in terms of rights and actual economic benefit. This was especially true of black men whose objectification in the US Constitution hardened in comparison to the rights awarded to whites. It is not an accident that as the gendered and raced outcomes of the revolutions unfolded, abolitionism intensified and Mary Wollstonecraft asked whether women had a country. Revolutions built vocabularies of rights, freedom, opportunity, and national belonging even as vocabularies applying to women emphasized domestic duty, republican motherhood, and ostracism from political and public life. For many black and indigenous women, the situation was becoming even worse.

Glossary

Maroon	Referring to escaped slaves.
Royalist	One who supports a monarchy.
Seneca	A North American Native American group.
Vodun	A West African religion that moved with slaves to the Western Hemisphere.

Notes

1 Quoted in Susan Migden Socolow, *Colonial Women in Latin America*, 2nd ed. (Cambridge: Cambridge University Press, 2009), 173.
2 Quoted in Marylynn Salmon, *The Limits of Independence: American Women, 1760–1800* (New York: Oxford University Press, 1994), 58.
3 Quoted in Ellen Carol DuBois and Lynn Dumenil, *Through Women's Eyes: An American History with Documents*, 2 vols. (Boston, MA: Bedford St. Martins, 2009), 1:146.
4 Quoted in Mary Beth Norton, *Liberty's Daughters: The Revolutionary Experience of American Women, 1750–1800* (Boston, MA: Little, Brown, 1980), 223–4.
5 *The French Revolution and Human Rights: A Brief Documentary History*, translated, edited, and with an introduction by Lynn Hunt (Boston/New York Bedford/St. Martin's, 1996), 124–9. https://chnm.gmu.edu/revolution/d/293/. Another version is available at http://www.olympedegouges.eu/rights_of_women.php.
6 Quoted in Mimi Sheller, "Sword-Bearing Citizens: Militarism and Manhood in Nineteenth-Century Haiti," *Plantation Society in the Americas*, 4 (1997): 244.
7 This interpretation follows that in Catherine Davies, Hilary Owen, and Claire Brewster. *South American Independence: Gender, Politics, Text* (Liverpool: Liverpool University Press, 2006), 39–41.
8 *The Asiatic Annual Register, or a View of the History of Hindustan, and of the Politics, Commerce, and Literature of Asia for the Year 1801* (London: Debrett, Cadell, and Davies, 1802), Miscellaneous Tracts 102, 105.

Further Reading

Adams, Catherine, and Elizabeth Pleck. *Love and Freedom: Black Women in Colonial and Revolutionary New England*. New York: Oxford University Press, 2010.

Barr, Juliana. *Peace Came in the Form of a Woman. Indians and Spaniards in the Texas Borderlands*. Chapel Hill: University of North Carolina Press, 2007.

Berkin, Carol. *Revolutionary Mothers: Women in the Struggle for America's Independence*. New York: Knopf, 2005.

Campbell, Leon G. "Women and the Great Rebellion in Peru, 1780–1783," *The Americas: A Quarterly Review* 42:2 (1985): 163–96.

Davies, Catherine, Hilary Owen, and Claire Brewster. *South American Independence: Gender, Politics, Text*. Liverpool: Liverpool University Press, 2006.

Dore, Elizabeth and Maxine Molyneux, eds. *Hidden Histories of Gender and the State in Latin America*. Durham, NC: Duke University Press, 2000.

Dunbar, Erica Armstrong. *Never Caught: The Washingtons' Relentless Pursuit of Their Runaway Slave, Ona Judge*. New York: Simon and Schuster, 2017.

Girard, Philippe. "Rebelles with a Cause: Women in the Haitian War of Independence, 1802–04." *Gender and History* 21:1 (April 2009): 1–52.

Hahn, Steven. *The Life and Times of Mary Musgrove*. Gainesville: University Press of Florida, 2012.

Jasanoff, Maya. *Liberty's Exiles: American Loyalists in the Revolutionary World.* New York: Knopf, 2011.

Meléndez, Mariselle. *Deviant and Useful Citizens: The Cultural Production of the Female Body in Eighteenth-Century Peru.* Nashville, TN: Vanderbilt University Press, 2011.

Murray, Pamela S. *For Glory and Bolívar: The Remarkable Life of Manuela Sáenz, 1798–1856.* Austin: University of Texas Press, 2008.

7

Industrialization and Work in a Global Society, 1800–1914

Eighteen-year-old Ann Eggly worked twelve-hour days in the coal mines pushing carriages filled with 800 pounds of coal from the mines. She had started when she was seven, alongside her sister who was two years younger. Neither of them knew how to read or write, and both often fell asleep before reaching their bed once the work day was over. In the 1830s, the coal they helped produce powered the steam engines that drove textile machines, also tended by children beginning in the late eighteenth century. At about that time, the apron of nine-year-old orphan Mary Richards, working a machine whose powerful rollers flattened fibers, got caught, drawing her in and whipping her body around. Every bone in her body was broken, her skull crushed with blood gushing across the factory floor. Poor children, among them teens and girls as young as five or six, were the workhorses of the Industrial Revolution that enriched many a factory owner.

The Industrial Revolution is said to be about such technology as Mary Richard's drawing frame and other machines created in England from the eighteenth century on. However, women utilized a range of technologies long before the rise of industry, with Chinese women's complex tools for weaving just one example, and African women's irrigation systems for agriculture as another. The preceding age of industriousness had brought about an interconnectedness of peoples and products and an expansion of markets across the globe. Because industrial economies spewed forth products such as textiles in even larger quantities than in the seventeenth and early eighteenth century, the Industrial Revolution could only survive where there were developed capitalist markets such as those in Amsterdam or the extensive commercial markets run by women in Africa and elsewhere. There had to be abundant consumers and an interconnected consuming economy across the globe, not just in large cities but in rural areas too to purchase industry's everyday products. Agriculture, in which women participated heavily and even dominated in many places, simultaneously developed efficiently enough that many individuals could be released from working the land and move to factories instead. In fact, thriving markets, expanding agriculture, and consumer engagement during the age of industriousness had prepared the way for mass production of goods by industrial machines.

Industrialization emerged first in England and then spread across the globe; the earliest factories for making textiles prospered by imitating non-Western products. Around the world, women continued to be both producers and consumers of new goods, and in parts of the world they controlled the marketing of them. Women slaves used their botanical and processing skills to incorporate new plants and generate the food that fed the industrial workforce, contributing to the ongoing development of a global division of labor. Women and men slaves also produced many of the raw materials crucial to industry: for example, cotton and various lubricants for machinery. As with slave families, industry generally weakened the family as a unit of production or severely wounded it through growing demands for productivity. Individuals, leaving the home for factory jobs, seemed to break the patriarchal grip on work. Strikes such as that of the Lowell mill "girls" and work actions of various types such as those of Chilean women cigar makers accompanied this new economic order and became part of industrial and postindustrial society. Industrialization attacked craft work. The desire of men to hold out in crafts despite losing money sometimes made artisans send their wives to work in factories or to take in industrial jobs that were open to outwork—a process of home piecework that continues to occupy women to this day. In India, for example, women were pushed into the jute mills to support themselves or their families when men couldn't.

All this said, the coming of the machine age did not eliminate patriarchy; rather, industry allied with it. Women were paid lower wages; the law in many cases awarded those female wages—large and small—to the men of the family; the upper levels of industry and commerce became male dominated; and the class, racial, and slave order maintained patriarchal power even where an old-fashioned monarchical political order gave way to the fraternity of equal male citizens, as in the United States and France. Some say that patriarchy died in the modern period, transformed into simple male privilege. Others, however, maintain that the industrial order was a boon to patriarchy, enriching more men than before and setting up structures that led to the greater impoverishment of women. Whatever the case in factories at the time, one historian has found that the preindustrial wage gap of the medieval period was the same as the overall difference between men and women's wages at the beginning of the twenty-first century.

What Is the Industrial Revolution and How Did Women Participate in It?

The Industrial Revolution that began in the middle of the eighteenth century was an organization of productive life around machines performing work through the use of water, steam, electrical, and eventually nuclear power that substituted for and augmented human power. A second ingredient was the socialization of production around these machines, as people and their work were generally taken out of family homes and individual workshops and then relocated, grouping larger numbers of unrelated workers in factories. A third ingredient was the snowballing innovation in the direction of more efficient industrialization; in other words, industrialization rarely moved backward but rather accelerated and diversified its own processes. Some write in terms of a first, second, third, and fourth Industrial Revolution, but we look at industrialization as a single unfolding process of the application of technology to the production and reproduction of human life in general.

Women had long participated in textile production, the sector of the economy from which the Industrial Revolution took off by using steam-powered machines to spin and weave. Eventually in almost every part of the world, they took jobs in wool, linen, cotton, silk, and various mixtures of these to produce fabric that then clothed and covered people and was marketed globally to that end. During the industrious era, global demand for textiles rose as did global population except in Africa, which was decimated by the slave trade and its accompanying warfare. Tinkerers had responded to rising consumer demand fostered by the industrious spirit of the age, carrying out mechanization that used nonhuman energy to multiply productivity exponentially. Chinese women spinners of silk thread at home gradually lost their livelihoods as did many European women in the countryside who had supported their families crafting linen and woolen textiles during the agricultural off-season. Yet, women also invented new processes that increased productivity: Japanese women brewed sake in greater quantity and cultivated new varieties of silkworms. In England, Ellen Hacking and her husband John devised a carding machine to straighten cotton and wool fibers for spinning. Much later, two American women invented the reaper and the sewing machine. In the United States, only men could take out patents, however, so their husbands gained the credit.

The first generations of textile workers in factories were often single women from rural areas whose families no longer needed them because of general improvements in farm techniques and technology. English industrial pioneers employed women and children, subjecting them to difficult working conditions. Orphans, such as Mary Richards, who did not need to be paid, were especially brutalized, even killed as was Richards, by the new, often hazardous machinery. For a while the young women workers of Lowell, Massachusetts, came as surplus labor from farms in the surrounding New England states and worked in the textile mills there under far better conditions. The Lowell Mill girls became legendary for their exceptionally civilized behavior and lady-like manner. They even produced a newspaper describing their lives and aspirations for education. Because industrialization was experimental at first, in various countries some factory owners also hired entire families because that was the unit of work on a farm. A head of household would bring his wife and children to the factory, direct their work as a team, and receive the family's wage.

Still, there was much variety among the workers. During the 1830s and 1840s, Betsey Guppy Chamberlain (1797–1886), a mixed-race young woman of English and Algonkian heritage worked in the Lowell mills after the death of her husband. She was also a writer, and many of her stories published in the mill workers' magazine focused on the unjust treatment of and attitudes toward Native Americans. In the story "A New Society,"

FIGURE 7.1 *Spinning machine powered either by water or steam, c. 1825. In this early factory, there is an apparent family division of labor, with a man (father), woman (mother), and to the left a child endangered under the machine perhaps cleaning up or mending broken threads. Sometimes small children were sent to mend threads atop the machines too. Courtesy of Ann Ronan Pictures Getty Images.*

she devised a set of rules that included the treatment of women and of all workers:

1. Resolved, That every father of a family who neglects to give his daughters the same advantages for an education which he gives his sons, shall be expelled from this society, and be considered a heathen.

2. Resolved, That no member of this society shall exact more than eight hours of labour, out of every twenty-four, of any person in his or her employment.

3. Resolved, That, as the laborer is worthy of his hire, the price for labour shall be sufficient to enable the working-people to pay a proper attention to scientific and literary pursuits.

4. Resolved, That the wages of females shall be equal to the wages of males, that they may be able to maintain proper independence of character, and virtuous deportment.[1]

In the long run, early industry was experimental and new ventures more often than not went bankrupt. Under the threat of failure, conditions deteriorated in order for businesses and their owners to survive. Initially, factory workers were usually paid more than artisans, who could not compete with the ever lower costs of industrially produced goods. Then, new groups, such as Irish immigrants in the United States, were hired in large numbers at ever lower wages. In Lowell, Irish immigrants replaced the "girls" who had first worked in the mills—an example of how cheap labor from across the globe displaced those already employed and would continue to do so down to the present. In sum, from the beginning, the course of industrialization was uneven, producing wealth for some, modest well-being for others, and perilous conditions for many more.

As women were paid less than men, they were often pawns in the race to pay low wages in new businesses. From England, industrialization spread across the European continent, followed by the United States whose industrial adventurers stole Europe's technological secrets and copied its machinery. One theme, however, from textiles to telephones and telegraphs down to the first computer programmers, cheap female labor proved the savior when it came to staffing innovative enterprise. After Europe, Japan, Latin America, South Asia, and almost every region of the world picked up on mechanized factory work for at least parts of their economies. In Argentina, some 2,800 women cigarette workers of the National Tobacco Company used rolling machinery to turn out 400,000 cigarettes per day by the end of the 1890s. As other nations copied England's technology, they also copied the practice of low wages for women to boost profits. Gender hierarchy funded industrialization.

Industry created jobs outside of factories proper. Even in the late twentieth century industrial jobs offered an alternative to working-class women that for many was far preferable to domestic service—another increasingly common female job when slavery and agricultural labor started to decline in many parts of the world. "I prefer the factory," one Brazilian textile worker said, "there we have all our rights. Living and working in the house of a family, you don't have any."[2] Not only did factories pay better than artisanal work, they also offered a higher wage than white- or pink-collar jobs when office and service work developed late in the nineteenth century. The transition to factory work was often gradual but nonetheless difficult for the livelihoods it increasingly affected: in the early days of the United States, men made the soles of shoes in workshops while women made the uppers, often at home. Gradually men's work on shoes mechanized, and then manufacture of the uppers did too.

Still, aspects of industrialization supported women without the necessity of leaving their homes. Women polished factory-made knives or decorated buttons made in factories; in China they carved the wooden characters for mechanical printing; in India they painted wooden or pottery animals. In many parts of the world, women at home made baskets, straw hats, paper umbrellas, pots, and other indispensable goods that had not yet been fully industrialized. They crafted toys and wrapped chocolates or made boxes for cheeses. They did much of this work away from the camaraderie enjoyed by those who worked in factories, though some worked with relatives or neighbors in small workshops. Isolation resulted in still lower wages, for which individuals had little solution because they could not exert group pressure.

Such was especially the case for women making garments and paid by the piece instead of by the hour. Employers could increase the number, say, of buttonholes that had to be made for the same pay. To make ends meet the seamstress work longer hours. This kind of work, known as sweated labor, has also remained a dominant form of women's work down to the present. Even doing piece work in workshops provided no recourse either because the women were not numerous enough or because the owner could easily replace them. He could also sexually harass them with little danger to himself; the worker had to give in or lose her job. Factory foremen, managers, and owners also harassed women at will. Russian workers in a rope factory reported enduring "pinches and searches" as they left the firm, while the atmosphere in a printing firm was "[nothing but] insults and obscene propositions."[3]

Finally, around industrial production urbanization occurred, creating even more jobs. More garments were needed, more restaurants and small stores with prepared foods, more boarding houses, laundresses, shop clerks, domestic servants, and barmaids—to name a few. All of these became jobs that women filled in growing towns and cities. Around these towns and cities were those who raised the produce to support the continuing increase in urban residents; in Japan and Korea, women divers brought in seaweed, sea urchins, abalone, and other food from the sea. Other women would then prepare such raw produce for the hardworking single laborers, far from their families, or for those families where the parents toiled long hours and lacked any facilities or time for cooking.

Though the vast majority of women worked as low-paid and exploited workers, some few women actually directed rising manufacturing. Women invested their dowries in industrial development from its beginning when there was general family financing of firms rather than public financing through selling stock, which would come later. While their husbands ventured out on sales trips to sell their pottery, textiles, and iron wares, some wives ran the businesses on a full-time basis, the task made easier by the fact that initially factories were located adjacent to owners' houses. They were tasked with tending the books for the firms because, as some noted, they were better at math and more methodical. Women of the super-successful Krupp metallurgical factories in Germany not only founded but helped run the enterprise, with Bertha Krupp so responsible for the firm's success that cannons were named after her in the First World War.

In Nishinomiyo, Tatsu'uma Kiyo (1809–1900) operated one of the most formidable and extensive sake industries in all of Japan. She headed the company from a backroom office, where she dealt with workers, made all decisions, and trained and married off her children with the idea that they would set up additional plants in the area. Up-to-date, she became concerned when bacteria contaminated some of the product and turned to scrubbing the large oak barrels with her own hands even while overseeing mass production of sake. Tatsu'uma also sensed the ups and downs of the business cycle and the uncertainties of the rapidly changing industrializing world. This awareness led her to diversify her capital by making business loans, buying her firm its own fleet of ships, and expanding into real estate. All decision-making and transactions, however, remained hidden from public view because women were never to appear to head the family even when like Tatsu'uma Kiyo they did.[4]

The Production of Raw Materials for Industry

With factories needing a variety of raw materials, the polyculture that had once supported families declined in favor of growing a single crop on a large scale. In many parts of the world, adventurers and officials of imperial powers pushed for the further development of plantation agriculture to replace family farms. They were joined by local entrepreneurs, some of them women, who sought to participate in supplying commodities, which included foodstuffs. Coffee, sugar, tea, chocolate, and any other raw materials that would fortify workers were in demand; many of these were farmed initially by enslaved women who became increasingly important as the slave trade was outlawed. Then as slavery itself was abolished before 1850—though not in the United States, Cuba, or Brazil—all of these major producers of raw material, whether grains and other foodstuffs or ingredients for manufacturing such as cotton, scrambled to adapt. The slave woman and then the freed woman with her agricultural knowledge and her reproductive capacity only gained in importance to land owners wanting to build wealth in this innovative and challenging economy. To their owners, African slaves had been a labor source, property for which they had paid, and often signs of status in the society; women slaves additionally provided the reproduction of the next generations of unfree workers.

In Brazil, slaves worked on sugar and coffee plantations, served as craftspeople and miners, or provided domestic help. At this time, far more African slaves were still sold in Brazil than in North America, with slavery only abolished in 1888. Their range of responsibility was wide, including prostitution and burglary benefitting their masters. Given the stakes, owners across the Western Hemisphere made great efforts to find slaves who had disappeared from their homes, shops, or plantations. Brazilian newspapers carried advertisements describing the physical descriptions of runaways along with offers of rewards for their return, indicating that they knew their female slaves intimately. One ad in the O Mercantil (Rio de Janeiro) January 15, 1845 went: "20$rs. To anyone who apprehends and takes to Rua da Alfandega No. 151 a slave woman named Claudina, Mozambique nation, who fled on the 1st day of the current month, is thirty years old, regular height, strong, big breasts, with a mark under her left eyes, has one of her fingers defective on her right hand. A protest is made against anyone who has hidden her." The ad shows that slaves had networks of "anyone who has hidden her" and that her body was completely familiar to the owner in these years as it had been earlier. Another ad for a girl half Claudina's age also indicated that slaves were not simply ciphers held in bondage but that there was an intimacy: "Fled or was led astray a black girl [meleca] named Maria of the Caande nation," the ad in the Diario do Rio de Janeiro of December 31, 1847 read, "who appears to be about 14 years of age and still does not have breasts, black color and thin, wore a dress of white calico with ribbons and pink flowers." The owner had clearly searched the neighborhood for her: "The said girl was missing yesterday afternoon when she went to the Campo de Santa Anna to get water, and it appears that she was crying because someone stole her water bucket. Whoever brings her to Rua de Santa Anna, 47B, upper floor, will be satisfactorily rewarded, or even someone who gives information about her so that her owner can get her back."[5] Every laboring hand, and in women's case, reproductive body counted in the struggle for profit in this transformational economy. Women played a doubly important part in it.

Relationships between slave and owner appear in the few accounts left by slaves themselves. Mary Prince (b. 1788–d. after 1833) was a slave born in the British colony of Bermuda; initially she worked for comparatively agreeable masters though sometimes laboring seventeen hours a day raking salt. This salt was necessary to food preservation, especially of meat and fish used to feed the industrial population, making Prince essential to the unfolding Industrial Revolution. Then Prince was sold to a pathologically cruel family in Antigua where she did odd jobs such as laundry to earn extra money. Both husband and wife beat their slaves regularly and with such rage that they themselves were often exhausted. Mary described two boys, for example, whose beatings she had just witnessed: "My pity for these poor boys was soon transferred to myself; for I was licked, and flogged, and pinched by her pitiless fingers in the neck and arms, exactly as they were. To strip me naked—to hang me up by the wrists and lay my flesh open with the cow-skin, was an ordinary punishment for even a slight offence." The work day was limitless: "My mistress . . . used to sit up very late, frequently even until morning; and I had then to stand at a bench and wash during the greater part of the night, or pick wool and cotton; and often I have dropped down overcome by sleep and fatigue, till roused from a state of stupor by the whip, and forced to start up to my tasks."

The abuse of Mary paled beside that of the slave Hetty, whose inhuman treatment shows the general attitude toward slaves as beings outside humanity and thus outside the normal protection of the law: "Poor Hetty, my fellow slave, was very kind to me, and I used to call her my Aunt; but she led a most miserable life, and her death was hastened (at least the slaves all believed and said so), by the dreadful chastisement she received from my master during her pregnancy. It happened as follows. One of the cows had dragged the rope away from the stake to which Hetty had fastened it, and got loose." Despite people's belief that masters so understood the monetary value of slaves that they sought to preserve their well-being, it becomes clear that the cow was more important to the master than the woman slave was: "My master flew into a terrible passion, and ordered the poor creature to be stripped quite naked, notwithstanding her pregnancy, and to be tied up to a tree in the yard. He then flogged her as hard as he could lick, both with the whip and cow-skin, till she was all over streaming with blood. He rested, and then beat her again and again. Her shrieks were terrible." Hetty then went into premature labor, giving birth to a dead infant. Once she appeared recovered, her owners took to beating her again. "Ere long her body and limbs swelled to a great size; and she lay on a mat in the kitchen, till the water burst out of her body and she died. All the slaves said that death was a good thing for poor Hetty; but I cried very much for her death."

Such beatings and murders disciplined slaves and showed them that they were beyond the edges of the community where they could be murdered at will: "The manner of it filled me with horror. I could not bear to think about it; yet it was always present to my mind for many a day." Mary's owners rented her out several times and then took her to London in 1828. "There was no end to my toils—no end to my blows. I lay down at night and rose up in the morning in fear and sorrow; and often wished that like poor Hetty

FIGURE 7.2 *Woman, carrying child, pounding corn in Cape Province, South Africa, c. 1900. As with coal to power industrial machines, traditional methods of growing or processing food were common in the nineteenth century to power the industrial workforce. Governments needed to import foodstuffs as agricultural land was converted to urban space for factories and urban housing. Courtesy of Popperfoto Getty Images.*

I could escape from this cruel bondage and be at rest in the grave."[6] So ill from beatings and abuse, Mary finally sought out help from neighbors and then the Moravian Church. Eventually she gained her freedom and wrote the brief, but galvanizing account of her life. This small glimpse of the everyday violence of whites and the horrific torture slaves endured was one provocation for abolition first of the slave trade and then of slavery itself in the Caribbean and other colonies. The treatment of these women slaves stemmed from the centralizing state's power: it decided who of those within its borders were not to have its protection. The state flexed its muscles in allowing that Hetty was unfit for life.

One job owners continued to offer their slaves was wet nursing. As shown, both wealthy and working women across cultures employed others to breastfeed their children for pay. As urbanization took hold, hardworking women in cities sent their babies to rural areas where a wet nurse would tend the newborn while the mother continued her job full time. Upper-class women often brought in a wet nurse for status reasons in addition to restoring their prepregnancy appearance more rapidly. Wet nurses also stepped in before the days of modern bottle feeding, when a mother's body did not produce the proper amount of milk to keep the child alive or when the mother was ill. In slave countries such as Brazil, slaves were used as wet nurses, with their own children either dead because of high infant mortality or simply taken from them by owners who wanted to rent out the new slave-mother as a wet nurse.

One owner wanting to profit from her slave's body placed this advertisement in a Rio de Janeiro newspaper in 1821: "For sale a black woman, wet nurse, without a child [cria], gave birth ten days ago from first pregnancy, 18 to 19 years of age, without any faults, knows how to wash, iron, cook, has learned the rudiments of sewing and is capable of full management of a house, in Rua do Sabao de Quitanda, upper section." A still different ad in 1827 gave far fewer accomplishments of the potential employee: "For rent, a wet nurse with very good milk from her first pregnancy, gave birth six days ago, in the Rua dos Pescadores, no. 64. Be it advised that she does not have a child [cria]."[7] The ads show on the one hand slave capacities and on the other, aspects of their lives as commodities, including a weakened tie to their own children who were not going to accompany them.

In urban Cuba, infant mortality among slaves was high, with many suspecting that mothers had killed their babies to keep them from the hardships of life on sugar plantations. Moreover, under slavery children belonged to the master. As noted earlier, slave–master relationships operated with a coercive intimacy—that is, sexual assault—not generally associated with the free male artisan or factory worker. A mother might well not want her child subjected to similar assault. Only the forced sex and abuse of the woman artisan or factory worker had any resemblance to the slave's relationship to her master.

As urbanization increased, enslaved women in the Western Hemisphere had more opportunity to buy their freedom. In Cuba, wet nurses were among those in the population who accumulated enough money to do so. Enslaved market women, laundresses, and seamstresses also dealt with the world of cash often enough to raise sufficient funds to end their enslavement. Market women working for women slave owners could make money dealing with their own commerce on the side. For wet nurses and perhaps for other intimate occupations devoted service occasionally earned manumission. Sometimes heads of family promised a wet nurse freedom if the baby survived and flourished—a considerable achievement in days of high infant mortality.

In 1804, Haiti abolished slavery, the first nation in the Atlantic world to do so, while in 1807, Britain criminalized the trade in slaves, followed by the United States in 1808. France, also a leader, abolished the trade in 1818. Thereafter, many of the new Latin American nations abolished slavery altogether, leading empire-builders and industrialists to replace slavery with a revived system of indentured workers who were technically free but forced to work for a set number of years. Some see these workers—Chinese, Indian, and others from Asia—as buffers between whites and blacks. They were able to have families, which slaves were not, and they were supposed to stand for cultures significantly different from Africans in the "New World." Although after the end of the slave trade, Africans were enlisted for indenture, the presence of indentured workers made discrimination more nuanced, allowing the imagined movement from slavery to full freedom as the regular life course of racial others. In this scenario, discrimination still abounded but in a revised form, and forced labor of one kind or another remained an ingredient of industrial development around the world down to the present.

Indentured workers were mostly men, but women also were taken into the system. Agents roamed different parts of Asia and Africa looking for workers to indenture. In some instances—that of British Guiana, for example, where the sex ratio was 41 women to 100 men—such a situation made for a range of problems. The initial issues, however, were in the home country where some women used indenture as a way to escape abusive or derelict husbands. Some South Asian women, looking for relief, went off with agents who promised them jobs as ayahs—that is, nurses for children—but then had them shipped off to the distant Caribbean or Mauritius. One young woman who had had an argument with her mother, escaped from home on a pilgrimage, accepted a job supposedly as ayah to a Calcutta family, but ended up indentured in South Africa. The cases of women fleeing from violent or unfaithful husbands were so numerous that the government in South Asia passed the Indian Emigration Act 1883 to stop women resorting to indenture as a cure for a bad marriage.

Still, new machines entered the production of crops as agriculture gradually became industrialized. These changes reduced the ability of farming to support families in times of famines and other disasters and simultaneously put farmers at risk of losing their land if they took on too much debt. In hard times, banks took over land whose farmers had difficulty repaying loans for modern heavy equipment, fertilizers, and seeds. Facing an evolving economy, women invented new kinds of cheeses or dairy machines; they devised an expanding array of food crops and prepared foods to sell to city workers. Others, however, took to the road or the seas in order to survive.

Transformations in Society

A society based on class relationships resulted from the rise of industry and trade and gradually came to shape everyday life for many. Class is seen as different from older forms of relationships such as lifetime serfdom or lifetime unfree labor, which diminished over the course of the nineteenth century, though remaining in some regions of the world. In industrial society, a class of workers arose having no guaranteed lands to farm; gradually their possession of large tools such as weaving and spinning machines declined too. The bourgeois or industrialist and merchant classes came to own these; additionally capitalists came to own great stretches of farmland-- the Countess of Sutherland in the late eighteenth century, for example. Class, unlike status based on genealogy or "purity" of bloodline in older societies, was fluid: one could rise from being a day laborer on a farm to being an industrialist. One's relationship to the tools, land, factories, banks and other instruments of capitalism determined one's class: one was either a worker selling his or her labor to gain life's necessities such as food or a member of the upper classes that owned the means for producing those necessities.

Work and the creation of one's property in wages or businesses or big farms were at the heart of values in this new age of industry and its global commerce. A class society's values differ from those based on purity and pollution, though both can coexist. Somewhat different values and class position characterized women. Increasingly across the West and in other regions influenced by the rise of industrialization, the goal was for women *not* to work outside the home. According to ideology, they were to remain "pure" in the home just as men were to work in the rough and tumble public away from the home. Domesticity, as this model existence for women came to be called, involved preparing a secluded spot away from the workplace and public concerns. In this supposedly sheltered space individuals first developed and refreshed their inner selves. There they constructed a sense of autonomy that allowed them, men in particular, to go out into the outer world and create property in the form of wages or capital. Women in the home were to cater to the needs of the male self—an ideal that existed mostly across Europe, the urban United States, and increasingly in areas where industrial capitalism and liberal institutions developed. The pollution and purity that were often seen as playing themselves out in women's lives could be contained in the inner quarters or the home.

The question arises whether these women with no engagement in property-creating work or in the public were part of the class system. Sheltered in the home as either an ideal or a reality, they supervised children, tended to the provisioning of the home's inhabitants with food, clothing, and a sanitary environment, and provided for the emotional well-being of all concerned. They were not, however, creating property or capital from their profits. In most of the industrializing regions of Europe and the United States, women could not own or amass property: even the clothing they wore belonged to their spouse. This set them apart from women in other parts of the world who could enjoy their dowries, invest their funds, and transmit it as they pleased in trusts or other charitable donations. For male commentators, the "true womanhood" reflected in capitalist domesticity constituted the peak of civilization and an institution that should be spread across the globe. As we have seen, however, such ideals were already powerful beyond the capitalist world.

Family organization changed dramatically, if gradually, with industrialization and the slow and incomplete end to slavery. As industrialization pulled people from multigenerational households in the countryside into a life in cities often as a single worker, households more generally began to shrink in size and in status. This shrinkage coincided with the idea of individualism in such places as western Europe and the United States, although not entirely. Single individuals who migrated there did so on their own, unconnected with their families, although some might have a relative or two who had made the first foray into the city. Although some factory owners had hired entire families, that practice soon gave way to hiring a single individual outside the orbit of the family. These factory hands, especially if they were women, might live in massive barracks or rooming houses run by the factory itself or by a business person—again, institutions entirely different from the household as a cluster of related people.

The reduction of slavery in many parts of the world, especially the United States and colonies run by western Europeans except Brazil, also reduced household size and influence. Large segments of the Ottoman Empire similarly saw a reduction in household size. Gradually, day laborers or live-in help replaced slaves; indentured servants did as well. Many of these factory or plantation workers were also unaffiliated with kin networks that might exist hundreds and even thousands of miles away. On the one hand, a bureaucratic state and domestic quarters for a more conjugal family replaced dynastic rule and the influence of powerful, extended families, their slaves and concubines and clients all housed together. On the other, the rise of modern industrial cities peopled with unmarried, isolated workers diminished the family as a productive unit. Industry took production from the home and made workers aligned with unrelated other workers the primary labor force. As these solitary individuals found partners and lived with them as an independent couple (workers often avoided the hassles and costs of legal, religious marriage) households and villages with large contingents of extended family members dwindled. Domesticity, separated from concerns for extended family power, became more prevalent across the globe, which is not to say that extended families no longer existed. Rather, domesticity based on a conjugal couple wrapped in their privacy and immunity from public life centered on reproduction, monogamous sexuality, and the raising of children.

Across the globe, rural daughters sent to the city with few, if any, resources filled the population of women in domestic service. Stories of their exploitation continue down to the present. Mean conditions and crushingly long hours were often standard for domestic workers, as were the additional jobs outside the household such as tending markets or working for neighbors as well as one's employer. Employers, imbued with racist attitudes, allowed themselves to treat Amerindians, mestizos, African Americans, and Asians in both North and South America with mental and physical cruelty. Men of such households felt themselves entitled to rape these defenseless domestic workers and then to have them fired should they become pregnant. Mexican widow Marcela Bernal del Viuda de Torres took her two daughters to Mexico City to find work for all three in its booming factories. As Marcela put it to her daughters, "I'm sure not going to let you end up as maids."[8]

Upper-class women increased their charitable efforts as industrialization destroyed older jobs, put people out of work, and left many an isolated worker without the protection of the extended rural family. Initially, many business people emphasized profit above all else, leaving large numbers in society impoverished, including their own workers. Philanthropy provided relief as part of a traditional sense of charitable duty. One solution middle- and upper-class women saw to poor women's economic vulnerability was charity—that is, providing medical, educational, and other assistance to the urban poor. In Mexico's large and small cities, Catholic women connected with the Society of St. Vincent de Paul worked by the thousands to bring the poor to participate in Church institutions such as marriage and regular worship and also to help them in their economic and family lives. They canvassed donors for funds for food, clothing, and living expenses and set up vocational schools to teach artisanal skills such as shoemaking and sewing. In San Luis Potosi, they urged women cigar factory workers to avoid prostitution and to worship regularly. For women and their children, these "Christian Amazons" set up medical dispensaries in urban areas along with networks of primary schools, soup kitchens, orphanages, and hospitals.[9]

Activism around women's situation in South Asia was also vigorous if more complicated by colonialism and a sturdy *caste* system based on levels of pollution and purity. In South Asia, local men worked with British officials to end customs like widow-burning and child marriage, while other efforts aimed to improve the well-being of people in scorned castes. Lower on the scale of purity, these people did the most menial jobs, though sometimes they had a good deal of responsibility for social order, carrying messages, policing village boundaries and safety, and the like. If men in the low castes were low, the status of low-caste women was lower still, leading some to undertake their education. To do so, reformers like Savithribai Phule (1831–1897) with her husband Jotiba Phule started the Satyashodhak Mandal of lower-caste people against the privilege and power of the Brahmins. The couple founded a school for young women in 1848 and others including one for lower-caste girls in 1851. They were berated for this undertaking even by their own families. In 1856, Savithribai's brother told her, "You and your husband have rightly been excommunicated. You help the lowly castes like the *mangs and majars* and that, undoubtedly, is committing sin. You have dragged our family name in the mud." Savithribai argued that the Brahmins owed their power and high position to the knowledge they had acquired. "Learning has a great value. One who masters it loses his lowly status and achieves the higher one."[10] The debate over aiding poor and low-caste women would continue, taking a new turn as industry spread across the globe.

As the Industrial Revolution was unfolding before their eyes, white women in Europe and North America became active around the abolition of slavery but the inspiration for many was less the issue of work, rights, and poverty than the affront to Christian morality and family values. However, across the Western Hemisphere, enslaved women persisted in their longstanding protests in everyday life and in alliance with broader abolitionist movements. In Cuba and Brazil, where slavery continued after its abolition in the new states of Latin America, emancipated urban women petitioned courts for their children's freedom. Cuban and Brazilian cities hummed with African-Latino ideas of freedom, around which both enslaved and freed women took legal action or continued to buy their freedom. Philanthropists sometimes set up funds to finance these legal suits. Like the high-caste women philanthropists, white women abolitionists learned that slaves and former slaves were as informed as whites were and usually more so. Moreover, mistreatment of women abolitionists under the law and by men also led them to think that they too could benefit from reform.

The Culture of Industry and Capitalism

Gender shaped the culture of industrialization, economic protest, and migration, as the technological and scientific foundations of industry promoted a new vision of masculinity as hyper-rational and practical. There remained a culture of the righteous warrior preserving or avenging family honor despite the inroads on that identity made by the rise of global trade. Trade was said to promote good, peaceful behavior more effectively than honor, as people needed to make exchanges and thus get along with one another. Merchants and the industry leaders who provided them with goods thrived on calculation that would allow them to make monetary profits. Instead of physically defeating an enemy, merchants engaged in the back and forth of commerce—a more civilized, intellectual occupation, as many saw it. For them, wars based on honor rather than rational interests could dampen trade. This way of thinking about life came to be associated with a "middle class" that behaved prudently, without swagger or brutality—or so the ethos of industrial life claimed.

Working-class men often upheld the notion of male honor based on the arduous work they performed. This work was somewhat similar to that of the soldier because of the courage needed to confront machines and endure the crushingly long working hours. However, business and commerce were believed to soften warlike instincts that erupted in lethal violence, subduing those instincts with mental activity and harmonious interactions of commercial and business people. Increasingly dependent on science for their goods, leading men of industry and trade also addressed masculinity, emphasizing the rationality of their work and the irrationality of women. Thus, women were said to be inferior in intelligence and erratic in temperament so that they could not perform the work of objective, high-level observation.

The belief that women were irrational confirmed the sexual division of labor in factories and workplaces but using a more up-to-date rationale. The sexual division of labor allowed for lower rates of pay for those doing the work of the less qualified or "irrational"—that is, women. Evidence for that line of thinking was most visible in the fact that women of the middle classes were pushed out of managing businesses during the process of industrialization. Whereas once wives had been business partners for their merchant/manufacturer spouses, cultural leaders in the nineteenth century deemed such work "unfeminine." French women, for example, had invested their dowries in their own and their husband's construction of textile factories and even managed them. By the end of the nineteenth century few women ran factories officially, though thousands across the globe— Tatsu'uma Kiyo, for example—worked behind the scenes to build industrial success. Despite an ideology of the emotional comforts of the home and the emphasis on men's "rationality," sexual harassment and assault were both common experiences of women in the industrial workforce, on the streets, and in the home itself. Men's claims to being logical and reasonable coexisted with the use of brute force against women.

Factories changed people's passage through time, as clocks determined people's work lives instead of the rhythms of nature telling individuals and communities when to begin and end the work or when to plant or harvest. Schools became an important social institution, instilling in the next generation of workers basic skills as well as the importance of living by the clock. People in rural areas and in the household, in contrast, continued to work by tasks and follow seasonal cycles. Urban women workers had a complicated relationship to time, in that they followed the clock as well as performing tasks according to the physical—that is, natural—needs of their families to be fed, clothed, and cared for in sickness. As the world industrialized, many housewives also lived in two time economies: that of the clock that men and school children followed and that of the household where life followed patterns of bodily health, mealtimes, seasons, and weather.

Addressing Women's Work: Solidarity, Unions, Strikes

Women had long participated in structured groups for mutual support. Guilds and mutual aid societies provided care in hard times including inability to work because of injury or sickness. Some collected funds to pay for a member's funeral. The challenges of industrialization called for better organization to match the power of manufacturers and other employers. Unions brought a new kind of organization. These combined the mutual support for the sick and incapacitated with the idea of solidarity in the face of factory conditions and low pay that threatened workers' very survival. In the Shanghai cotton mills, girls formed sisterhoods dedicated to mutual support when confronted by organized gangs that grew up amid rapid urbanization and its disarray: "We would go to work together and leave work together because then it was not good to walk alone." After a while, groups of these girls would pledge loyalty to one another, vowing to protect one another from the gangs who stole paychecks or street women who seized these young girls to sell to brothels.[11] In Italy and Spain, rural women joined anarchist groups opposing the increasing immiseration of day laborers and sharecroppers. When conditions became too oppressive, members as a whole sent representatives to negotiate with owners. Lacking success, the collectivity of workers would stop work and go on strike. In the 1880s, match girls in London struck because of the dangers in working with phosphorous, bad working conditions, and a fining system that could cost them a day's work for the smallest infraction such as being slightly late. Many women did join unions, but the percentage of women's participation was lower than it was for men. They hardly had time because of their double burden of factory and housework. As important, because their pay was usually half that of men, they could not afford union dues. Moreover, the union ethos was unfriendly to women, as men saw themselves as the breadwinners and women as competitors in achieving good wages. Women working in factories or participating in union activity undermined masculinity. Women had many other ways of protesting, however. When prices rose too high, housewives banded together, fighting in groups against merchants. They invaded food shops and sometimes took all a storekeeper's goods. In times of hardship, merchants even harassed customers by demanding sexual favors in exchange for food. Women workers in the Ottoman Empire held dramatic protests against unfair competition and the destruction of jobs across the second half of the nineteenth century.

The sexual division of labor persisted into the industrial age and may have become even more pronounced and possibly more patriarchal over the nineteenth century. Team organization of work soon gave way to factories where one sex tended the spinning machines, another the weaving machines. Although the work might be segregated, its assignment to teams of men or women was completely arbitrary. In one city the custom could be for men to tend weaving machines, and in another, women would do this job. This segregated workforce was then paid according to its gender composition: a workforce of women was always paid less than a workforce of men. On the other side of things, justification for the sexual division of labor was changeable, though matters were not quite so clear cut as alleged, given that women performed almost every kind of work that men did. In the jute mills set up around Calcutta in India beginning in the 1850s, women could be weavers, while in cotton mills they were seen as polluting and thus forbidden to weave. They were allowed, however, to spin cotton. Logic could not explain such paradoxes, which is not to say that people did not try. The mere existence of a sexual division of labor and the gendered complexities around longstanding ideas of pollution and purity and the newer ones about equality and profit allowed employers to reap benefits when they employed women, even in a mixed labor force.

Sex segregation and the low wages accompanying it provoked an array of responses, some corrective, others organizational, and still others backed by violence. Women mounted ad hoc actions, such as in Barcelona where they protested working conditions by taking over streets and large stores—that is, occupying public space with their protests. Indentured workers and former indentured workers struck too and conducted strikes. Sugar cane workers in Jamaica in 1900 protested the precariousness of their lives caused by sugar beets competing with cane sugar. Strikes erupted over bad working conditions and minimal wages that arose because cutting the cane could be entirely women's work, men's work, or men's and women's work, showing that the "natural" division of labor by sexes was created entirely by humans in order to keep wages low.

Alongside the rise of global commerce, industry, and protest, ideologies including Marxism, liberalism, anarchism, and Social Darwinism developed. Liberalism, the earliest of these political/economic philosophies, announced the equal rights of the individual as a person on this earth whose main necessity was to feed, clothe, and house him- or herself. Not a soul or spirit, individuals freely amassed property as they worked to provide these necessities; they might also work for someone else, freely exchanging labor for pay. This free exchange of one's labor was at the foundation of liberalism. If such freedom or liberty operated in the economy, liberals believed, society would be harmonious, balanced, and prosperous. Such was the optimism of liberalism, and even this optimism was revolutionary as a secular theory of the way society could operate in peace and prosperity. It removed the deity in religions from the functioning of society and made way for social scientific understandings of the world.

The individual became prominent in this political idea, replacing the family and divine hierarchies. Still, John Locke, the primary theorist of liberalism in the seventeenth century, saw the family as an important part of human organization. As mentioned, though the family was composed of equal individuals endowed with rights, Locke maintained, the father should command. If government became tyrannical, citizens were justified in rebelling against it and demanding new, more just leaders and institutions. It was on these grounds that women and minorities continued to demand their rights, especially in Western societies but increasingly across the globe.

Anarchism and Marxism sought to combat the inequities in the new industrial capitalist system; Marxism in particular espoused revolution to achieve this goal. Anarchism, inspired especially by the work of the printer Pierre-Joseph Proudhon, believed that no governing structures were necessary to society. Though women in both industrial and rural society became anarchists—even ardent ones—Proudhon so believed in women's inferiority that he did not want them involved in anarchist activism. Instead, they should maintain a well-run household that would benefit the men in their lives. Still, women agrarian workers in Italy, women urban workers in Barcelona, and women activists in Japan engaged in anarchist politics, carrying their strikes to the fields and city streets alike.

Among the Marxist activists, German Clara Zetkin and a host of other women across the globe protested not just the harms done by industry on the factory worker but especially the double burden it made women bear. They pointed to the long working hours women labored in industry or in the peripheral outwork system as the first burden and then the responsibilities for childcare and housework as the second. Marxist activists believed that the working classes should overthrow the capitalists who owned industries, banks, and all the land used for commercial agriculture. Then they would form a socialist society without that kind of money-making private property. Without private property, women would automatically be liberated. The antipathy of Marxist and other union men toward women, however, repulsed many women, though some became committed in almost every country where Marxism took hold. One of the most active and accomplished Marxist theorists was Polish-born Rosa Luxemburg who emphasized worker participation in revolutionary struggle.

In a climate of rising worker discontent over the century, European and US politicians turned to protective legislation to regulate women's work, often at the instigation of men who disliked women competing with them for good jobs. This legislation set maximum numbers of hours that women could work and in some cases banned them from working in industries such as mining. In this latter case, the ban pertained only to work in the mines themselves but did not prevent women from doing back-breaking labor hauling heavy ore or other products. The idea was that women were more fragile than men and that work impeded their childbearing. To this end, British legislators blocked women from working in the potteries because they supposedly fell ill from such work. However, medical studies showed that men became ill far more often than women did. Another excuse for banning women from certain jobs or reducing the hours they could be employed was that their fertility was lowered. At the time, many countries were worried about their falling birthrates. However, women protested that the limitations on their work as florists, barmaids, or potters—none of this especially strenuous—were designed to keep them from good-paying jobs, not to protect their health. Women could be "protected," that is, removed from higher-paying jobs—because they were not citizens.

Still other consequences for women sprang from the uneven rise of industry. In Japan, excess agricultural workers followed the call of government officials to make the state more prosperous. Officials striving to develop the nation's industry after 1868, called on families to release their young daughters to the patriotic duty of working in factories. There they lived in large unheated dormitories and survived on meager meals and lack of sleep. Though they might have worked under bad conditions in struggling rural areas, in these factories they were isolated and easily exploited, succumbing to disease and deprivation including emotional deprivation. These Japanese workers produced "Song of Living Corpses" with varying verses:

Excited I arrived at the gate,
Where I bowed to the gatekeeper;
I was taken immediately to the dormitory,
Where I bowed to the room supervisor.
I was taken to the infirmary,
Where I risked my life having a medical examination.
I was taken immediately to the cafeteria,
Where I asked what was for dinner.
I was told it was low-grade rice mixed with sand.
When I asked what the side dish was,
I was told there weren't even two slices of pickle to eat.
When I return to my room,
The supervisor finds all manner of fault with me,

FIGURE 7.3 *Mines in Scotland, 1848. The Industrial Revolution could also involve backbreaking work, as with these children and a woman hauling coal from mines. The parliamentary testimonies of women's and children's work in the mines led to protective legislation limiting hours and setting other conditions. Courtesy of Oxford Science Getty Images.*

And I feel like I'll never get on in this world.
When next I'm paid I'll trick the gatekeeper
And slip off to the station,
Board the first train
For my dear parents' home.
Both will cry when I tell them
How fate made me learn warping,
    Leaving nothing but skin and bones on my soul.[12]

Rural women in India, driven from the land by high taxes or by the closing down of home textile production because of cheap goods from England attracting consumers, traveled to cities in search of work. As Indian cities filled with single men and women, women often competed unsuccessfully for industrial jobs. Urban areas offered them an array of more poorly paying jobs: serving as runners and load-carriers for businesses; working in boarding houses and inns; doing laundry, barbering, and other maintenance tasks; and prostitution. Alone on city streets, they faced verbal abuse, robbery, kidnapping, rape, and even murder. After the middle of the nineteenth century, young girls beginning their working lives at the age of twelve or thirteen and even grown women were especially vulnerable. The same work alternatives and urban dangers characterized virtually the entire industrializing and urbanizing globe.

Female prostitution soared in cities worldwide because of this huge population shift and the economic exploitation of ordinary people during industrialization and ever-rising global commerce. Men and women alike, arrived in cities without family members and without any other support system. They found work, sometimes in industry, other times in sweatshops, and still other times in outwork done in their tiny dwellings. Even then, hard pressed or more likely completely destitute families in cities like Shanghai sometimes sold their girls to traffickers or to families wanting household slaves. When women found themselves strapped to the point of starvation they would go into casual prostitution to make ends meet, then move back to more "respectable work once jobs opened up." Because there was still a seasonality to many jobs including seamstressing, pulling silk, collecting eggs, and artificial flower-making, exchanging sex for food was not uncommon in the off-season.

The study of prostitution connected to urbanization, manufacturing, and the growing population of solitary individuals far from their roots in the countryside emerged alongside those focused on changes in family life and work patterns. Urbanization appeared to be altering familial and work stability, involving fleeting individual sexual satisfaction than a more anchored, supposedly traditional existence. Doctors and social critics worried about the transmission of disease and the rise in criminal elements benefitting from the arrival of solitary girls in cities. Governments passed legislation legalization the incarceration of prostitutes so that they could be regularly examined for venereal infections that might infect soldiers and fathers in turn. The idea was that disease originated in women, not in men. The study of prostitution and calls for overturning its regulation—and thus ending the incarceration of women who had committed no crime—ended. Women reformers were outraged that poor, vulnerable women both in the British metropole and in colonies such as India lost their civil rights, were assumed guilty, and imprisoned though innocent of any crime. In contrast, their male clients were always seen as blameless.

Conclusion

The Industrial Revolution, though it brought about explosive growth in productivity and new abundance for many people, when it came to women workers, traditional values persisted in the midst of change. They were paid less and not infrequently abused and harassed in the workplace; slave and indentured labor were the backbone of providing commodities for industrial societies. Yet the Industrial Revolution and the urbanization that followed produced opportunities, some of which women created with their sheer inventiveness and others that they simply seized. Conditions in early factories varied but they were usually harsh. However, factories offered a solution to the problems of underemployment in the countryside. Moving to cities provided new types of jobs and also harbored dangers, including that of high-risk sex work.

Women and men alike developed policies, projects, and new ideas for bettering the conditions caused by the rise of cities and the hazards of factory life. One early solution was providing charity to poor and underemployed women; a second was "protecting" them through legislation that removed them from so-called dangerous jobs or that monitored sex workers. A third solution was protest and political activism. Women's protest was often spontaneous, such as taking over streets to demonstrate for their cause or confiscating foods that were too high priced. Other women were better organized, signaling that women were preparing themselves to be more active citizens of industrial nations and to demand their equal rights.

Glossary

Caste	A system in which people's place in society (including occupation) is fixed, according to heredity and birth.
Mangs and majars	Low caste groups, though majars (mahars) are higher because of doing administrative tasks.

Notes

1 Betsey Guppy Chamberlain, "A New Society," New England Historical Society, http://www.newenglandhistoricalsociety.com/betsey-guppy-chamberlain-promotes-radical-notion-indians-people/ Accessed November 7, 2017.

2 Liliana Acero, *Textile Workers in Brazil and Argentina: A Study of the Interrelationships between Work and Households* (Tokyo: United Nations Press: 1991), 103.

3 Quoted in Barbara Alpern Engel, *Women in Russia, 1700–2000* (Cambridge: Cambridge University Press, 2004), 96–7.

4 See Joyce Chapman Lebra, "Women in an All-Male Industry: The Case of Sake Brewer Tatsu'uma Kiyo," in Gail Lee Bernstein, ed., *Recreating Japanese Women, 1600–1945* (Berkeley: University of California Press, 1991), 131–51.

5 Robert Edgar Conrad, *Children of God's Fire: A Documentary History of Black Slavery in Brazil* (Princeton, NJ: Princeton University Press, 1983), 363.

6 Mary Prince, *History of Mary Prince: A West Indian Slave* (London: F. Westley and A. H. Davis, 1831), 8–9. http://docsouth.unc.edu/neh/prince/prince.html.

7 Robert Edgar Conrad, *Children of God's Fire: A Documentary History of Black Slavery in Brazil* (Princeton, NJ: Princeton University Press, 1983), 133–4.

8 Quoted in Susie Porter, *Working Women in Mexico City: Public Discourse and Material Conditions, 1879–1931* (Tucson: University of Arizona Press, 2003), 3–4.

9 This account is from Silvia Marina Arrom, *Volunteering for a Cause: Gender, Faith, and Charity in Mexico from the Reform to the Revolution* (Albuquerque: University of New Mexico Press, 2016), especially chapters 3 and 4.

10 Letter of Savithribai Phule to Jotiba Phule, October 10, 1856, in Susie Tharu and K. Lalita, eds., *Women Writing India: 600 BC to the Early 20th Century*, 2 vols. (London: Pandora, 1993), 1:213.

11 Quoted in Emily Honig, "Burning Incense, Pledging Sisterhood: Communities of Women Workers in the Shanghai Cotton Mills, 1919–1949," *SIGNS*, 10:4 (Spring, 1985): 704.

12 "Song of the Living Corpses," in E. Patricia Tsurumi, "Serving in Japan's Industrial Army: Female Textiles Workers, 1868–1930," *Canadian Journal of History*, 23 (August 1988): 172–3.

Further Readings

Arrom, Silvia Marina. *Volunteering for a Cause: Gender, Faith, and Charity in Mexico from the Reform to the Revolution*. Albuquerque: University of New Mexico Press, 2016.

Bahadur, Gaiutra. *Coolie Woman: The Odyssey of Indenture*. Chicago, IL: University of Chicago Press, 2013.

Cowling, Camilla. *Conceiving Freedom: Women of Color, Gender, and the Abolition of Slavery in Havana and Rio de Janeiro*. Chapel Hill: University of North Carolina Press, 2013.

Gordon, Andrew. *Manufacturing Consumers: The Sewing Machine in Modern Japan*. Berkeley: University of California Press, 2011.

Hunefeldt, Christine. *Liberalism in the Bedroom: Quarreling Spouses in Nineteenth-Century Lima*. College Park, PA: Penn State University Press, 2000.

Lowe, Lisa. *The Intimacies of Four Continents*. Durham: Duke University Press, 2015.

Ranta, Judith A. *The Life and Writings of Betsey Chamberlain: Native American Mill Worker*. Boston, MA: Northeastern University Press, 2003.

Robb, George. *Ladies of the Ticker: Women and Wall Street from the Gilded Age to the Great Depression*. Urbana: University of Illinois Press, 2017.

Sen, Samita. *Women and Labour in Late Colonial India: The Bengal Jute Industry*. Cambridge: Cambridge University Press, 1999.

Tsurumi, E. Patricia. *Factory Girls: Women in the Thread Mills of Meiji Japan*. Princeton, NJ: Princeton University Press, 1992.

8

The Lure of Modernity,
1830–1914

In 1868, Japan threw off its old political organization dating from the twelfth century and brought back an emperor to rule with a constitution and to help steer the nation toward becoming more business-like and industrially focused. Becoming "modern" through a more knowledge-based administration would also help prevent Japan from succumbing to European and US imperialists, hungry for resources from territories beyond their shores. Opponents of a government focused on change resisted the transformation unfolding around them. Among these opponents were many women, who, dressed as men, provided supplies for the traditional male warriors (samurai), and even took up arms themselves. In the fortified castle of Aizu-Wakamatsu, they made cartridges for the men's guns and prepared rice balls and other food for those defending the castle. They dragged wounded fighters to the women's quarters so that they could be nursed away from the flying bullets. As the situation became dire, some took to the battlefield: "[W]e cut our hair so short that we looked like men," Mizushima Kikuko remembered of the "women's brigade" formed in Aizu. The men objected to women's going into battle. "Nonetheless, we managed to thrust [at the enemy] with our halberds," she recalled of making herself over into a soldier at age twenty. When one of her companions was killed by a bullet in the forehead, her sister "cut off her head, and wrapped it in her white silk headband" so that it could be ceremonially buried and wouldn't be disgraced by falling into enemy hands. Close to 200 women died in this failed skirmish against modernizing and nation-building forces, while dozens of others at this one site committed suicide in the face of defeat.[1]

Modernization may be said to include a scientific politics and the use of technology, such as the Japanese Meiji government planned. A modern nation was said to be a streamlined and centrally run unit, not a collection of disconnected small territories run by petty and locally minded rulers.

The building of railroads and steel plants, the rise of chemical industries, and the waging of war on diseases through medicine are all part of the belief in modernization through knowledge, especially of technology and the social sciences. To progress, such innovations needed an efficient and unified government that would allow products to flow, build infrastructure to accommodate trade, and advance ideas, including those of science, so that they might have their greatest impact. The word modernization is also used as a slogan, with some nations calling themselves "modern" compared to other peoples who were supposedly "backward" or "traditional" in their culture. Women's ways of life, even women themselves, often fell into the category of the backward or traditional. Reformers saw family rule in the form of aristocratic privilege in government and the dominance of a single family in an inherited, absolute monarchy as backward. Women themselves stood on both sides of the politics of modernization.

Leaders in the West and imperial reformers around the world often came to equate national modernization with the rule of law and unity of spirit among peoples living within a nation-state's borders. Reforming individuals bonded together to create the modern nation, which stood as the opposite of an authoritarian emperor or a small-time king or chieftain—a sign of backwardness. The content of political backwardness was thus that a state was run according to the will of a single individual of "royal" descent or by the command of religious authorities who could rule subjects as they wished. Some of those wanting to reform society and make it more modern criticized men's power over women in the family as similar to such absolute rule. Their idea was that women, like men, needed to develop as individuals to be self-regulating and rational, even participating in determining the course of the nation-state. Others, sometimes women themselves, disagreed.

The creation of the nation was usually a struggle, but one in which many women took part. Behind the "modernizing" inclusiveness of a nation's social order were the marks of oppression within national and, more broadly, global bounds. Many were excluded from the nation, moved to the margins as "exceptions" to the inclusivity of nation-building rhetoric expressed by both revolutionaries. People of different ethnicities and races were seen as exceptions to inclusivity, as were women whose relationship to the nation was seen as "different" and also "naturally" inferior given their feminine bodily form and biological functioning. All of these—women, ethnic and racial others, members of different religions, the poor—all needed to be commanded, whether in the family or in the nation instead of being rights-bearing citizens.

Modernization was thus theoretically for the many but also exclusive. The arts, cultural criticism, and feminist thought brought these issues to the public, showing citizens the nation-state's seamier side especially in terms of race and gender. Women opponents to the nation-state included those like the devoted samurai women who wanted conditions to remain as they had always been. Other activists demanded that the nation-state extend the benefits of political modernity to them and the generally excluded as well as to men. To make that happen, women worked to become full-fledged citizens with equal, individual rights. They also became theorists, writers, and artists concerned with all issues of modernity. The debate and activism have continued down to the present.

The Nation and Modernizing Masculinity

Gender figured in the creation and representation of nations—from France and the United States to Japan, Latin American states, and beyond, as the nation became an increasingly dominant form and as citizenship became the mark of belonging. Nations, whether with constitutional monarchies, representative democracies, or other republican forms of government, were based on the notion of citizen participation and consent. A nation-state of unified citizens replaced the kingdom in which a monarch's will dominated a cluster of subjects. In monarchies, all privileges flowed from that monarch—in most instances a king. When a male heir was lacking, in many countries a queen might serve as a replacement without changing the preference for men. In its early formation during the eighteenth and nineteenth centuries, the nation, as opposed to a kingdom, was a kind of fraternity of equal men, with women excluded from many rights, even those they had once possessed. These citizens' rights included political representation, the ownership of property, and the right to vote. Jointly, usually through representatives, men ruled. Rights and rulership for this fraternity of men and their equality as citizens were part of a reworking of masculinity politically, though not a reduction in their power. The "modern" nation-state thus combined old and new: in the household a man commanded his subjects as individual monarchs had once done. In traditionally run kingdoms elite, noble women might own wealth and enjoy high status. In contrast, each man as a citizen in the newly devised nation-state was part of a community of consenting male individuals all endowed with equal political, economic, and social rights, including expansive rights over women.

The new institution of the nation demanded that masculinity reject an older chivalric and hierarchical ideal of a few privileged fighters loyal to a lord, with a higher level of military aristocrats serving the topmost person in a dynasty—a king or an emperor. In Japan, the reformer Sakamoto Ryoma (1836–1867) penned this indictment of the old *daimyo* elite: "The great majority of the daimyo are generally persons who have been born and nurtured in the seclusion of the women's apartments; who have been cherished as tenderly as if they were delicate ornaments of jewels or pearls; . . . never having mastered the details of business, they feel no sense of responsibility in approaching affairs of state."[2] This critique of a traditional arrangement based on knightly loyalty to a superior equates it with femininity, charging that the old daimyo and samurai elites lacked the modern and manly spirit of business, individual enterprise, and military professionalism. The feminist Mary Wollstonecraft decades earlier had also equated the nobility or aristocracy with the decorative ways of women. Unlike the new male citizen, aristocrats were simply not manly.

The male citizen of the nation was potentially an equal member in the new citizen-based army. This army lacked the traditional hierarchy in which the highest rank went automatically to high-born aristocrats and into which recruits from prisons and poor or unprotected rural areas were coerced to serve by royal officials. As modern nations took shape, many aristocrats, whether in Japan or France, resisted the leveling in which all men might serve and advance in armies and navies as had Napoleon during the French Revolution. Many samurai, strongly supported by women as in Aizu, rose up against the new constitutional monarchy established in Japan in 1868 as it dissolved the samurai order and instituted a society of opportunity based on individual deeds not on privileges of birth. Soon the samurai were replaced with a conscript citizen-army derived from the German model—an army that crushed samurai outbursts, leading some samurai to adapt by becoming businessmen and government officials. Japanese modernizers fostered education, even sending men and eventually a few women to other countries to experience modernity in the form of individual development—whether in terms of an active mind or active engagement with modern science and business. These armies were bands of brothers serving their nation. A muscular soldier-citizen was coming to the fore as the guardian of propertyless and weak women and children worldwide.

Full of paradoxes, the new nation grew up around the band of equal brother-citizens, and also heterosexual ones with female subordinates in their households. Even though a nation might be represented on coins, for example, by a strong woman such as "Liberty" in the case of the United States or "Marianne" in the case of France or the goddess Amaterasu from whom the emperor in the new Japanese nation was descended, only strong and modern citizen-soldiers were the proper leaders who could defend the weak and inferior family members. Another paradox in Japan was that poor men and women alike were enlisted for the most menial tasks in the name of national strengthening. Besides poor rural women being driven into factories, others from rural areas agreed to become prostitutes in far off, growing cities such as Singapore. Paid more than factory workers, these young women were told that by undertaking foreign sex work they would "serve the emperor and their country, . . . pay off their debts, and . . . become decent citizens."[3] Japanese and other men were also encouraged to make money for the nation by traveling to these same growing cities for work. The funds they earned could then be sent back home. In this scheme, then, the exploitation of prostitutes and male migrants was a paired necessity for Japanese modernization.

In the early twentieth century, other women served as still different tools in the achievement of national modernity. In the Qajar state of Iran/Persia, reformers pointed to the situation of women to arouse support for the creation of a modern nation state. In reformers' eyes, ruling elites were tied to one another through networks of privilege, influence, loyalty, bribes, and corruption with little concern for the public good. Iran, late in the nineteenth century, had been losing its territorial autonomy to Russia on the north and Britain to the southeast, while Turkemen and other tribes constantly crossed borders to get their share of people to advance their trade in slaves and their capture of Persian people for their own households. As the peasantry early in the twentieth century suddenly suffered from the arrival of millions of locusts that destroyed crops, they were unable to pay their taxes. Instead of lightening up on the tax burden, local elites at the behest of the monarchy told them to sell their daughters and wives to the Turkemen traders.

In 1905, a large number—exactly how many is unknown, though some estimated the amount as several thousand—of girls and women were sold from the town of Quchan. As modernizing reformers caught wind of these events, the sale of girls—the "daughters of Quchan"—became a cause of shame that discredited the older Qajar regime. Ballads, poems, drawings, drama, and gossip about the "daughters of Quchan" traveled the country, providing ammunition for reformers against the "backward," ineffective leadership and ultimately leading to a revolution that brought in a constitutional government of modernizing men.

Nation-builders accused rival societies or those it wanted to conquer of being backward and standing in the way of progress—as had reformers in Iran. Communities or states where women had power were especially susceptible to being overpowered by ambitious nations, the justification being that they represented roadblocks to progress. For example, citizens of the young United States were as eager as other nation-building imperialists to take over the resources of local peoples—in this case the land of Native Americans. By the early nineteenth century, some Native Americans were settled farmers, had converted to Christianity, and were well-educated, but this made no difference to North Americans who often accused these groups in which women owned the land and were politically influential as not being forward thinking. The propaganda went that such prosperous Native Americans were "savage." As such their land should be taken for more progress-oriented male settlers.

In 1818, a council of *Cherokee* women, who possessed land for domestic farming and their other enterprises and who were the actual heads of household, confronted the threat of dispossession. They were empowered because they had more rights and political influence within their communities than did white women in the new United States. "We have heard with painful feelings that the bounds of the land we now possess are to be drawn into very narrow limits," they declared. "The land was given to us by the Great Spirit above as our common right, to raise our children upon, and to make support or our rising generations." In support of their claim, they raised the legal concepts of first settlement and of possession as cementing their rights to property, begging "the head men and warriors, to hold out to the last in support of our common rights, as the Cherokee nation have been the first settlers of this land; we therefore claim the right of the soil." They raised still other issues: "Our Father the President advised us to become farmers, to manufacture our own clothes, and to have our children instructed. To this advice we have attended in every thing as far as we were able." Moreover, the women continued, they feared that being moved thousands of miles that they would become "savage" again, losing the "enlightened" mindset that they are acquired. They had learned the gospel, followed the advice of missionaries, and even become Christians. Finally, these council leaders accused the white men who had married into the tribe of betraying their families by making deals to hand over Native American farms and other lands. These very men then agreed to have their communities emigrate. "These ought to be our truest friends but prove our worst enemies. They seem only to be concerned how to increase their own riches, but do not care what becomes of our Nation, not even of their own wives and children."[4] Early on, these women leaders had understood the "brotherhood" or male bonding of nation-building, including men's privilege when it came to ownership of property and other wealth. In 1835, the US government drove tens of thousands of Cherokees from Georgia to the other side of the Mississippi, so that whites could prosper instead.

The Nation and Women's Modernity

As the dispossession of Native Americans was wrecking individual lives and entire communities in the name of the US nation, Muhammad Ali (1769–1849), an early nation-builder in Egypt and leader in driving Napoleon from his attempted takeover of Egypt in 1799, set out to provide better institutions. He energized economic activity by taking control of Egyptian land and trade and using forced labor to work both. In a more "modern" vein, he set up scientifically oriented medical and other sanitary services. Another project was the education of women, for which he encouraged schools for girls and the opportunity for higher education after that. One reformer aided him by finding words of the Prophet endorsing women's intellectual growth and publishing a book on the subject. Muhammad Ali encouraged schools for midwives and the development of nursing, ultimately aiming for the training of women as doctors to tend to female patients and their children. Although Egyptian girls continued to have schooling down through the century, opposition arose from religious leaders who gave other interpretations of Islamic thought forbidding such instruction. When the British took Egypt over in 1882, education for girls and women continued to be a priority. By 1913, girls constituted 13 percent of the student body in state-sponsored schools, which is not to mention those attending private religious and secular ones. Still, hierarchy remained, enmeshed in a debate over whether women should be modernized inhabitants of the country or traditional ones.

In the 1850s, a Chinese experiment in changing women's lives arose in the Taiping movement. To bring about a "Heavenly Kingdom of Great Peace" the movement inflicted vast destruction in many parts of the Qing Empire. It especially promised improvement in women's condition. In 1851, its leader Hong Xiuquan, who believed himself to be the brother of Jesus, announced that he was king of the Heavenly Kingdom. Hong had spent years in study for exams that would allow him to become a government official but failed them several times. After taking over some of the richest areas of China with his followers, he set up headquarters in Nanjing. At first he insisted that those he conquered remain celibate, while he and his leading advisors kept large retinues of women for sex. Meeting resistance, Hong Xiuquan devised a wide-ranging program of equality for women, beginning with an end to foot-binding but also opening a range of positions to women that included soldiering. They were also promised access to property of their own. These programs attracted some women because of the refreshing, forward-looking improvements they seemed to offer.

Hong came from the Hakka ethnic group within China—a poor and much abused people. Hakka women did not bind their feet nor were they barred from working outside the home. Instead, they farmed alongside male family members or undertook urban jobs even in construction. These wider opportunities of Hakka women Hong now offered to all women under Taiping control, even forcing new ways of life on them. His followers threatened those who refused to unbind their feet with execution and most often the leadership demanded that women work in menial jobs. Good jobs, although promised, usually went to men, while Taiping leadership was virtually all male.

The Taiping Rebellion brought chaos and violence. The devastating civil war killed some 60 million people, while under the Taiping most women's safety was imperiled because of sexual and other violence that became increasingly common. Women committed suicide to avoid rape and other physical harm; in the general deprivation and turmoil the Taiping inflicted on the country, prostitution became a major means of support. For women, charged with provisioning their families often in the absence of husbands, conditions of everyday life were dire. Add to that, rumors of coming invasions kept everyone fearful: "With my feeble constitution I am definitely useless./ Sad feelings engulf me even more," Qing poet Wang Qingdi wrote of the uprising in 1856. This 28-year-old mother understood the wider world from her constant flights to safety: "Signal fires startle me. They are signs of our land's disorder./ Now I know the inconstant ways of the world." The Taiping had challenged the Confucian system of prescribed gender and other relations but ended up heightening male dominance in its deeds. The cost was catastrophic both in terms of the individual and the Qing Empire as a whole even as the question of fixing gender hierarchy became a political issue. Ironically perhaps, it was the Empress Cixi who enlisted the European military to help modernize the Chinese army (though not fight in its place) sufficiently to defeat the Taiping.

The Taiping promised women's modernity for China but failed to deliver much except vast destruction and loss of life. In contrast, the US Civil War of 1861–5 initially aimed only at preserving national unity. Before the war, women such as escaped slave Harriet Jacobs (Linda Brent, 1813–1897) and middle-class white author Harriet Beecher Stowe (1811–1896) had broadcast the cruelties of slavery, including on women and the family. Harriet Jacobs did so from her own horrific experience of rape and her seven years of hiding to escape her master. The shocking account in Stowe's *Uncle Tom's Cabin* joined Jacobs's *Incidents in the Life of a Slave Girl* in revealing a world of terror far different from enlightened rule that modernity was supposed to entail. Alongside the publication of these two books visions of modernity for women, especially their rights to freedom and equality, were already brewing in the activism of abolitionists and reformers such as Harriet Tubman, Elizabeth Cady Stanton, Susan B. Anthony, Sojourner Truth, Ernestine Rose, Margaret Fuller, and others. They pushed the cause of abolition as war erupted in 1861 with the presidency of Abraham Lincoln.

Women participated in the US Civil War as they had participated in others, provisioning units of the armies from their home towns, doing laundry, and tending wounds. Notoriously, as in most wars at the time, they stepped in when a wounded soldier's rifle became available or they took up male garb and became full-time fighters. There were other forms of participation: Harriet Tubman (1822–1913), a major figure in the underground railway that helped slaves escape their masters, returned to the US South to serve as a spy for the North and to continue her work freeing slaves. Her reconnaissance forays made possible the escape of some 800 slaves in the Combahee River area of South Carolina. Tubman's dangerous work, like that of hundreds of other women, made possible the re-unification of the United States and ended up modernizing it by ending the Atlantic plantation system based on slave labor. It gave African American and other slaves their freedom, but it did not give these women or any women the full rights of citizenship.

When in 1868, as black men were gaining the right to vote in the United States, Japan became an industrial and more constitutionally based state despite having an emperor. To modernize, government ideology promoted women as being "good wives, wise mothers." To bring children to readiness for modern citizenship, leaders felt that education was necessary not just for citizenship but to understand and perform in an advancing economy. Mothers would provide the first lessons in that citizenship and be responsible for developing offspring into striving adults but also stable ones—something not provided for in liberal theories of capitalist economies in the nineteenth century but implied in the attention to domesticity. For these reasons, leaders in many parts of the world came to favor the education of women

FIGURE 8.1 *Drawing of Harriet Tubman as soldier and spy. After her escape from slavery in 1849, Harriet Tubman spent her heroic, if notorious, life helping others to escape from captivity. During the US Civil War she armed herself as a soldier and through her work as a spy directed Union soldiers in the Combahee River Raid that freed an additional 800 slaves. Courtesy of Hulton Archive / Stringer Getty Images.*

who would have to teach children and be companionate partners to men. They were to learn household skills and often religion. Utako Shimoda (1854–1936) taught Chinese exchange students and Japanese women how to be modern homemakers but her curriculum went beyond that. Born into a samurai family, she traveled to Europe and became committed to higher education for women, founding three schools for them, one of which was Jissen Women's University. Like other reformers Utako Shimoda also advocated physical education for women—breaking with the ideology of women's frailty and daintiness. She herself was an expert in judo. More than one woman across the globe was radicalized by book learning: Utako Shimoda's Chinese pupil Qiu Jin became an outspoken revolutionary.

Reforming Women

Aside from bringing women and men to awareness of the nation and to provide them with skills for a gendered modern life, reformers sponsored a range of programs that would eliminate the worst abuses of the past and bring other forms of modernity besides education to women in India, Russia, the United States, Great Britain, and elsewhere across the globe as part of sharing the nation's bounty, especially its "civilization." Like the attribute of being "modern," being "civilized" was one claimed by strong nations. Education alone was not enough. It was intermingled with erasing the old ways. Local reformers in India, for example, saw practices such as child marriage, widow-burning, and women's seclusion as practices that blocked the progress of their society. Early in the nineteenth century Indian men began a campaign against child marriage, in which girls just entering puberty and lacking any schooling were taken away from their parents, married to a stranger, and forced to take up in all their ignorance and inexperience the chores of running a household and caring for an extended family. Imperialists and local reformers saw child marriage as an "uncivilized" practice and relic of barbarism.

Ideas for reform rolled from the pens of critics such as Japanese journalist Fukuzawa Yukichi (1835–1901). Dressing in Western clothing like other Japanese men and advancing programs for national power, he supported changes in the gender order that had earlier appeared in the Taiping program and in theories that were in the wind globally. Like the Taiping, he advocated gender equality in all areas of life and for women to have rights to divorce and property ownership. He wanted prostitution and the system of concubinage abolished, but this could only occur with creation of good jobs for women and the development of their skills through education. Others took the Taiping movement as a wake-up call by pointing to the decadence of the Qing state and of women's situation more specifically— conditions making for weakness that many linked. For Liang Qichao (1873–1929), China's defeat by the British in a series of wars over opium resulted from the poor education of women and their lack of access to good jobs. Additionally, women's health weakened the empire overall and added to its fragility. Focusing on the need for women's advancement, many male modernizers were showcasing modern ideas, not practicing them: Fukusawa, for example, forced his daughters to marry the men he chose for them.

Amidst such debates where both men and women urged respect for women's talents and capacities, a global event was taking place when in

1879 Norwegian playwright Henrik Ibsen produced his play "A Doll's House." The story features a typical middle-class housewife, Nora, who forges her father's name on a bank loan so that her desperately ill husband can be cured by a stay in Italy. Back in good health, the husband finds out about the forgery and loan, which his wife has been paying off. He scorns her, saying that he will only continue their marriage as a formality to keep up appearances so much has she ruined family honor. Soon, the holder of the forged loan document destroys it, making the husband happy and eager to restore the marital relationship. Nora will have none of it. At this point she decides that the relationship is over and that she needs to develop herself as an individual. Nora walks out of the house, leaving both husband and children behind.

"A Doll's House," shocking enough in Europe where many theaters demanded that the ending be changed, traveled the world to both controversy and acclaim. It played in Egypt, Japan, China, Australia, and the United States, to name a few locales. In each venue it caused a scandal but also revolt among both women and men. As the play's influence was unfolding, Japanese activist Kishida Toshiko (1863–1901) and other women who advocated rights went public. Kishida took to the podium, traveling the country picking up on the message of improvement of women's condition as pivotal to nation-building. For her, gender hierarchy in which women were represented as polluting and disruptive of order infected both official and popular culture. The other side to such degradation was the privileging of men who were seen as worthy and important; as such they deserved better treatment than women did. Women activists wanted an end to it.

Other women joined in, though in different ways. Inspired by "A Doll's House," five Japanese women university graduates founded the Bluestocking Club and took to daring behavior such as drinking liquors in public. In 1911, they also started the journal *Seito*, with Raicho Hiratsuka opening the first issue with the words "In the beginning woman was the sun." The periodical went on to publish essays about sexuality and other taboo subjects. Citing national security and the needs of a modernizing economy, in 1890, the Japanese government had made it illegal for women to be public orators. Now it invoked the cause of national well-being to censor issue after issue of *Seito*. Nonetheless, reform-minded Japanese women were soon promoting contraception and women's control of fertility as essential to modernity.

Liberating the Body, Modernizing the Household

The call for change targeted not just public causes but the well-being of the body and the household. There were places such as Vietnam where women's bodies were already relatively unconstrained, operating in slim garments that allowed for easy movement. Saris in South Asia, or wrapped garments in Africa and Indonesia were also more accommodating than various garments in the West or in China, for example. Across the Western Hemisphere, long skirts and petticoats offered protection from the cold in northern climates but the ubiquitous corsets also worn in Europe were injurious to health. The corsets broke bones and injured internal organs while voluminous long skirts dragged around the ground picking up dirt, excrement, and other health-threatening material. Long, infrequently washed hair common in most countries was also a site for breeding germs and vermin. In China, bound feet limited women's movements, broke bones, and served up a range of health hazards. Different societies around the world began to look at male/male sex and at the sexual initiation of boys by older men with disdain, even outrage and disgust.

Liberating the body was actually a project involving global exchange of customs, first among the middle classes and some workers. For example, the anti-foot-binding movement in China looked to the bodily freedom of women's feet experienced in other cultures. As anti-foot-binding societies sprang up and took action, advocates signed pledges not to bind the feet of their daughters. Christian missionaries also encouraged these activities, though not women's overall equality. Along the same lines, Western women abandoned their corsets to have the upper body freedom enjoyed by Asians and Africans. Dress-reform became part of organized feminist movements. In some cases, they slowly adopted the loose-fitting trousers of Chinese, Burmese, Vietnamese, and Ottoman women, while their skirts and dresses were progressively less voluminous and became shorter. Hairstyles also evolved, with women in the United States, for example, first adopting hair puffed up around a rat to surround the face; then the short hair styles of modern girls eventually became almost universal; that is, fashionable women from Africa to Brazil to Britain and the Netherlands began experimenting widely as they also came to do with make-up. The chemical industry facilitated the introduction of the permanent wave that made hair curly or wavy like that of African women, another sign of the globalization of women.

Developing the modern household became a century-long project infusing the care of families, the provisioning of kitchens, relationships among spouses, and manners at home. With the scientific discovery of bacteria, viruses, fungi, and health hazards, sanitation took on new urgency, beginning with some upper- and middle-class housewives, filtering down through education, and advancing the rise of home economics. This was never a uniform process, and some took such knowledge to extremes, but the importance of domestic sanitary conditions rose alongside the drive to be modern. Medical knowledge traveled the globe, while the discovery of vitamins also added to the modern tasks of women who organized subsistence in the household. The toolkit of the mother, spouse, or housekeeper was supposed to be well-stocked with knowledge of germs and vitamins to

FIGURE 8.2 *Japanese empress Haruko c. 1890. To escape being colonized, Japan aimed to become "modern" like Western imperial nations. A special focus was on women, shown by the Western dress and overall look of the Japanese empress. Still, Western women were imitating Japanese and other East Asian women by eliminating their corsets and voluminous skirts. Courtesy of Hulton Deutsch Getty Images.*

promote well-being and restore health in case of illness. Modernization of family health was to serve the nation just as education would.

Modern conceptions of time started shaping family members' mindset and behavior. Although task-oriented around cooking a meal and doing household chores, those in a modern family had suddenly to worry more about observing time. This time-orientation involved arranging and observing schedules for getting to school and work on time, having meals on time, and clothing and other needs ready in time. As the empire modernized, women in Ottoman cities felt the pressure of the clock. For one thing, industrial and bureaucratized men insisted on efficiency, often placing their families on a time regimen. Education emphasized habits of modern techniques such as getting assignments in "on time." The intersection of on-timeness or punctuality with a more traditional sense of time often made everyday life contentious, even wrenching as family members inhabited different realms of time.

Muslim author Altaf Husain, writing in northern India, produced works that aimed to show that even secluded in the home, women needed to be modern. In fact, "modern" or "up-to-date" was the meaning of "Hali"—his pen name. Hali felt that uninstructed women polluted domestic life and sociability when they got together. Their conversation consisted mostly of complaints and negativity. "In contrast, the educated woman immersed in the Qu'ran and classical literature will have a diplomatic outlook on life and will aim for understanding and reason. These will help her see that the many household superstitions about the evil eye and folk explanations for illness or accidents lack any basis in reason. Additionally the instructed woman will keep a clean, healthy household and one that is financially well-run—all of these modern attitudes and practices leading to the well-being of her immediate and extended family."[5]

"A Doll's House" had put the focus of reform squarely on the relationship of the husband and wife—that is, on the conjugal couple. Globally, the abolition of slavery and increasing publicity to citizens' rights as part of modernity continued the reduction in the size of some households. In Egypt, an autonomous region of the Ottoman Empire but one dominated by Britain, changes unfolded around the structure of the household and women's role, in part to challenge the British and to assert Egypt's difference from Ottoman ways. As the household became more streamlined with the gradual elimination of slaves and the multiethnic staff, including concubines, reformers highlighted a more intimate household centered on a conjugal couple that was Egyptian—and not distracted from attention to one another by outsiders within its walls. Although "Egyptian" did not necessarily exclude other ethnicities, in this rising household configuration the wife/mother gained a cultural role, preparing her children to be instructed Egyptians and herself to be instructed so that she could exercise maternal leadership. As the modernizing nation began to emerge despite foreign domination, Egyptian cultural leaders pointed to great women of the ancient past who served as rulers, leading scientists, high priestesses, merchants, and other active professionals. Leading women nationalists asserted their place as "Mothers of the Nation." Motherhood—once seen as comprising a simple act of breeding—gained status or at least increased verbiage as part of modernization.

Prostitution, even as it might be promoted by governments, military personnel, industrialists, and urban developers albeit quietly, also fell victim to paradoxical concerns for modernity and health because of the unchecked prevalence of sexually transmitted diseases in the population—a situation that hindered the development of the nuclear couple. For one thing, women were often kept ignorant of the cause of any genital issues they might have. Additionally, with the nation's strength and power a major concern, the health of men came into focus. The military thus needed protection. Both national and imperial governments targeted prostitutes as the main source of venereal diseases, and with this in mind passed legislation calling for their regulation. With the rise of policing, medical doctors would examine ever more women in houses of prostitution, known street-walkers, and even women alone on city streets and incarcerate them. Meanwhile, concern for men's status led to a wife rarely being informed if her husband had a sexually transmitted disease.

With attention focused on women in nation-building, their appearance in public life was used to indicate either chaos or an ordered, integrated society. In South Asia, middle-class reformers and public officials focused on Indian temple women and other women performers in public as signs of backwardness in the late nineteenth century. Temple dancers, who had performed sacred rituals with honor for more than a millennium, were said to represent the divine. Those local people influenced by the British, however, now called them prostitutes, most likely because many performers in Britain itself took wealthy married men as their sexual partners. (In 1988, temple dancing was declared illegal in India.) Eager to establish their credentials as "modern," local reformers tried to rid the public world of women performers, driving them into the seclusion of the household so that their region could be up-to-date and thus worthy of self-rule instead of British domination.

Meanwhile, African American women had organized themselves to fight the historic but still real effects of their own oppression, including rape. In 1896, several of their organizations formed the National Association of Colored Women (NACW), which in 1904 became the National Association of Colored Women's Clubs (NACWC). As co-founder, the highly educated Josephine St. Pierre Ruffin (1842–1924) used her wealth in supporting black organizations, including the National Association for the Advancement of Colored People (NAACP) in 1910. Middle-class women in cities found solidarity in working for their churches and living spiritually rich lives shared with their neighbors. They organized book clubs and study groups and became active in charity work—all of this aiming at emotional and intellectual as well as household health. Simultaneously, they were carving out a modern place in public for themselves.

Much of their outreach aimed to raise the level of ordinary African American women's lives. It especially sought to combat the stereotypes created by whites that African American women were sluts and whorish in their everyday lives—a characterization used until the present day to paper over white men's continuing sexual violence against black women through blaming the victim. As with white women, a sense of class superiority and responsibility fueled their social attitudes and their efforts to make lower-class women "respectable" but as a way of "lifting" the race. Mary Church

Terrell, founding and longtime president of the NACW, was one who used the expression "lifting as we climb." In so doing, she, like middle-class activists around the world, articulated the hierarchy at work among women in their drive for rights and overall household wellness.

Professions and Other New Jobs for Women

Sentimental images of the maternal and obedient, if instructed wife vied with the single, "new women" who served as nurses, missionaries, service and other workers. As nations came to compete with one another, their skills were in fact needed to bolster efficiency and well-being. Except for Western societies at the middle of the nineteenth century, women globally held an array of responsible public positions. Where societies were segregated according to gender, they could still practice law and medicine in order to attend to women's legal and health-care needs. Royal palaces and the segregated homes of the very wealthy employed women doctors, accountants and bookkeepers, personal secretaries, household managers, and a variety of attendants for bodily needs as they had centuries earlier. In other societies, middle-class women were taking a wider range of jobs outside the home.

By the end of the nineteenth century, women in Western societies were serving as nurses and other health-care professionals, including the few who joined the ranks of doctors. Several active women popularized health care and medicine as realms for women's professional activity, notably through their activity in wartime. In 1855, Mary Seacole (1805–1881), daughter of a free black Jamaican woman and a Scottish army officer, arrived in the Crimea where the British, French, and Ottomans were fighting the Russian Empire. Seacole had learned about medicine from her mother and from doctors who passed through Kingston and stayed at the family hotel. In addition to a gift for healing, Mrs. Seacole (as she was always called) had a passion for travel, which she supported by tending other travelers, especially during an outbreak of cholera in Panama. When the Crimean War erupted in 1853, she wanted—like Florence Nightingale—to be at the battlefront. Once there, Mrs. Seacole tended to desperately ill soldiers for whom armies offered little organized medical care.

What allowed these pioneering nurses a place was the lack of concern for medical care and supplies of food by armies in those days. As Mary Seacole noted, "[Sick soldiers] could and did get at my store sick-comforts and nourishing food, which the heads of the medical staff would sometimes find it difficult to procure." Like many women, she had health-care experience: "I was very familiar with the diseases which they suffered most from and successful in their treatment (I say this in no spirit of vanity), were quite sufficient to account for the numbers who came daily to the British Hotel for medical treatment," she wrote in her autobiography. Seacole also discerned the emotional side to recovery and again was part of a movement toward women's hospital philanthropy, which a century earlier would have been more or less unthinkable. "That the officers were glad of me as a doctress and nurse may be easily understood. When a poor fellow lay sickening in his cheerless hut and sent down to me, he knew very well that I should not ride up in answer to his message empty-handed. And although I did not hesitate to charge him with the value of the necessaries I took him, still he was thankful enough to be able to *purchase* them. When we lie ill at home surrounded with comfort, we never think of feeling any special gratitude for the sick-room delicacies which we accept as a consequence of our illness; but the poor officer lying ill and weary in his crazy hut, dependent for the merest necessaries of existence upon a clumsy, ignorant soldier-cook, who would almost prefer eating his meat raw to having the troubles of cooking it (our English soldiers are bad campaigners), often finds his greatest troubles in the want of those little delicacies with which a weak stomach must be humoured into retaining nourishment."[6]

Mrs. Seacole's nursing during the war was matched in Russia during the same conflict and in Britain where the celebrated reformer Florence Nightingale began taking groups of women to nurse in the Crimea as well. She also produced statistical studies of the sanitation and other supply needs of armies. Nursing, however, became her major claim to fame, as she helped convert it—again through the publicity given to her work in Crimea—from a job for the lowest possible class of women, even prostitutes, to one for educated women from "respectable" families. A few years later, Clara Barton helped spearhead similar services during the US Civil War, ultimately founding the American branch of the Red Cross—a philanthropic organization rapidly becoming transnational and attracting women volunteers and professionals like Barton herself. Still, these efforts marked a course in which women would be channeled into lower-paid ranks of health-care professionals and discouraged from practicing medicine and other healing.

The struggle in the West for women to become doctors was difficult and only a few women before the First World War succeeded. Medicine was becoming professionalized in the nineteenth century, with the state granting doctors the power to determine who could practice. The attack on women's access to healing came in several ways: midwives and other caregivers were increasingly driven out, while women university graduates were not admitted to professional training. Thus a hierarchy of practitioners arose, with men only allowed into training as highly paid experts and women confined to more lowly, though crucially important, "helping" roles. Still, a few women trained in the sciences gained access through determined struggle: Elizabeth Blackwell in the United States, Elizabeth Garrett Anderson in Great Britain, and Maria Montessori in Italy. Anandi Gopal Joshi, the first Indian woman to gain a medical degree in the United States, set up an obstetrics practice but died of tuberculosis at age twenty-two.

Like others entering the field Joshi helped what many thought was a population ill-served by male doctors—that is, women. In 1879, Aletta Jacobs became the first woman in the Netherlands to earn her doctorate in medicine. Like Joshi, she surmounted hurdles to do so, including having to gain permission from the Dutch minister of education to attend high school, because at the time girls were forbidden by law to do so. Jacobs focused her medical skills on poor women and prostitutes, offering wellness education and setting up clinics for the working class. In this effort she recognized the need for birth control among working women whose multiple pregnancies and harsh working conditions undermined their health. In her clinics, she improved and thus widely advanced the use of the diaphragm, invented around 1880 by a male doctor. Her work led diaphragms to be known as "Dutch caps."

The rise of women journalists in the Middle East, Europe, India, and the United States helped in this production of global culture, although male journalists also became advocates for women's modernization and even for their entry into the professions. Women journalists had long existed but their reach expanded in the late nineteenth century as literacy rates rose in many parts of the world and as the technology for inexpensive print media developed. This generation popularized the development of clothing reform, household modernization, and the professionalization of women through their journalism. Often they had access to political leaders, again increasing women's access to information. In some societies they started newspapers of their own, especially advocating for women's rights. Also doing work for newspapers, they became photographers, and as the condition of women sold papers, they described lurid scenes of oppression and even photographed them. Indian, Syrian, and Egyptian women journalists amplified the discussion of rights alongside some reform-minded men, but they added to their commentary their region's right to independence, notably from the British and French. The feminist press reached a peak of first-wave development around the world with many publications such as the Japanese feminist periodical *Seito* and the French *La Fronde*. The latter publication would only employ women printers.

As literacy improved, other service or white-collar occupations opened to women. They flocked to work as telephone and telegraph operators, sales clerks, office workers, and teachers. Their low pay allowed some of these new, experimental technologies to establish themselves and for national bureaucracies to build efficient staffs at low cost. A modern mentality took hold, competing with a familial task-oriented one as women worked on an industrial schedule and even punched into time-clocks. Moreover, they had to display the modern skills of reading, writing, and arithmetic. Indeed these "clean" jobs could pay less not just because of the wage gap but also because so many women from the educated classes competed with one another for jobs. As with Florence Nightingale, statistical work and jobs in social welfare took shape. Women inspected factories for compliance with protective legislation and investigated conditions of outwork for those performing jobs at home, often intruding on families to the point of taking their children away on health and other grounds.

While opportunities arose for some women, for others they declined. The use of women in domestic jobs rose, as some well-educated women with children took jobs in the professions. More prevalent was the job of child-nursemaid or nanny or ayah who cared for the children in an upper-class family or in a middle-class, professional one where the mother worked. Women flocked to domestic jobs because, as in India or Europe, for example, they were pushed out of some industries by protective legislation or by displaced male artisans taking factory jobs. The emphasis on childhood education and well-being as important to national modernization additionally enhanced the importance of the ayah or nursemaid to the well-off middle classes who came to believe children needed constant attention to build character. Sexual harassment and abuse continued to be regular features of these and almost all jobs held by women, determining whether one would advance in the position, earn a good salary, or even keep the job in the first place.

Women in great numbers also wrote histories, novels, and theoretical works expressing the complexity of social and political change. Although constantly active in public, albeit in a wide variety of ways, women joined in the creation of secular, even political organizations that can be interpreted as national. In Britain, they provided a range of support services for the Conservative and Liberal parties. Though forbidden to participate in political meetings in France, in fact they did so. In 1889, ten women were delegates to the India National Congress. One of those delegates, Pandita Ramabai (1858–1922), founded orphanages and schools for girls across the subcontinent and also traveled to Britain as daring political acts.

In the first decades of the century, Latin American women's groups met to promote women's voting rights, their access to good jobs, and their welfare in general. These feminists were especially concerned about the well-being of children, particularly the "warehousing" of poor, orphaned, abused, or otherwise underprivileged ones. Providing education for girls and women was another major concern as well as giving women access to teaching positions. Reformers in China helped the country gain some 134,000 schools for girls, instructing 4.5 million students before the First World War. Higher education for women also advanced, with women's colleges established in Great Britain and the United States late in the 1860s and early 1870s; Women's University in 1901 and Chukyo Women's University in 1905 in Japan; Ginling College founded in 1913 in China; and, in India, the conversion of an ashram for widows and girls founded in 1896 converted into a college for women in 1916 and then into a university. As the number of women's universities swelled across the globe before 1914, men in most emerging countries were active in debating women's right to education, good jobs, property ownership, and the vote. Many sought to bring women's considerable energy into the fight against colonialism on behalf of national independence.

Women and Modernity at the Turn of the Twentieth Century

In this retreat from command of a massive household, masculinity might appear to be diminished. Whereas men had been tasked with protecting the household's honor, especially the honor of its women either through killing a soiled girl or woman or marrying off a compromised daughter, honor came to be a matter of defending the historical nation. The defense of the nation's honor used the tradition of defending a woman's honor to build a state-oriented unity. For instance, in June 1906 an Egyptian woman was shot by a group of army officers at Dinshaway on the road to Alexandria, arousing villagers to protest. Because a British soldier died later, though the cause is in dispute, four villagers were hanged, others tortured, and still others imprisoned. Ballads and poems followed: "The problem started with a woman—an Arab—in the barn. One of the English loaded his gun and fired./ In order to shoot pigeons, they let fly upon the hill,/ And so they burned the woman, also her barn and her father's house." The song ended with by invoking the "Sons of the Fatherland." The event and its retelling became "a crucial cornerstone of the collective Egyptian national memory,"[7] once more rallying soldiers to the nation with a story of abused or problematic women.

Either blaming women or protecting them as a national cause occurred in the context of women's organizing in public beyond the nation-state. International feminism developed, with women engaging in a growing number of international causes while creating global contacts. In the nineteenth century Susan B. Anthony of the United States had launched the International Council of Women (1888)—the first women's NGO or nongovernmental organization it has been called. This group expanded into the International Women's Suffrage Alliance founded in 1902. By the end of the 1930s, the Alliance had met in a range of countries, including Turkey in 1939. Other international efforts included the Pan-American International Women's Committee founded in 1916. Most of these groups included well-established women who worked within the political systems and social networks of their individual countries. Many of them would become diplomats and government officials in subsequent decades.

Women's activism on behalf of their rights occurred alongside the fact that women in some corners of the world held significant power and that women's causes went beyond explicitly feminist concerns. Britain's Queen Victoria did not favor feminists even as she became Empress of India in 1876 and as such an inspiration for many seeking women's advancement. In Qing China, the most powerful person between 1861 and 1908 was the

Empress Dowager Cixi, who was poorly instructed as a girl but eager to learn in her adulthood. As a ruler, however, she was expert in manipulating factions within the government so that Chinese policies seemed paralyzed between advancing toward reform and moving backward in its policies, losing ever more of its autonomy to the imperial powers. As the century opened she stomped on reform movements that called for relaxing the grip of fathers and elder brothers on women in the family while making other efforts to modernize.

Yet as a result of women's activism and attention to modernity in such realms as health and education, they gained more rights as the twentieth century opened even while remaining the topic of public debate. The right to guardianship of one's own children, the right to divorce, and opportunities for education were hard-fought victories in many countries. Some women in Western nations gained the right to their wages and other property. All this seemed to culminate in the right to vote that women in New Zealand won in 1893—the first parliamentary government to grant women's suffrage. The campaign, led by Kate Sheppard of the Women's Christian Temperance Union and supported by the original inhabitants—Maori women—was opposed by many, including the entire liquor industry, which feared for the survival of its business. Women in Finland achieved the vote in 1906 and just before the First World War women in the Netherlands did too.

In 1905, Rokeya Shekhawat Hossein (1880–1932) of Bengal published a short story in *The Indian Ladies Magazine*. "The Sultana's Dream" described a perfectly run, advanced technological society called Ladyland. It was the perfect expression of women's modernity—a modernity where they showed themselves to be far in advance of men. Women professors in the universities of Ladyland had harnessed the power of the sun, electricity, mechanical dispensers of water, and other technologies to produce flying cars, solar power, electrically farmed agriculture, among many inventions. Another advance, according to the plot, was reworking of sex segregation, maintained according to Muslim tradition but with men, who had earlier failed so badly in running the society, now confined to the harem or zenana. In this excerpt the visitor to Ladyland hears from a guide about how it came about that men entered the harem and gave political and economic control to women.

> Soon afterwards certain persons came from a neighbouring country and took shelter in ours. They were in trouble having committed some political offense. The king who cared more for power than for good government asked our kind-hearted Queen to hand them over to his officers. She refused, as it was against her principle to turn out refugees. For this refusal the king declared war against our country.
>
> Our military officers sprang to their feet at once and marched out to meet the enemy. The enemy however, was too strong for them . . . [I]n spite of all their bravery the foreign army advanced step by step to invade our country.

A meeting of a number of wise ladies was held at the Queen's palace to advise as to what should be done to save the land.

"If you cannot save your country for lack of physical strength," said the Queen, "try to do so by brain power."

Then the Lady Principal of the second university (who had collected sun-heat), who had been silently thinking during the consultation, remarked that they were all but lost, and there was little hope left for them. There was, however, one plan which she would like to try, and this would be her first and last efforts.

The Queen thanked them heartily, and asked the Lady Principal to try her plan. The Lady Principal rose again and said, "before we go out the men must enter the zenanas. I make this prayer for the sake of purdah." "Yes, of course," replied Her Royal Highness.

On the following day the Queen called upon all men to retire into zenanas for the sake of honour and liberty. Wounded and tired as they were, they took that order rather for a boon! They bowed low and entered the zenanas without uttering a single word of protest. They were sure that there was no hope for this country at all.

Then the Lady Principal with her two thousand students marched to the battle field, and arriving there directed all the rays of the concentrated sunlight and heat towards the enemy.

The heat and light were too much for them to bear. They all ran away panic-stricken, not knowing in their bewilderment how to counteract that scorching heat. When they fled away leaving their guns and other ammunitions of war, they were burnt down by means of the same sun-heat. Since then no one has tried to invade our country any more.

"Please let me know, how you carry on land cultivation and how you plough the land and do other hard manual work."

'Our fields are tilled by means of electricity, which supplies motive power for other hard work as well, and we employ it for our aerial conveyances too. We have no rail road nor any paved streets here.'

Then she screwed a couple of seats onto a square piece of plank. To this plank she attached two smooth and well-polished balls. When I asked her what the balls were for, she said they were hydrogen balls and they were used to overcome the force of gravity. The balls were of different capacities to be used according to the different weights desired to be overcome. She then fastened to the air-car two wing-like blades, which, she said, were worked by electricity. After we were comfortably seated she touched a knob and the blades began to whirl, moving faster and faster every moment. At first we were raised to the height of about six or seven feet and then off we flew. And before I could realize that we had commenced moving, we reached the garden of the Queen . . . .[8]

In Ladyland, women had become modern citizens indeed.

Conclusion

Did reformers have Ladyland in mind as the outcome of their efforts to modernize women? For decades, the cause of women's modernity shaped one aspect of political discourse during the rise of the nation-state. Displacing absolute monarchies and advancing the modernization of the male citizen, nation-state advocates saw women's modernity as crucial to a nation's success. However, achieving their education and modernizing housekeeping were disconnected from political and citizens' rights, which women were not supposed to have. Yet in the course of modernizing, women across many regions came to political activism on behalf of equal citizenship and access to modern jobs. Some became doctors and scientists and a few even got the vote. These opportunities, however, only accrued to women unevenly and after several centuries of struggles. They were often open to women of the right race, class, or religious background. Simultaneously women in colonized areas were taking up those same struggles and developing a political will and savvy on behalf of independence—their own as women and their nation's—that would last into the twenty-first century.

Glossary

Cherokee   Local, Native Americans of the southeastern woodlands, known for the leadership of their women and for their expulsion from their homes in the early nineteenth century.

Daimyo   The great lords of Japan, before the Meiji Restoration.

Notes

1 Quoted from and described in Anne Walthall and M. William Steele, eds. and trans., *Politics and Society in Japan's Meiji Restoration: A Brief History with Documents* (Boston, MA: Bedford/St. Martins, 2017), 137–40.

2 Walthall and Steele, *Politics and Society in Japan's Meiji Restoration*, 119.

3 Quoted in James Francis Warren, "Japanese Brothel Prostitution, Daily Life, and the Client: Colonial Singapore," in *Sex, Power, and Slavery*, Gwyn Campbell and Elizabeth Elbourne, eds. (Athens: Ohio University Press, 2014), 292.

4 Theda Purdue and Michael D. Green, eds. *The Cherokee Removal: A Brief History with Documents* (Boston, MA: Bedford/St. Martins, 2005), 131–3.

5 As described in Gail Minault, *Secluded Scholars: Women's Education and Muslim Social Reform in Colonial India* (New Delhi: Oxford University Press, 1998), 38–52.

6 Mary Grant Seacole, *Wonderful Adventures of Mrs. Seacole in Many Lands* (New York: Oxford University Press, 1988), 125–6. Online versions available at Project Gutenberg and the Internet Archive.

7 A description of the event, its interpretation, and the ballad are found in
   Beth Baron, *Egypt as a Woman: Nationalism, Gender, and Politics* (Berkeley:
   University of California Press, 2005), 43–45.
8 Rokeya Shekhawat Hossein, "The Sultana's Dream," *The Indian Ladies
   Magazine* (Madras, 1905) http://digital.library.upenn.edu/women/sultana/
   dream/dream.html and many other websites.

Further Reading

Anderson, Marnie. *A Place in Public: Women's Rights in Meiji Japan*. Cambridge:
   Harvard University Press, 2010.
Baron, Beth. *Egypt as a Woman: Nationalism, Gender, and Politics*. Berkeley:
   University of California Press, 2005.
Kosambi, Meera. *Pandita Ramabai: Life and Landmark Writings*. London:
   Routledge India, 2016.
Kozma, Liat. *Policing Egyptian Women: Sex, Law, and Medicine in Khedival
   Egypt*. Syracuse, NY: Syracuse University Press, 2011.
Lowy, Dina. *The Japanese "New Woman": Images of Gender and Modernity*. New
   Brunswick: Rutgers University Press, 2007.
Maksudyan, Nazan. *Women and the City, Women in the City: A Gendered
   Perspective on Ottoman Urban History*. New York: Berghan, 2014.
Najmabadi, Afsaneh. *The Story of the Daughters of Quchan: Gender and National
   Memory in Iranian History*. Syracuse, NY: Syracuse University Press, 1998.
Najmabadi, Afsaneh. *Women with Mustaches and Men without Beards: Gender
   and the Sexual Anxieties of Modernity*. Berkeley: University of California
   Press, 2005.
Nimura, Janice P. *Daughters of the Samurai: A Journey from East to West and
   Back*. New York: W. Norton, 2015.
Pollard, Lisa. *Nurturing the Nation: The Family Politics of Modernizing, Colonizing,
   and Liberating Egypt, 1805–1923*. Berkeley: University of California Press, 2005.
Sommer, Matthew H. *Polyandry and Wife-Selling in Qing Dynasty China: Survival
   Strategies and Judicial Interventions*. Oakland: University of California
   Press, 2015.
Walthall, Anne, and M. William Steele, eds. and trans. *Politics and Society in
   Japan's Meiji Restoration*. Boston, MA: Bedford/St. Martins, 2017.
White, Deborah Gray. *Too Heavy a Load: Black Women in Defense of Themselves,
   1894–1994*. New York: W. W. Norton, 1998.

9

Expanding Empires, Resisting Empires, 1870–1914

Empress Myeongseong (1851–1895), known as Queen Min, was the influential wife of Korea's emperor in the last third of the nineteenth century. She came from the powerful Min clan and built a reputation—both approving of and rejecting her—for political maneuvering but also for advancing modernizing projects such as education for girls and women. Korea, a proud and independent state, was nonetheless a client of China as well as a target for Japan, Russia, the United States, and other powers that craved greater contact with and, more importantly, greater control over the peninsula. By 1894, Japan was in a position to overpower the Korean monarchy even as Queen Min lobbied for keeping Korea independent by tacking between China and Russia. Global opinion was on the side of Japan as an up-and-coming, modernizing power, especially after it defeated China in the Sino-Japanese War of 1894–5. Young Asian women, for example, went to Japan to study and become more up-to-date. In the fall of 1895, when Queen Min tried to oust resident officials representing newly victorious Japan, its henchmen assassinated her and burned the body to make it appear that she had simply disappeared. Despite Queen Min's efforts at preserving Korean independence, in 1910 Japan took the country over as a colony to be ruled by the military.

From the 1850s on, colonial rule expanded with as much tumult and violence as ever, much of it affecting and even costing women their lives. Some imperial nations pushed to annex more land including women's farms; foreigners joined in the rush for territory; older empires frequently struggled to survive or modernize. Japan, the United States, Belgium, and Germany were just four newcomers striving for transoceanic holdings. Britain and France pushed deeper into Africa, while *Zulus*, the Spanish, Koreans, and Chinese struggled and mostly failed to hold onto their power. Like Queen Min, strong women such as the Rani of Jhansi in India, Queen

Victoria in Britain, Dowager Empress Cixi in China, and Yaa Asantewaa of West Africa's Ashanti Empire influenced the unfolding drama of imperial expansion.

Intensification of empire from the last half of the nineteenth century on was also about masculine prowess as muscular killers and conquerors: at the time not only were women notable rulers, but the health of masculinity was worrying given women's wide-ranging activism and falling birthrates in many parts of the world. Declining fertility seemed to threaten national power. Yet, one ploy of imperialists was to call conquered males as a group "effeminate" and weak like women and girls. Empire thrived on gender-talk and gendered action, including in the very communities at the mercy of armed invasions. Amid the painful uprooting, rape and murder common to empire, and the many forms of imperial exploitation, colonized women's and men's daily experiences were often as chaotic and unpredictable as imperial rule itself.

A Few of Empires' People

As elsewhere, women's lives even under colonialism were complex in their mixture of joys, sorrows, drudgery, and menace. Rashsundari Debi (1809–1900), born in a small Bengali village under British, produced a rare account of everyday lives. At the age of twelve, she was married to a landowner and gave birth to her first child at the age of fourteen. The occasion of her wedding and removal from her family brought heart-break, while her married life was full of hard work, caring for an extensive household from the time of her marriage and raising her family. She found great joy in her early twenties when in secret she learned to read; then she began to write. At the age of fifty-nine, Rashsundari Debi published the first autobiography written in Bengali, a precious work she continued to revise and enlarge well into her eighties. Advocating education for women, Debi's autobiography showed the ways in which the patriarchal tradition perpetuating women's intellectual ignorance intermingled with empire. In combination, they layered one form of domination on another. Still, her publication put her at the forefront of the resistance found in the growing number of South Asian writers, poets, playwrights, political thinkers, and artists.

Like education, the ongoing movement of rural people to cities globally was seen to offer opportunities. With more individuals at work away from farms and local networks, market women picked up the slack, expanding their array of home-prepared food along with the home-grown produce that traditionally prevailed in markets. In India, they collected wood from forests, milled flour to sell, or spun thread for weavers. Migration enhanced market life, which remained women's sphere, because many no longer had time to make labor intensive products or seek access to sources of produce in fields and forests. Working in the bustling city of Accra, Ghana, Naa

Kowa credited her stepmother teaching her to practice a wide range of craft and marketing skills: "We sold cloth beads, [red] pepper and groundnuts [peanuts, for example], and smoked and salted fish." Naa Kowa also helped tend a "rum shop" for her father. "When I returned home from the shop I would polish beads, or smoke some fish if they were abundant."[1] There was usually solidarity alongside competition among traders, but trade networks were strong and would eventually become the sites of women's activism against empire. For the moment, however, market women could support themselves under colonialism, if not in the highly organized and political way that would later define them.

In large colonial cities, courtesans offering sexual, cultural, and political services might attain high levels of influence and wealth. In colonial Lucknow, the royal seat of the Awadh monarchy in northeast India, those courtesans interacting with noble and wealthy men themselves enjoyed stunning riches. Their reputation as teachers of social behavior and even important knowledge drew young men, often sent by their families, for training and enjoyment. Generations patronized these women and their offspring. In addition, the courtesans' establishments offered refuge and

FIGURE 9.1 *Indian ayah, Maria de Sousa, c. 1870. The ayah or children's nurse appears with the three European children she cares for. Serving as an ayah gave temporary security in the chaotic imperial world and European families liked having such women as servants. As women without resources, ayahs might be more docile and do extra chores without complaining. Courtesy of The Royal Photographic Society Collection/National Science and Media Museum/SSPL Getty Images.*

jobs as sex workers to women seeking many types of escape, for example, from abusive husbands. Despite the role played by men in their success, the courtesans of Lucknow created a woman-centered community of wealth and influence. All their funds went to daughters who advanced their finances through banking, real estate, and other investment skills. As one said, they deliberately erased the ways of housewives in their community and instead developed different skills, notably the manipulation of men, especially those who would contribute large sums of money. The courtesans wore burkas while in public, keeping people from seeing them and only allowing men who paid for it that privilege. Theirs was one way of dealing with both empire and the dominance of local men in the household and family.

Empires' Gender Tensions and Their Civilizing Mission

The Spanish, Chinese, and Portuguese empires were in decline by this time, while other European, Japanese, and US empires expanded. For most advocates of empire, nation-building and imperial expansion were intertwined in the further development of bureaucracies and military forces. Through them, ambitious states aimed to overtake numerous independent peoples in Africa, the Pacific, and various Asian regions and to impose an order on them that would more easily extract wealth. In the context of foreign political rule and the immigration of settlers, the lives of ordinary people whose regions were targeted for conquest were further changed by such acts as confiscating women's lands, spreading the system of plantations and mines, imposing new taxes and laws, and inflicting violence with ever more powerful weaponry.

Britain's imperial holdings swelled to include India, Burma, Australia, New Zealand, and other islands in the Pacific as part of its extensive possessions. In line with its gendered policies, the British dispossessed women of traditional influence they had as rulers and as owners of property. In confiscating property from women, they awarded it to loyal white and local men. One special British ploy was to lay claim to the territory of a deceased local ruler instead of allowing it to pass to his children or consorts. In the case of India, in 1853, the British declared the kingdom of Jhansi ceded to Britain after the death of its aged ruler. His queen, Lakshmibai, the Rani (1828–1858), protested the confiscation and the seizure of her jewels and other valuables, the British having offered her a pension instead. Soon members of the British Indian armies began to contest such outright theft and administrative takeovers by the British. Muslim and Hindu soldiers, protesting the rumored use of pork and beef fat on cartridges, rebelled.

The Rani, trained in archery, horsemanship, and swordsmanship, took command of her own troops, while other regiments took to the field as well.

Ultimately, the British defeated the massive resistance to their rule in which thousands died and during which the British blew cities and fortresses to bits. The Rani died in battle, asking that her body be cremated in a Hindu observance, at which point the telling of the Indian Rebellion itself became highly gendered. Eventually, the Rani of Jhansi was commemorated as a heroine of the imperial period, while Hindu troops were seen as cowardly savages for rising up against their masters. The Gurka, Sikh, and Scottish troops who had suppressed the Hindu soldiers became in British lore the model of soldierly masculinity—the martial races they were called even as elite Hindus were seen as cowardly, especially in their numerous rapes of British women. The stories of these rapes, which were actually found not to have happened, only added to the luster of the martial races, as they were acclaimed for having slaughtered rapists without mercy. Learned Indian officials working for the British civil service, many of them Hindu, went from being seen as cultural leaders to being called womanly and unfit to rule. This gendered depiction and the gendered account of Hindu men's alleged cowardly behavior during the rebellion, repeated nonstop, came to justify the ongoing grip of the British on India and its economic wealth.

As the French along with other European powers, now protected by quinine from deadly malaria, invaded the interior of Africa, they too transformed gender regimes. For one thing, similar to the British the French employed African men in their armies and allowed them to accumulate traditional symbols of power—women and slaves—as payment for conquests. Europeans also chose local men to perform bureaucratic functions such as collecting taxes and maintaining order in villages. These men often took over positions of power from chiefs—including women leaders—or became an additional layer of exploitation, allowing them to profit from the labors of their neighbors. The French and other Europeans stopped forging political relations with powerful families and clan networks and instead saw women as strictly useful for sexual pleasure. Rather than building their trading and political interests through partnerships with Indian and African women, for example, they sought out a sexual relationship only. In the 1890s, French officer Emile Dessaulx based in West Africa wrote his brother letters full of boredom and longing: "nothing but my paperwork and schedules await me impatiently at bedtime." Instead, he watched with disapproval his comrades' casual arrangements for regular sexual intimacy with local women. Finally, however, he succumbed, taking a fifteen-year-old in "marriage" and paying "royally" for her. Unlike liaisons a century and more earlier, Dessaulx did not seek entrée into the heart of a powerful clan in this arrangement but only his personal satisfaction. Mama, the name of his sexual partner, was a "charming companion in my exile" but hardly a political intermediary or economic advisor as had been the case in the past.[2]

Belgian treatment of Congolese people was notoriously brutal in the late nineteenth century when the quest for rubber was at its height there. Belgian officials and their African agents enforced quotas of rubber on African men, maiming and even killing them if they lagged in collecting increasingly sparse supplies. Not only were women left with all agricultural and family responsibilities, but Congolese soldiers hired by Belgium were allowed to seize the wives and daughters of escaped or laggard rubber workers. They cut babies from the bellies of pregnant women; threatened with death, boys were made to have sex with their mothers. In one case, the wife of a rubber worker at home alone was told by a soldier to have intercourse with him. When she refused, he shot her and then cut off her foot to confiscate her bronze ankle bracelet. The woman was still alive but even as her foot was amputated, she played dead, subsequently walking on one leg supported by a hefty stick. Guards put fresh clay to dry in the genitals of a woman worker in a brick factory and cut off a single breast of other women. White soldiers, supposedly the representatives of a higher white "civilization," were often the onlookers, laughing at the scenes of torture and humiliation as empire's gendered power was on full display.[3]

Despite the accomplishments, hard work, and family values of women in colonized countries, imperialists used the charge of cultural backwardness to introduce what it called the "civilizing mission"—a set of practices designed to erase local cultures and force colonized peoples to adopt the supposedly superior habits of their imperial masters. As those who would raise the next generation of the colonized, women's behavior and values were especially targeted. Missionaries and others taught girls in their colonies to dress and behave like women in the metropole—though not quite. They should see their education as training them for domestic life, not for jobs other than as household servants to whites. As for domestic life, its practices were to be those from the colonizer's culture. Some women who received an education in the colonizer's skills looked back and appreciated the chance to learn to read, write, and do math. They also liked learning about the world, because most schools did not teach local children about their own culture and history but about that of their imperial rulers. Many others, however, were of an entirely different opinion: individuals from both sides of the schooling debate were among those women joining resistance movements or rejecting domestic service to become politically and economically active.

Women were especially targeted because of Western beliefs in republican motherhood and the Japanese idea of "good wives, wise mothers," but there was more to the education of women ruled by empires. Russian officials, for example, wrote directives aimed at reeducating Muslim women in the expanding empire so that they would educate their children to be obedient laborers. The idea was that these women would see the value both for themselves and their families in a certain kind of education and gain a willingness to play along with imperial powers rather than resist them. Teachers themselves were respected and commanding, again providing a lesson in deference to superiors. In this education and in colonial rule generally, the family was supposed to be removed from a network of clans with its own political practices and transformed into a lowly element of empire. The enlistment of women to impart imperial rules to the family would ideally convert ethnic, religious, and clan loyalties into imperial obedience, easing the tensions of empire.

US treatment of Native Americans also involved taking their lands and subjecting them to a similar civilizing mission. In her forties, Zitkala-Sa (Red Bird, 1876–1938) described her removal as a child from her Native American family along with others from her Sioux community to a white missionary school where she was renamed Gertrude, supposedly as a way of civilizing her. In the boarding school the Native American children were subjected to what Zitkala-Sa called "iron discipline." Each day meant being subjected to relentless monitoring in contrast to the warmth of her maternal clan's everyday habits. "A paleface woman, with a yellow-covered roll book open on her arm and a gnawed pencil in her hand, appeared at the door. Her small, tired face was coldly lighted with a pair of large gray eyes." The woman's only interest seemed to be in attendance, not in the children's well-being, she remembered. "[I]t was inbred in me to suffer in silence rather than to appeal to the ears of one whose open eyes could not see my pain, I have many times trudged in the day's harness heavy-footed, like a dumb sick brute." Zitkala-Sa called the process "the civilizing machine."

According to her account, children died with little appreciation of the white culture that aimed to remake them. "Once I lost a dear classmate. I remember well how she used to mope along at my side, until one morning she could not raise her head from her pillow. At her deathbed I stood weeping, as the paleface woman sat near her moistening the dry lips." Not Native American rituals but white people's rituals prevailed. "Among the folds of the bedclothes I saw the open pages of the white man's Bible. The dying Indian girl talked disconnectedly of Jesus the Christ and the paleface who was cooling her swollen hands and feet. I grew bitter, and censured the woman for cruel neglect of our physical ills." Zitkala-Sa described her ever-changing relationship to white culture: "I blamed the hard-working, well-meaning, ignorant woman who was inculcating in our hearts her superstitious ideas." Soon she went back to being rebellious: "Within a week I was again actively testing the chains which tightly bound my individuality like a mummy for burial."

Being renamed and taught American skills was supposed to make Native Americans "civilized" enough to hold low-level jobs in the US economy, she realized. After being exposed to schooling, Zitkala-Sa, however, wanted both to keep her own culture and play the violin and piano and write books. Of one thing she was sure: she rejected the "menial" jobs white Americans intended her for. Zitkala-Sa became an author of Native American stories and of her memoir describing life as a child. She also founded the National Council of American Indians in 1926—two years after passage of the law finally granting many Native Americans the rights to citizenship.[4]

Other women experienced acculturation differently but with equal complexity. The *Berber* Fadhma Amrouche (1882–1967), who lived in a mountainous region of colonized Algeria, was born after her mother's husband had died. As Amrouche described the situation, her twenty-three-year-old widowed mother was not only beautiful, but "young and foolish. In her own courtyard there lived a young man from the same family as her old husband. She fell in love with him. And the inevitable happened. She became pregnant and the young man denied that he was the father of the child." The mother was completely ostracized by her community and delivered Fadhma herself, as both of them became outcasts. Fearing that she or her daughter, "the child of sin," would be killed—her social offence was that grave—the mother at several instances heard of childcare and then educational opportunities available from French officials, religious personnel, and charitable volunteers. All the while, she petitioned French officials to extract funds from Amrouche's father and did so with only small success.

Fadhma's first asylum from village life involved placement with the French order of White Sisters, but their cultural mission involved drastic punishment for a small mischief of throwing thimbles into the cesspool somewhere around the age of four or five. She had to climb into the container filled with human waste to retrieve the lost items and then stand in her excrement-soaked garments with a bag of additional excrement around her neck. In addition she was whipped bloody. Her mother removed her from the Sisters' care: "Was it for this I entrusted her to you?" she asked the nuns. Meanwhile, a charitable French laywoman had founded a boarding institution for Berber girls, which suited Fadhma much better and where she was renamed Marguerite. She learned to read and come in contact with European literature and ideas. "I loved French," she remembered, "except when I had to explain proverbs and maxim . . . " and history was a favorite too. French colonial administrators ultimately decided that Berber girls should be trained to do more practical tasks that could earn them money, perhaps as domestics. French culture was not for lowly North African girls.

The school was eventually closed and Fadhma returned home in her early teens, only to be given a job in a Catholic-run hospital, where she eventually converted to Catholicism. "As for the Catholic religion, I don't think I was ever truly convinced . . . When the Fathers declared that only those who had been baptized would go to heaven, I didn't believe them. I thought of my mother, of all that she had suffered, the three months a year she spent fasting (for besides Ramadan, she imposed supplementary fasts on herself), of the heavy loads of water she took it upon herself to carry to the mosque in all weathers and I thought, 'Is it possible that my mother will not go to heaven?'" Fadhma Amrouche's life story proceeded under the complexities of colonialism, as multiple cultures, ways of life, and differing values intermingled. She came to the end of her life with this judgment: "in spite of my basically French education, never have I been able to become a close friend of any French people, nor of Arabs. I remain for ever the eternal exile."[5]

Women living under colonial conditions became special tools of empire beyond their production of raw materials for industry. The new and growing medium of photography focused on them, producing images of them clothed in local garb. On the one hand such images provided a glimpse of imperial life and globalization for those living in the imperial heartland or metropole. Their sense of a wider world grew, if in an imperialist format. Even people in the countryside of the United States or Germany could view women's situation thousands of miles away. On the other hand, such images exoticized the women themselves, showing them in an array of dress far different from that in the metropole. They often wore copious jewelry and lavish styles in these images or at other times, they might appear bare-breasted, offering soft pornography to the male viewer. The US magazine *National Geographic*, founded in 1888, offered this multifaceted education in the exotic ways of the world for its subscribers and for patrons of public and school libraries. The exoticization of women in some locales deflected from the message of reformers and feminist activists at home that women had important contributions to make to the public, that they were rational, needed educational opportunities, and that they should vote. Imperial misogyny displayed women as fleshly and "backward."

Women's dominance in African agriculture continued, but that dominance came under attack by colonial officials as part of the gendering of the civilizing mission. Under imperial rule, foreign officials and their agents increasingly attempted to deal with men only. They awarded men land that women had formerly cultivated because male ownership was customary—and indeed the law—in European countries. Colonial developers of plantations aimed to break up subsistence farming for the household in favor of farming of single crops for the market on large tracts, with men serving as the cultivators in order to have cash to pay imperial taxes. Such was the goal of the male "breadwinner" model, and by the twentieth century women's household needs competed with the economic "development" model in which large-scale farming for international markets took up land that families needed to survive. Woods, streams, and swampy areas providing an array of foods, including wild herbs, fruits, greens, insects, and water life, disappeared as trees were felled, swampy lands filled in, and dams constructed to support the beginnings of agribusinesses on which the imperial future was supposed to depend. Although some women traveled to areas where such forestlands remained intact, others, stripped of their farmland, became domestics or laborers for the colonizer.

At the other end of the social scale, women mobilized their ingenuity, even in defeat at the hands of invaders. Among these stubborn resisters was the Hawaiian queen Liliuokalani (1838–1917), whose kingdom was a target of US oceanic expansion in the nineteenth century. After taking most continental lands from Native Americans, the US government helped businessmen and missionaries to depose Queen Liliuokalani in 1893 and annex the islands. It then encouraged uprisings against Spain, helping defeat its empire too. Though promising independence, the United States quickly made a direct takeover of the Philippines and instituted more indirect rule in Cuba and Puerto Rico. To many, such as Queen Liliuokalani who had been imprisoned for an uprising against US annexation, the US use of force to take over independent governments such as that of Hawai'i contradicted its announced belief in rights and fair play.

Liliuokalani described her house arrest, where she was guarded by soldiers. A visitor arrived, who asked "if, in the event that it should be decided that all the principal parties to the revolt must pay for it with their lives, I was prepared to die? I replied to this in the affirmative, telling him I had no anxiety for myself, and felt no dread of death. He then told me that six others besides myself had been selected to be shot for treason, but that he would call again, and let me know further about our fate." It was a tense waiting game, once she had been threatened with death for resisting the takeover. Soon another envoy arrived with what appeared to her a document certifying her abdication, which she was to sign: "For myself, I would have chosen death rather than to have signed it; but it was represented to me that by my signing this paper all the persons who had been arrested, all my people now in trouble by reason of their love and loyalty towards me, would be immediately released. Think of my position—sick, a lone woman in prison, scarcely knowing who was my friend, or who listened to my words only to betray me, without legal advice or friendly counsel, and the stream of blood ready to flow unless it was stayed by my pen." More waiting and then a group of people was brought to see her sign the abdication so that US officials and businessmen could say that the abdication was entirely voluntary. "So far from the presence of these persons being evidence of a voluntary act on my part," she wrote later, "was it not an assurance to me that they, too, knew that, unless I did the will of my jailers, what Mr. Neumann had threatened would be performed, and six prominent citizens immediately put to death. I so regarded it then, and I still believe that murder was the alternative." Her only consolation was that "there is not a drop of the blood of my subjects, friends or foes, upon my soul."[6] Liliuokalani used her exile to publish the celebrated memoirs of her imprisonment and ultimate overthrow to show the world US global greed and conniving. Recourse to the press became one of the weapons used by those whom imperialists attacked.

At about the same time, other women rulers faced the increasing violence of empire as ambitions clashed. Dowager Empress Cixi of China handled foreign incursions by supporting an anti-foreign movement called the Boxers that arose in the 1890s. After a series of so-called Opium Wars and the Sino-Japanese War (1894–1895) in which Japan quickly crushed Chinese forces, Chinese autonomy declined, with the winning powers demanding ever more access to the empire and ever larger reparation payments. Women were prominent among the invading missionaries determined to Christianize the Chinese and to "upgrade" their culture, especially the status of women and the running of family life. They targeted child marriage and foot-binding in particular, all the while working to undermine traditional spiritual beliefs and practices.

As foreign intrusions multiplied, the militant "Boxer" activists blamed a series of natural catastrophes, including drought and devastating famine, on the presence of foreigners on Chinese soil. In particular, they targeted Chinese Christians and Christian missionaries for undermining the empire, and used their martial prowess, murder, and the burning of buildings, especially churches, to revive the empire. Women Boxers, called Red Lanterns, also appeared, for the most part practicing martial arts though not in combat, circulating messages, and providing support. Although it is generally believed that the Red Lanterns were unimportant strategically or tactically, the Red Lanterns and women in general played an important symbolic and propaganda role. Most societies at the time mobilized beliefs in women's pollution and other bodily powers to explain events. The Boxers often attributed the success of their fires to the Red Lanterns reducing their bodily size to that of an egg and cruising the skies to start fires and otherwise promote the Boxers' cause. Boxers likewise attributed their defeats to a woman's pouring of dirty water in front of a house scheduled for torching and thus upsetting well-laid Boxer plans. The presence of naked women or menstruating ones had a similar destructive effect on the Boxers, it was said. Ultimately the Boxers suffered defeat, despite the support from Cixi. The collapse of the long-standing Qing Empire was underway, often blamed on its woman ruler.

Gender and the Colonizers' World

Officials anchored empire through celebrations featuring military bands and marching soldiers as well as ceremonies such as durbars in India. Two lavish durbars occurred in 1877 and 1903, bringing thousands of Indian princes and their subjects as well as military and colonial officials into a public display of loyalty to the empire. The second durbar in 1903 was a massively expensive and lavish affair with British King Edward VI and Queen Alexandra in attendance. In 1877, the first durbar celebrated the proclamation of Queen Victoria (1819–1901) in the previous year as Empress of India—a title she had long craved. Victoria reveled in the trappings of empire, with her favorite servant being Abdul Karim, a South Asian man, who acted as her secretary and confidant in the last fifteen years of her life. A consumer of imperial goods, she regularly gave shawls imported from India as gifts but more importantly encouraged politicians to expand British power around the world. Her statue adorned more than one city in the empire to indicate the enduring nature of the British presence.

Confident in their superiority, imperialists pushed their way of life right down to the very food they put in their mouths even when far from home. Women and men maintained properly gendered attire, with European women wearing corsets and heavy skirts in tropical climates, while European men wore woolen suits and full evening garb even in the tropics. They also promoted eating heavy meals and following exhausting ceremonial behavior. Local women wisely rebelled from many of these customs because they undermined health; they objected to other customs such as wearing cumbersome Western underwear because it was believed that such items weakened young women's reproductive systems.

The march of the British, French, Belgians, and others into the interior of Africa after the discovery from Amerindians of South America of quinine's uses against malaria also reworked gender even as it depended greatly on gender as justification for conquest. Although a primary reason for extending empires to the interior of the continent was to gain raw materials for industry and to exploit cheap local labor in agriculture and mining, another ingredient of empire had to do with the belief in empire's fortifying effects on men and their nations. Generals were celebrated, their military likenesses displayed in the newly colorful advertising posters of the day. Conquest was a display of individual masculine heroism and character, for strength and bravery in facing the perils of savage territory created the strong male persona. In this regard, the well-publicized masculinity of the modern nation meshed nicely with the world of masculine imperial conquest.

Behind the myth of masculine ruggedness, however, lay the reality: most men in Africa would have died without vast caravans staffed with hundreds of porters, cooks, guides, and negotiators to ensure safe passage and secure supplies of food. Men in uncharted, tropical territory went out of their minds, became alcoholics and drug addicts, or wasted away from any number of unknown diseases. In the face of this reality, survivors often turned vicious or acted out. German imperialist Carl Peters (1856–1918) was a rabid nationalist, white supremacist, and overall rapacious individual who founded The Society for German Colonization to lobby for overseas expansion. A committed Social Darwinist believing in white and male superiority, Peters was among the early German adventurers in East Africa who put his beliefs into practice, stealing land from local people and using his gun as his chief negotiating tool. During his time in the region, often serving as an honored representative of the German elite, he had one of his African concubines executed for having a relationship with another man. Peters ran roughshod over African humanity, even as he called on Germany authorities to bail him out of his scrapes, either financial ones or those resulting from his wanton brutality. Such was the gendering of empire.

The British and Americans also gave no quarter when it came to the display of muscular empire. In 1900, US senator Albert Beveridge explained the benefits to emerge from a successful campaign for the annexation of the Philippines: "It means opportunity for all the glorious young manhood of the republic—the most virile, ambitious, impatient, militant manhood the world has ever seen."[7] Unstated was the possibility that women might also aspire to be conquerors. Not only had they been conquerors in the past but

FIGURE 9.2 "The Conquest of Africa," *1900 Georges-Antoine Rochegrosse. Europeans portrayed colonization as altogether beneficial and nurturing, erasing its violence from the white public's mind. In this depiction empire is represented, like the nation, as a frail, very white woman. If the fragile, female nation needed protection by muscular men, the female empire would need military protection as well. Courtesy of Leemage/Corbis Getty Images.*

they themselves had worked to conquer others, leading troops among the Zulus, for example. White women had also joined the drive to invade other countries as explorers and settlers, especially in Australia and New Zealand where opportunity abounded, it was believed.

The religious toleration and power of the Ottoman and early Mughal empires were replaced by the cultural and technological pridefulness of Western nations in these years and by their continued efforts to convert people to their religions. Increasingly, these imperial leaders justified controlling distant peoples by pointing to the inferior treatment of women by local men. It made no difference, for example, that Muslim women in the Middle East, West Africa, and South and Southeast Asia often were more advantaged economically than women in the imperial heartland of western Europe and the United States. One accusation was that because women in colonized countries were covered in textiles from head to toe, they were oppressed. Paradoxically, in regions where women wore far less clothing than in the West, they were also said to be oppressed. Increasingly, states used the examples of women's clothing and their levels of formal instruction in schools as a rationale for invading a region and overturning its government. Women's and men's religious beliefs in these countries also signaled to invaders and colonizers that these regions were backward. It was also true that some of these societies did oppress and even physically harm women—as did Westerners.

Women settlers from the invading imperial countries benefitted from leaving their homelands. Some were eager to leave domestic life or to find work or husbands. Margarethe von Eckenbrecher (1875–1955), who settled in German Southwest Africa with her husband in 1902, prospered and raised a family. She came to believe that she had a god-given right to the territory. Von Eckenbrecher had nothing but scorn for the Herero ethnic group who pastured their cattle in the region and had long done so. For her, these were inferior people and dangerous because of it. She noted that the Herero always seemed to be threatening, her Herero washer woman even singing a song about white people including little children soon dying in Herero country. According to von Eckenbrecher, the washerwoman warned her not to sleep too deeply. In the early twentieth century, the Herero rose up against German confiscations, as the colonial army ordered them off their own land. Having superior weaponry, the Germans ultimately took over Herero farms and wealth, forcing survivors into areas where they starved for lack of pasture and farmland. After the First World War, when Germany surrendered its colonies, Margarethe von Eckenbrecher still believed the region to be literally her own—her real homeland and rightful possession.[8]

Women from many imperial centers were ardent imperialists for economic and nationalistic reasons. Frieda von Bülow, like von Eckenbrecher from an increasingly nationalist Germany, went to German Southeast Africa with Carl Peters for the adventure but also to instill German ways as part of perpetuating German superiority. In the late nineteenth century, Germany had just conquered France (1870–1) in the Franco-Prussian War. Patriotism became aggressive, connected less to values such as the rule of law and citizenship than to military might and swagger. Frieda von Bülow enjoyed that might, which she saw in the commanding military presence of strong men like Carl Peters. As Peters became more erratic and unfaithful, von Bülow left him, though she remained loyal to the cause of empire.

Simultaneously, an ideology of imperial motherhood developed across the colonizing powers. Not only did the birth rate among the conquerors need to increase but the master races needed to ensure the fitness of the young. Local officials and charities set up wellness clinics across imperial nations and began programs to ensure that people from the poorer classes had shoes, clothing, and enough food. In 1907, British officer Robert Baden-Powell organized the Boy Scout movement to make young boys strong, preparing them to participate if necessary in imperial conquest. The Scouts were to be loyal and honorable when dealing with one another—an element in constructing an imperial masculinity. Soon thereafter, the American Juliette Gordon Low founded the Girl Scouts. In these efforts girls were to build character and self-reliance. Mothers gained new responsibilities for ensuring that their children participated in these programs in order to create a strong master race.

Women endorsed and even led reform efforts such as the temperance and eugenics movements that would boost the overall fitness of the entire population. They saw alcoholism as a scourge of families that needed to be eradicated. Working men, after a hard day, went to pubs and cafes, using funds better directed toward their families for drink. Proper nourishment for children suffered and fathers returned home abusive and unable to behave as responsible heads of their families—that is, unable to serve as building blocks of the race. Not only did they beat their children, but they also beat their wives—women who themselves were malnourished and even tempted to alcoholism because of the father's selfishness in family life. The Women's Christian Temperance Union blanketed Western society and even regions beyond it in its effort to get men to take the pledge not to drink. Women of marriageable age were encouraged for the sake of future generations and of the empire to avoid men who drank. They should seek fit and upright men to be their sexual and marital partners.

Even as the weaknesses of the so-called master races were in plain sight, imperial officials showcased empire in blockbuster exhibitions such as world fairs, colonial expositions, or other events celebrating global mastery. Britain, France, and the United States held some of the most spectacular of these events, but individual women's groups took similar initiatives. In 1898, activist women held a fair in The Hague, capital of the Netherlands, to display ways of life in the Dutch East Indies (Indonesia). Based on Indonesian crafts and village life, the fair turned out to have surprises when the imported "natives" rebelled at their conditions. In addition to sparking huge interest in colonial life and its "exotic" ways, the women sponsors piggybacked an industrial exhibit of women's craft and industrial skills onto the colonial display. Women and colonialism were right at home in this massive presentation of imperial life.

Women in the imperial countries often felt empowered when following the lure of freedom by migrating. Both single and married women moved globally in great numbers. For single women, movement brought several opportunities: the first benefit for women in Western countries was to escape what they felt an oppressive domestic ideology that saw their fundamental nature best expressed in domestic activity. Migration, initially to cities in their home countries but then to colonized regions, brought freedom to gain different kinds of opportunities and even adventures. A second benefit in their eyes was to find a sexual partner, especially a husband, given the financial security most women believed men could bring them. Third, some women wanted the same kind of adventure that publicity showed men enjoying. Hunting, shooting, trekking, and collecting were just some of the dreams that women followed. Margaret Fontaine (1862–1940), a clergyman's daughter, escaped England to collect butterflies (and lovers) in some sixty countries. In 1878, she began keeping diaries of her travels, collecting, and newfound acquaintances met along the way. The diaries were so unusual, even scandalous, that she banned their use until 1978— that is, a century after she had begun keeping them. Other women became spies, archeologists, and translators, to name just a few of the adventurous occupations they found internationally. Many, like Fontaine, found freedoms seldom enjoyed by middle-class women.

Religious women sought opportunity in bringing Buddhism and Christianity to different regions of the world. Religious women from India brought the Ramayana to the Caribbean for indentured workers to study it and observe performances. Catholic religious founded more schools, orphanages, and hospitals that they used both to provide assistance in distant lands and to gain converts for their religions. Protestant women had the same goals, often traveling with their clergymen husbands as a team. Some Western missionaries prepared themselves by studying health care and then promoted their own sanitary practices, many of them based on such Western commodities as soap. Alongside these enthusiastic volunteers were convict women forcibly transported to Australia and other distant colonies for punishment and exile.

Other Western women were among those engaged in committed borrowing and collecting of non-Western objects, although by this time exchange was multidirectional given the shipment of both raw and finished goods worldwide. The Rockefeller women, enriched by the oil and other business ventures of John D. Rockefeller, particularly focused on Asian art. Beyond that, American-born artist Mary Cassatt used the Japanese palette of colors, arrangement of figures on the canvas, and even the subject matter of mothers and children in eighteenth-century Japanese prints to create her paintings. She was just one among many who did so, with women studying with Asian and other artists to learn their techniques.

Writers such as German poet Else Laske-Schuler wrote of her love for her partner as akin to an Oriental rug in the beauty of colors, craft, and overall harmony of the finished product. Somewhat later, Virginia Woolf, whose diaries suggest a non-Western mysticism, produced *Orlando* in the 1920s. It featured a young man of the early modern period, who, by the twentieth century, had been reincarnated as a woman. At the same time, Western women including feminists practiced yoga and even non-Western martial arts not to mention practicing meditation and communication with spirits.

Russian-born Helena Blavatsky (1831–1891) attracted a widespread following across the globe to her new doctrine of theosophy. She had culled its precepts from "the masters" whom she professed to have visited in India and from secret Egyptian and other Middle Eastern knowledge. Blavatsky's followers engaged in occult non-Western rituals including automatic writing and seances where spirits would visit. An eccentric person, she captivated many, including scientists, philosophers, and artists in a variety of genres, exercising a heavy-handed leadership of her sect even after her death and spawning other globalized movements such as anthroposophy still in existence today. Among the followers of theosophy and its offshoot anthroposophy was Swedish avant-garde painter Hilma af Klint (1862–1944), who invented abstract art based on mystical faith in the power of colors and geometric shapes.

Race and gender intertwined in Charles Darwin's *Origin of Species* (1859) and *Descent of Man* (1871), both of which provided a supposedly scientific explanation for the so-called inferiority of colonized and exploited peoples and of women. Darwin's main point was that "with women the powers of intuition, of rapid perception, and perhaps of imitation, are more strongly marked than in man . . . [and] characteristic of the lower races, and therefore of a past and lower state of civilization."[9] Darwin tied race and gender into one package, just as he had in his initial take on the subject of evolution, that is, the progress of life through various ascending stages of development. In the *Origin of Species*, Darwin allowed that on the scientific scale of evolution, white men were more highly evolved and accomplished than either men of other races or women of any race. This had occurred because white men had struggled and reasoned like no other race nor like women. Thinkers and ideologues seized on Darwin's pronouncements, using the "science of race" to justify imperialism and discrimination against women. Having been denuded of their goods by rapacious empire builders, poor people of other races were seen not as victims of oppression but seriously deficient in intelligence and civilization. Women too, similarly prevented from gaining an education and in many cases from having any funds of their own, were said from "scientific evidence" to be inferior and lacking in aptitude like the "savages."

During this age of resistance to empire, these Social Darwinists worried about a falling birthrate in many parts of the globe. In places like Africa, they feared a shortage of labor to do crippling work and menial labor in households. In imperial centers, the worry was different. Given the falling birthrates across most of Europe and the United States, Social Darwinists worried that savages would overpower the white races. President Theodore Roosevelt thought birth control "unpleasant" and feared a deterioration of white masculinity. In fact, commentators at the center of empire constantly invoked a crisis in masculinity evidenced by the falling birthrate and the defeat of white armies. Roosevelt hunted, did martial arts, and constantly tested himself physically, as his boy children were supposed to do too. Outside the United States, military training geared up to make men better able to survive attacks by "savage" races.

Eugenics grew as an overarching theme in politics. The "best" people should breed with one another, while the lower people such as the unfit poor should be discouraged from having children. What alarmed imperialists the most was that the poor seemed to be having great quantities of children, while the middle and upper classes were cutting their fertility—in large part because a new emphasis on childrearing had increased the costs of having a large family among these more privileged groups in society. Eugenics advanced racial thinking in heterosexual relationships and reproduction, eventually leading to sterilization programs for the poor and non-whites followed by genocide in the twentieth century.

Organized Resistance to Empire and State Power Grows

Even as Darwinism and eugenics thrived in expanding empires such as Britain, Japan, and the United States, minority and colonized people were opposing racist, imperial values. In Africa, the Caribbean, and the United States pan-Africanism developed to unite all people of African blood as a way of countering white oppression. One particularly strong, parallel movement was the anti-lynching campaign in the United States, advanced among others by Ida B. Wells (1862–1931), a teacher and journalist in Tennessee. In 1889, she had acquired a part interest in the pro-African-American newspaper, *Free Speech*, and used it to mobilize protest over the lynching of a black store owner whose business success was challenging whites. Wells also pointed out the tendency of whites to claim that African American men were raping white women. This claim, she and other anti-lynching advocates noted, covered up the prevalence of white men raping black women and the fact that some white women were having intimate relations with black men, preferring them to whites. Wells was threatened with death so vigorously that she was forced to leave town. Women's anti-lynching campaigns increased, however, in the twentieth century, with lynching continuing nevertheless for more than half a century.

A different kind of opposition arose with the discovery of gold and diamond mines in South Africa, which led to illicit gender relations and sexuality. European colonizers imposed taxation on those they conquered, although no longer in the form of produce but rather in the form of cash. To pay these taxes, men left their communities and families to earn the funds needed. The mostly male composition of the mine workers led to new relationships, including erotic ones with other men. They formed into same-sex couples, who devised special partnerships complete with sexual practices unique to the mining community's couples. When the stint in the mines finished, the men went back to their original families, aware that they had explicitly acted against the norms of the colonizer.

Others came to oppose imperial expansion and oppression more directly. The oppression of local women was easy to see in the break-up of families and the harsh conditions. A few women became prophets, leading their people to a variety of actions against empire. At the time, prophetesses arose in the colonized and non-colonized world alike In 1856, while fetching water, the teenaged Nongqawuse (c. 1840–c. 1900) of the Xhosa of South Africa met with two spirits, who had a solution to the deadly disease plaguing Xhosa cattle. The Xhosa should kill all their cattle as well as their crops and food supplies. After that, new and better cattle would appear in a purified form; new and better crops would spring up. The Xhosa had successfully fought off the British earlier in the 1850s, with some suspecting that a British official had somehow gotten to the teenager and encouraged her to have the cattle and crops destroyed. The result was famine among the Xhosa and a British takeover of their land. Other prophetesses appeared in these menacing times, often to fortify their families and neighbors. They were part of a tradition of millennialist leaders who had grown in influence and number as colonialism advanced. As a woman, Nonquawuse, pregnant and unmarried, symbolized the mother who would give birth to the savior of the people.

Indigenous women in newly colonized areas of the Pacific, the interiors of Africa, and the Western Hemisphere were in fact dispossessed as never before, their children sometimes taken from them. They themselves were also forced to renounce local ways of thinking and behaving. In 1840, when a Maori chief, Rangi Topeora (c. 1790–c. 1870), signed a treaty with the British, she believed it was a grant of British citizenship, whereas the British took it as an acknowledgment of their sovereignty. Hundreds of thousands of immigrants flooded New Zealand, setting up missionary and commercial outposts as the Maori themselves dwindled from disease. In Australia and New Zealand British officials seized thousands of young children for re-education, putting them in orphanages or with settler families. As for women chiefs and authorities like Rangi Topeora, missionaries there as elsewhere tried to "civilize" them with lessons in domesticity even as local women leaders maintained their positions of authority and were at the forefront of many unsuccessful battles to keep the interlopers from taking their lands. Ironically, Maori women, the first colonized women to get the vote, engaged in resistance against the invading whites.

Along with women in the West, many women living under colonialism cut their fertility, causing real concern among imperial officials late in the nineteenth century as it had done in the past. In the Belgian Congo, for example, rates of childbirth collapsed under the lethal rule of King Leopold. Reduced fertility may well have occurred because of insufficient food—even starvation or other punishing physical conditions. The decline in births, however, importantly meant fewer laborers in mines and on rubber, palm tree, coffee, and other plantations. Maori women, mentioned above, had a higher fertility rate than white settlers or than colonized women elsewhere, but infant mortality among the Maori was high as well. In other places, repressive imperial rule discouraged child-bearing. Women's deliberate practices of birth control resulting from despotic imperial policies constituted yet another form of opposition.

Colonized women and men were becoming rebelliously nationalistic across Africa, the Middle East, East and South Asia, and the Pacific Islands. South African–born teacher, Adelaide Dube, had earned her bachelor of science degree in the United States and then returned to South Africa to become an influential teacher. She married the owner of a prominent newspaper supporting the Zulu cause. In 1913, her poem "Africa: My Native Land" appeared in her husband's paper, marking the burial of the Zulu king but the simultaneous promulgation of the Natives' Land Act confiscating African land and moving Africans themselves to the confinement of official reservations.[10] At the turn of the century, nationalists also objected to both actual marriage and concubinage of local women with European men: as one newspaper columnist asked, would you "continue indifferent when you see your sister, your daughters sold for *prostitutes*, while you aspire to rise?"[11]

Women's nationalist participation accelerated, becoming more cohesive. As Westerners spread the idea of non-Western women's backwardness, some non-Western women organized beyond issues of women's status and behavior. In India, as we have seen, middle-class reformers had attempted to eliminate the occupation of street performer as degrading to all women but also because their supposed degradation served as imperialists' excuse to control India further. Periodicals sprang up in India, Egypt, various other regions of the Ottoman Middle East, and China to debate the condition of women and to improve their education, rights, and treatment in the family and across all of society. The province of Bengal in India by the end of the nineteenth century alone had some twenty magazines edited by women or for which they wrote. Their participation spoke to a rebellion against older restrictions. Other women in India joined the Indian National Congress lobbying for more general reforms in the colony. An ocean away, authors and activists such as Zitkala-Sa saw women's cultural advances as a way to strengthen their people.

Anti-colonial activism took other forms. Women regularly worked across the globe, a fact that made imperialists salivate over the prospect of controlling and taxing that work or reducing its political potential. Among their many occupations was beer-brewing, which imperial governments increasingly outlawed. It continued, with women using a variety of strategies to circumvent the prohibition, including employing scouts to look out for inspectors. In South Africa, women working in markets were so harshly regulated that they were forced into domestic service for the invasive white settlers. Again, officials aimed to control their movements, tax any work they were doing, and prevent them from leaving abusive employers, seeking better-paid work, or acting politically.

The mechanism for this control in South Africa became the "pass" system, by which people were obliged to carry an identification paper charting their movements. The person violated the pass if he or she moved outside a given

FIGURE 9.3 *Dahomey Amazons, women warriors, c. 1897. These warriors evolved from the early modern palace guards into a full-blown and highly disciplined fighting force. Although respected as soldiers and even feared by Africans and Europeans alike, eventually superior French weaponry defeated them after several dozen battles at the turn of the century. Courtesy of Chris Hellier/ Corbis Getty Images.*

territory without the express permission of an employer. Women rose up to protest this white-imposed "pass" system in their own lands.

One of the first protests came in the Orange Free State, officially part of Britain's South African colony by the early twentieth century. In the 1890s, a "Pass law" enacted there ordered all African women to carry government registration cards. As soon as it came into effect, police, employers, and officials used these cards to restrict women's movements in the public sphere, especially when it came to employment or activism. In 1913, African women in the Orange province petitioned the governor with a list of their grievances. The first was that they were simply not allowed the freedom of movement that women in other parts of South Africa had and that the pass itself subjected them to onerous taxation that women earlier had not paid. The economic consequences were that they could not participate in the ordinary labor market in which workers could find the most remunerative employment. "It is an effective means of enforcing labour, and as such, cannot have any justification whatever on the ground of necessity or expediency," they protested.

There were cultural consequences as well: according to them the pass "lowers the dignity of women and throws to pieces every element of respect to which they are entitled." In fact, the pass law had a chilling intent: "it is the most effective weapon the governing powers could resort to to make the natives and coloured women in the Province of the Orange Free State ever feel their inferiority, which is only another way of perpetuating oppression regardless of the feelings of those who are governed."[12] Not being able to move freely and needing a pass from an employer forced them to gain outside employment in the first place rather than conducting their own businesses such as running market stalls, laundering and brewing at home, or doing other jobs that might take them on the streets. As they marched by the hundreds in protest, their slogan was "We have done with pleading, we now demand," these women declared. Thereafter, women continued demonstrations against the law during which they burned their passes. As the pass system spread and evolved into full-blown Apartheid rule across all of South Africa, their activism established a tradition of women's protest against the increasing violence against African peoples by the Boers and British.

The Irish in the British Empire were equally active against foreign control and built political and cultural wings to their movement. Long oppressed by demands for ever higher rents and driven from their lands by wealthy British landowners, Irish men organized Sinn Fein (We Ourselves)—a party focused on Irish independence. Women sought membership in the various Irish independence groups, but their political help was usually rejected unless they would cook and sew for the men. Still, committed women persisted in their activism, organizing signal corps and training in medicine and the care and use of weapons. Activists such as Maud Gonne and Constance Markiewicz took leadership roles, with Gonne promoting the substitution of Irish culture for British, thereby building a deeper allegiance to Ireland. They offered alternative celebrations for children whenever royal visits occurred so that they would not have to participate in events that included parroting patriotic British poems or singing about the virtues of empire. They also sponsored Irish theater instead of performances of English plays, in which Markiewicz participated. However, Markiewicz, for her part, took a far more militant role, organizing and financing troops for a future uprising, selling her jewels and other assets to do so. From a society aesthete, she became a soldier, announcing that women should wear short skirts, sturdy boots, and "buy a revolver."[13]

In 1910, Mexican men and women rose up against a government that took farms from ordinary peasants to give to wealthy landowners and to US citizens eager to expand their agricultural and mining holdings in Mexico—a form of business *imperialism*. Among the many factions in the Mexican Revolution (1910–20), Emiliano Zapatista mobilized the peasantry to restore their land ownership while others worked for a variety of political goals including liberal constitutionalism. Amid factionalism, women provisioned armies for which there were no other sources of food or medical care. Individuals went along with their soldier-partners to provide these and also sexual services, while still others actually took up arms and became *soldaderos*. Landowner Margarita Neri (1865–?) raised an army of some thousand fighters, which, as an excellent marksman, she led herself.

Before the Revolution, Mexican women had weighed in on policy and politics and would continue to do so during it. Already in 1901, journalist Juana Belen Gutierrez de Mendoza was publicizing government corruption; she later joined the Zapatistas. Others provided news and commentary while also agitating as feminists. Amid ongoing battles, a Feminist Congress took place in Yucatan in 1916, leading to new property and other rights for women. Still, as the war progressed, women soldiers were often equated with loose, even immoral women despite their heroism. The public sang ballads and listened to romantic songs about individual heroine soldiers, but officials worked to erase their pivotal contributions, including their manning of guns and shaping of new constitutional principles. Such erasure eventually strengthened the Mexican budget, as women veterans were then denied the pensions awarded their male comrades at the Revolution's end.

Conclusion

Empire came in many forms. Of whatever type, imperial rule—including US business imperialism in Mexico—affected and oppressed women, especially as older empires such as that of Spain declined and new more vigorous ones like that of Belgium advanced. Imperialism added further tools of domination to the male privilege that already existed; it increased demands on colonized women to be reproducers and producers and to endure the assaults by brutal colonizers such as Carl Peters. Although officially slavery ended, slave-like conditions continued to shape the image and the reality of most colonized peoples—men and women alike. At home, colonizers exoticized portrayals of colonized women, while enjoying all the products they worked to produce on plantations. Officials devised programs to make citizens of the dominant powers into hearty imperial races. As imperial managers drove the colonial workforce, women's opposition to imperialism grew in word and deed. Those deeds included fighting in the Mexican Revolution or facilitating the work of secret societies in the Ottoman and other empires. Meanwhile, the imperial powers continued to compete with one another in building military capacity to control the activism of colonists and to fight one another for empire. Massive global warfare followed.

Glossary

Berber	A North African ethnic group, some of whom have intermarried with Arabs.
Business imperialism	Investment in less powerful regions and states that gives foreign states the influence that an imperial state might have but without the costs of direct rule.
Durbar	Large public ceremonies or receptions in India sponsored by princes or high British officials.
Opium Wars	A series of conflicts beginning in 1839 between China and Britain over British merchants/smugglers illegally bringing opium into China.
Theosophy	A mixed set of beliefs and rituals based on ideas from India, Egypt, and other parts of the world that aimed to find the hidden or occult secrets of the cosmos.
Xhosa	The second largest ethnic group in South Africa.
Zulu	A South African ethnic group that comprised a powerful kingdom in the nineteenth century. The kingdom was ultimately conquered by the British but Zulu people comprise a major population group in South Africa today.

Notes

1 Quoted in Claire C. Robertson, *Sharing the Same Bowl: A Socioeconomic History of Women and Class in Accra, Ghana* (Bloomington: Indiana University Press, 1984), 129.

2 Emily Lynn Osborn, *Our New Husbands Are Here: Household, Gender, and Politics in a West African State from the Slave Trade to Colonial Rule* (Athens: Ohio University Press, 2011), 130–1.

3 These examples are treated most effectively in Nancy Rose Hunt, "An Acoustic Register, Tenacious Images, and Congolese Scenes of Rape and Repetition," *Cultural Anthropology*, 23:2 (2008): 220–53.

4   Gertrude Simmons Bonnin/Zitkala-Sa, "School Days of an Indian Girl,"
    Atlantic Monthly, 0085:58 (February 1900): 190.
5   Fadhma A. M. Amrouche, *My Life Story: The Autobiography of a Berber
    Woman*, translated and with an introduction by Dorothy S. Blair (New
    Brunswick, NJ: Rutgers University Press, 1989. First published by Librairie
    Francois Maspero, Paris, 1968), 3–18, 43–8, 159.
6   Liliuokalani, Queen of Hawaii. *Hawaii's Story by Hawaii's Queen*
    (Boston: Lee and Shepard, 1898), Chapter XLIV "Imprisonment—Forced
    Abdication." As digitized at http://digital.library.upenn.edu/women/
    liliuokalani/hawaii/hawaii.html.
7   Quoted in Amy Kaplan, "Romancing the Empire: The Embodiment of
    American Masculinity in the Popular Historical Novel of the 1890s, *American
    Literary History*, 2:4 (December 1990): 659.
8   M. J. Daymond, et al., eds., *Women Writing Africa: The Southern Region*
    (New York: Feminist Press, 2003), 148–52.
9   Charles Darwin, *The Descent of Man and Selection in Relationship to Sex*
    (New York: D Appleton, 1879 [1871]), 563.
10 M. J. Daymond et al., *Women Writing Africa: The Southern Region*
    (New York: Feminist Press, 2003), 106.
11 Quoted in Carina E. Ray, *Crossing the Color Line: Race, Sex, and the
    Contested Politics of Colonialism in Ghana* (Athens: Ohio University Press,
    2008), 8.
12 Native and Coloured Women of the Province of the Orange Free State,
    "Petition," 1912 from the National Archives of South Africa, Pretoria,
    Transvaal Archives Depot, National Archives Repository [Ref: GG1542
    50/284 as reproduced in M. J. Daymond et al., *Women Writing Africa: The
    Southern Region* (New York: Feminist Press, 2003), 159–60.
13 Gina Sigillito, *Daughters of Maeve: 50 Irish Women Who Changed the World*
    (New York: Kensington, 2007), 87.

Further Reading

Amrouche, Fadhma. *My Life Story: The Autobiography of a Berber Woman*. New
    Brunswick, NJ: Rutgers University Press, 1989.
George, Abosede. *Making Modern Girls: A History of Girlhood, Labor, and
    Social Development in 20th Century Colonial Lagos*. Athens: Ohio University
    Press, 2014.
Bay, Mia. *To Tell the Truth Freely: The Life of Ida B. Wells*. New York: Hill and
    Wang, 2009.
Clancy-Smith, Julia Ann. *Mediterraneans: North Africa and Europe in an Age of
    Migration, C. 1800–1900*. Berkeley: University of California Press, 2011
Hunt, Nancy Rose. *A Colonial Lexicon: Of Birth Ritual, Medicalization, and
    Mobility in the Congo*. Durham, NC: Duke University Press, 1999.
Hunt, Nancy Rose. *A Nervous State: Violence, Remedies, and Reverie in Colonial
    Congo*. Durham, NC: Duke University Press, 2016.
Kent, Susan Kingsley. *A New History of Britain: Four Nations and an Empire*.
    New York: Oxford University Press, 2017.

Kent, Susan Kingsley. *Queen Victoria: Gender and Empire*. New York: Oxford University Press, 2016.

Oldenburg, Veena Talwar. "Lifestyle as Resistance: The Case of the Courtesans of Lucknow," *Feminist Studies* 16: 2 (Summer 1990), 259–287.

Ray, Carina E. *Crossing the Color Line: Race, Sex, and the Contested Politics of Colonialism in Ghana*. Athens: Ohio University Press, 2015.

Sarkar, Tanika. *The Making of Amar Jiban: A Modern Autobiography*. New Delhi: Zubaan, 2013.

Wildenthal, Lora. *German Women for Empire, 1884–1945*. Durham, NC: Duke University Press, 2001.

10

Global Warfare, 1914–45

In 1937, Carolina Maria de Jesus (1914–1977) moved to Sao Paulo where she built herself a shack out of cardboard, tin, and other refuse—a shelter like others in the favelas (slums) across urban Brazil. Carolina Maria de Jesus had been born in the countryside to a single mother who forced her to go to school. During her brief stint there, she learned to read, but it was in the favela that she began writing a diary of life during the economic depression of the 1930s and the Second World War that followed. De Jesus's diary affirmed her African heritage and the existence of her three children, each born of a different father. Every day she battled for food and survival in a neighborhood where neighbors seemed jealous of her, sociability was often tense, and violence lurked. The already precarious life of slums declined during hard times as rural people flocked to cities, often competing to survive. Carolina Maria de Jesus led a life not unlike that of others across the globe during the economically catastrophic 1930s.

De Jesus's life was sandwiched between two world wars—also catastrophic—and the global struggle for independence and justice in the colonies. Yet, empires relentlessly expanded during these decades, especially where new raw materials such as oil appeared to entice imperial leaders to take over resource-rich regions. In the process, societies became militarized and gender came into play: in wartime resources were shifted from civilians—mostly women and children—to soldiers, the majority of whom were male; millions of ordinary people suffered deprivation that women were often tasked with remedying. Authoritarian and male military leadership became an ideal in many places, leaving democratic principles far behind and unleashing repression on targeted civilians. The First and Second World Wars disrupted life worldwide. The war against civilians flourished in such acts as the artificial famines in Greater Syria and India, bombing and firebombing of cities in Japan and Germany, and the horrific acts of genocide and the Holocaust.

As revolutions erupted in Mexico, Ireland, Russia, and elsewhere in the early twentieth century, women were often at the forefront of activity, including frontline fighting. Equally, they were conscripted into the world wars in a variety of ways, ranging from forced labor in colonies to serving on the front lines as doctors and nurses. Gender disorder seemed to take hold in many parts of the world, for example, in the Ottoman Empire or Africa where men and provisions alike were stripped from communities. There and elsewhere women assumed the physical work of men on farms, in the factory, and in the maintenance of transportation and a range of civic institutions. Rape and starvation were also their lot. Many urban women were stunned by the transformation into barbarity of their increasingly sophisticated consumer lives, the dynamic culture of radio, film, and the arts and the more open sexuality of the 1920s and 1930s.

The First World War in an Age of Revolutions

Amid the cataclysmic civil war in Mexico and resistance to imperialism, in 1914, the First World War broke out among the imperial powers, with Britain, France, Russia, Italy, and eventually Japan and the United States fighting Germany, Austria-Hungary, and the Ottoman Empire. Each nation was eager to preserve or expand both territory and imperial stature. At first, governments closed down factories making consumer goods or converted them to the manufacture of wartime materiel. Women working in these light industries were sacked. By 1915, as millions of men on the front lines lost their lives or were incapacitated from war wounds, women were enlisted to take up the slack in munitions and other factories and in transportation, farming, education, and trade. Women also served as nurses on the front lines and in Russia they formed all-women military units. In places with segregated men's and women's jobs, gender expectations blurred, sometimes causing disturbances. The combination of women's and men's full effort in military struggle on the battle field and on the home front is called total war.

Wartime conditions in the First World War also brought uprisings. Muslim women in the Russian Empire took to the streets against the relentless conscription of men. Soldiers on the battlefronts in Europe rebelled against their slaughter—a rejection of male sacrifice and a sign of pent-up anger. The cost of living soared when the production of goods from civilians dropped off in favor of diverting resources to combat soldiers. Anti-Semitism rose, as citizens blamed Jews for the wartime tragedy. Women refused to pay the sky-high prices, including rent, and saw big- and small-business people as immoral profiteers. "Either deport us all to another place or cast us into the sea,"[1] starving Ottoman women wrote the government in 1917. In 1916, as discontent rose, Constance Markievicz (1868–1927) participated in the Easter Uprising against British rule over Ireland—a rebellion that was brutally repressed and its leaders executed. Markievicz was spared, despite her history of activism and outright call for women to revolt and despite her public hatred for British colonial rule in Ireland. Across Europe civilians took to the streets, though in the war-torn east of the continent many were often too weak from hunger and displacement to do so. Like soldiers, they were shell-shocked from rape and destruction of their homes and villages.

Even before 1914, European military buildup and news of colonial wars had led to activism on behalf of peace. In the face of increasingly lethal and accurate weaponry, German Bertha von Suttner persuaded Alfred Nobel to found a peace prize for outstanding efforts to prevent or end conflict. It was first awarded in 1901, and in 1905, she herself received the award. In 1915, during the First World War, a group of women from twelve countries met in The Hague, establishing the Women's International League for Peace and Freedom (WILPF) and agreeing to visit the heads of states of a number of combatant countries and lobby them to negotiate peace. The effort was unsuccessful, but the declaration of principles these women drew up and circulated to heads of state was remarkably similar to American President Woodrow Wilson's Fourteen Points, issued some two years later.

In the late winter of 1917, as conditions worsened across Eurasia because of the deprivation and wartime slaughter, women workers began taking to the streets of St. Petersburg. Across the Russian Empire they had protested the high cost of living since 1916, but on International Women's Day of 1917, soldiers joined in their protests against prices, food shortages, and government disregard for civilians and the military alike. Protests escalated, and within ten days the tsar had abdicated. First among the major powers to do so, the new civilian government gave women the right to vote. The next fall the Bolsheviks—a group of Marxist socialists—took power and by January 1918 had formed a renamed "Communist" government that ended the ownership of private property in industry, finance, and agriculture. As Marxism promised that a workers' revolution would benefit women, some changes soon took place in the social sphere but mostly because women activists made it so.

Marxist thinkers had advertised that women needed liberation from oppressive conditions. Aleksandra Kollontai (1872–1952) became a major spokesperson for the new Communist government in Russia, especially embracing the cause of women. Like other Marxists, she denounced "bourgeois" or middle-class feminists for ignoring the needs of working women and mothers and for pitting women against men. In the early twentieth century, most feminists were middle- and upper-class even though they organized employment agencies for working women and groups to check on working conditions for women in factories and workshops. These socialist-feminists were militant in their attacks on the suffrage movement and many opposed the war. From a wealthy family herself, Kollontai had been a leading organizer and opponent of war and a leader in the Bolshevik takeover in 1917. Named minister of public welfare, she organized social programs, including childcare for working parents, public clinics to provide health care, and welfare assistance for those who needed it.

Kollontai pointed to feminism's creation of a worldwide movement. "Its main objective was the achievement of equal rights for women, equal rights with men in all spheres of life within the limits of a bourgeois capitalist society." Yet feminists were always deceptive, acting "to woo the support of the female proletariat, to bribe their sympathy and thereby enhance their own political significance." She attacked the "universalism" of feminists of her generation, appearing to be "the advocates and spokesmen of the demands and aspirations of all women. . . ." In reality, they only spoke to benefit themselves, she claimed. The accusation of classism would be leveled at feminists down to the present alongside charges of racism, homophobia, able-bodied pride, and general discrimination against diverse peoples.

Kollontai claimed that middle-class feminists concentrated on the vote instead of addressing the real needs of working-class women: that is, those connected with their triple burden of working full time, bearing and raising children, and doing all the tasks of ensuring a healthy and functional household. "The feminists made yet another mistake: they absolutely refused to take into account that woman bears a twofold responsibility towards society and that the 'natural right' which they were so fond of quoting not only demands that women should effectively contribute to society but also that they should provide society with healthy offspring. . . ."[2]

In the early 1920s, Kollontai also supported those Communists who believed that their revolution should feature workers' interests at the grass roots. Bolsheviks, who believed in elite party leadership, used her ideas that sexual partnerships should not be coercive but rather free and sincerely maintained to discredit her support for more democracy in Russia. Her opposition to the double standard in sexual conduct by which men might have multiple relations, as did the male Bolshevik leadership, but women should not was another strike against her. Kollontai became persona nongrata for both of these positions though mostly for rejecting the elitist view of the Bolshevik Revolution.

Many women followed the Communist leadership of the new USSR (Soviet Union, 1923) who were creating a modern industrial state. The male-dominated bureaucracy enlisted women to be tractor drivers and lathe operators, shining publicity on their newfound industrial skills. In part, the state needed women because a cohort of young men had been killed in the war, had become maimed, or died of the influenza that broke out as the war was ending. Moreover, enlisting women was a sign of modernity and the creation of the new Soviet person. Yet Communist leaders of the USSR inflicted famine by taking control of peasant land and by executing hundreds of thousands of both ordinary and high-level citizens. To rebuild the population, they ended support for birth control and abortions and outlawed homosexuality. Women's participation as leaders declined to virtually nothing.[3]

Women in Motion

The Bolshevik revolution turned into a civil war between its supporters and opponents, causing a surge in migration from Russia. Wealthy and poor alike headed for western Europe, the Middle East, and other parts of Asia. This was, however, just part of the flood of migrants around the world due to the violence of empire, the horrific wartime conditions, the postwar settlement in Europe and the resulting economic downturn, especially caused by the further mechanization of agriculture and the drop-off in orders for wartime supplies. The Peace of Paris of 1919 that ended the First World War created new nations based on the racist implications of Woodrow Wilson's idea that nations be based on distinct "peoples" or ethnicities forming independent states. As Poles, Czechs, Hungarians, Greeks, and Turks violently drove other ethnicities from their borders, millions of people lost their lives, homes, livelihoods, and the lands on which their families may have lived for centuries. Because of the great loss of men's lives and the disabled condition of others from the war, women and children formed the majority of refugees.

Simultaneously, in the US South conditions deteriorated for blacks, who lost positions as sharecroppers in the countryside or artisanal work in the cities. Men often migrated first, with women forming a human network to spread information about those northern cities that flourished because of wartime needs and booming manufacturing. These African American migrant networks were especially active, as women sought information on the possibilities of travel and jobs from those who had already left and from black newspapers. There were also rumors, such as that of a "Great Northern Drive on the 15th of May," about which there is no record: "I am a reader of the Defender and I am asked so much about the great Northern drive on the 15th of May. We want more understanding about it for there is a great many wants to get ready for that day & the depot agent never gives us any satisfaction when we ask for what they don't want us to leave here." In this case, white people aimed to discourage the migration of those poorly paid workers on whom their own comfort depended and thus suppressed or falsified information about transportation such as railroad schedules. Women then turned to family and other networks, plus the black press in the North. "I want to ask you to please publish in your next Saturdays paper just what the fare will be on the day so we all will know & can be ready. So many women here are wanting to go that day. They are all working women and we cant get work here so much now, the white women tell us we just want to make money to go North and we do so pleases kindly ans. This in your next paper."[4] Workers' quest for the empowerment that mobility could potentially provide and their resistance to whites paralleled women's protests against government measures to prevent their mobility in South Africa.

The tradition of forced, lethal migration that Germans used to decimate the Herero in Africa before the war also reappeared during it as well. In a forced migration campaign during the First World War, the Ottoman military drove Armenians from their homes, the men often separated from the women and children. Then the women and children—both girls and boys—were most often raped. Some young girls of seven or eight years old were raped so badly that they had difficulty continuing the march, in which case they were simply shot. Some might be sold to traffickers. Such was the reporting from missionaries, German allies of the Ottomans, and other witnesses. The widespread trafficking in unaccompanied women seeking relief and opportunity was yet another component of the wartime and postwar cruelty that millions of eastern and southeastern Europeans suffered.

Further Expanding Empires Meet Further Expanding Activism

At the end of the First World War in 1918, empires still expanded even as others—Russian, German, Ottoman, and Austro-Hungarian—failed to survive the conflict, causing a rush to revive masculinity that had taken such a beating in the war. Destruction of arms, legs, genitals, faces and other body parts shredded the image of an invincible masculinity. Some among the wounded were unable to survive without round-the-clock care. Other fighters, asserting their physical prowess and warrior status, refused to disband, while governments—the Japanese, British, French, and their allies—rushed to claim possessions of the losing powers. Men in the colonial armies had often gained new fighting skills on the European, African, and Middle Eastern fronts in the First World War. From their experiences of this brutal war, anti-imperial activism escalated too. This activism and the repression of it added to the violence and tumult of the wartime and postwar years.

Women such as those in China and the Middle East grew even more active because of the Peace of Paris, and protests became legion, even leading to massacres. In 1919, young Chinese women took part in the May Fourth Movement protesting the award to Japan of territorial rights to Germany's sphere of influence in China following the First World War. The May Fourth Movement, like similar movements seeking independence, claimed that patriarchal control of women had to be reduced in order for the country to become free and modern to the same degree that women in the West were. Women writers escalated the pace of their stories, essays, and autobiographical writing. In 1930, a new code of laws allowed women free choice of marriage partners and the right to equal inheritance. Conditions did not change for most women, however; despite growing urbanization the vast majority lived in rural areas where patriarchal customs prevailed.

FIGURE 10.1 *Women attendants of Marcus Garvey marching up 7th Avenue in New York, 1924. African American women who had migrated north participated in growing activism, often expressing postwar militarization. Here, women supporters provide a uniformed escort for Jamaican-born Marcus Garvey, who advocated black nationalism and Pan-Africanism. Garveyism connected local followers to one another and to the wider world of African liberation movements. Courtesy of George Rinhart Corbis Getty Images.*

Ba Chin's *Family*, a novel written in the 1920s and published in 1931, was an indictment of the ways in which women in typical Chinese households— young women in particular—were harassed to the point of gruesomely taking their lives. During various street protests in China, close by in Korea, Ewha University student Yu Gwan-sun (1902–1920) participated in the March 1 demonstrations also against Japan's colonialism. When the colonial government closed the universities, she still worked to organize protests. In 1920 she was arrested and tried for her participation in the commemorative demonstrations on March 1. In the process, her parents were shot and killed and Yu imprisoned. Even from prison, she continued organizing but eventually died there, many believed from torture. Women's activism remained a sign of modernity for nationalist activists and indicated to them the promise of the reformed nation-state to come.

African women were similarly active under colonialism, and many had been further politicized by the war, as forced recruitment upset family life and caused hardship especially where fighting also brought seizure of goods and destruction of property. Drawn into global economic and cultural networks,

some African women bonded with activists or religious and family networks
in Latin America, the Caribbean, Europe, and the United States. They also
continued to resist government encroachment on their livelihoods: in 1925,
Igbo women in British-run Nigeria had undertaken the Dancing Women's
Movement, protesting the deterioration of living conditions that included
the devastation from influenza, the increased taxation on men, and growing
supervision of women's traditional undertakings, including their markets.
In 1929, Igbo women rebelled more massively against their own taxation
and the encroachments of colonial officials. Mobilizing kin networks and
women's associations and painting their bodies, some ten thousand women
blocked colonial roads, invaded factories, and shamed African collaborators
with the imperialists. The result: the women were attacked, arrested, abused,
and killed in the dozens by the army to put down this "Women's War"
against colonial rule. Few in Britain, however, were concerned by the
slaughter of unarmed women.

To the north, an uprising in 1919 and early 1920s, brought Egyptian
feminists out from the sex segregation of the harem to join men seeking
national independence from Britain. Among women of all classes, ages, and
religions engaged in the uprising, Muslim women took off their veils in
public demonstrations, showing themselves to be modern and their country
thus worthy of self-rule. Despite the male-female alliance, once Egypt gained
its nominal independence in 1923, the male allies refused to give women
the vote or to fulfill other promises of political rights. Huda Sha'arawi,
a pioneer in the movement, analyzed the situation in her memoirs: "In
moments of danger, when women emerge by their side, men utter no protest.
Yet women's great acts and endless sacrifices do not change men's views of
women ... Men have singled out women of outstanding merit and put them
on a pedestal to avoid recognizing the capabilities of all women."

Huda Sha'arawi (1879–1947) was born into a wealthy family in Cairo,
Egypt, where she received instruction in the Qu'ran, Arabic and Turkish
languages, and other subjects. At age thirteen, her parents arranged for her
marriage to a prominent and much older cousin, with whom she did not live
for eight years after the marriage. During the First World War, Sha'arawi's
husband became a leader of the Wafd, the movement for Egypt's autonomy
from Britain; Huda, having reconciled with him, led the Wafd Women's
Committee. In this cause, the women marched and demonstrated across
Cairo, often coming face to face with armed soldiers during their first
demonstration in 1919 when hundreds of wealthy women broke loose from
the harems to march against the British.

Huda Sha'arawi described the scene: "On the morning of 16 March,
I sent placards ... bearing slogans in Arabic and French painted in white on
a background of black—the color of mourning. Some of the slogans read,
'Long Live the Supporters of Justice and Freedom,' others said 'Down with
Oppressors and Tyrants' and 'Down with Occupation.'" During their March,
Sha'arawi noticed that the marchers were leaving the agreed-upon route

because of soldiers holding machine guns to halt the women's progress. She challenged a British soldier who aimed his gun at her: "I shouted in a loud voice, 'Let me die so Egypt shall have an Edith Cavell' [an English martyr in World War I] . . . Continuing in the direction of the soldiers, I called upon the women to follow. A pair of arms grabbed me . . . , 'This is madness. Do you want to risk the lives of the students? It will happen if the British raise a hand against you.' At the thought of . . . the Egyptian losses sure to occur, I came to my senses and stopped still. We stood still for three hours while the sun blazed down on us."[5]

In South Asia, Mohandas Gandhi became the most prominent postwar opponent of empire, gathering around him millions of followers. As the Indian National Congress became a mass movement, the British army became trigger happy across the empire, killing some 1,300 pilgrims gathered at a shrine in Amritsar, India, in 1919, and wounding thousands more—men, women, and children alike. A "mob" the British called the dead and wounded and then declared martial law. From London, Sarojini Naidu, Indian nationalist poet, who would become leader of the Indian National Congress in 1925, gave so accusatory a speech that members of Parliament loudly denounced her. In it, she pointed to "blood-guiltiness of the British, not just for the murder and maiming of thousands in the massacre" but for "the insult and agony inflicted upon the veiled women of the Punjab." Her denunciation was direct and pointed: "Englishmen, you who pride yourselves upon your chivalry, you who hold more precious than your imperial treasures the honour and chastity of your women" then assaulted Indian women at Amritsar. "My sisters were stripped naked, they were flogged, they were outraged." Her final judgment of Britain rang out: "You deserve no Empire. You have lost your soul; you have the stain of blood-guiltiness upon you; no nation that rules by tyranny is free; it is the slave of its own despotism."[6]

Women's active opposition to British rule mounted in the 1920s, in some cases joining with Gandhi's nonviolent supporters and in others serving as members of his inner circles. They raised a loud outcry on the publication of US author Katherine Mayo's *Mother India* in 1926. The book invented an inflammatory list of women's mothering practices, accusing them of sexually stimulating their male children until they became incapable of adult male rationality and achievement. Indian feminists were outraged at the insults. In other instances, women used violence in hopes of ejecting the British from their lives. In India, Kalpana Dutt served nine years in prison for participating in planning an attack on a European club whose warning sign read "No Dogs and Indians Allowed." Preeti Waddadar, who took part in the actual attack and then swallowed a cyanide capsule rather than surrender to police, illustrated women's commitment to suicidal anti-colonial agitation. In 1932, Bina Das attempted to assassinate Sir Stanley Jackson at the Calcutta University convocation ceremony: "I had been thinking—is life worth living in an India, so subject to a wrong and continually groaning under the tyranny of a foreign government or is it not better to make one supreme protest against it by offering one's life away? Would not the immolation of a daughter of India and of England awaken India to the sin of its acquiescence to its continued state of subjection and England to the iniquities of its proceedings ... All these [sufferings of the people] and many others worked on my feelings and worked them into a frenzy."[7]

Anti-imperial protest was determined and multifaceted. African women— and men too—took to writing to defend the practice of genital cutting, which indicated that a girl or young woman was ready for marriage and motherhood. Jomo Kenyatta, leader of Kenyan resistance, stressed genital cutting as intrinsic to the ethnic group's values. Since the early twentieth century and especially in the interwar years European missionaries, reformers, and government officials waged a campaign to stamp out the practice. To do so, some imperial officers directed local councils to outlaw it; some enforced the law with inspections of girls' genitals or they used missionaries to try to assist them through religious persuasion. The imperialists' concern, when it came down to it, was that infant mortality and low birthrates were due to genital cutting, thus depleting the supply of labor from which their regimes could profit. They announced, however, that the practice indicated a backward culture, while feminists protested that any prohibition denied women their autonomy and rights and that male outsiders were enforcing their will on helpless girls and young women.

African women resisted these self-proclaimed reformers, believing that their local practices actually enabled fertility and prevented catastrophes during childbirth. They supported genital cutting for men and women alike as part of community building and networking among groups of similarly aged children or "age-grades" from whom the next generation of leaders would emerge. Ceremonies around this cutting seemed to indicate a parity with men, who underwent circumcision and other interventions in the sexed male body. Thus, as inspectors set themselves up in villages to monitor the practice, individual Africans had these procedures done in out-of-the-way places beyond where an inspector's mental horizons would lead him to look. As Westerners, including feminists, persisted in their hostility to genital cutting, resistance to imperial meddling remained entrenched across the colonies.

International activism also thrived. The WILPF, composed of women who had opposed the First World War, continued to be active in opposing imperial power during the 1920s, the US branch protesting the US occupation of Haiti in 1926 and its invasions in Latin America and Asia in the interwar period. These Western women were increasingly distrusted by women from the colonized "south," because they flaunted their supposed racial superiority. When German activists at an international meeting of WILPF sponsored a resolution condemning the presence of black troops in their country after the First World War on the grounds that blacks would rape white women, African American women had to lobby hard to block the motion even though they could not stop the hateful racist speeches. Local women in India, additionally, did not want British women with their claims to greater knowledge and intelligence to start an Indian branch of WILPF. They would do the organizing themselves. During the interwar years, women in the Middle East lobbied the League of Nations to protect Palestine and to allow women in the colonized world to participate in committee discussion on women's issues. Women from Britain and the United States in particular worked successfully to suppress these Middle Eastern women's voices while perpetuating the idea that these women were in fact silenced by their own "backward" men.

Postwar Mass Culture and the Great Depression

Wartime is a life-and-death affair—very basic and without frills. Even as it proceeded to starve bodies, break hearts, and maim and kill, a military ethos was taking societies firmly in hand and moving them to a militarized peacetime. In the 1920s and 1930s, peacetime unfolded around mass society and standardization that had developed during the war. Governments of combatant countries introduced mass rationing during the war, forcing most homemakers to follow state guidelines on what people could eat and even the recipes they should follow. A mass "look" began to take shape in the form of muscular, lithe bodies. Before the war extra flesh was a sign of prosperity, while rural bodies were of necessity muscular and lean, though they might often be worn and weary. The desirable postwar bodies were slim and athletic, shaped to an imagined military perfection. Postwar women, especially working women in offices, stripped away layers of cloth that slowed their movement and essentially shrouded their bodies and exchanged these garments for more standardized slim ones. Like men, who had streamlined clothing far earlier, the wartime need for textiles to make uniforms for millions of soldiers led women of necessity to free up their bodies too. Leaders such as Mustafa Kemal (Atatürk) of the new republic of Turkey used the law to mandate this transformation in clothing, making it so that women were brought into mass society based on a "modern," streamlined look in fashion.

A world of images arose to direct women in achieving this new look. Film studios began showing slender, active women, while beauty contests worked to the same end. Novels such as *Naomi*, serialized in the mid-1920s by Japanese author Tanizaki Junichiro, portrayed modern women as not only complicated in themselves but also complicating the social order as a whole. Tanizaki's heroine in this work is a seductive young woman, entirely taken up with modern Western culture. The film industry also portrayed modern women as vamps, screwballs, and earnest forces for good, thus introducing this new incarnation of women via multiple interpretations of their modernity. The stars of this period such as Butterfly Hu in Shanghai and Louise Brooks in Hollywood were adept at creating such standard depictions of the modern woman—from heartbreaker to heart-of-gold. Other modern girls became sports stars, aviators, or like former star Leni Riefenstahl of Germany, filmmakers themselves. Around the world, films became a prime form of instructive entertainment in the 1920s and 1930s for women, who in many places constituted the majority of the cinema-going audience.

New values often clashed with traditional culture. Turkish women entertainers sang in cafes and private clubs, cutting records for still another media device—the phonograph, which was fast becoming the basis for a thriving industry. Also outside traditions, African American women performed jazz and the blues both in clubs and on records. Now considered classic, their artistry matched that of women painters and sculptors. Frida Kahlo (1907–1954), Mexican painter, mingled the imagery of native peoples, Catholicism, and Mexican forms in her stirring, sometimes grim and lush portraits of herself as the Virgin Mary, a wheelchair victim, or a tortured woman wrapped in chains while garbed in vividly colored clothing. In the Soviet Union, women were additional pioneers in the coming of modern art that was abstract. Olga Rozanova, who would die in the influenza epidemic, painted shimmering lines of color on a white background, hoping to make color and form themselves—not "accurate" representations of people and nature—count as capturing a deeper reality. In Japan, Uemura Shoen, while following many of the conventions of Japanese print-making focused on women's sensuality, broke with those conventions by showing women hard at work both in the home and outside it.

As authors, women of the Harlem Renaissance advanced modernity in literature, writing about race, sexuality, and the tensions of modern society. Zora Neale Hurston (1891–1960) moved to Harlem in 1925 where she published fiction about black women's concubinage and other unsavory aspects of US culture. Her celebrated *Their Eyes Were Watching God* benefitted from her training as an anthropologist, her research in Haiti, and her own life in Florida. Other novels such as *Passing* by Nella Larson captured the mental dilemmas of postwar migration and racial hybridity resulting from African American–White relationships.

Even as writers and artists explored their identities and the experiences often resulting from the drive for modernity, public leaders such as Madame Chiang-kaishek (Mai-ling Soong), wife of the post-Qing Empire leader, publicly emphasized good health and hygiene for the Chinese masses. As a founder of the *New Life Movement* she was widely photographed as a sleek, extremely fit and modern citizen of revolutionary China. The same emphasis occurred in the Soviet where vivid posters showed women in overalls tending machinery or driving tractors—again, fit and vigorous. Women in cities and, to some extent, in the countryside were shown as healthier: their

FIGURE 10.2 *Frida Kahlo, "Me Twice," 1939. Celebrated Mexican artist painted colorful depictions of herself, including this study of her complex identity as Spanish/Mexican woman and as Amerindian. Kalho portrayed her tortured emotional and physical life in other works. One shows a thorny necklace piercing her skin, another features a miniature of her husband Diego Rivera planted in her forehead. Courtesy of Getty Images.*

bodies followed new hygienic procedures and were militarized to this new health. In photographs from across the globe they appear doing energetic tap dancing in kick lines or engaging in robotic-looking aerobic exercises while clad like soldiers in uniforms.

The fit and energetic young women ironically lived under dictators who preached the importance of women's domestic roles, especially their child-bearing potential. Their aim to boost the population was sparked by the ongoing drop in fertility, now augmented by the loss of life in revolutions and world war and by the global birth control movement that also progressed in the 1920s and 1930s, making knowledge of fertility limitation increasingly available. Knowledge of women's ovulatory cycles and mechanical birth control spread, resulting in a drop in fertility by almost half before 1930, especially in the West. A number of women became prominent in the twentieth-century worldwide birth control movement, foremost among them American Margaret Sanger, who made world tours in 1922 and 1935 and influenced such rising leaders as Kato Shidzue (1897–2001) of Japan to become activists too. Kato and Sanger, like most advocates, were concerned with the welfare of poorer women but also wanted all women to have access to family limitation. From the start, Kato's inspiration was Margaret Sanger, who sponsored Planned Parenthood internationally. Privileged through wealth, she read theoretical works that focused on the problems of the working class, especially in the economy.

"I felt instantly her [Margaret Sanger's] magnetism," Kato wrote in 1920. "Listening to her account of the birth control movement, the memory of the overcrowded miners' huts in Western Japan came back so vividly that the idea of my true mission in life flashed over me." She forged ahead on her own in 1923 and worked to transform people's practices, especially such harmful ones as infanticide. She also saw family limitation as a way of making the lives of laboring people less stressful. Above all, Kato believed that birth control would bring about the "elevation of women" and "the betterment of the human race."[8] In the 1930s the Japanese government banned birth control and arrested her.

Governments were often hostile to family planning efforts, as the century was one of rising militarism and politicians made their name with militaristic statements promoting virility, measured not only in martial but sexual prowess. The growing war machines of the interwar years in Italy, Japan, and Germany needed more population not less. Despite much activism against contraception, it continued to spread, bringing the birth rate in 1930s Europe, for example, below replacement rate. People, including those in rural areas, widely used abortion as well as infanticide—mostly of girl babies—to control family size. Other conditions also affected access to birth control as seen in Bolshevik and French response to the severe population loss caused by the First World War and events thereafter: both outlawed abortions and birth control, the French in 1922 and the USSR, as mentioned earlier, in the 1930s.

The great reforms announced by strong men such as Mustafa Kemal, Turkish leader of the successor state to the fallen Ottoman Empire—literacy for women, wearing reform clothing, for example—did not blind their women collaborators to their weaknesses, including the tendency toward authoritarian government and crediting themselves with women's modernity. Many women, for example, had helped modernize societies even before the wartime and promoted the integration of women into the fabric of modern nations. Halide Edib Adivar (1884–1964) was a prominent political activist and novelist in Turkey and became a major promoter of Turkish independence, aiding Atatürk (Mustafa Kemal) in his struggle to free Turkey from an attempted Allied takeover of the country. However, once Atatürk succeeded and assumed dictatorial power, Adivar became a critic. Noting that Atatürk credited himself for such reforms as the modernization of clothing and the elimination of Islam as a state religion, she criticized Turkey's authoritarianism in a series of speeches in the United States in 1928.

"[W]hat is of supreme interest is the change of a democratic state, of five years' standing, into a dictatorial one," she wrote, "without even an altering of the form or the closing of the National Assembly . . . ." To her mind, his rise to supreme power was hardly original. "After all, the Turkish dictatorship was not and is not unique in the world. The postwar world favors dictatorship . . . ." After the failure of the old political institutions to stop the recent catastrophic wars and revolutions, the postwar world "seeks something new." Would-be dictators pointed to democracy's "slow growth," she maintained, whereas "[dictatorships] have the appearance of "doing" all the time, whether they accomplish lasting changes and effect internal reconstruction or not."

Adivar maintained that the congratulations journalists awarded Atatürk for upgrading women's lives and giving them jobs were misplaced. Women had long enjoyed both education and jobs and to hold them had left their seclusion decades before the First World War. "All Turkish men of the progressive type ... especially from 1908 on, have been in favor of the progress of women and have helped to give them rights and opportunities—educational, economic, and social. From the moment Turkish women entered the economic field there has been no discrimination whatever of the kind which European feminists complain of." The war, however, had strengthened their position, as women went to work to provide for their families in the absence of men, thus enhancing their "natural social freedom" already enjoyed before the great conflict.[9] Adivar's unmasking of men's claims to being the main benefactors of women was timely as was her emphasis on the appeal of dictators in the period after the First World War. Her critique mirrored that of feminists elsewhere, who challenged men's claims to having "given" women the vote in Britain, Germany, Scandinavia, the eastern European states, and the United States at the war's end. For decades, women had fought for their rights. The Great Depression that erupted in 1929 and encompassed the globe, made her evaluation of dictatorship troublingly forward-looking.

Economic Depression and the Rise of Authoritarian Saviors

Mass society came into being during the "Great War" and flourished in the Great Depression. The economic crash of 1929 followed a drop in agricultural prices in the 1920s because of postwar overproduction; then financial risk-taking caused a rapid fall in stock markets; finally, businesses collapsed or laid off millions of workers as money went out of circulation and buying of consumer and other goods tumbled. Gender order was once again upset as men lost their jobs, while lower-paid women could piece together stints as laundresses and domestics, and by undertaking other menial work. Single, literate women could still survive as secretaries and the many low-paid service jobs.

The Great Depression of the 1930s was a global phenomenon, but often affecting men and women differently. Strikes abounded among unemployed soldiers as well as producers of raw materials even as militarization took place in many societies. Women in unions redoubled their efforts and in places they rose to the top, calling out directions to "stop the line" or making the hard decisions as to who would get a full-time position or who would be laid off. Among the coffee sorters in Cordoba, Mexico, Sofia Castro Gonzalés began work at age eleven and gradually built a patronage network through which she exercised power. She was known as a great speaker and one who "had no qualms about speaking her mind," as one contemporary put it.[10] Highly religious, she wore men's boots and carried a gun, using it on men when necessary. Breaking through the ideology of men's right to dominate, she and many others of the growing number of union leaders produced change. Still others took different action in hard times: in Northern Nigeria in early 1930s, women revived textile weaving in Igbirra and Kabba, which substituted African fabrics for both costly European textiles and unwanted, inferior Japanese ones. They thus gendered the economic revival in their area. They used their profits to pay for men's migration to seek jobs in Lagos. Likewise, they saved funds by hiding children, which cut their taxes.[11] Less successful under- or unemployed people across the globe continued to resort to selling their children as slave laborers, even to sex traffickers.

The Great Depression crushed the spirit of many men even as these working women showed stubborn resistance. Adolf Hitler (1889–1945) became dictator almost immediately on being selected as chancellor of Germany in 1933 and appealed to those men. He promised to make them "men" again, and women "women," provided they were not tainted by Jewish and other inferior "blood." "The feelings and, above all, the soul of woman have always complemented the mind of man," he announced to an organization of Nazi women. In the 1930s, he described the division of male and female tasks at that moment as "blurred along an unnatural line." Society could only function peacefully "as each sex fulfills its natural mission"; he claimed that feminism had been devised by Jews. In the good old days, there was never a push for women's emancipation. "[A woman] controlled exactly that which nature freely gave her as her due to administer and preserve—just as the man in good times did not have to fear that woman would oust him from his position." Men were by nature to control the larger world—the public and the government—while women's was the "smaller world" that attended to the less significant aspects of life. Yet, Hitler announced to his audience of women, "the great world can only be built upon this smaller world . . . ." In fact, "it is not correct for a woman to invade man's world . . . respect demands that neither sex encroach upon the sphere of the other."[12]

Despite Hitler's appeal to gender differentiation based on women's confinement to the home, many women around the world needed to work. Factory worker Joana de Masi Zero (1916–?), in her *Reminiscences* of the 1930s, described her family's poverty when first her father and then her grandfather died when she was only five years old. She and her sisters went to work, her sisters in a factory and she in a private workshop sewing carpets. Brazil suffered great turmoil in the 1930s, not unlike other countries facing the hardships of the Great Depression. So she went from job to job, finally getting a factory job when she was fourteen. She was actually younger but lying about her age was necessary to get the job. From there she continued her quest for work, finally finding a job that she kept for twenty-five years.

As in other nations, the result of economic and social stress was the rise to power of a dictator: Brazilian dictator Getulio Vargas (1882–1954) served his first term from 1932 to 1945, appealing to the poor and stating that his aim was to provide them with government assistance and good jobs. Vargas crushed opponents and helped the wealthy to regain prosperity but he continued to put programs in place to help the poor. Brazilian workers and the poverty-stricken in these desperate years of the Great Depression often called Getulio Vargas the "Father of the Poor." Joana de Masi Zero agreed: "Many people said that he was a dictator, but he did many things for us workers." She appreciated the fair labor laws, the pension system into which everyone had to pay, and the lack of inflation. She and her sisters had enough money to go to the movies even as they made their own clothes. "We ate well, we lived well. They say he was a dictator, but for us he was good."[13]

Second World War

It was not surprising that this era of technology saw the slaughter of civilians on an unprecedented, massive scale once the Second World War (1937–45) broke out, first in Asia, then Europe, and finally across a wide swath of the globe. This second total and worldwide war, said to be one of tyranny versus democracy, appeared as one to expand or preserve empires. In it, Japan, Germany, and Italy (the Axis powers) fought China, Great Britain, France, the Soviet Union and eventually the United States (the Allies). It is believed that civilian deaths far outnumbered military deaths with women's mortality being higher than that of men. In one example, European Jewish women were less likely to migrate to safety from Nazi Germany's lethal anti-Semitic policies, staying behind to help older family members and thus caught up in Germany's genocide machine. The Japanese seemed to target Chinese women in such acts as "The Rape of Nanjing" of 1938 when tens of thousands were sexually violated and mutilated before being murdered. German, Italian, and Japanese dictators (the Axis) invoked women's sexuality—as virtuous mother or castrating professional woman, for example—to inspire masculine prowess. Among the "Allies" (primarily Britain, France, the United States, the Soviet Union, and China) full use was made of women as factory and service workers and even as soldiers and pilots. Simultaneously the Allies also created images of alluring, scantily-clad women as dangerous: "Loose lips sink ships," such depictions read.

Axis gendered ideology muted the appeal of work outside the home for women, diminishing their war efforts in comparison with Allied women's service as fighters, factory workers, and other essential laborers. With men taken from their homes by the millions, whether as combatants for their nation or as conscripts from the captured in foreign lands, women became the main citizens to keep civil society and the economy going. Chinese women from all political parties, for example, rallied to the war effort, setting up organizations of various kinds. The National Association of Chinese Women for the Cheering and Comforting of the Officers and Soldiers of the War of Self-Defense and Resistance against Japan made massive contributions to soldier morale and to their physical well-being by providing goods to sustain them. Because civilians were so at risk in wartime, the Wartime Child Welfare Protection Association and the Women's Directorial Committee of New Life Movement Promotion Federation took action in China. Other Chinese organizations worked to entice women into the war effort and to protect those in areas vulnerable to Japanese attack.

Everyday life in wartime was a mixture of dodging bombs, hiding from invaders, facing sexual and other violence, being taken hostage along with one's children, and watching men in their families shot while they themselves were spared. Alongside the violence and even when violence was hundreds of miles away, there was also a desperate search for food, especially because fighting soldiers took priority to keep up their strength. In Chongqing China, for example, as people migrated southward after the Japanese capture of successive Chinese headquarters, shopkeepers at first made good amounts of money provisioning the refugees. However, as the war progressed and food supplies uniformly disappeared, women scrambled, often selling possessions and their bodies to help their families survive. Suddenly, the ideal of delicate womanliness of necessity gave way, while the competent woman who could make do in any circumstance became valued.

Similar situations existed in all the theaters of war and even beyond. African daily life was torn apart as resources were confiscated and men caught up for forced labor or combat. Even where fighting did not occur, soldiers were privileged and women were to hold society together. Amid government-driven civilian deprivation, they faced starvation, created in an effort to aid the troops. Winston Churchill, holding South Asians in contempt, inflicted a famine in their region in 1943 by taking out grain and refusing Allied offers to bring in surplus grain from Argentina and North America. Naturally, women and children who remained in the region formed a large number of those who perished, as men were off at the front. In the siege of Leningrad from 1941–4 women and old people not at the front ate glue from wall paper and resorted to other desperate measures to stay alive. In Manila in the Philippines, hostages and prisoners of war held by the Japanese became skeletons, as did in many cases the Japanese themselves. "No one grew fat during the war," one woman living in Nazi-occupied France remarked.[14]

Despite their responsibilities on the home front, women were often suspected of being spies, collaborating with the enemy, and irresponsibly giving away secrets and otherwise undermining the war effort. These suspicions were not far from the truth, as they actually did play a large role in the resistance to the Axis powers. The European front, for example, was alive with women resisters, hiding Jews and soldiers, protesting food shortages and the incarceration of civilian suspects, and participating in assassinations. Seducing enemy officers, they often could wring crucial information from them. Because women were part of the "smaller world" in the minds of Axis personnel including the police and the military, they could carry bombs and other weapons unnoticed to meeting points. Eventually, Hitler's insistence on the importance of women in their "smaller" world of the home backfired. Many German women stayed in their homes during the Second World War and were hard to coax into much-needed factory work, unlike in Allied countries where they worked in essential industries, formed combat units, and flew airplanes.

On the Front

In one sense, the front lines in the Second World War were everywhere, as civilians were targeted as much as soldiers through bombings of cities or blockades of ports preventing the entry of food and supplies necessary to everyday life. The Holocaust—that is, the systematic rounding up and extermination of Jewish people by the Nazis—was the largest single targeting of civilians, again with women and children the majority of victims. Those women not immediately gassed with their children kept themselves alive wherever possible through creating alliances and friendships, celebrating birthdays, and observing religious holy days. Others survived through serving as camp prostitutes. Nazi women, in contrast, participated in inflicting punishment and everyday discipline. Those women who survived the camps endured further suffering as refugees and in some cases rejection and even murder when they tried to reclaim their homes.

Still, the battlefront remained a site of massive slaughter, and Stalingrad was perhaps the most horrific single battle of Second World War and at the same time the war's turning point on the European continent. Casualties in this lengthy battle were enormous on both sides (some 2 million dead, wounded, or imprisoned and likely to die in the camps). The battle began in July 1942 and continued into February 1943 when the German army surrendered, after house to house combat amid starvation and death from cold.

FIGURE 10.3 *Soviet women in the Second World War. The 125th Guards Bomber Regiment performed some 30,000 nighttime raids on German positions in outdated planes. They were known as the "night witches" by Germans because of their stealth and skill. Their service reflected both the Soviet need for replacing men lost in battle and the "can-do" spirit of Soviet women. Courtesy of AFP Getty Images.*

Although Stalingrad is depicted as an entirely male event, in fact, women served in the Soviet army and air force over the entire course of the Second World War and participated in its military updating. Vera Ivanovna Malakhova, a medical doctor in the Soviet army for four years, described surviving Stalingrad as a feat of cooperation among medical personnel and soldiers—men and women who used ingenuity to escape the enemy. In one crisis, a comrade led her out of an encirclement, forcing her to don men's clothing to escape advancing tanks on horseback. At another time, some medical personnel disobeyed her orders and headed off to find drinking water in a town.

We already knew that we had been encircled [again] by the Germans . . . "Guys, we're done for. What have you got for weapons?" It turned out one person had a carbine, some had automatics . . . And Natasha, who was in charge of medication, was there, too—I don't know how she got there—and Andrei, the medical orderly, crept up... [and] said to Natasha—Natasha was a member of the Komsomol [a group for Communist youth activists]—"Natashka, . . . Let's crawl out of here . . .

Let's crawl over there and get a drink," said Andrei. "Don't you dare,"
I said. "I'm senior to you in rank; don't you dare." He crawled off and so
did Natasha; neither of them returned. Later, after we had gotten out of
the encirclement, we were told that everyone in the village had been lined
up and questioned: Who is a Communist? Who is a Komsomol? Who is a
Jew? . . . Well, by all accounts, they were among those who were shot. The
Germans finished everyone off: all the communists, all the Jews! There
were a lot of Jews in our medical battalion, and they were all shot—every
last one of them . . . June of '42. That's when the most horrible battles
took place, that's when we retreated.[15]

Like the Soviet medical personnel, women worldwide served in multiple
battlefront capacities, including as both forced and voluntary sex workers.
In the United States, some 35,000 women joined the armed services. Their
numbers, it is believed, would have been larger had men in the military not
worked to keep them out so that there would be at least some "safe" jobs
available for men in the military. There was also a quota on African American
women in the military but the number of women in general was low because
of harassment and the military's rumor-mongering that women joined the
military because they were lesbians. That said, transport and other ships
were sites of sexual adventures of all types. At the other extreme, military
nurses at the battlefront had dangerous and daunting tasks, dealing with
foreign soldiers, tending atrocious wounds, and addressing the aftermath
of fire-bombings of cities such as Tokyo and the dropping of two atomic
bombs. German women also inflicted pain and even death as personnel in
extermination and concentration camps.

As in daily life in empires, in this war of atrocities victors subjected
women to rape and sexual abuse. The so-called comfort women of the
Second World War were the Japanese-enslaved Korean, Chinese, and other
women from conquered regions confined to military brothels. Many of these
brothels passed to the Allied forces occupying East Asia at the war's end in
1945; they maintained the use of forced sex workers during the Korean War.
The situation was abusive and ultimately so traumatic and humiliating that
for many decades the survivors would not speak of it. Korean sixteen-year-
old Ch'oe Il-rye was captured by two Japanese soldiers and taken along
with several dozen other girls to Manchuria. After receiving new names and
housed in barracks with round-the-clock guards, they were examined by a
doctor.

After the test, a high-ranking officer summoned me to have sex. Until then
I had no knowledge about the male sexual organ, let alone about coitus.
The officer raped me, and I tried to accept everything as my fate . . . For
twelve or thirteen years, from 1932 to 1945, I labored as *wianbu*, serving
only officers most of the time. Officers sent their men to fetch me to their
places. My colleagues and I also worked as nurses and washerwomen

for the soldiers. We would send soldiers to battle, tend the wounded, and attend the funerals of those killed in combat, wearing black hats and kimonos . . . Toward the end of the war, when life became harder, without enough food to go around, an officer whom I served regularly told me to flee without telling the other women. He provided me with three white identification cards and explained to me in detail how to run away.[16]

Conclusion

Tens of millions of women worked in factories and other civilian jobs during the Second World War and even earlier in the First World War. Except for Axis countries, women also served in military roles. When both wars ended, the goal was to restore civilian life and values. After the First World War the "new woman" or "modern girl" came into her own, while after the Second World War a stern domestic ideology emerged worldwide, in part to signal a return to clear gender roles and in part to replenish the c. 100 million war dead. The legacy of genocide and the Holocaust affected women and men alike, though historians still tend to see the unspeakable cruelty as somewhat nuanced by gender. Many women received the vote after one or the other of these world conflagrations and in the face of male casualties temporarily became public officials after the Second World War. Women resistance fighters in Europe, however, faded into the background, while in contrast women in colonized areas joined independence movements, because many during the wars had hardened and militarized themselves. Activists forced the new United Nations to concern itself with women's rights and their well-being, but it was a struggle. The war itself was seen as a purely male event for which they deserved rewards, not competition from women.

Glossary

Harlem Renaissance	An upswelling of African America cultural life in Harlem New York featuring jazz, works of fiction and poetry, dance, and other aspects of artistic production especially in the 1920s and 1930s.
Igbo	An ethnic group in Nigeria, whose women were pivotal in the 1929 "women's war" or resistance to British taxation.
New Life Movement	A cultural effort to reform, reinvigorate, and modernize the Chinese population, instituted by the Nationalist Party in the interwar period.
Wianbu	This word translates into "comfort woman," a nicer term than a wianbu was—a sex slave.

Notes

1 Yigit Akin, "War, Women, and the State: The Politics of Sacrifice in the
   Ottoman Empire during the First World War," *Journal of Women's History*,
   26:3 (Fall 2014): 13.
2 Aleksandra Kollontai, "The Labour of Women in the Evolution of
   the Economy" (1923), translated and reprinted in *The Family in the
   U.S.S.R.: Documents and Readings*, Rudolf Schlesinger, ed. (London,
   Routledge, 1949), 45–8. Excerpted in *Women, the Family, and Freedom: The
   Debate in Documents. Volume Two, 1880–1950*, Susan Groag Bell and Karen
   M. Offen, eds. (Stanford, CA: Stanford University Press, 1983), 2:289–90.
3 On this point, see the strong evidence presented in Yuri Slezkine, *The House
   of Government: A Saga of the Russian Revolution* (Princeton, NJ: Princeton
   University Press, 2017), 484, 559, and passim.
4 *Journal of Negro History*, Letter from New Orleans, Louisiana to the *Chicago
   Defender*, April 23, 1917 and October 1919 as quoted in Ellen Carol DuBois
   and Lynn Dumenil, *Through Women's Eyes: An American History with
   Documents* (Boston, MA: Bedford St. Martins, 2005), 468.
5 Huda Shaarawi, *Harem Years: The Memoirs of an Egyptian Feminist*, Margot
   Badran, trans. and ed. (New York: Feminist Press, 1987), 113–14, 131.
6 Sarojini Naidu, "The Agony and Shame of the Punjab," in *Sarojini Naidu: A
   Biography*, Padmini Sengupta (London: Asia Publishing House, 1966), 161–2.
7 Quoted in Geraldine Forbes, "Ideals of Indian Womanhood: Six Bengali
   Women during the Independence Movement," in *Bengal in the Nineteenth and
   Twentieth Centuries*, John R. McLand, ed. (East Lansing: Asian Studies Center,
   Michigan State University, 1975), 64. Emphasis in the original.
8 Ishimoto Shidzue, *Facing Two Ways: The Story of My Life* (1935; repr.,
   Tokyo: Ozorasha, 1997), 183, 234, 349–50, in Taeko Shibahara, *Japanese
   Women and the Transnational Feminist Movement before World War II*
   (Philadelphia, PA: Temple University Press, 2014), 86, 88, 89.
9 Halidé Edib, "Dictatorship and Reform in Turkey," in *The Middle East
   and Islamic World Reader*, Marvin Gettleman and Stuart Schaar, ed.
   (New York: Grove Press, 2003), 128–31.
10 Heather Fowler-Salamini, *Women Workers, Entrepreneurs, and the Mexican
   Revolution: The Coffee Culture of Córdoba, Veracruz* (Lincoln: University of
   Nebraska Press, 2013), 174 and Chapter 4 passim.
11 Moses E. Ochuonu, *Colonial Meltdown: Northern Nigeria in the Great
   Depression* (Athens: Ohio University Press, 2009), 16–17, 86–7.
12 Adolf Hitler, Speech to the Nationalsozialistiche Frauenschaft, September
   8, 1934, Nuremberg; reprinted in *Hitler, Reden und Prokomationen*, Max
   Domarus, ed. 2 vols. (Wurzberg, 1962), I:449–54, in Susan Groag Bell and
   Karen M. Offen eds. 2 vols (Stanford, CA: Stanford University Press, 1983),
   375–7. Susan Groag Bell, trans.
13 Robert M. Levine and John J. Crocitti, eds., *The Brazil Reader: History,
   Culture, Politics* (Durham, NC: Duke University Press, 1999), 120–1.
14 Bonnie G. Smith, *Confessions of a Concierge: Madame Lucie's History of
   Twentieth Century France* (New Haven, CT: Yale University Press, 1985).

15   Barbara Alpern Engel and Anastasia Posadskaya-Vanderbeck, eds., Sona
     Hoisington, trans., *A Revolution of Their Own: Voices of Women in Soviet
     History* (Boulder, CO: Westview Press, 1998), 190–4.
16   C. Sarah Soh, *The Comfort Women: Sexual Violence and Post-Colonial
     Memory in Korea and Japan* (Chicago, IL: University of Chicago Press,
     2008), 125–7.

Further Reading

Clements, Barbara Evans. *A History of Women in Russia: From Earliest Times to
     the Present*. Bloomington: Indiana University Press, 2012.
Danke, Li. *Echoes of Chongqing: Women in Wartime China*. Urbana: University of
     Illinois Press, 2010.
Dooling, Amy D. *Women's Literary Feminism in Twentieth Century China*.
     New York: Palgrave Macmillan, 2005.
Edwards, Louise P. *Women Warriors and Wartime Spies of China*. Cambridge:
     Cambridge University Press 2016.
Faison, Elyssa. *Managing Women: Disciplining Labor in Modern Japan*. Berkeley:
     University of California Press, 2007.
Fowler-Salamini, Heather. *Working Women, Entrepreneurs, and the Mexican
     Revolution: The Coffee Culture of Córdoba, Veracruz*. Lincoln: University of
     Nebraska, 2013.
Grossmann, Atina. *Jews, Germans, and Allies: Close Encounters in Occupied
     Germany*. Princeton, NJ: Princeton University Press, 2007.
Hawkesworth, Mary E. *Globalization and Feminist Activism*. Lanham, MD:
     Rowman & Littlefield, 2006.
Krylova, Anna. *Soviet Women in Combat: A History of Violence on the Eastern
     Front*. Cambridge: Cambridge University Press, 2010.
Matera, Marc, and Susan Kingsley Kent. *The Global 1930s: The International
     Decade*. New York: Routledge, 2017.
Matera, Marc, Susan Kingsley Kent, and Misty Bastian. *The Women's War
     of 1929: Gender and Violence in Colonial Nigeria*. New York: Palgrave
     Macmillan, 2012.
Metinsoy, Elif Mahir. *Ottoman Women during World War I: Everyday Experiences,
     Politics, and Conflict*. New York: Cambridge University Press, 2017.
Mickenberg, Julia L. *American Girls in Red Russia: Chasing the Soviet Dream*.
     Chicago, IL: University of Chicago Press, 2017.
Sinha, Mrinalini. *Specters of Mother India: The Global Restructuring of an
     Empire*. Durham, NC: Duke University Press, 2006.
Soh, C. Sarah. *The Comfort Women: Sexual Violence and Post-Colonial Memory in
     Korea and Japan*. Chicago, IL: University of Chicago Press, 2008.
Wingfield, Nancy, and Maria Bucur-Deckard. *Gender and War in Twentieth-
     Century Eastern Europe*. Bloomington: Indiana University Press, 2006.

11

Creating New Nations, Decolonizing Women

Shan Xiuzhen's family disintegrated in the 1930s and 1940s because of the drought, famine, disease, and death that plagued rural China during the Depression and the Second World War. Added to that were the destruction and uncertainty of troop movements, bombings, and confiscation of the already meager crops that Xiuzhen grew. On her own or with her mother or mother-in-law, or children she had walked hundreds of miles across the area inhabited by her family and her in-laws to find food, even as her family dwindled in size, dying off. In 1949, when the war ended and Communists took over, however, Shan Xiuzhen got a new lease on life. The Communists chose her, as they chose capable women across China, to be a leader of rural women and to rally their efforts, instructing them in being modern and Communist. As one delegate recalled of her trip, carrying backpacks: "How enthusiastic I was . . . When leadership orders would come down, we would set out at two in the morning . . . From Xixiang to Shahe was [twenty-seven miles]. We covered it in one day."[1] All this served the cause of instilling Communist energy in the female population after decades of discouragement and death.

Even though the Second World War had been catastrophic in many regions of the world, its end brought hope that a page had been turned in human history. Imperial powers had drafted men, taken resources, and left the colonial home front to fend for itself even as it was pillaged. The combatant powers had requisitioned agricultural harvests, manufactured items, and raw materials for the war effort from colonies and occupied regions. These resources were directed away from rural people to major cities to keep the civilian and military forces there in the best shape possible, while people in the colonies or occupied regions experienced impoverishment, destruction of their homes, and farmland, and even starvation. Still, at war's end, there was the expectation that from all that suffering new and better societies would emerge, including for women and their families.

Many colonized men and women were politicized, ready to resist a return to rule by their imperial masters and to build a future on a foundation of liberty. The kinds of postwar governments that would replace wartime ones remained open to question, as in many cases there was much debate about the shape of both new nations and old empires. Even as the former imperial powers prepared to restore their domination of distant lands, the call for reform and an end to colonialism was loud and sustained. It was a call for which neither the victors in the war nor the defeated were fully prepared.

Conditions across much of the globe were dire in 1945. So many men had been killed or were prisoners of war that heavy burdens continued to fall on women across China, Korea, eastern Europe and the Soviet Union, and many other areas as well. The victors humiliated, raped, imprisoned, and even murdered women who had in any way benefitted from enemy occupation. In some cases, mass rapes occurred simply as the right of the victors and as a form of revenge. The Allies also kept open Japanese brothels filled with forced sex workers or completely destitute victims of the war for the use of the soldiers from victorious Allied armies. Still, during the war and in its immediate aftermath, colonized women formed militant resistance groups and also bore arms themselves.

Even as the postwar world seemed hopeless given the millions of homeless refugees, for some, the idea was that such suffering could not have been in vain and that evil's defeat opened a path to a better future. Women authors condemned their treatment in fiction and in so doing created a politics of reform, equality, and social justice. Others threw their intellectual weight toward eliminating racism, anti-Semitism, sexism, and other forms of oppression now that dictators and their thugs had been defeated. As colonialism was overthrown, women from Latin America and socialist countries lobbied the new United Nations, formed in 1945, to pay attention that women be included in guarantees for justice and equality and as members of the institution itself. The irony was that amid positive developments a new Cold War was brewing between the United States and the USSR. Women participated in the Cold War proxy wars—that is, wars in which the two superpowers took sides but did not confront one another directly on the battlefield. Women also took up a range of anti-colonial and civil rights activism, all of which cost tens of millions of additional postwar lives.

Women's Postwar Lives

The status of women was among the many issues rising to the surface after the Second World War, leading in some cases to actual improvement. French and Italian women received the vote at the war's end, while Douglas Macarthur, head of the occupying Allied army in Japan, demanded that the nation's new Constitution also include women's right to vote. Such political participation, he claimed, was necessary to tame the extreme and brutal militarism evident in the horrific treatment of women in Nanjing and other regions. That accomplished, those in charge of finding collaborators with the militarist Japanese government rounded up leading feminists who had supported the war. Temporarily women had postwar jobs, especially given the desperate quest for food; one of the most lucrative and widely held jobs was serving as prostitutes for American soldiers and staff. Any permanent place that feminists might have wanted women to hold in the service, factory, and professional sectors soon disappeared as the ideology of women as good wives and wise mothers was reinvigorated and the feminist movement itself discredited as not sufficiently anti-communist. Still, numerous colleges and universities for women sprang up after the war in Japan.

As in Japan, destruction was massive across the world's battlefields, although not just from Allied bombs but also from the German program of genocide and scorched earth. Soviet women had piloted planes, fought in the army, served as medical personnel at the battlefront, and worked long hours while caring for families during the conflict. At the war's end, their participation in the workforce was critical given the horrific USSR casualties during the conflict—sometimes estimated at over 40 million—and the loss of hundreds of thousands of homes and other buildings, among other destruction. Simultaneously, however, the government encouraged them to have babies to make up for these population losses. While still working long hours and searching for scarce food, they were also to make themselves glamorous to reinvigorate men and additionally to serve them. A shattered masculinity needed fortification and women's subservience as inferiors to men would, once again, right the many wrongs men had suffered. In the USSR veterans and men more generally surrendered political ambitions in exchange for control of women and the household. Additionally, although women had held positions of responsibility during the war, afterward they became the major sanitation workers and farmhands while surviving men returned to become managers, engineers, military officers, and the well-paid industrial workers. Nonetheless, the USSR maintained its official stance as it expanded into eastern Europe that its women were entirely equal to men while unofficially degrading them.

After years of similar destruction, dramatic change came in 1949 when Communist forces in China, which had united with Nationalist armies to block Japan, defeated the troops of this former ally. For some two decades, women had participated in the Chinese Communist movement before and during war. Officially, the Communist Party's stand on women's work and family was Marxist, based on the principle of total equality after the overthrow of the backward Chinese society. In power, the Communists expanded the reforms that the Nationalist government had made in the 1930s legal code, especially giving women the right to own property in their own names. Their place in the workforce was endorsed by a Communist backed Women's Federation. The collectivization of agriculture followed, taking land from peasants and reapportioning it to communities headed by men. Women's inequality resurfaced but some rural women were caught up in the project despite regional officials' favoring men. Communist party leaders called Women's Federation's protests of the situation obstructionist and ultimately forced the Women's Federation to shut down.

The government advanced the cause of women's education: although girls were 28 percent of students in primary schools in 1950, they constituted 44.8 percent in 1985. While women composed only 22 percent of students in universities in 1951, by the twenty-first century they made up 44 percent of the student body. Moreover, the government trained local leaders like Shan Xiuzhen—uneducated but savvy—to explain the new concept of equality in marriage and counsel couples with marital and other family problems. These leaders explained that the cause of pre-communist unhappiness had been loveless arranged marriages: "Many women and men had no way out and jumped into wells or hanged themselves. How well marriage problems are solved determines whether people will live a happy life or a bitter one . . . So this is not only an issue about husband and wife about family, but also about liberating social productivity, democracy and solidarity . . . This is the responsibility of all men and women, of all revolutionary comrades."[2]

Alongside those gains, the simultaneous persecution of women Communist leaders was a setback, as they found themselves classified as enemies to Chinese development. The context for this attack on women's leadership was the failure of Mao Zedong's economic programs in the 1950s, which caused the death of millions due to famine. The resulting drive for a Communist revival—the Cultural Revolution of the 1960s— singled out for punishment many women leaders and activists along with men as counterrevolutionaries. Simultaneously, Mao's fourth wife Jiang Qing (1914–1991) rose to power in part ironically by forcing the theme of women's activism and parity with men under Communism.

An actress by profession, Jiang Qing had not been treated well by cultural power brokers in the 1930s. Allied with Mao, she focused on bringing women's past achievements to the fore as justification for her own prominent role and then for her own seizure of political authority. For this, she revitalized the tale of the Red Lanterns in the Boxer Rebellion by giving them the kind of decisive influence that few believed they had actually had in the uprising. Her opera "Hongdeng ji" had as its centerpiece the heroism of a young woman holding aloft the Red Lantern of resistance and justice. As the Cultural Revolution of the young attacked the old ways, punishing cultural authorities and destroying cultural treasures, Jiang's popularity soared. Young men and women allied themselves so completely with Jiang that she became a unique power in China both then and briefly after Mao's death in 1976. The modernizers, who came to power shortly thereafter, were pragmatists and advocates of technological and economic development. They arrested her and her chief allies. At her trial in 1980–1, Jiang renounced the Mao myth and her own. Highlighting Mao's arbitrariness and brutality rather than his Communist wisdom, she announced, "I was Mao's dog. What he said to bite, I bit."[3]

Ordinary people learned the rules of the proclaimed Chinese Communist utopia. Sansan, as Soo Chin-yee was nicknamed, was an infant left behind in China when her parents went to the United States. As a toddler when Mao announced the creation of the People's Republic of China, life changed for Sansan: her parents stayed in the United States and old ways of doing things were replaced by authoritarian Communist ones. Attending school was a challenge because of the Maoist ideas of right-thinking and self-criticism as foundational to the new society. The situation became extreme for youth as well as adults; Sansan's fellow students were punished for failure in right-thinking. She explained the experience: "We were to be more involved in political campaigns than ever; along with my courses in zoology and botany, physics, chemistry, geometry and algebra, physical education, music, Chinese literature and grammar, there was a new class called 'political discussion.' Beginning in 1957, all students in all schools were assigned to weekly political-discussion groups . . . Soon we all learned and tried to find a way to fulfill our obligations without making a mistake."

She learns that this class was not about expressing one's own ideas even as one was expected to voice an opinion. "At this meeting we were asked our views of Han's violating the rule against social dancing for students. A teacher had discovered music scores for dance tunes in Han's desk, and after scolding him severely, asked that he be reprimanded by his own classmates." Sansan knows that Han likes to hum the music and doesn't dance at all. She says so.

"I had hardly finished and each person in turn reprimanded me. After that I knew better than to speak my convictions . . . only opinions that echoed the ones suggested by the group leader." She discovers that the best solution was to volunteer to take notes and thus usually not have to talk at all.[4] Life took a more violent turn for girls and young women under the Cultural Revolution of the 1960s when instead of being verbally attacked, they were often raped and otherwise abused by the male members of the Red Guards.

Similarly enduring the effects of postwar chaos and destruction, women across eastern Europe also suffered postwar rape at the hands of the occupying armies but especially soldiers in the Red Army. Such abuse and the fact that Germany was so devastated in the war, many German women felt themselves the real victims of the war. Nor did Nazi racism die easily: one young woman, a former Nazi leader, explained her attempts to hitch a ride in order to escape back home at war's end: "everywhere there were Jews and they wanted a lot of money or material and I had already lost everything to Poles."[5] Given that the losses of men were so high, and the participation of men in the Nazi party so thorough, women had to make a supreme effort to survive: in fact some temporarily became important politicians, holding a range of public offices amid the brutality and chaos. Grassroots activism also took shape as cooperation on the local level became important to survival. With their male relatives often dead or in prison camps, women banded together to find food, share housing, and take care of both children and one another. Occupying armies saw women among the defeated as guilty and rounded them up to do forced labor clearing rubble and generally all other tasks of public sanitation. Meanwhile wartime participation in the Resistance in France and elsewhere was celebrated, with male resisters rushing to take control of their liberated countries while women resisters were relegated to the background—another way to help men recover their masculinity by women's erasure of activism beyond domesticity.

The Creation of New Nations

Across Africa and Asia, women participated in the resurgence of independence movements that had already existed before the war; some of these movements such as Communist groups in Southeast Asia also preached the equality of women. In most nationalist movements, women had historically been treated as "auxiliary" to the supposedly more intelligent men. Most women also found their own concerns secondary to those of male nationalists, even though women often gained promises of equal rights once independence had been achieved. In Africa, however, there was virtually no independence activism that did not include women from the outset. In the Côte d'Ivoire (Ivory Coast), a French colonial holding, women began a hunger strike in 1949 to protest the arrest and incarceration of nationalist leaders. Even as the French shot and wounded some forty strikers, it became clear that colonialism would not hold and the French negotiated independence there and in many other countries thereafter.

Simultaneously, Funmilayo Ransome-Kuti (1900–1978), president of the Nigerian Women's Union and the Abeokuta Ladies' Club, came to focus her group's activism on confronting British imperialism, taking strong action that ultimately brought Nigerian independence. Before that struggle, she had fought British taxation of women and worked to support poor women and men. Ransome-Kuti and other African women returned to traditional clothing, thus rejecting the claims of British and Europeans to superiority when it came to women. For Ransome-Kuti this meant wearing *Yoruba* clothing and for others various local forms of cotton garb and headpieces. Once Nigeria became independent in 1960, as elsewhere women were pushed to tend the household and nothing more. Ransome-Kuti fought reigning dictators and the lack of democratic participation; government soldiers murdered her in 1978.

Women elsewhere joined in the effort to create free nations. In the independence organization called Mau Mau in Kenya, women served as suppliers of weapons, food, and communications for fighters, as they themselves were dispossessed of their land, thrown into the British concentration camps, and tortured just as men were. In the war for Algerian independence in the 1950s, women freedom fighters, once again disguised as "women," worked for the independence forces in a variety of ways such as intelligence gathering and terrorism. As Algerian resistance fighter Jamillah Buhrayd put it, there were thousands of women who "moved, just like me, from the Qasbah to the French Quarter. Carrying bombs in their handbags and throwing them into cafés."[6]

During the 1950s, after the outbreak of hostilities between the Algerian National Liberation Movement (FLN) and the French army, both sides tortured not just combatants but ordinary citizens suspected of aiding the enemy. After the actions described by Buhrayd became known, the French army tortured women too. Soldiers invaded homes where women were secluded and brutalized them in public, seeming to spare no one. After the Nazi record of torture, people across the globe were shocked at reports of its revival, as the Algerian struggle for independence came to be a war of words. In that effort, the FLN published the record of assault and torture of the young woman Djamila Boupacha. Here is her published account, some of which is too barbaric to print:

FIGURE 11.1 *French military operation in 1955 in Algeria. The French army was desperate to keep Algeria as part of France, especially because it had large stocks of oil. To flush out opponents, they combed the Algerian countryside, even rounding up women and children in this mountain village. When it came to empire, no one was safe. Courtesy of Michel DESJARDINS/Gamma-Rapho Getty Images.*

On the night of 10th and 11th of February 1960, the police, Arab collaborators, and police inspectors—about fifty in all—got out of their jeeps and military trucks . . . and stopped at my parents' house where I lived in Algiers . . . On the spot and without being taken away, I was beaten savagely. My brother-in-law Abedelli Ahmed who was also there, suffered the same fate as did my father Boupacha Abdelaziz, 70 years of age.

We were taken to the triage center El-Biar. There I received terrible blows that made me fall to the ground. That was when the soldiers, led by a parachutist captain, crushed my ribs with their boots. I still suffer today from deviated ribs on the left.

After four or five days, I was transferred to *Hussein-Dey*. It was, they told me, to receive "the second degree." I soon found out what that meant: electric torture to begin with (the electrodes placed on my breasts did not stick so one of the torturers glued them to my skin with scotch tape), then they burned me in the same way on my legs, groin, genitals, and face. Electric torture alternated with cigarette burns, punches with fists, and water torture: suspended over a full bathtub, I was made to drink until suffocating.[7]

Many other women were in the vanguard of independence movements, like Ransome-Kuti explicitly combining their feminist activism with struggles for national independence. In most African countries they took up arms: in Eritrea they were some thirty-five percent of active soldiers. Across the globe, independence groups forged alliances with a range of women's federations, promising equal rights and leadership positions after successful struggles. Meanwhile, as in wartime they struggled to feed their families. Homes were destroyed, farms burned, and entire families relocated, sometimes to concentration camp-like enclosures. Women had to maintain life when in fact the means to maintain life had been seized or demolished. Yet in many postindependence African nations, women's groups were nonetheless disbanded and the atmosphere toward women changed: as the postwar dictator of Zaire (Democratic Republic of Congo) put it, "there will always be only one head in each household . . . he who wears the pants." Women needed to behave with "revolutionary submission."[8]

The struggling British government also let go of its hold on India in 1947. Independence came about as a contest among various religious groups that resulted in large part from the British having emphasized differences among Muslims, Hindus, Sikhs, and others. In fact, the Indian population comprised many religions that had lived together for centuries. Once independence became inevitable, Britain supported the formation of India and Pakistan as opposed to a unified India—a form of divide and rule. Before and after the August 15, 1947 date for partition approached, the seizure of property, kidnapping of women and children, physical violence, and murder increased among these groups and continued into the 1950s. All groups went on the attack, targeting women in particular for sexual violence and disfigurement; female suicide was widespread; between 1 and 2 million died.

Women survivors gave varying accounts:

> On October 19 [1947] we noticed a massing of tribals [local groups] on the hills around our village. Mehta Dhuni Chand, the DC [Deputy Commissioner?], was the first target—he was killed. Many Hindu families, including ours, gathered in a large haveli [mansion]. Some had rifles and guns with which we kept the tribals at bay for a couple of days. After this, we were overpowered and had to surrender. All our money was taken and we were told to march across the bridge over the Krishanganga. My three sisters swallowed poison—our hospital compounder distributed poison to anyone who wanted it—my bua [aunt] gave the signal to the other women to jump by jumping off the bridge first. Then other aunts, my bhabis [aunts, cousins, and sisters-in-law], six in all, killed themselves. No one tried to stop them, not even my father. We tried to persuade Veeran, a young cousin, to take opium, but she refused.[9]

South Asian women survivors volunteered for and even set up hostels and support centers on their own for those who had been wounded and assaulted. They began to live on their own, sometimes disobeying the men in their families in so doing. For Bibi Inder Kaur, who moved from Karachi to Bombay during the turmoil, the shattered unity of "India" actually worked to her benefit. "I spread my wings," she claimed. While her husband found his medical practice weakened and he himself depressed, she used the breakdown of community and family bonds to do something unusual. She went to school, getting advanced degrees and then a series of responsible and well-paid jobs. She accomplished all this against her husband's will; nor did community traditions hold her back. "There are millions of women like me who want to do something but cannot. I managed to because Partition gave me a chance." She had gained strength from surviving the horrors of Partition, proceeding thereafter to "spread her wings."[10]

Many of the promises for women's equality did not come to fruition. Where these movements entailed military violence and because of imperialism's own legacy of violence, military leaders arose to rule many of the new nations—a situation that Ransome-Kuti and other women protested. Despite imperialists' calls for colonized men to reform their attitudes toward women, in fact imperialists themselves had privileged men, for instance, awarding them women's agricultural land in exchange for their service to empire. In West Africa, the French targeted lands that had once yielded wild plants that enriched food in nutrition and flavor for conversion into male-controlled agribusiness, even after independence.

While other empires and systems of racial oppression appeared to be struggling and even collapsing, the *apartheid* regime in South Africa fortified itself after the Second World War. It simply took lands owned by blacks and then drove these landless victims into crowded ghettoes called "townships." Strict segregation laws were enforced with brutality and those who protested them were often tortured and then murdered. As other regions liberated themselves from colonial control, apartheid became increasingly murderous and oppressive of blacks, whose movements were monitored ever more tightly.

Nonetheless, under this regime, activism prevailed in the form of union organizing, worker protest, and student resistance. There were also many African organizations that operated along ethnic lines and other political parties such as the African National Congress that struggled for a better future. Union leader Emma Mashinini began as an inexperienced worker but soon helped organize her fellow workers to achieve a shorter workday and insurance for workers in the 1950s and 1960s. Under apartheid, she was arrested and put in solitary confinement for being a union leader. "I had no visits, no interrogation, no word from anybody whatsoever." Instead, she was constantly teased into thinking she was going home when in fact the government was adding new charges against her.[11] Yet, as in the case of Nigeria, the experience of activism in earlier protest such as the Women's War of 1929 formed a foundation for women's alliances and union strikes that persisted during these decades. In 1994, South Africa held its first, postapartheid democratic election with no small thanks to such women's activism, which was recognized in founding documents of the new regime.

Another, very different contribution to independence and nation-building in the postwar period came in the world of film, music, song, and culture generally. Umm Kulthuum, for example, began her career singing passages from the Qu'ran but then expanded her repertoire to include traditional desert songs, religious verses, and romantic ballads. Traffic came to a stop in Cairo on the first Thursday of every month in the 1950s when Umm Kulthuum's radio program was broadcast. She was a nationalist, traveling the Arab world on behalf of anti-Westernism and the integrity of Arab culture. Others revived and perpetuated the cultural canons of their newly independent countries. In India, Suchitra Mitra used her musical talent to spread the song of Rabindranath Tagore as well as popularizing a range of Indian musical culture. Cultural nationalism fortified political independence.

The USSR and the United States sold guns to the male military in the new nations in order to win their allegiance in the Cold War between the two superpowers that began just as the Second World War ended in 1945. Still, a few women assumed leadership positions. Indira Gandhi (1917–1984) was the third prime minister of independent India and the only woman to serve as such. Daughter of Jawaharlal Nehru, the first prime minister, Gandhi already had political knowledge and diplomatic skills that smoothed her way in politics. Her party was the Indian National Congress, which was founded by reformers in 1885; at its head she proved a strong, if authoritarian leader. She worked on poverty and other social problems: in the name of resolving these, her administration carried out thousands of forced sterilizations. She fatally blundered when in 1984 she ordered the army to take over the holiest Sikh site—the Golden Temple. The death of more than 400 Sikhs in the massacre enraged Sikhs across the country; that year a Sikh body guard shot her, while a second riddled her body with bullets. As in many cases, tensions whipped up under imperialism endured to poison nation-building.

Women also lobbied at the United Nations, founded at the end of Second World War, for a commitment to equal citizenship and for basic human

FIGURE 11.2 *Eritrean People's Liberation Front Muslim woman soldier. The EPLF believed in the equality of women including in service as soldiers. They thus composed 25 percent of frontline troops. This woman fighter carries with a Russian-made Kalashikov AK-47 rifle. Courtesy of Alex Bowie Getty Images.*

rights. They were particularly concerned because of being kept from most meetings of the Allies and especially the establishment of the United Nations at Dumbarton Oaks in 1944. As decolonization unfolded, representatives Minerva Bernardino of the Dominican Republic and Bertha Lutz of Brazil led the successful drive for a statement on gender equality in the UN charter. Only with great difficulty did they obtain a guarantee of equal employment opportunities at the new international institution. They and women diplomats from around the world failed to get an independent Commission "of women" to monitor the status of women because of opposition from the United States. Eventually a Commission on the Status of Women was subsumed under the UN Commission on Human Rights, as a strong group of activists began working on a range of pro-women issues.[12]

Women's Cold War

After the war, civilians and governments alike turned to restoring everyday life, but this effort became part of the Cold War contest for global leadership. The two nations did not conduct actual warfare against one another but tried to show that their way of life was better. In the non-communist world, a revival of well-being built support for capitalism and for women to return to domesticity as a sign of the full restoration of freedom. As in the nineteenth-century West, the idea was that a dominant man would have a thriving work life as well as an emotionally satisfying life in his home or domestic interior. This interior life would develop with the help of a full-time housewife. This plan ran up against the reality that women across the postwar world continued in the workforce, in part because there was so much demand for labor to rebuild war-torn areas but also to produce weapons and other ingredients of the Cold War. At the same time, communism had great appeal for millions worldwide because of the Red Army's heroism in Europe and the efforts of Communist forces in defeating Japan in China. Communists also stressed a happy civilian life, even though capitalist societies provided more material goods and better appliances.

New welfare state benefits featured the postwar expansion of education, pensions for seniors, and guaranteed access to health care (except in the United States). The welfare state's needs encouraged the arrival of newcomers from former colonies. They filled the labor shortages resulting from the war and the expanding needs of the Cold War, taking up menial work such as clearing rubble and rebuilding, scrubbing and cleaning, and other low-paying jobs. They were still treated like colonial subjects, the women sexually abused as before, their intellectual capacity and experience disregarded: highly trained nurses from the Caribbean and Southeast Asia, for example, were hired to janitorial jobs and the work of aides in hospitals. A brisk business in "docile" women brought brides from Asia to European men. They signed up believing in promises of a better life.

The communist way of life was somewhat different in that Communist countries were poorer, not receiving the massive postwar aid that the United States gave to western Europe or to emerging nations as a way of maintaining their loyalty. Consumerism flourished in the USSR and its satellites, although Communist tastemakers worked to distinguish communist from capitalist style in furniture, clothing, and design generally. Advertising itself looked different, focusing more on utilitarianism and less on excess, but a comfortable private life was important, especially when an active public or political life was less of an option.

The Cold War's effects on women's lives came in many forms, from outright war and civil war, to attacks on dissidents and persecutions of individuals. An exception to the "decolonization" trend across the globe was the expansion of the Soviet Empire to include many nations in eastern Europe. Women participated in the Communist takeover of governments in Czechoslovakia, Hungary, Poland, Romania, and other countries. They never became leaders, however, as Cold War leadership was coded masculine and heterosexual. The Western press often accused gay men of being spies; in fact, the great mathematician and a primary contributor to development of the computer Alan Turing lost his security clearance because he was discovered to be gay.

Purges were thus a feature of the Cold War. These began in the Soviet sphere as soon as the Second World War ended. In the late 1940s and 1950s the political climate in both the United States and the Soviet bloc became one of hysterical fear, in large part as both governments maintained that there were traitors in their midst. These traitors, it was said, were plotting with the enemy government to overthrow democracy in the case of the United States or to overthrow socialism in the USSR. Milada Horáková (1901–1950) was one victim: she was accused of being the leader of a terrorist organization in Czechoslovakia and executed. Guided by Soviet advisors, Horáková's trial in 1950 was the largest show trial in eastern Europe to that time. In fact, Horáková had studied law in Prague, received her doctorate in 1927, and lobbied for feminist reform. She had been captured and sentenced to death by the Nazis. Released from prison when the Soviets liberated Czechoslovakia, she returned to being a democratic, instead of a Communist politician—a fatal mistake. She was charged with attempting to destroy the "paradise" of Communist rule—a criminal—the prosecutor maintained, "who joined against the people of this republic in order to thrust a dagger in their back" and a member of "a political underworld which is preparing a new Munich and a war against its own people . . . ." Albert Einstein, Winston Churchill, and Eleanor Roosevelt—among others—worked to save her life, without success. She was executed in June 1950.[13]

In the United States, Ethel Rosenberg, believed to be entirely innocent, was convicted of espionage and executed in June 1953, with the prosecution and press heaping great abuse on her as the ringleader of a spy network. Rosenberg, who was heftier than her frail-looking husband, became the

FIGURE 11.3 *A model at the Fashion House, 1955 Moscow. Depicted as grim and unfashionable in anti-Soviet Cold War propaganda, Russian women were interested in looking good, going to the hairdresser and manicurist, and finding bright textiles. They favored a somewhat more utilitarian style and far less ostentation than in "capitalist" women's dress and home furnishings. Courtesy of Aleksandr Grinberg Foto/Soyuz Getty Images.*

satanic woman. Her apparent flaunting of gender roles in her appearance made her look guilty, displaying the masculinity of Soviet working women in contrast to American women's femininity. In the United States, women union leaders and other women activists, especially those in the peace movement and ban-the bomb organizations, were called before Congress. Harassing them made Americans both fearful of attacks on sexual hierarchy and reassured that the men in Congress could beat back women's drive for rights and equality.

The Cold War was also a military one, consisting of "proxy wars" in which the USSR and United States faced off by supporting competing independence movements in many parts of the world. In the wars in Indochina/Vietnam that began in 1945, pro-independence women served in combat, manufacturing, and transport to escape the Western powers. Some 1 million Vietnamese women were active soldiers in the struggle against the French, who were defeated in 1954, and then against the United States, defeated in 1975.

The experience of noncombatant women in this excruciating war entailed moving back and forth between sides as one or the other force took control of villages. Le Ly Hayslip passed her childhood and young adulthood in this warzone—caught between forces fighting for South Vietnamese big landholders and those allied with the North Vietnamese Communists. Vietnam itself had been divided in 1954 after the French loss of their colony. Trapped in the struggle for the country that followed, Le Ly described the frightening back-and-forth that people in South Vietnam experienced, especially as US soldiers with their extraordinarily powerful weapons appeared on the scene to fight for Cold War control. Later she would be raped by soldiers and forced to earn a living by accommodating the sexual demands of both Viet Cong and Americans and their allies. Ultimately Le Ly Hayslip moved to the United States, where she began working for Vietnamese-American reconciliation.

Le Ly Hayslip described what life was like when she was about eleven years old.

In school, the pressure to take sides was enormous. Our teacher, a villager named Manh, who was paid by the government, asked us, "What will you do if you see a Viet Cong [Communist soldier], or hear about someone who's helping them?" We answered in chorus, "Turn him in to the soldiers!" Manh praised us for our answer and told us that the Republicans would pay our families big rewards for every Viet Cong we helped them capture.

In 1960, Madame Ngo Dinh Nhu, the sister-in-law of Ngo Dinh Diem and first lady of our country, came to a nearby village with the idea of organizing the local children—and, particularly its young women—into Republican defense brigades: the *Phu Nu Cong Hoa*, "women warriors" who would repel the Viet Cong terrorists . . . We learned new patriotic songs proclaiming our loyalty to the Republic and took target practice with rifles that were quickly confiscated when we were finished. We heard lectures about how to keep ourselves safe from the Viet Cong, then acted out what we had learned in little plays in which the enemy was always defeated.

[Then the Viet Cong takes control of the region.] "From them we learned that, like the French, men of another race called *Americans* wanted to enslave us . . . We learned that cheating, stealing from, and lying to Republican soldiers and their allies were not crimes, and that failing to do these things, if the situation demanded it, was treason, of the highest sort . . . We then sang songs to celebrate those brothers and fathers that went north to Hanoi in 1954—I sang loudly."[14]

Only in 1975 did US troops withdraw.

The Korean War began a similar scenario, as women's activism sprang up when the forces of North Korea invaded the South in 1950 after skirmishes from both sides. At the end of the Second World War, Korean women were excited about the possibilities of a far better future than had existed under Japanese rule. With the outbreak of war, Pak Chongae wrote a rousing essay to her fellow women in North Korea: "All Korean Women Rise in Support of the War of Justice to Wipe out the Enemy of the People." Likewise the government of South Korea enlisted women to do every type of job and to work long hours doing it. They rebuilt bombed-out infrastructure and cut back on food for themselves and their children in order to support the war effort. Most of all in the South, women served as sex workers for the hundreds of thousands of US soldiers and, in separate brothels, for Korean soldiers. This was seen as a patriotic duty, no matter how awful for the individual. As another result of the war, there were some half million widows, many of them destitute, broken, and shunned.[15]

The politics of decolonization remained trapped in Cold War ideology and contests for hearts and minds. In June 1963, Celina Simango from Mozambique attended the International Women's Congress in Moscow to urge support for Mozambique and its women. Neither she nor her activist husband was a Communist, but the National Front for the Freedom of Mozambique [Frelimobut] was. In 1979, amid political and ideological struggles, her husband was executed and soon thereafter she was rounded up and presumably executed as well. Before that, however, she took advantage of the Congress, where the USSR wanted to prove itself on the international stage and hosted some 2,000 delegates from 119 countries. Simango was eager for the chance to speak to representatives.

My country is one of the least known in Africa, if only because we had the misfortune of being controlled by Portuguese imperialism for many centuries.

The whole economy of our country is geared towards the satisfaction of the European settlers. In order to make certain that the European settlers get the fullest economic advantage from the African worker, the Portuguese government has used many techniques of forcing our people to work in European farms, industries and commercial enterprises, mostly in menial jobs . . . The women and younger people are also forced to work in European plantations within Mozambique.

If any women in the whole world should understand the need for peace, it is the African women in general and the Mozambican women in particular. As an African woman I am extremely aware of the need for peace partly because Africa has not yet known peace for the last one hundred years. Since the European imperialist parceled our continent into enclaves of European capitalist exploitation, they have been taking away the best of our men to feed their economic enterprises with cheap labor, while leaving the women and children behind to fend for existence in the poorest conditions . . . Therefore the people of Mozambique have decided to fight for their freedom.[16]

The remains of colonialism were most visible in the Middle East where the two sides grew increasingly hostile. On one side of this growing divide was Golda Meir, born in Kiev (1898–1978) and educated in the United States, who migrated to Palestine as a young woman in the 1920s. Meir's goal was to be part of the establishment of a Jewish homeland. She joined other "pioneers," living on a kibbutz. "No one helped us settle or learn Hebrew or find a place to live . . . It never occurred to us that anyone else was morally obligated to assist us."[17] This last remark was critical of later immigrants, who complained if state assistance wasn't up to their high expectations and former way of life. For Meir, the kibbutz experience was transformative, not just of individuals but of the land of Israel itself. Meir increasingly criticized Arabs for whom she had only harsh words. Colonialism advanced and with it, the usual imperial contempt for those colonized as settlers fought to create the state of Israel from parts of Palestine.

On the other side, Fadwa Tuqan (1917–2003) lived in Nablus in Palestine and, growing up in the women's part of a sex-segregated household, had little deep knowledge of outside events. The poetry that she came to write focused on private life and nature. She recorded in her memoir, however, the gradual change in women's attire until it became more or less "Western." With the defeat of Palestinians by Israel in 1948 and the increasing impoverishment and loss of Palestinian lands she awoke to a wider political reality. She traveled to England, returning to the Israeli occupation of her birthplace. Her poetry became political as the Seven Days War in 1967 saw even further erosion of Palestinian well-being. Israelis and Europeans came to hate her, whereas Arabs had once criticized her for being too Western. The situation remained unsettled as millions of Palestinians were driven out by the increasing number of settlers who simply took their property. For many, the struggle was unrelated to Cold War issues.

Fighting communism or fending off imperialist capitalism justified atrocities, both USSR and US leaders believed. Thus dictators could remain in power and thrive using brutality and even murder in nations allied either with one or the other side. In Latin America a string of dictators were active in the postwar period, mostly allied with the United States because they backed businesses and promised to keep out Communists. These military dictatorships began "disappearing" citizens who discussed politics, mostly criticizing dictatorship. It became known that the high school and college students, workers, journalists, and others so "disappeared" were usually tortured, raped, and killed, babies ripped from their mothers' bodies, genitals beaten or sliced up, and living victims dropped from airplanes to their death.

Mothers started protesting across South and Central America. In the late 1970s a group of Argentinian mothers of these "disappeared" ones began silently walking in the Plaza de Mayo in front of the government's headquarters. Many were detained or "disappeared" themselves, but new participants joined. The movement spread to other Latin American countries where the United States government was similarly using billions of dollars to prop up dictatorships in the name of fighting the Cold War. Often women protestors in El Salvador and elsewhere received support from some clergy but Catholic clergy also supported the political power structure and worked against the anti-authoritarian activism. The Argentinian Mothers platform went as follows:

We have no political objective. No one has called us together nor tells us what to do. We are against violence and terrorism of any sort, whether individual or state-inspired. We want peace, brotherhood, and justice. We wish for a democratic system that respects the fundamental rights of people [individuals] in Argentina. Whether believers or not, we adhere to the principles of Judeo-Christian morality. We reject injustice, oppression, torture, murder, kidnappings, arrest without due process, detentions followed by disappearances, and persecution based on religion, race, ideology, or politics.

We do not judge our detained-disappeared children. We don't even ask for their freedom. We only wish to know where they are and what [crimes] they are accused of; and, for them to be judged in accordance with the law and the legal right to a defense—if it is determined that they have committed some crime . . . Can there be a more simple, more basic, more correct, more human, more Christian plea?.

As mentioned earlier, our first objective is to get the country's civil, military, and judicial authorities to answer the questions that haunt us: Where are our children? What has become of them?[18]

These activists against Latin American dictators emphasized their motherhood and the family. This strategy had some advantages, as the authorities seemed to treat them somewhat less brutally than they would have treated male protestors. Their example spread worldwide and influenced protests elsewhere, for example, the "Women in Black" movement operating in the Middle East, Europe, Africa, and elsewhere in the world.

Critics, however, find the strategy of focusing on womanhood and family as somehow less legitimate than underscoring the human rights of all people.

Remembering, Portraying, Struggling

Women were among the notable authors and political thinkers who recorded, imagined, rebelled against, and theorized both postwar and postcolonial conditions. Across the transition from colonized to liberated, some women gained an education that eventuated in extraordinary memoirs and new feminist deeds. Women such as Nelly Sachs memorialized the Holocaust in poetry, for which she was awarded the Nobel Prize. African women produced insightful novels of Africa after the Second World War, during both the struggles of decolonization and their aftermath. Formerly colonized men also examined the effects of colonialism on their psyches. Imperialists had called them effeminate and irrational, lacking the sturdy rationality of Western men. After India became independent, the hypermasculinized American president John F. Kennedy mistrusted Jawaharlal Nehru, its new leader. Nehru wore the garb of the region that included a long skirt-like garment with a flower affixed to it. Frantz Fanon wrote about the terror aroused by the colonized male because of his dark skin, which was said to be an indication of his monstrosity and frightening nature. The preference for white skin as a sign of superiority remained active even in areas that had broken free from colonialism centuries earlier, Latin American societies being foremost among these.

In the immediate aftermath of the Second World War and as independence from colonialism unfolded, Nigerian-born Flora Nwapa (1931–1993) produced one of the most influential postcolonial novels—*Efuru* (1966). The work told the story of a young African woman, whose child dies and both of whose husbands abandon her. She is thus without the two central ingredients of a woman's identity in Nigeria. Instead of remaining bereft and unhappy with herself, she becomes a follower of the goddess Uhamiri, who tells her to be proud of her well-being and beauty and to continue to use her talents to the full. Nwapa worked a revolution in this and successive stories by turning the narrative of African women away from the pathos, despair, or resignation found in African men's heroines and instead toward an awareness of their strength.

Women's literature flowered globally as never before, many novels outlining their plight in less than happy terms but mostly showing women's resolve and fortitude in the face of hardship. Kamala Markandaya (1924–2004) published her *Nectar in a Sieve* (1954) focusing on peasant life in India, where adversity arose at every turn. In Africa, women were rejected as candidates to stand for elections and called "lazy" of mind despite promises of postwar treatment as equals while fighting for independence.[19] Daughter of a white mother and African father, Bessie Head, a South African writer who had escaped the apartheid system to live in Botswana, developed Fanon's themes in her novels. Her characters danced on the edge of madness because of their complicated identities springing from colonialism, clashing ethnicities, and education. A teacher in Head's novel *Maru* (1971) has had an English education but is despised and disdained by other Africans because she belongs to the darkest-skinned group of Bushmen or Bushies. Myriam Ba's *So Long a Letter* (1979) recounted the trials of marriage in a Muslim society where men could take new wives at will and abandon their families. However, the heroine's plight had less to do with religion than with her husband's lack of character. Bad character made male power all the more oppressive. Women characterized independence as something emotionally conflicted for individuals, with the meaning of freedom still to be puzzled out.

Other African writers focused on the promised access to the "good life" that Europeans led. Buchi Emecheta (1944–2017) remembered her days as an educated young woman in Nigeria and then her disenchantment on arriving in England in the 1960s. Not only did her husband become lazy, abusive, and unfaithful but the promised equality of the "West" never materialized in her life. She was, as she titled one book, a "Second Class Citizen." Still, she persevered, gaining an education and becoming not only a librarian but also an author. After memorializing her own experiences, she set down those of her grandmother during the influenza epidemic and those of her mother as an African woman living under colonial rule. In *The Slave Girl* (1977), a brother sells his sister into slavery to an African market woman in order to make his own life easier after their family's decimation during the epidemic, which the British had brought to their shores. Emecheta's books were earnest yet seriously critical of the society she had left and the one she had joined.

As the Cold War and its resulting proxy wars expanded, culture was militarized, with war, espionage, and gangland films with their largely male casts dominating the scene. Hong Kong films satirized the violent masculinity of Western films. With destruction of male bodies rousing little outcry, another popular genre was the happy filmmaking of India, nicknamed Bollywood. In these, the heterosexuality that underlay the nation-state thrived, as Bollywood films worked in tandem with military ones. Western militarization protected happy heterosexuality—a heterosexuality emphasizing a lusciously sexual female body and joyful coupling.

Ideas from the decolonizing world came to infuse protest culture in the United States and Europe, where minority women and men were treated as subject peoples. Americans still stigmatized racial minorities and increasingly tried to keep them impoverished, for example, providing them only segregated, underfunded education. In 1955, NAACP (National Association for the Advancement of Colored People) activist Rosa Parks (1913–2005), sitting in the section of a Montgomery Alabama bus designated for blacks, refused to get up when a white man could not find a seat. Parks' arrest galvanized women to organize a boycott of buses in the city. The boycott lasted more than a year and accelerated the massive civil disobedience on the part of African Americans, Hispanic Americans, and their allies in the name of ending racial and ethnic discrimination in the United States.

Minority women across North America now accelerated their organizing and participation in nonviolent activism including sit-ins at segregated restaurants and lunch counters that began in 1960. Aiming to overcome the suppression of African Americans in politics, they joined with whites to achieve African American voter registration. In the early 1960s only 3 percent of eligible African Americans voted because whites prevented even their appearance at the ballot box. Women's activism was by then a tradition: when the US Supreme Court ruled in 1954 that schools had to be desegregated, girls were chosen to be on the front lines of school desegregation. They endured taunts, threats of rape, violence, and a range of other psychological and physical abuse in this cause. Older girls and women joined both the many nonviolent and Black Power groups that sprang up in the 1950s and 1960s.

The extraordinary women leaders such as Fannie Lou Hamer and Ella Baker soon discovered that men in their movement only tolerated women's participation if they did the cleaning, cooking, and secretarial work for the male leadership. Baker, despite her crucial role in founding the Student Nonviolent Coordinating Committee (SNCC) realized that she would not be an acknowledged national leader in the civil rights movement: "First, I was a woman. Also, I'm not a minister,"[20] They spoke up, giving white women activists at the time an example of protest within the civil rights and anti-war movements themselves, being called "bridge leaders" because they brought people together and into the streets and organizational meetings. The idea of "women identified women" took shape, and while African American women's organized activism had behind it more than a century of protest it now took off in powerful and formative ways for activism generally.

African American women, coming to the effort from many political directions, were often, as one woman put it, "terrified" of what would happen as they registered voters or tried to integrate lunch counters. In 1972, Shirley Chisholm (1924–2005) became the first woman to run for the Democratic presidential nomination and the first black woman to run for the nomination of either major party. Before that, in 1968, she was also the first black woman member of Congress—a position to which she was elected seven times. Philosopher Angela Davis was more radical than Chisholm: as an active Communist her criticism of the United States was biting. Flo (Florynce) Kennedy (1916–2000) represented a far edgier activism, especially given the tradition of respectability fostered by many middle- and upper-class African American women. Kennedy pushed to get admitted to Columbia University's law school over the objection not that she was black but that she was a woman. Thus, she felt the force of intersectionality at an early stage of joint feminist-civil rights activism. Representing plaintiffs on both civil rights and feminist grounds, including Black Panthers and other Black Power activists, Kennedy's transgressions extended to organizing a mass urination on the campus of Harvard to protest its lack of bathrooms for women.

It was black women activists who brought to the fore issues of sexuality and who made the most vivid advances in recognizing intersectionality—that is, the interaction of categories such as religion, class, race, and gender in politics, society, the law, and economics. In 1965, white women had launched NOW, an organization for women to gain legal and political rights, but the movement that grew up around these issues seemed mostly concerned with white women's economic, cultural, and heterosexual issues, factoring out the situation of non-whites. White feminism exploded in hundreds of marches, manifestos, and the founding of magazines, academic programs, and legal initiatives. Across Europe, they fought as well for the right to birth control, abortions, equal rights in divorce, finance, the law, and wages. Many of these initiatives, including access to such fields as law, medicine, and higher education, were successful.

Still, exclusions were visible, and in 1977, a group of black feminists in Boston laid these out in the Combahee River Collective statement. The manifesto was named after the river by which Harriet Tubman's spy network allowed some 800 slaves to reach freedom during the US Civil War. It brought to the fore the lack of attention in the white women's movement to issues of race, "third world" feminism, and sexuality. The Collective gained allies among lesbians who similarly felt that white heterosexuality was privileged in the so-called "mainstream" movement. As the 1970s closed, there had been achievements when it came to achieving reproductive rights. However, many influential people were unconvinced, Prime Minister Indira Gandhi of India being a prime example: "You know I am not a feminist in the accepted sense of the word," Indira Gandhi explained to a friend. "Women in India, perhaps in most of the world, are so dominated and discriminated against. There is so much unnecessary cruelty and humiliation . . . I have taken my own decisions throughout my life. I can stand alone."[21]

Conclusion

Women had enormous responsibilities for cleaning up after the destruction of the Second World War. Amid their work to clear rubble and to overcome the scarcity of food, the superpowers were already involving the world's peoples in new conflicts. Activism continued in the wars against imperialism across the globe. Vietnam, Korea, and Algeria were just three sites where women were engaged and millions killed. In all of these places, despite promises, equal citizenship seemed hopeless. Nonetheless, freedom fighters persisted in South Africa, Kenya, Nigeria, the Middle East, and beyond.

When independence brought poverty and civil war because the imperialist countries had left new nations threadbare or conflict-ridden, all the while supplying male leaders with weapons, women composed a vast river of migrants. They set up new lives and found new sources of employment and political participation in distant lands.

To finance state-building, newly independent governments cut needed education and health care for women and their families. However, women wrote, made art, and prospered as they charted postwar life. Novels were amazingly complex, glorying in women's strength while laying out struggles with cheating husbands and continuing racism. Activists took heart in images not just of women's survival but also of their triumph over the most difficult conditions in everyday life. Many of them did this while taking sides in the Cold War. The art and writings of African, Asian, and Latin American women plus news of women's activism around the globe fortified a feminist uprising worldwide. All of this was a good preparation for the challenges that technology and a new wave of globalization were to bring to the world's peoples.

Glossary

Apartheid	The South African policy of complete segregation of whites and other ethnicities, especially local African people that included confiscating their property, pushing them into ghettos, and imprisoning, torturing, and murdering critics.
Hussein-Dey	A district of the greater Algiers area in Algeria.
Qasbah	The citadel or fortress area of a North African city around which a neighborhood develops.
Yoruba	An ethnic group in parts of Nigeria and Benin.

Notes

1 Quoted in Gail Hershatter, *The Gender of Memory: Rural Women and China's Collective Past* (Berkeley: University of California Press, 2011), 73.
2 Hershatter, *Gender of Memory*, 111.
3 Quoted in Ross Terrill, "Jiang Qing," *Oxford Encyclopedia of Women in World History*, Bonnie G. Smith, ed., 4 vols. (New York: Oxford University Press, 2008), 2:652.
4 Soo Chin-yee, *Eighth Moon: The True Store of a Young Girl's Life in Communist China* [as told to Bette Lord] (New York: Harper and Row, 1964), 47–9.
5 Quoted in Mary Fulbrook, *The People's State: East German Society from Hitler to Honecker* (New Haven, CT: Yale University Press, 2005), 28.
6 Gerhard J. DeGroot and Corinna Peniston-Bird, *A Soldier and a Woman: Sexual Integration in the Military* (Lexington: Longman, 2000), 227.

7   Sworn testimony, published in *El Moudjaid n*, no. 66, June 20, 1960, reprinted in *Les femmes algériennes dans la guerre* (Paris: Plon, 1991), 68–9. Translation by Bonnie G. Smith.

8   Mobutu Sese Seko quoted in Iris Berger, *Women in Twentieth Century Africa* (Cambridge: Cambridge University Press, 2016), 102.

9   Rita Menon and Kamla Bhasin, *Boundaries and Borders in India's Partition* (New Delhi: Kali for Women, 1999), 51.

10   Menon and Bhasin, *Boundaries and Borders in India's Partition*, 214–15.

11   Emma Mashinini, *Strikes Have Followed Me All My Life: A South African Autobiography* (New York: Routledge, 1991), 53–4, 61–2.

12   Mary E. Hawkesworth, *Globalization and Feminist Activism* (New York: Rowman and Littlefield, 2006), 88–9. See also Jan Lambertz, "'Democracy Could Go No Further': European Women in the Early United Nations," in *Women and Gender in Postwar Europe: From Cold War to European Union*, Joanna Regulska and Bonnie G. Smith, eds. (London: Routledge, 2012), chapter 2.

13   Wilma Iggers, *Women of Prague: Ethnic Diversity and Social Change from the Eighteenth Century to the Present* (New York: Berghahn, 1995), 300–1.

14   Le Ly Hayslip, *When Heaven and Earth Changed Places: A Vietnamese Woman's Journey from War to Peace* (New York: Doubleday, 1989), 34–42.

15   Barbara Molony, Janet Theiss, and Hyaeweol Choi, *Gender in Modern East Asia: China, Korea, Japan as Integrated History* (Boulder, CO: Westview Press, 2016), 375–9.

16   Celina Simango, Speech at the International Women's Congress in Moscow, from *Mozambican Revolution*, no. 1 (December 1963) in Todd Shepard, *Voices of Decolonization: A Brief History with Documents* (Boston, MA: Bedford/St. Martins, 2015), 149.

17   Golda Meir, *My Life* (New York: G. P. Putnam's Sons), 80.

18   Asociacion de Madres de Plaza de Mayo, *Boletin*, January 1980 (#1), p. 1–2. Trans. Lynda Jentsch in Pamela S. Murray, ed., *Women and Gender in Modern Latin America: Historical Sources and Interpretations* (New York: Routledge, 2014), 240–1.

19   Quoted in Iris Berger, *Women in Twentieth-Century Africa* (Cambridge: Cambridge University Press, 2016), 101.

20   Quoted in Belinda Robnett, *How Long? How Long? African-American Women in the Struggle for Civil Rights* (New York: Oxford University Press, 1997), 94.

21   Pupul Jayakar, *Indira Gandhi: A Biography* (New Delhi: Viking Books India, 1992), 265–7.

Further Reading

Alegre, Robert F., and Elena Poniatowska, *Railroad Radicals in Cold War Mexico: Gender, Class, and Memory*. Lincoln: University of Nebraska Press, 2014.

Ardener, Shirley, Fiona Armitage-Woodward, and Lidia Dina Sciama, eds. *War and Women across Continents: Autobiographical and Biographical Experiences*. New York: Berghahn, 2016.

Berger, Iris. *Women in Twentieth-Century Africa*. Cambridge: Cambridge University Press, 2016.

Devlin, Rachel. *A Girl Stands at the Door: The Generation of Young Women Who Desegregated America's Schools*. New York: Basic Books, 2018.

Guy, Donna. *Women Build the Welfare State: Performing Charity and Creating Rights in Argentina, 1880–1955*. Durham, NC: Duke University Press, 2009.

Hershatter, Gail. *The Gender of Memory: Rural Women and China's Collective Past*. Berkeley: University of California Press, 2011.

Kaplan, Temma. *Taking Back the Streets: Women, Youth, and Direct Democracy*. Berkeley: University of California Press, 2003.

Mackie, Vera. *Feminism in Modern Japan: Citizenship, Embodiment, and Sexuality*. Cambridge: Cambridge University Press, 2003.

Menon, Rita, and Kamla Bhasin, *Boundaries and Borders in India's Partition*. New Delhi: Kali for Women, 1999.

Olcott, Jocelyn. *International Women's Year: The Greatest Consciousness-Raising Event in History*. New York: Oxford University Press, 2017.

Shepard, Todd. *Sex, France, and Arab Men, 1962–1979*. Chicago, IL: University of Chicago Press, 2017.

Thomas, Lynn M. *Politics of the Womb: Women, Reproduction, and the State in Kenya*. Berkeley: University of California Press, 2003.

12

Women's Globalization in a High-Tech Age

In 2009, at the age of eleven, Malala Yousafzai began blogging from her home in northwest Pakistan. The region was controlled by an extremist group known as the Taliban, which wanted women segregated and kept from schooling. Under the title "Diary of a Pakistani Schoolgirl," Malala advocated education for girls and declared her own love of study. Many in the West turned Malala into a heroine, emblematic of forward-looking thinking and modern behavior, enabled by technology such as the internet and World Wide Web. In 2012, members of the Taliban shot Malala, who, as she fought for life, became even more celebrated in adversity and eventually a co-recipient of the Nobel Peace Prize. Critics, while praising Malala, emphasized that children in her region could not go to school anyway because of US and allied drones that blanketed her region, killing hundreds of innocent children like Malala. They accused Westerners of using Malala to paper over their own complicity in Malala's plight: like many a schoolgirl she faced death from technology despite her humane use of the internet.

Connected to this situation, a multifaceted scientific revolution took place after the Second World War, affecting the reproductive, social, cultural, and work lives of women, not to mention their personal safety. New reproductive technologies sprang up and a telecommunications revolution linked the world's people as never before, leading to the creation of a relatively dispersed but interlocking global workforce. The participation of women in all aspects of work life, including the high-tech sector made economies around the world hum with activity. In that workforce, women faced the unprecedented power of global businesses and of governments with massive financial, military, and administrative resources: businesses went wherever and whenever they found the cheapest—often female—labor; militarized states rained bombs and drones down on civilians living thousands of miles away. Simultaneously, civil and other wars erupted locally; genocide threatened peoples; women most often led the list of victims of these wars. They were robbed of their household goods and funds, raped, and murdered; if they survived, they migrated whenever possible with their children to escape. An age of opportunity was also an age of discrimination and violence for millions.

Amid it all, women contributed to the arts, intellectual, technological, and general cultural life of their communities even while maintaining vigorous activism for subsistence, rights, and a better world. More than ever, they became highly visible leaders on the world stage. The causes they championed included stamping out the immense and rising poverty of many women across the globe, as income inequality soared in the first decades of the twenty-first century. While many in Africa eked out a bare living, for example, local women created networks of support amid economic distress and constant violence. In Liberia, social worker Leymah Gbowee mobilized women to protest the eleven-year civil war in 2002 and peacefully to force that war to end. As a new government formed, Ellen Johnson Sirleaf was elected president—the first woman head of state in modern Africa. Activism was global and increasingly interconnected, thanks in part to the paradoxical effects of technology.

Scientific Advances in a Knowledge Society

The Second World War showed the increasing importance of technology and innovation based on scientific and other formal knowledge, which in the postwar world came to influence everyday life more than ever. The standard of living improved around the world as electrification and hygienic improvements benefited rising numbers of people. Refrigeration and more reliable cooking appliances improved the safety of food; safer water supplies and public sanitation advanced personal health. To this day, the benefits remain unequally distributed: large areas lacked and still lack water and food security; conditions allowing for personal hygiene and sanitation remain abysmal across sections of the globe. Although, in general, human longevity increased globally, women in the global North, which included the former imperial powers, gained the most from these developments. Even here, however, progress varied: in the wealthy United States, the longevity of white women began to decline, attributed to declining standards of health, education, and overall well-being in rural areas. Across the globe, those in power appeared little concerned for the poor or for the general welfare of the population. Such neglected women lacking access to basic, healthful resources have been labeled as "out-of-the-way" people.

That said, a major development in modern times was that on average women lived longer than men did. This inversion from the days when women lived fewer years than men resulted from the lowered rate of maternal death, thanks to greater understanding of overall health and obstetrics and to the widespread drop in fertility rates. However, maternal health and infant mortality also reflected priorities: both Great Britain and the United States had higher rates of infant and maternal death than all other developed economies and even some developing states did. Biologists developed and tested a birth control pill in the 1950s on women in the Caribbean and the United States, most of whom were eager to benefit from fewer pregnancies. By the end of the 1980s, women in Africa and Asia who had once aimed to have as many children as possible because children shaped a woman's identity, changed their mind. They cut fertility dramatically too, in part because more children were surviving to adulthood thanks to new medicines and improving sanitation. The uneven distribution of these improvements cannot be emphasized enough.

On the other side of the equation, a biological revolution in reproductive technology and medicine permitted women in wealthier economies who might have remained childless to bear children through in-vitro fertilization. The first "test-tube" baby was born in Britain in 1978 after she had been incubated in a jar; thereafter tens of thousands of couples and individuals of means were able to conceive in this manner, but the high cost limited the benefits to those who were well-off. In general, women's bodies were medicalized as never before, with childbirth in hospitals and clinics growing in frequency along with medical interventions such as caesarean sections. Sonograms, fetal monitoring, amniocentesis, and other in-utero technological procedures, including surgery, were applied to the fetus and the pregnant woman. Motherhood remained a major and even *the* major component of women's identity in certain regions of the world. In East Africa, for example, few women were childless; if they did not bear children themselves, members of their community would offer children for adoption, so harmful was it seen to group life and the woman herself for anyone not to have children. In other regions, forced sterilization programs tried to control women's fertility and thus population growth. Because money was involved, violence erupted against women who refused to submit.

In China, government policy early in the 1980s mandated that no couple could have more than one child. Women who became pregnant faced pressure to have an abortion, although such restrictions affected higher status or wealthier people far less. The policy had other consequences that were often unsavory: girl fetuses were often aborted; parents and grandparents treated the one child in a family as a special pet to be spoiled; children grew up without siblings and other close relatives with whom to interact and negotiate; a shortage of women made it difficult for Chinese men to find a woman to marry. These social problems encouraged government officials to allow larger families in 2015. Across the globe, the state made women feel the intertwined force of political rhetoric and policy, while advertising, public opinion about motherhood and women's identity, ups and downs in the economy, and scientific advances in reproductive technology on their fertility affected their entire life course.

In the face of globalization motherhood remained as high-pressured as ever, as children's education made a big difference in their future. Nations such as Germany and the United States had less available childcare. That in the United States was more costly than virtually anywhere else in the world. Many women worked simply to advance their children's educational credentialing and skill acquisition. In addition, the competitive pressures made it important for mothers to lend psychological support to ensure success. In dangerous societies, the preservation of life came first, and single mothers often faced insurmountable challenges in supporting and protecting. Mothers needed to foster mental health and a host of technical skills in their children. At the extremes, where life was precarious, parents might pawn children out to brickmakers or owners of sweatshops.

Scientific knowledge was also the context for the passage from one sex to another via hormonal treatment and surgical procedures. For long, physicians had intervened in the bodily formation of intersex people. In cases where infants had the secondary sex characteristics of both sexes, physicians, sometimes with the consent of parents, determined which to remove surgically in order to establish a clear sexual identity. Activism developed to prevent medical interventions in infants who had no say in the modifications to their bodies. Simultaneously other individuals decided that their own bodies did not conform to their gender identities. For centuries people had blurred and some even refused sexual categories altogether, seeing in them outsiders' exercise of power over their being. As shown earlier, across history people had developed a range of new sexual identities and original practices of those identities. Other people accepted gender identities but not those that society assigned to them by virtue of their physical characteristics. Where societies were unaccepting of anything but a binary sexual range, transsexual people became more insistent on their right to a chosen identity and sexuality. Medicine and technology became major factors in accomplishing such targeted changes even as others objected to that intervention. As with the satellites that allowed global communication but also targeted locations of individuals to bomb, so technologies of the body had complex potential.

Work in a Globalizing, Neoliberal Economy

For centuries women have worked in a globalizing economy, with Chinese women making silk, for example, that in the sixteenth century might be transported and sold in western Europe. From Russia to Africa and the Western Hemisphere, people also migrated 500 years ago—both freely and as forced or slave labor—to serve a brisk, globalizing economy that absorbed workers from many parts of the world. That movement only increased so that even in the late twentieth century women's work could involve cycles of migration—from rural areas to cities, from city to city, or continent to continent even when that entailed traversing thousands of miles and crossing oceans. For many, migration involved a desperate move out of poverty or out of military danger; for the few, migration was part of career advancement. Migration depended on conditions in the home country but also on global information and ever more powerful marketing to get people to move, especially to take menial jobs.

A mobile female workforce mostly involved low-paid labor, often unfree or forced. Because of the continuing privilege accorded to men in the form of higher wages and greater social power, most women remained poor and some two-thirds of those living in poverty around the world remained women and children. Where conditions were desperate, indebted mothers continued to pawn children to work for no pay, while girls continued to be part of forced and international prostitution rings. Some women became prostitutes through agencies deceptively advertising office and other kinds of appealing work. Despite these worst aspects of international work, there developed more reliable networks for nurses and other health-care workers. Skilled women traveled for opportunities as technicians, physical therapists, nurses' aides, especially as health care became a way for states to show concern for citizens. Still, downgrading by bureaucrats and employers below their level of training to reduce costs of both businesses and the welfare state continued. Even young mothers migrated to get cash to send back home, as family members, including husbands, took up the task of childcare.

Women continued migrating to serve as domestics. Women from Southeast Asia sought out jobs as domestic help or as caretakers of children in China or Japan. They worked long hours but received food and shelter and some form of wage. Such jobs still carried the threat of abuse, including the age-old one of rape by male householders or their grown children. In the twenty-first century, domestics under the worst conditions worked long hours and were often beaten by women and men alike, their passports and wages confiscated so that they could not escape. Any complaint could lead to their own arrest. Still, some very brave women went to the authorities, with the result that abusive conditions were publicized and the abusers sometimes arrested.

At the other extreme, women stood on the frontlines of the scientific and technological breakthroughs of these decades. In Finland, Britain, the United States, and other countries many of the first computer programmers were women despite the much-believed cliché that women are not able to understand technology. The six main programmers of the first digital computer were all women. Although the computer was a super-sophisticated technology for its time, so was weaving as it had developed millennia earlier. In many technologies, once women had developed them, men then entered the field, often driving off women as the technology became increasingly lucrative. Still, women also lobbied to have legislation and customs preventing them from being lawyers and stockbrokers in Western societies overturned.

A global economy in which jobs could as easily be done in China as in Argentina created opportunity and took opportunity away. Jobs popped up everywhere, as the world's labor market became "liberal" or "neoliberal"— that is, in the seventeenth-century understanding of liberal, individualistic and free from restrictions. In the 1990s, neoliberalism as pioneered politically by British Prime Minister Margaret Thatcher a decade earlier became a central business model for promoting growth. Reducing social programs such as health care and education for ordinary working people would lower taxes for employers and boost the employer's profits and investment. Cutting taxes for the wealthy gave them extra funds to invest, which would theoretically increase the number of good jobs for workers. Neoliberal policy encouraged business mergers, the elimination of rules for the industries and banks, the free flow of capital across national borders, and cutting jobs to increase profit. A longstanding neoliberal business practice was to pay workers the most minimal of wages and to move should they demand more. One retired woman in Medellin, Colombia, saw neoliberalism changing the textile industry of fifty years earlier for the worse: "the industrialists of that time . . . were not only very intelligent, very advanced, but also very human." Compared to the present, she felt that her textile factory had been "an *earthly paradise*."[1]

The neoliberal model opposed the postwar welfare state in which many governments tried to create a minimum level of well-being for society as a whole. Although many still believed that government should provide social services and education for all, the tightening of budgets in the European Union and emerging states alike reduced these services. The Swedish government drastically cut pensions, leading one union member to complain: "It means that we have to work our entire life."[9] Because employers (like workers) paid taxes for social service programs, any reduction in benefits or education costs meant smaller employer contributions and more income for the owners. A major US education official aimed to eliminate public education entirely, thus cutting the taxes for owners of industry and creating a pool of less educated workers to take menial, low-paid jobs. Despite neoliberal convictions, some nations believed that certain services were too important to be abandoned in the name of profit rather than the public good; for that reason, these governments continued to run high-quality transportation systems, pave roads, and support free public education for the next generation of citizens. Developing economies such as South Korea, China, and Vietnam, however, made it a top priority to use low-paid young women as workers to attract manufacturers from around the world.

As tens of millions of people in the twentieth and twenty-first centuries migrated from countryside to the city and from nation to nation to find work or to escape wars, conditions varied. Male engineers, doctors, and other well-educated people had fewer problems migrating, while those lacking advanced education often moved illegally, facing dangers and even death. Once arrived, they might be exploited in sweatshops, their passports confiscated and wages not paid. This was the case of Rojana Cheunchujit, a Thai woman smuggled into the United States. Born in 1970, she went to school for nine years, then worked in sewing factories and got married so that her parents wouldn't worry about her. She arrived in the United States when she was 24, after being spotted by a recruiter:

> He said that if I wanted to come to the US, he would be able to arrange it for me for 125,000 baht [US $5,000] which I paid him.
>   I came to the US with my friends, not with my family. I thought I would stay and work in the US for three years . . . I was locked up in the sewing shop by the owners. They fed us poorly . . . As soon as I arrived in this country, they . . . basically told me I would have to work continually, non-stop and only have a day off from time to time. This was completely the opposite of what I had been told in Thailand . . . I realized I had been duped.
>   There were over 70 Thai workers at the shop. We worked 20 hours a day for the whole one year and four months I was there—until the day I was liberated. I cooked for myself. We ordered food from the owners, but they charged us really high prices, at least twice the amount.

"After paying the $5,000 to get here, they told me I had to pay an additional $4,800. They said they would keep me as long as it took to pay off the . . . debt." These menacing employers threatened to harm the families back in Thailand of anyone who left the workshop. When someone tried to escape "they beat him up pretty badly . . . They did this to intimidate us."[2] Eventually US officials liberated the entire enslaved workforce from this common treatment of migrant workers. Such an imposition of standards by the US government went against neo-liberal theories of maximizing profits by minimizing any regulation of business, no matter what happened to workers.

Women workers, even in the most menial of jobs, experienced falling levels of fertility and rising levels of education, as did their children. By the second decade of the twenty-first century women's fertility had declined to 2.5 children and in countries such as Japan and in regions of Europe was below the replacement level of 2.1 children. Some of this was due to intensive programs to boost women's employment and in turn ramp up national economies. The rise of the Pacific "Tigers in the 1980s and 1990s," for example, happened because these nations mobilized single and married women alike to work in electronics and other factories for Western firms at low wages. At the same time, to advance women's contribution to both reproducing the next generation and thus growing the workforce, emerging states provided maternal care and childcare on a more regular basis. Birth control became more available in order to keep a segment of the workforce active. Still, those who remained "out of the way" in rural areas of the global South lacking adequate food, clean water, and good medical services saw their conditions decline with declining social welfare budgets.

Earning wages, working women became consumers of electronic devices such as smart phones, which could make life easier for some and could help them make connections among themselves. In some instances they could become more active in protecting their families or improving conditions at work. Some women made money simply by owning a phone and renting it out. They also became international entrepreneurs, using global connections to ship prized local goods from West Africa, for example, to West African migrants working temporarily in Europe or other parts of the world. Many women used globalization to their advantage. Others used technology differently: one Jamaican woman made organizing transoceanic migration for herself and her family her mission in life: "She's always been the person with a very global vision," as one child described her mother's efforts to benefit her family economically.[3]

From the 1980s, tens of thousands of Chinese young women moved from rural areas to cities where the manufacturing of inexpensive goods for the global market helped make China's economy the second largest in the world by 2010. Conditions were often horrendous and hours long and with little relief. Suicide rates rose. At the same time, young women developed urban networks along which passed information about firms that offered the best working conditions and about job openings. They appreciated learning languages, such as those used on shipping packages or on directions for producing or assembling parts. Workers said that their networks became much wider than in the countryside, providing not just employment information but also friendships and new social ties.

For some, globalization and technology, despite their uncertainties created pathways, skills, networks, information, and know-how that could serve women and their families. In the 1990s, single young women moving from the countryside to Port Said, Egypt, to work in the clothing factories developed new connections, including with their male coworkers. Factories there focused on the overall productivity of these workers, while the workers themselves used the factories to save money to pay the costs of getting married. They also used their resources to promote the well-being when necessary of their distant families. However, blended into the conduct of industrial life were highly coded mating practices that modified traditionally strict Islamic values when it came to interactions, friendships, and courting between men and women. Marriage for love intruded on the practice of arranged marriages all in the context of globalized and technological manufacturing.

Gender identity in the workforce came under pressure in many regions of the world, as values shifted in a neoliberal workplace. The salary man in Japan was a stereotype of the overly hardworking white-collar office worker, who often labored sixty hours a week and was expected to socialize after that with office companions and on weekends with managers, leaving his stay-at-home wife alone. In Egypt, the workplace altered the dominance of marriages arranged by parents and modified traditional codes of

FIGURE 12.1 *Telephone workers in Kowloon, Hong Kong, 1990. These women, perhaps from the Chinese countryside, are the workers who helped China achieve its rapid growth so that by 2010 it had created the second largest economy in the world. Women powered many other emerging economies across the Pacific region, making sacrifices but also achieving personal gains. Gerhard Joren/LightRocket Getty Images.*

gendered behavior, even as those codes remained relevant to many people. Factories there, for another example, saw the hijab sometimes take on new, often sexualized, meanings that young women created with this single item of apparel despite the presence of phrases from the Qu'ran on the workplace walls.

Still, varieties of protest took place across the new globalized workplace. On the one hand, workers competed with one another worldwide for jobs; on the other, conditions could become too onerous to ignore. In the 1970s, women in South Korean low-wage factories staged so many protests over the horrendous conditions that police beat and even killed them. The head of the Korean CIA shot and killed dictator Park Chung Hee during a dispute over how to handle the women's strikes. Elsewhere, as in the Egyptian textile factory, people had other strategies, moving to another workplace in the enterprise zone without warning when their pay was late or vocally standing up for themselves when treated unjustly. As one woman said loudly on the shop floor, referring to an extra load of work but addressing no one in particular though in hearing range of her supervisor: "A new system has been set up at my expense! I'm having more work than Tamer . . . My blood is boiling. I want my [just dues]." The worker then invokes the supervisor specifically: "If he wants extra merits in heaven, he is *not* to load me with yet more work this afternoon."[4] Women's strategies ran the gamut of protest in the workplace, but by this time public activism had also become global as well as wide-ranging in demands for local and national change.

Activism

Exciting new activist voices stressed the importance of diversity, sexual transformation, environmental concerns, and intersectionality of condition. Seeking change, women from around the world contested the claim to leadership of Western organizations, whether directly at the United Nations or in other global settings. At UN Decade for Women conferences in the 1970s and 1980s, working-class women from Latin American nations along with elite Communist women from the Soviet bloc brought practical issues to the fore. Both before and after these conferences, dissenters had been bold in opposing dictators in South Korea, the Middle East, Latin America, and across the Soviet bloc of European communist countries. Some pointed to the unchecked violence against women and girls and had led the way in getting women's issues acknowledged at the United Nations. Activists increasingly put their lives on the line in numerous situations. In the postcolonial world, activism was also deliberately local despite being widespread. Whereas those women from the global South, for example, who had helped get the UN to acknowledge women's rights in the postwar UN, were privileged and wealthy, a wider range of activists such as Malala Yousafzai at the end of the twentieth century fought to correct the effects of globalization, neoliberalism, and violence against women but also against their neighbors.

Local Initiatives. Although the wives of high-ranking politicians in the Philippines united to work for "reforms," grassroots activism spread across this dispersed island nation. For one thing, many rejected the male dominated Catholic religion and its vision for women of suffering and virtue that arrived with European colonization. Instead, the *babaylan* or ancient priestess endowed with wisdom and insight became their touchstone. Local groups especially fought to end trafficking and to assist prostitutes as emblematic of working women. Like local favela residents surrounding Brazil's cities, their activism had nothing to do with middle- and upper-class feminism. For the impoverished women living alongside the massively wealthy families connected to corporations dealing in oil and other natural resources, their favelas—that is, the urban neighborhoods of shacks surrounding major cities—were the stage for activism. In Rio de Janeiro's slums, women organized the social services such as sanitation that the city denied their neighborhoods. They set up schools for themselves in which they could learn to read, write, and gain basic civic knowledge that would allow them access to basic resources such as health care and clean water. They fought for medical attention for their children and themselves in addition to adequate schooling. Women of all classes circled the world in dense patterns of activism, much of it avoiding the projects and values of elites.

Environment. During these decades, women won the coveted Nobel Prize not only for their scientific and literary accomplishments but also for their activism on behalf of oppressed people, the environment, and pacifism. As in the case of Rigoberta Menchu or Wangari Maathai, their efforts were often directed toward change benefitting their society as a whole, not just women. In many parts of the world—including both the global South and North—they came to hold the highest offices in their nations. Menchu wrote of the relationship that her K'iche' people had with nature and their activities on behalf of preserving nature. She chronicled the racist treatment that Ladinos—or descendants of Europeans—dealt Amerindians of Central America. As members of her family were killed by the army for protesting oppression, Rigoberta Menchu documented those murders and the only slightly less lethal everyday abuse of farm and domestic workers. Her goal and that of her people was multifaceted, but like many activists she objected to the ways in which global entrepreneurs were destroying nature and thus the heritage of her people. When some found discrepancies in Menchu's story, she demonstrated that such a composite account was part of traditional history-telling in which the entirety of a community's experience was represented—not that of a solitary story-teller providing details of her own slice of life. Rigoberta Menchu won the Nobel Peace Prize in 1992.

Wangari Maathai of Kenya teamed up with Mary Robinson of Ireland to promote human rights and the environment based on the sense that these were intertwined. Both led the way in their respective countries—Kenya and Ireland—in activism, with Robinson serving as Ireland's first woman president. Maathai involved women at the grass roots in planting trees in Kenya against the wishes of business people and politicians who had profited from destroying forests to sell their wood and who had hurt the environment in other ways. She received numerous death threats from these interests, but in 2004 the Nobel Prize Committee awarded her the prestigious Peace Prize. As High Commissioner for Human Rights at the United Nations and President of Ireland from 1990 to 1997, Robinson joined forces with Maathai to explain the relationship between human well-being and sustainable economies—that is, economies that did not decimate the earth's natural resources in the name of making money.

"Women leaders must insist we address environmental and development challenges in tandem. A more coherent approach also requires much greater attention and action to address the particular challenges facing women and girls and their role in advancing sustainable development," they wrote. In particular, they noted the effects of decades of industrialization based on plundering raw materials. "In Sub-Saharan Africa and other regions, drought exacerbated by climate change is contributing to chronic crop failures, deforestation and water shortages, with devastating impacts for

FIGURE 12.2 *Wangari Maathai and the Green Belt Movement. 1977. Wangari Maathai motivated thousands of Kenyan women to work to achieve reforestation of their country after it had been ravaged, ultimately because of poverty, corruption, and exploitation. Simultaneously she used her program to build democracy and community among the women planters of trees as they cooperated to achieve their massive project. Courtesy of William Campbell/Sygma Getty Images.*

girls and women. The primary food producers and procurers of water and fuel for cooking are women." Few people, they maintained, took note of the specific gender impact of climate change and economic devastation of nature. "Environmental changes are resulting in women being forced to travel farther to secure food, water and fuel for their families. This has been shown to have negative impacts on nutritional levels, educational attainment and work opportunities, to say nothing of quality of life issues overall."

For them, the solution was the activism of women: "But not only are women bearing the brunt of environmental and development setbacks—they are also a powerful source of hope in tackling climate and other environmental threats, and their voices must be heard. As the success of the Greenbelt Movement in planting millions of trees in Kenya has demonstrated, women can be an extraordinary force for positive change. Their knowledge and experience are fundamental to mitigating the effects as well as adapting to the inevitable changes wrought in local communities by shifting climatic patterns. "The absence of women, particularly those from the global South, from national and international discussions and decision-making on climate change and development must change," they insisted.[5]

The Nongovernmental Organizations. Women took up reform in formal nongovernmental organizations (NGOs). These organizations promoted wide-ranging causes, including those for the environment. Women from the northern countries raised money from their localities but more often from state and national governments and from transnational entities such as the European Union. Wealthy philanthropists such as the George Soros gave millions of dollars to fund education in support of democratic institutions that allowed both women and men active political participation. In some cases, philanthropists, including Soros, sponsored the beginnings of Women's and Gender Studies programs in such places as the former Soviet Union. Wealthy NGOs such as the Ford Foundation did the same as a way of capacity building among women who had not had the opportunity to participate in civil society. Their achievements were often enduring: as authoritarians worked to close down democratic and other rights in Poland in 2016 and 2017, women were among the most organized and effective opponents of antidemocratic politicians. Authoritarian Hungary worked to eliminate Women's and Gender Studies instruction from universities and schools.

NGOs also worked for extension of individual rights for women and ultimately for girls. In large part, they based their activism on the UN Declaration of Human Rights of 1948 and on CEDAW or the Convention on the Elimination of All Forms of Discrimination against Women, which went into effect in 1981. In 1975, the United Nations had sponsored an international women's conference in Mexico City. It was a momentous event, especially as women from South America and other parts of the global South announced that Western and other wealthy women had no idea of women's real problems: the lack of clean water, medical care, education, personal safety, and good jobs, to name a few. Women at the conference called for a Bill of Rights for women, and a UN committee focusing on social and economic rights created a document addressing those basic needs. Adopted by the UN General Assembly in 1979, CEDAW went into effect in 1981. Six member states of the United Nations had recently not ratified CEDAW: Iran, Palau, Somalia, Sudan, Tonga, and the United States (although the United States did sign the agreement). The beginning of the document is general and then moves to more specific issues of defining discrimination and its effects.

Article 1

For the purposes of the present Convention, the term "discrimination against women" shall mean any distinction, exclusion or restriction made on the basis of sex which has the effect or purpose of impairing or nullifying the recognition, enjoyment or exercise by women, irrespective of their marital status, on a basis of equality of men and women, of human rights and fundamental freedoms in the political, economic, social, cultural, civil or any other field.

The Convention then proceeded to detail the specific areas in which governments needed to address problems of discrimination against women. This entailed enacting laws and taking a variety of measures—"other appropriate means . . . including sanctions where appropriate"—to protect them from the harms of inequality. It suggested the creation of tribunals to ensure that such discrimination was not taking place. Another path to equality was fostering women's education, including providing access to schools with the same curricula and high quality teachers that men benefited from in their schooling. The convention specified that stereotypes of women and men had no place in the classroom; this was a foundation of educational equality. The elimination of stereotypes held for all textbooks and other curricular material, examinations, and teaching methods and needed to be maintained in rural as well as urban schools. Schools needed to cut the disparity in drop-out rates, higher for girls than for boys because parents did not want to bear the costs of girls' education. Coeducation, CEDAW determined, was the best way of ensuring the elimination of stereotypes and unequal facilities and opportunities.[6]

In 2013, after the transfer of CEDAW's enforcement and advancement to the High Commissioner of the United Nations in 2008, findings showed that one-quarter of the world's population were women living in rural areas. On all measures of human development, rural women—out-of-the-way people—across the globe were worse off than rural men and also worse off than all urban people. They did most of the agricultural work, while also bearing responsibility for all domestic and child-rearing work. Had CEDAW been enforced, the reports went, there would have been a drastic improvement in the lives of a quarter of the human race.

Although NGOs participated in UN commissions on women and other threatened groups, some politicians disliked and even condemned their work. This was especially true in the early twenty-first century—an era of rising authoritarianism that featured attacks on democratizing efforts to create citizen awareness. Authoritarian leaders in Russia and some eastern European states struck out at feminist activists, including pop culture stars. In post-Soviet Russia, born of the fall of the Soviet Empire at the end of 1991, members of the feminist punk rock group Pussy Riot were arrested and jailed in 2012 after performing in a Moscow church. The group pointedly criticized authoritarianism, especially that of Russia's president, Vladimir Putin. After their release late in 2013, they performed at the Olympics in Sochi, Russia, where Cossacks whipped them and nonuniformed thugs also assaulted them so that they were hospitalized. Such imprisonment and attacks made the group the object of worldwide support and protest. Although not an NGO, Pussy Riot was the kind of comparatively weak organization that bullying officials liked to discredit and turn into targets to build public support for themselves.

In the twentieth and twenty-first centuries, women's groups from the global South also organized without support from the large transnational NGOs.

In fact, these groups developed programs not just for their communities and nations but transnationally—that is, across national borders. For example, indigenous women of the Americas had often been left out of transnational meetings, or, more specifically, participation in the leadership. When accepted as participants, they were eliminated from determining policy. In the twenty-first century they became especially active on behalf of their way of life, their community's values, and the economic well-being of their families and local networks. Manifestos from indigenous women often protested the seizure by international corporations of their natural resources including their farmland. They also strategized on how to recuperate some of the influence they had had centuries earlier—that is, before the arrival of Europeans and other foreigners, including both feminists and activists in NGOs.

In 2009, the Coordinating Committee of the First Continental Summit of Indigenous Women meeting in Peru issued its first manifesto. The Committee represented an activism headed by strong, local women or Commandantes, who objected to being cast as "Indians" or, in some cases, "indigenous." For them, as for many "out-of-the-way" peoples, Western ideas had mostly brought them poverty and violence. Their public statement, thus began: "We, indigenous women gathered in the sacred lands of Lake Titicaca, after two days of discussions and deliberation raise our voices in these times when Abya Yala's [the Continent of Life] womb is once more with childbirth pains, to give birth to the new Pachakutik [era] for a better life on our planet." The members pointed to a range of issues—different from those of middle-class or Western feminism but with similarities:

With the goal of finding new ways to eliminate injustice, discrimination, violence against women, and machismo and to restore harmony and mutual respect on the planet, we gather here at this summit, uniting our hearts, minds, hands and wombs. As we women are part of nature and the universe, we are called to care for and defend our mother earth. From her, comes the ancient history and culture that makes us what we are: indigenous peoples under the protection and spiritual guidance of our parents and grandparents who gave life to all the human beings that now inhabit this wonderful planet—though a few oligarchs and imperialists threaten to destroy it out of greed.

We demand that our worldview not be "folklorized" by governments and private businesses.

To eliminate machismo, racism and ethnic discrimination, it is vital to return to the values associated with our communally-based worldview the basic principles of which are: complementarity, duality, balance and respect.

We indigenous women must not be passive when it comes to public policies. We must be able to shape these and oblige governments to consult us and let us participate in all matters in which our rights may be at stake.

The aforementioned initiatives will be undertaken by our own organizations and not by NGOs [non-governmental organizations], thus enacting our own agendas, not ones foreign to our principles and worldview.

Establish strategic alliances with other, like-minded sectors of society such as: organizations of mestiza, campesina [rural], and black women, female domestic workers, environmental organizations, unions, among others.[7]

Maasai women in Tanzania similarly moved in their own directions, staging several protests in the early twenty-first century. Living in a pastoralist society, land for animal grazing was central to the health of their community, though the government acted otherwise. It had confiscated large tracts of their rangelands since the 1950s for tourism and hunting. In 2009, it confiscated additional land, awarding it to a brigadier general from the United Arab Emirates for big game hunting and to a US safari tourism company. These persistent seizures of land condemned the Maasai to impoverishment and by 2010 even to starvation. Organizing themselves Maasai women protested, marching to the seat of Tanzanian government and turning in their membership cards in the ruling party. It was a shocking gesture.

For NGO leaders from the global North, and in fact, for an array of onlookers, the gesture was a trivial one made by "backward" people. Women's NGOs had insisted that the Maasai and other women across North and sub-Saharan Africa take up the cause of anti-female genital cutting as a way to protect the individual rights of women. However, these Tanzanian women acted on behalf of community and family well-being because they did not prioritize individual rights more than community and family well-being. In so doing, they were seen as out-of-touch, a remnant of "tribal" Africa; indeed, they were often displayed in tourism posters as such—bejeweled and colorful for visitors to savor. According to NGOs, the poverty of these women was their own fault for not modernizing, especially organizationally, and not the result of unjust confiscation of their means of supporting themselves.[8] Concern for families and communities instead of a focus on individual rights was evidence of backwardness.

Others objected to the ways NGOs had made women's poverty a big business, noting, for example, that those offering small loans, or microfinance, often charged high rates of interest that would-be small businesswomen could never pay. Moreover, many recipients of such loans had little training in running a business in the cutthroat, neoliberal world. The sheer force of outside sponsors of microfinancing put women at the mercy of male relatives who were eager for women to get the cash. On the other side of the equation, NGOs and financiers offering funds to alleviate poverty assumed the power to invade women's lives by directing the use of loans or by overseeing women more generally. In sum, as activism took its many forms it also posed many questions: foremost was the relationship between local women of the global South and wealthier institutions, many of them created by women, of the global North.

The Work of Culture

Cultural work by women proliferated, no matter the race, religion, or national origin, and provided multifaceted explorations of the human condition. Toni Morrison became, in 1993, the first African American woman to win the Nobel Prize for Literature. In works such as *Beloved* (1987), *A Mercy* (2008), and *Home* (2012), Morrison describes the nightmares, daily experiences, achievements, and dreams of those who were brought as slaves to the United States and their descendants. Similarly cross-cultural, *Reading Lolita in Tehran* (2003), a memoir by Iranian author Azar Nafisi, an immigrant to the United States, details the powerful influence of Western literature under conditions of censorship and oppression. Nafisi, who left her post at a Tehran university during the Iranian theocracy, writes of bringing a group of young women to her home to read forbidden literature. Fatou Diome's *Belly of the Atlantic* (2004) describes young Senegalese boys' dreams of being soccer stars and the crushing of those boys' very lives by unscrupulous Europeans. Their dreams are smashed, as are hers, by the duplicity of a lingering but powerful white supremacy; white greed, in the past as in the present, destroys the hopes and dreams of the colonized, or in her case the formerly colonized.

Women's writing focused on clashes of cultures across the globe. Novelist and filmmaker Tsitsi Dangarembga grew up in colonial Southern Rhodesia— now Zimbabwe—in the 1960s. A superior student, for a while she studied medicine in England and worked across Europe as a writer of novels and drama. The title of her first novel *Nervous Conditions* (1988) refers to a sentence of Frantz Fanon: "The condition of native is a nervous condition." In it, Dangarembga crafted a coming-of-age story full, not only of the aches of growing up but also the sensibility of those young people living in a world where whiteness was prized. On the cusp of Rhodesian independence first as the white-dominated Republic of Rhodesia and then as the new nation of Zimbabwe, the teenage heroine is torn between the values of her own culture and those of the "modern" West and the white people who even a distance away from her village subtly influence its inhabitants. She strives to make her family proud in white-run schools but also to fulfill her desire to use her mind in new, challenging ways, especially as her cousin Nyasha breaks down. The heroine's mother, often appearing to be too traditional and out of touch with modernity, is the one who pinpoints Nyasha's problem: "the white people."[9]

Still different tales of slapstick mishaps flowed from the pen of another British author Zadie Smith (b. 1975), whose novel *White Teeth* (2000) featured an array of immigrants, following a host of religions, pushing scientific projects, and protesting a range of situations in their society. Bizarre situations point to the bizarre nature of society that replaced so-called perfection of Western whiteness. Of Caribbean descent, Smith's other novels such as *Swing Time* (2016) raise issues of identity among a multi-raced cast of women—some migrant, others descendants of newcomers, and still others British born.

Authors charted the horrors of twentieth- and twenty-first-century history—among these Stalinist communism, colonialism, and US domination. Svetlana Alexievich was a migrant journalist and writer, spending her life investigating women's testimonies of the Second World War, the reaction to Chernobyl, and the sweep of Russian history under Stalin, Gorbachev, and Putin—among others. For taking on these subjects, she passed long stretches of her life in exile, though winning the Nobel Prize for Literature in 2017. A more voluntary exile, Chimamanda Ngozi Adichie, depicted the complexities of living in West Africa after colonialism had spawned authoritarian governments that crushed people's lives (*Purple Hibiscus* 2003). Her *Americanah* (2013) featured a Nigerian heroine in the United States attempting for the first time to understand race as she experiences it in this strange Western nation. Literally, thousands of other artists and writers became models for old and young women alike with their art, pop songs, dance, poetry, and plays.

Debating Alternative Feminisms

By the beginning of the twenty-first century, feminists coherently, though not identically, debated an array of issues, created innumerable organizations, or reinvented old ones. They disagreed and adopted varying solutions to gender inequity and oppression. For example, many women in India believed that the complex of ideas and practices today clustered under the cultural feminism and "post-feminism" rubrics did not address the issues of violence, poverty, and education. To them Western feminism seemed to assume that one could easily move past such basic issues and that essentially all was well in the world. In fact, Indian policies toward women and feminist reactions to them focused on the perils of developmentalism as fostered by elites, on the universalizing attitude that women were all the same and that one policy fit all, and on the legacy of the anti-colonial nationalist movements that saw rights as a universal priority when in fact policies of an independent government treated women differently and as religious subjects. Activism by other women outside the West focused on remedying other bread-and-butter issues, many of them long included in CEDAW and in the principles agreed upon at the Beijing international conference of women in 1995: girls and women's freedom from violence and safety in their person; equal and safe access to medical resources, educational advancement, and sanitation; opportunity in the workplace and in the operation of political institutions.

A different sense of women's place in the world came to shape the attitudes of a generation of young women in the twenty-first-century West. A large group of internationally and nationally minded feminists saw that the recognition of diversity needed to be a primary issue, especially addressing intersectionality in policies for and treatment of women. Many others believed it was time to move into an era beyond feminism. They mustered arguments often based on the "mission accomplished" scenario. Aren't women everywhere in the seats of power, in the work force, and in the university, they asked. Women's lives are good and fulfilling, many of these "post-feminists" declared, ending the need for feminism. They argued against the continuation of legal and economic activism, even seeing Women's Studies as no longer relevant because everything there is to know about women was integrated into the curriculum from kindergarten through the university. In the late twentieth century, women entered the top ranks of governmental power across the world and influenced growing, if unsteady and uneven global prosperity. Indira Gandhi kept the momentum for a healthy independent India alive in the 1970s and early 1980s, while Corazon Aquino was likewise seen as advancing development as president of the Philippines. Across Latin America and Scandinavia women had come to power in even greater numbers, as they also had in the rest of Europe. Like Prime Minister of the United Kingdom Margaret Thatcher in the 1980s, German Chancellor of Germany Angela Merkel in the twenty-first century shaped the economic future of the world in a variety of ways. In the twenty-first century, Merkel was seen as perhaps the single most important person in determining the economic health of the world. Mission definitely accomplished, some maintained.

Other postfeminists argued that teenagers and adult women no longer have road blocks to getting contraception or other reproductive counseling. The world is now accepting of many sexual orientations. For one woman, equality for women existed naturally: "In college, I was introduced academically to feminism as the belief in equal rights and opportunities for both sexes. Well that's just American, I thought."[10] Others called older feminists from the 1960s and 1970s "negative and ugly and inappropriate."[11] These early feminists were prejudiced and hateful of men, with plenty of class privilege, it was said, while contemporary women around the world bonded with men, either as comrades in suffering oppression as the African activist stated or as pals in the "gender-enlightened" workforce as depicted in the media since the 1980s. In addition, networking electronically, today's women are politically sophisticated worldwide. They have watched or heard of feminists meeting globally in successful, well-publicized congresses from the 1970s to the present and they see women's sexuality flaunted instead of repressed. Finally, post-feminists stress that cross-racial friendships flourish.

Post-feminists are innovators, adopting and being adopted by technology of which earlier feminists had no idea (except the South Asian writer Rokeya Shekawat Hossein who imagined the successes of high-tech women more than a hundred years ago). Post-feminists jettisoned their gender online or with the help of medicine embrace a host of normative or nonnormative embodied selves. Trans people trouble the boundaries of gender while simultaneously acknowledging that these boundaries exist and can be constraining. Because of technology, trans people over the past half century and more have enacted new biologies identified by feminist scientists such as Anne Fausto-Sterling decades ago. Trans identities upset more than perhaps any other groups binary male/female on which feminism has long been built. Moreover, queer theorists have aimed for the same overcoming of fixed gender and other identities in challenging old categories of gender and traditional feminist thought.

Critics find much in post-feminism and other new feminisms to dislike and call it valueless, producing commodity-driven lives and supporting neo-liberalism; instead of joining together for collective action and social improvement, they concentrate on sexual satisfaction and owning material goods with designer labels. They are thus apolitical and fail in their duties as citizens to participate responsibly in public life. Younger generations, dispute this, finding that organized movements are outmoded. In the digital age, if the self is positively attuned to the world, communication can create political change in minutes and in serious cases can mobilize tens of thousands for activism almost instantly. Witness the Arab Spring when crowds of disparate people were created out of nothing via social media and ousted dictators. Witness the immediate calling to order of protestors to any harms done to women during such events. Witness the connections maintained by migrants across oceans providing virtual lifelines and political rapport, even to strangers. Debates and disagreements flourish.

Simultaneously, other forces have aimed to block efforts and reform, especially when it comes to women's well-being and their activism. Logging companies were behind the murder of Catholic nuns in South America who opposed the destruction of rain forests and who sheltered activists. In 2006, Russian journalist and human rights champion Anna Politkovskaya was assassinated in her Moscow apartment as a critic of Vladmir Putin. Extremist groups such as ISIS and the Taliban have attacked women mercilessly in the name of Islam, with ISIS soldiers taking vast numbers of women as sex slaves or as post-rape victims to slaughter. In the 1980s, the United States had armed and financed the Taliban to fight the Soviet Union's attempted takeover of Afghanistan. After the Soviet withdrawal, the Taliban came to power and issued new rules on the behavior and treatment of women. These *Decrees* from 1996 restricting women's autonomy, along with alleged Taliban sponsorship of terrorism against the United States, were an official justification for invading the country in 2001:

Women you should not step outside your residence. If you go outside the house you should not be like women who used to go with fashionable clothes wearing much cosmetics and appearing in front of every men before the coming of Islam.

Islam as a rescuing religion has determined specific dignity for women . . . In case women are required to go outside the residence for the purposes of education, social needs or social services they should cover themselves in accordance with Islamic Sharia regulation. If women are going outside with fashionable, ornamental, tight and charming clothes to show themselves, they will be cursed by the Islamic Sharia and should never expect to go to heaven.

All family elders and every Muslim have responsibility in this respect. We request all family elders to keep tight control over their families and avoid these social problems. Otherwise these women will be threatened, investigated and severely punished as well as the family elders by the forces of the Religious Police *(Munkrat).*

Female patients should go to female physicians. In case a male physician is needed, the female patient should be accompanied by her close relative.

During examination, the female patients and male physicians both should be dressed with Islamic *hijab* (veil).

Male physicians should not touch or see the other parts of female patients except for the affected part.

During the night duty, in what rooms which female patients are hospitalized, the male doctor without the call of the patient is not allowed to enter the room.

Sitting and speaking between male and female doctors are not allowed, if there be need for discussion, it should be done with *hijab.*

Female doctors should wear simple clothes, they are not allowed to wear stylish clothes or use cosmetics or make-up.

Female doctors and nurses are not allowed to enter the rooms where male patients are hospitalised.[12]

As we have seen, in 2009, Malala Yousafzai countered the spirit of such regulations when she began her blogging and attracted the world's attention. Yet as her long and difficult recovery unfolded and as critics announced the problematic nature of celebrating her heroism, the complexity of Malala as feminist heroine and in fact the complexity of many struggles on behalf of women's rights became apparent. As many pointed to Muslim men's bad treatment of Malala, others pointed to the dangers white Christian men inflicted on women and girls across the Muslim world. The situation also showed the vast differences among women across the globe, including the dangers many faced because of weapons technology deployed to kill them, while also being deprived technology's basic sanitation and medical help. Yet, amid it all, women went to unbelievable lengths to overcome the challenges of gender hierarchy. The debates over women were always riddled with disagreement and at the same time with agreement that women's lives were valuable and even worth celebrating. The threats to those making such efforts and upholding beliefs in women's worth were, however, greater than ever before.

Conclusion

Women's accession to power as heads of state was noticeable by the end of the twentieth century and continuing into the twenty-first. The most significant person in Europe in 2015 was judged to be Chancellor of Germany Angela Merkel (b. 1952) who came to power in 2005. In effect, Merkel led not just Germany but the world's largest single market—the European Union— because of her nation's prosperous economy and her own steady hand in the face of many emergencies. Preceding Merkel, as we have seen, were the many heads of state and women leaders across Asia after the Second World War: Golda Meir headed Israel; Indira Gandhi, India; Corazon Aquino and Gloria Macapagal Arroyo, the Philippines; Benazir Bhutto, Pakistan; and Megawati Sukarnoputri, Indonesia. Except for Meir, these Asian leaders were members of powerful families, many of whose men had served as heads of state and whose networks were major factors in their achieving power. Opposition leader Aung San Suu Kyi was also a political force because of her decades of opposition to dictatorship in Myanmar; she too came from a powerful family yet once in power seemed to preside over the ethnic cleansing of the Muslim Rohingya people in the north of the country.

Additionally, women became heads of state in Finland, Ireland, Iceland, Britain (once again), Ukraine, Mozambique, Bangladesh, Liberia, Brazil, Chile, and Argentina—to name a few. Again, the accession of some of them to lofty and responsible positions resulted from family power and included elements of corruption and cronyism. In other cases, however, it became apparent that the feminist emphasis on equality, fairness, and women's capacity for leadership had been effective and that women's activism had been a progressive force. The visibility of women in national and local politics showed that to some extent political conditions had evolved and that women's participation from a broad strata of society had achieved change. That said, infants, girls, and women faced a world of constant international violence that included potential death from bombs launched by distant powers and neighbors alike, individual murder and rape in civil and religiously inspired wars, and the ordinary, all too-present sexual and domestic violence against women. Still, international activists and women in their local, daily lives had with great effort brought about an evolution in many people's consciousness—though an uneven one—about women's equal worth. It remained to perpetuate that awareness and the activism surrounding it into the future.

Glossary

Taliban   A militant Sunni Muslim group operating in Afghanistan and to some extent Pakistan.

Notes

1 Quoted in Ann Farnsworth-Alvear, *Dulcinea in the Factory: Myths, Morals, Men, and Women in Colombia's Industrial Experiment, 1905–1960* (Durham, NC: Duke University Press, 2000), 3.
2 Miriam Ching Yoon Louie, ed., *Sweatshop Warriors: Immigrant Women Workers Take on the Global Factory* (Cambridge, MA: South End Press, 2001), 235–42.
3 Quoted in Elaine Bauer and Paul Thompson, "'She's always the person with a very global vision': The Gender Dynamics of Migration, Narrative Interpretation and the Case of Jamaican Transnational Families," *Gender & History*, 16:2 (August 2004), 364.
4 Quoted in Leila Zaki Chakravarti, *Made in Egypt: Gendered Identity and Aspiration on the Globalized Shop Floor* (New York: Berghahn, 2016), 89.
5 From Wangari Maathai and Mary Robinson, "Women Can Lead the Way in Tackling Development and Climate Challenges Together," quoted on *The Huffington Post,* September 20, 2010. Internet Resource: Green Belt Movement http://greenbeltmovement.org/a.php?id=488&t=p.
6 Office of the UN High Commissioner for Human Rights, UN: http://www.ohchr.org/Documents/ProfessionalInterest/cedaw.pdf and many other UN websites.
7 Excerpted from "Mandato de la Primera Cumbre Continental de Mujeres Indigenas de Abya-Yala" posted on Abya-Yala Net, http://www.abyayalanet.org/index.php. Pamela Murray, trans., ed., *Women and Gender in Modern Latin America: Historical Sources and Interpretations* (New York: Routledge, 2014), 328–30.
8 Account taken from Dorothy L. Hodgson, *Gender, Justice, and the Problem of Culture: From Customary Law to Human Rights in Tanzania* (Bloomington: Indiana University Press, 2017), 133–56.
9 Tsitsi Dangarembga, *Nervous Conditions* (London: Women's Press, 1988), 202–4.
10 Jenna Goudreau, "Who's Afraid of Post-Feminism? What It Means To Be A Feminist Today," *Forbes* (December 13, 2011) http://www.forbes.com/sites/jennagoudreau/2011/12/13/afraid-of-post-feminism-means-feminist-today-gloria-steinem-jane-fonda-ursula-burns.
11 Ibid.
12 From Ahmed Rashid, *Taliban: Militant Islam, Oil and Fundamentalism in Central Asia* (New Haven, CT: Yale University Press, 2000), Appendix 1, 217–19.

Further Reading

Abbate, Janet. *Recoding Gender: Women's Changing Participation in Computing.* Cambridge: MIT Press, 2012.

Alidou, Ousseina. *Muslim Women in Post-Colonial Kenya: Leadership, Representation, and Social Change.* Madison: University of Wisconsin Press, 2013.

Berger, Iris. *Women in Twentieth-Century Africa.* New York: Cambridge University Press, 2016.

Bhavnani, Kum-Kum, *Feminist Futures: Re-Imagining Women, Culture, and Development.* New York: Zed Books, 2016.

Chakrabarti, Leila Zaki. *Made in Egypt: Gendered Identity and Aspiration on the Globalized Shop Floor.* New York: Berghahn, 2016.

Cole, Jennifer, and Lynn M. Thomas, eds. *Love in Africa.* Chicago, IL: University of Chicago Press, 2009.

Fidelis, Malgorzata. *Women, Communism, and Industrialization in Postwar Poland.* New York: Cambridge University Press 2010.

Fong, Mei. *One Child: The Story of China's Most Radical Experiment.* New York: Houghton Mifflin Harcourt, 2015.

Genz, Stephanie and Benjamin A. Bravon. *Postfeminism: Cultural Texts and Theories.* Edinburgh: University of Edinburgh Press, 2009.

Ghodsee, Kristen R. *Lost in Transition; Ethnographies of Everyday Life after Communism.* Durham, NC: Duke University Press, 2011.

Hodgson, Dorothy. *Gender, Justice, and the Problem of Culture: From Customary Law to Human Rights in Tanzania.* Bloomington: Indiana University Press, 2017.

Macnaughtan, Helen. *Women, Work and the Japanese Economic Miracle: The Case of the Cotton Textile Industry, 1945–1975.* London: Routledge, 2005.

Najmabadi, Afsaneh. *Professing Selves: Transsexuality and Same Sex Desire in Contemporary Iran.* Durham, NC: Duke University Press, 2013.

Sanos, Sandrine. *Simone de Beauvoir: Creating a Feminist Existence in the World.* New York: Oxford University Press, 2017.

Susan Stryker. *Transgender History: The Roots of Today's Revolution.* 2nd ed. New York: Seal Press, 2017.

Veldman, Meredith. *Margaret Thatcher: Shaping the New Conservatism.* New York: Oxford University Press, 2015.

ACKNOWLEDGMENTS

This book is a stab at writing a chronological history of the world's women in modern times, while integrating some of the recent scholarship on gender and on world history. It rests on the amazing primary research produced over the past half century by the pioneering scholars in the field of women's and gender history. Because so many brilliant works have appeared and because this is a work of synthesis with page limit determined by smart editors, *Women in World History* necessarily covers the surface of women's past.

I have been fortunate during this time to work at Rutgers University, where scholarship in women's history flourished, thanks to early "enablers" like Dean Mary Hartman. Equally, scholars across the United States and the globe have shared their work and insights. Then, there are former students, who now produce works that are constantly astonishing for their insights and rich global scholarship. Two young scholars—Nova Robinson and Shikha Chakraborty—whose book-length manuscripts will soon appear have contributed to my current knowledge. It is tempting to continue naming everyone individually but there is also the fear of omitting someone pivotal, as happened a few books ago when Daniel Sherman somehow didn't appear in the acknowledgments. To extraordinary friends and fellow students and researchers of the past, infinite and heartfelt thanks. Imagine that your faces and books are floating through my memory at this moment and inspiring gratitude.

Thanks go to the many editors at Bloomsbury, who first broached undertaking this work and who allowed the delays while pushing for completion. Most recently Dan Hutchins vetted and secured the images, while the efficient and truly competent production team at Bloomsbury and Newgen, especially Kalyani, have ensured that the book materialized. My beautiful family breathes love in and out, most notably Donald Kelley who knows more history than anyone and who works in marvelous ways to keep scholarship alive.

This book is dedicated to my much loved and loving sister-in-law Beverly Graziani Sullivan and to the memory of my brother William W. Sullivan (1948–2018). The sorrow of this loss is forever, as is the grace of his existence.

INDEX

Note: Because this is a book about women, many terms will not begin with "Women" or "Women's." The assumption is that in the term "Activism, environmental," there is no need to add "women's" to precede "environmental activism." Or, under the heading "African Americans, post-First World War migration" it is not necessary to specify "women's" migration.

Note: Page numbers in **bold** denote Figures.

Abeokuta Ladies Club 264
abolition of slave trade 170
abolitionism 174, 192
abortion
  China 287
  infanticide as 15, 248
  right to 280
  USSR outlaws in 1930s 238
Abu Talib Khan, Mirza 154
acculturation, by women of Native
    peoples 93
activism
  Cherokee women 189–90
  environmental 295–6
  favelas, Brazil 294–5
  First World War 237
  financing 297–9
  Maasai women 300
  Philippines 294
Adam and Eve, in Protestantism 72–3
Adams, Abigail 140
Adiche, Chimamanda Ngozi 302
Adivar, Halide Edib 248–9
af Klint, Hilma 225
Africa
  agricultural development 217
  agriculture 113
  changing views of African women
    107

  early modern population decline 111,
    161
  increasing internal violence with
    Atlantic slave trade 113
  religions mixed with Catholicism
    103–4
  women's politicization 228–30,
    241–2
Africa: My Native Land 228
African Americans
  jazz performers 246
  "lifting the race" 199
  organizations 199–200
  post-First World War migration
    239–40
  post-Second World War activism
    278–80
  pro-Marcus Garvey march **241**
  Second World War participation 255
African National Congress 268
age grades 244
agency, in women's history 6–7
Agnesi, Marie 127
agriculture
  Chinese 27
  early modern West Africa 26, 95–6
  Mandan women 27
  seventeenth and eighteenth centuries
    revolution 113, 119–20

Aguirre, Francisco de 95
Aisha, as interpreter and wife 56–7, 68
Aizu-Wakamatsu Castle 185
Akbar (Mughal emperor) 41, 46
'al-'Adawiyya al-Qaysiyya, Rabi'ah 69
Alexandra (Britain) 219
Alexievich, Svetlana 3, 302
Alexios I 24
Algeria
  independence 280
  independence struggle 265–6
  round-up of women and children 265
Altahualpa, Juan 137
ambassadors, Southeast Asia 49–50
Americanah 302
American Revolution 138–41, 155
  blacks' exclusion from citizenship
    140–1
  boycotts 139
  camp followers 139
  heterosexual ethos 141
  women's loss of rights following 140
Aminah bint Wahb (mother of
    Muhammad) **69**
Amritsar Massacre 243
Amrouche, Fadhma 215–16
Analects 54
  and women's writing 78
anarchism 176, 177–8
ancestor worship 20–1
Anderson, Elizabeth Garrett 201
Anishinabe, women as traders 89
Anthony, Susan B. 192, 204
anti-colonial freedom fighters, post-
    Second World War 280
anti-environmentalists 304
anti-feminists 298
anti-footbinding societies 196
anti-lynching campaigns 226
anti-Semitism, in First World War 236
anti-women discourses, Cairo and Black
    Death 24
Antigua 167
Apartheid 267–8
aristocracy, versus citizen army 188
armed guards 38
armed virtue 141
Armenians, persecution of 240
Army, Germany as model for Japan 188

artisans 28, 29, 160
artists, early modern 62
Arwa (Yemeni queen) 57
Aquino, Corazon 303, 306
Arab Spring 304
Arroyo, Gloria Macapagal 306
Asante 135
Asma (Yemeni queen) 57
Atlantic plantation system 192
Atlantic slave system 135
Aung San Suu Kyi 306
Australia, "A Doll's House"
    performance in 195
Austria-Hungary 236
authors, sixteenth- and seventeeth-
    century defense of women 82
authorship, in early modern China 62
Avalokitesvara, bodhisattva of
    compassion 64
Axial age, reinforces male superiority
    18
Ayah Maria de Sousa **211**
Ayisha Sultan Begim 42, 49

Ba Chin 241
Ba, Myriam 278
babaylan 294
Babur, Zhiruddin Muhammad 42,
    78
Baden-Powell, Robert 222
Baker, Ella 279
Ban Zhao 54, 112
Barcelona 177, 178
Barton, Clara 201
basketry 29
Bassi, Laura 127
Bastidas, Michaela 137–8, 150
Beauvoir, Simone de 3–4
Beijing International Conference on
    Women 302–3
Belair, Sanite/Suzane 148
Belgian Congo 213–14
Belly of the Atlantic 301
Beloved 301
Berbers 215–16
berdache 41
Béreté, Sassooma 74
Bermuda 166
Bernal del Viuda de Torres, Maria 173

Bernardino, Minerva 270
Beveridge, Albert 220
Bhago, Mai 68
Bhakti movement 70–1
Bhutto, Benazir 306
Bible 62, 130
biology as destiny 3–4
birth control 248
Black Death 24–5
Black Panthers 280
Black Power 279
Blackwell, Elizabeth 201
Blavatsky, Helena 224–5
Bluestocking Club 195
body, conditions of pre-1600 7, 12,
    13–14
Bois Gaillard, Flore 147
Bolívar, Simón 151, 152–3
Bolsheviks 237
Bonaparte, Napoleon 146, 151
Book of the City of Ladies 80
Bora, Katharina von 73
bound feet 196
Boupacha, Djamila 265–6
Boxer Rebellion 219
Boy Scouts 222
Bradstreet, Anne 81
Brazil 166, 169, 251, 294–5
brewing 29
bride price 22
Bridgetown, Barbados 97
Britain
    First World War 239
    imperial expansion 212
    loses India 266
    opposition to its rule 1920s
        242–3
    post-First World War expansion 240
    torture of Kenyans 264–5
British East India Company 154
Brock, Severine 96
Brooks, Louise 246
brothels, postwar 260
Buddha 82
Buddhism 7, 65
Buddhism, Tibetan 64
Bülow, Frieda von 222
Butterfly Hu 246
Byzantine Empire 24

Calcutta, jute mills 177
capitalism 171
Cassatt, Mary 224
caste, reforms of 173
castration 25–6
Castro Gonzalés, Sofia 250
Catherine II (Russia),
    continental expansion 88
    promotes literacy 128
Catholic Church,
    censors Sor Juana 125
    enforces Amerindian monogamy 94
    in Spanish America 103–4
    in Spanish Mexico 104–6
Cavell, Edith 243
celibacy, attacked in Reformation 72
Ceres 64
Chamberlain, Betsy Guppy 162–3
Chandrav(b)arti 66
Charles VII (France) 75
chastity, sexual abstinence, Inca 30
Châtelet, Emilie du 127
Chernobyl nuclear plant 3
Cheunchujit, Rojana 291
chieftains, West African 149–50
childbirth, Africa 31
childbirth, rituals 12
children
    Aztec training of 19
    costs of raising, twenty-first century
        288
    early modern training of 18
    Napoleonic Code 147
    pawning, twenty-first century 288
    raising, early modern China 28
    work in Industrial Revolution 159
China
    attacks on women's leadership 262
    bound feet 196
    Boxer Rebellion 219
    Communists to power 261
    courtesans in Ming dynasty 75
    cultural revolution 262
    defeat in Opium and Sino-Japanese
        Wars 218
    "A Doll's House" in 195
    effects of Industrial Revolution 161
    fears of idle women 118
    girls' education 203

industriousness **115–16**
internal migration, late twentieth–
    twenty-first centuries 292
literary tradition 82
literary women 128–9
Marxist platform on women 261
May Fourth movement 240
neglect of correct behavior 80
New Life Movement 246
nineteenth-century reform of women
    194
one-child policy 287
post-Second World War education
    262, 263
postwar family and marriage
    counseling 262
Qing imperial decline 212
Qing officials on women's work,
    seventeenth–eighteenth centuries
    118
Qing takeover 93
seclusion as mark of status 124
shortage of women 287
Women's Federation 261–2
Chisholm, Shirley 279
Chonghu 131
Churchill, Winston 252, 271
citizenship, male
education for in Rousseau 154
French Revolution 146–7
male fraternity 187
new United States and 141
revolutions against Spain 151
civil service samples 2
civilizing mission, nineteenth century
    214
Cixi, Empress China 204–5, 210,
    218–19
Taiping 192
clans 42, 89, 155
empires want to break loyalty to 214
class
domesticity and 171–2
industry and 171
clergy, not celibate in colonies 95
clothing
rationale behind invasions 221–2
unconstrained in South Asia 196
Yoruba, as patriotic 264

Cold War 260
dictators supported by both sides 275
proxy wars 273
USSR-US competition for emerging
    nations 268
violence in Latin America 275–6
collecting 224
colonial rule 138, 214, 284
expansion in 1800s 209
in Ireland 237
Women's War attack on 242
colonization, Australia and New
    Zealand 221
Colonna, Victoria 72
Columbian exchange 86
Columbus, Christopher 85
Combahee River Collective 280
Combahee River Raid 192
comfort women 255–6
commerce
culture of nineteenth century 174
integration of foreign goods 117–18
revolutionized in expansion 113
commodities, slave and indentured
    labor in producing 181
Commission on the Status of Women
    270
communism
in Cold War 270
in Russian Revolution 237
community
early modern monitoring of
    reproduction 18
in individual and household decision-
    making 39
life rituals 12
work as creating community 21
Comnena, Anna 24
complementarity 12
Aztec gender roles 41
concubinage, in royal courts 48
concubines
in French West Africa 213
selected by lead wife 46
condition of women 130–2
Confucius 112
precepts 66
in Taiping ideas 191
writings of 112

consumerism 118, 292
conquest
  North African women make use of
    91
  oceanic 85
"Conquest of Africa" **221**
conscription 235–6
continuity and change in history 4–5
contraception 15
Convention on the Elimination of All
    Forms of Discrimination against
    Women (CEDAW) 297–8
Coordinating Committee of the
    First Continental Congress of
    Indigenous Women 299–300
corsets 196
Cortes, Hernando 94
Côte d'Ivoire 264
Coudray, Madame du 127
courtesans
  adept in arts 62
  Lucknow 211–12
  Ming dynasty 75–6
  sexual symbolism in paintings 78
dourts, legal, women's use of 106
Coya (Incas) 40
Crillo (creole) 124
Crimean War 200–1
Croatans **90**
cross-dressing
  a capital crime among Aztecs 16
  Native Americans 16–17
Cuauhtlatoatzin (Juan Diego) 104
culture
  Cold War 278
  decolonization and 268
  middle-class 174
  1920s and 1930s 236
  women's irrationality 175

Da Gama, Vasco 85
Dahomey, fighters in Haiti 148
Dahomey warriors **229**
Daimyo elite 187
Dangarembga, Tsitsi 301
Dancing Women's movement 242
daoism 65–6
Darwin, Charles 225
Das, Bina 243–4

"Daughters of Quchan" 189
Davis, Angela 279
De Gouges Olympe 143, 146
De Jesus, Carolina Maria 6, 235
De la Cruz, Sor Juana 124–5
Debi, Rashsundari 210
Declaration of the Rights of Man 143
Declaration of the Rights of Woman
    143
democracy 3
Descent of Man 225
Dessault, Emile 213
development, agricultural, in Africa 217
Devi, goddess 53
"Diary of a Pakistani Schoolgirl" 285
Diego, Juan (Cuauhtlatoatzin) 104
Diome, Fatou 301
disease, among Amerindians 86
divers 165
Doan Thi Diem 64–5
doctors, medical, struggle to become
    201–2
A Doll's House 195
domestic service 173
  nineteenth-century perils of 173
domesticity
  after industrialization 172
  as purity 171
dowry
  early modern China 22
  potential for disorder, early modern
    China 22
  transfer of Amerindian wealth 93
  transfer of royal territory 39
  United States 22
Dube, Adelaide 228
Durbars 219
Dutch East Indies, portrayed in world's
    fair 223
Dutt, Kapana 243
dyes, Mexican 29

East Africa
  German rule over 220
  motherhood in 287
Easter Uprising 236
Eckenbrecher, Margarethe von 222
education
  Catholic in colonial Algeria 216

China 155
colonial 214
in home 127
Native American children seized for
    215
Rousseau ideas for 154
Wollstonecraft ideas for 154
writings on in post-revolutionary
    United States 155
Edward VI (Britain) 219
Efuru 277
Eggly, Ann 159
Eguiluz, Paula 103–4
Egypt
    activism vs. British 242–3
    "A Doll's House" performed 195
    Dinshaway massacre 204
    factory workers, late twentieth
        century 292
    journalists 202
    reforms in women's education and
        training 190–1
Einstein, Albert 271
Elizabeth I (England) 81
    state-building 43–5
    supports expansion and piracy 88
Elizabeth, Countess of Sutherland
    119–20
embroidery 118
Emecheta, Buchi 278
empire
    commercial in Indian Ocean 88
    decline Spanish, Portuguese, Chinese
        212
    European social life in 219–20
    false dealing, New Zealand 227
    masculinity and 210
    post-Second World War overthrow
        260
    Russian attitudes toward Muslim
        women in 214
English Revolution 113, 131
enlightenment 112
enslavement 85
environment, activism in Central
    America and Kenya 295–6
equality, French eighteenth century
    debates on 142
Eranso, Catalina 88

Eritrea, women soldiers 266
Estrada, Maria de 88
Eugenics 225–6
Eunuchs
    Ming and Ottoman empires 16
    roles and sexuality 26
    seclusion and 25–6
Europe
    attraction to Indian textiles 116
    effects of Industrial Revolution in
        161
evolution 225
Ewha University 241
exclusion of women and racial
        and ethnic others from full
        citizenship 141
exoticism 231
expansion, imperial 135

factories, conditions in early 181
Family 241
family
    dynastic state and 42
    extended family decline 172
    governance and hierarchy 21
    Industrial Revolution and 160
    liberal thought and 177
    under industrialization 172
    size declines after slavery 172
famine
    Allies induced Greater Syria 235
    Britain induced in India 258
    early modern blamed on women 67
    USSR inflicted 1930s 244
Fanon, Frantz 277
fashion, Moscow **272**
Fatima, as model for women 56–7, 68
Fausto-Sterling, Anne 304
feminism 7
    Hitler and 250
    ignores "Third World" issues 280
    international 204
    Kollontai criticizes 238
    post-feminism says "time to move
        beyond" 302
    queer theory upsets premises 304
    "white" 280
Feminist Congress (Mexico) 231
Ferdinand of Aragon 40, 43

fertility
    birth control pill 287
    community, household control of 20
    drop in Belgian Congo 227
    falling, late nineteenth–early
        twentieth centuries 210, 225
    of late twentieth and twenty-first
        century workers 291
    post-Second World War push for in
        USSR 261
    programs to boost, 1920s and 1930s
        247–8
film, interwar 245–6
Finland, suffrage 205
fire eaters 33
First World War
    early protests of Muslim women in
        Russia 236
    opposing sides in 236
    post-First World War imperial
        expansion 240
    women's occupations in 236
Flores, Dona Maria Josefa 120
Fontaine, Margaret 224
food
    availability First World War 236–7
    processing as skill 22
    processing early modern Africa 28
    processing in South Africa **168**
    provisioning cities 165
footbinding
    under Manchus 100–1
    missionary campaigns against 218
Ford Foundation 297
Fourteen Points 237
France
    concubinage in empire 213
    erasure of women's resistance
        activism 264
    First World War 236
    post-First World War expansion 240
    torture of Algerians 265–6
French and Indian War 138
French Revolution,
    counter-revolution 145
    market women to Versailles 144, **145**
    Mary Wollstonecraft observes 153
    undoing reforms in 152
    women's activism 141–7

French Revolutionary wars 146
La Fronde 202
Fukuzawa Yukichi 194
Fuller, Margaret 192

Gandhi, Indira 268–9, 280, 306
Gandhi, Mohandas 243
Garvey, Marcus 241
Gbowee, Laymah 286
gender
    definitions 3, 8
    Hungary eliminates study of 297
    plasticity, in work 29–30
    religious and ethical prescriptions 55
    roles in Mulan's story 74
    roles in Protestantism 72–3
genital cutting, Kenya 244
genocide
    late twentieth and twenty-first
        centuries 285–6
    Second World War 251, 253, 256
Gentileschi, Artemisia 78
Georgia (USA), Cherokees removed 190
Germany
    First World War 236
    genocide of Herero 222
    nationalism and colonialism 222
    rule in East Africa 220
    women in WILPF protest black
        soldiers in Germany 244–5
    women in postwar 263–4
Ghana 210–11
Girl Scouts 223
Global South, condition of women 291
Glückel of Hameln 113–14
go-betweens, Native women 47, 87
goddesses 12, 63–6
    Aztec 51
    Hindu 55
    models 82
    mother 63
Golden Temple Massacre 269
Gonne, Maud 230
Great Depression 249–51
Green Belt Movement 295–6
Gregory, widow 119
Guanyin 55
    metamorphosis 64
    religious syncretism 104–5

guerilla war, Jamaica 135
guilds and craft organizations 30
Gutierrez de Mendoza, Juana Belen 231
Gul-Badan Begum 78–9
Guru Angad 68
Guru Nanak 68

Hacking, Ellen 161
Hacking, John 161
Hadith, women's interpretations of 67
hairstyling 196
Haiti, abolishes slavery 170
Haitian Revolution 147–9, 155
  blacks in France 148
  Constitution 148–9
  tropical diseases in 148
Hajj 67
  Gul-Badan Begum 70
Hakka people 191
Hamer, Fanny Lou 279
Haruko (Empress Japan) 197
harem, Mary Wortley Montagu visits
      125
harems, as places of work,
      reproduction, and power 41–2
Harlem Renaissance 246
Hatun, Mihri 80–1
Hawaii, seized by United States 218
Head, Bessie 277–8
heads of government 306
healers 135
healing 103
health 286
Heard, Betsy 121, 136
Henry VIII (England) 42
Henry (Navarre) 46
Herero 222
Herschel, Caroline 127
heterosexuality 9, 141, 154
hierarchy
  Christianity 55–6
  family 21
  gender hierarchy funds
      industrialization 163
  in nunneries 106
  religious and ethical teachings 55
  royal courts 39
  world religions 58
history 1–5, 10

History of Humayun 79
Hitler, Adolf, on women 250–1
Home 301
homosexuality, mobilized in Cold War
      271
Hongdeng ji 262
Hong Kong factory workers 293
Hong Xiuquan 191
Horáková, Milada 271
Hossein, Rokeya Shekhawat 205–6
House of Chosen Women 30
household
  Egypt, modernization of 198
  formation 18
  matrilocal 21
  modernization 195–6
  practices as religious 53
  rites and ancestor worship, China 67
  royal as site of government 42, 43
  royal women's control 78–9
  size reduced with industry,
      urbanization, end of slavery 172
  West African, multiple wives in 21
  West African early modern royal 45
Housing, Mandan 27
Huang Yuanjie 129
Humayun 79
Hurrem Sultan 43, 45
Hurston, Zora Neale 246
Husain, Altaf 198

Ibsen, Henrik 195
identities
  under Atlantic colonialism 107
  as shown in clothing (Quito) 121–3
imperialism 231–2
in-vitro fertilization 287
Incidents in the Life of a Slave Girl 192
indenture
  culture of 224
  replaces slavery 170–1
  strikes and protests 177
  women's escape route 171
independence movements 264–8
independence struggles, everyday life
      during 266
India
  Amritsar Massacre 243
  forced sterilizations 269

Industrial Revolution in 160
journalists 202
partition and independence 266
reforms to modernize women 194
urbanization and women 180
Indian Emigration Act (1883) 170
Indian National Congress 203, 228,
    243
Indian Uprising (1857) 212–213
Industrial Revolution 159–61
    definition and characteristics of 161
    industriousness paves the way 160
    patriarchy and 160
    preconditions for 159–60
    textile workers in Europe, China 161
industrialization
    agriculture 170
    Communist USSR 238
    work removed from household 172
industriousness and Industrious
        Revolution,
    in China 115
    Chinese poem on women's overwork
        119
    early modern causes of 111–12
    slave women and 120–1
industry
    Argentina cigarette workers 163
    clock time 175
    culture of 174
    forms of resistance in Egypt 293–4
    innovation and women's low wages
        163
    mechanization of women's work 164
    preference for factory 164
    slavery enables Industrial Revolution
        165–70
    women's direction of early industry
        165–6
infanticide 15
inn-keeping 120
inoculation 125–6
International Council of Women 204
International Women's Congress 274
International Women's Day 237
International Women's Suffrage Alliance
    204
Internet 285
intersectionality 7–8, 279–80

intersex, twenty-first century 288
inventions, free women for other jobs
    119
Ireland, resistance to British rule 230–1
Isabella of Castile 40
    Catholicism as state-building 43
    possessions in New World 88
    state-building 43
ISIS 304
Islam
    African slave trade 150
    conversion to achieve freedom 97
    devotion to Mary 68
    history and tenets 56–7
    in Sundiata story 74
Italy, First World War 236

Jacobs, Aletta 202
Jacobs, Harriet Ann (pseud. Linda
        Brent) 6, 192
Jackson, Sir Stanley 243
Jahanara 128, 129
Jahangir (Mughal Emperor) 45
Jamaica 135, 177, 292
Jambi (King of) 37
Japan
    anarchist politics 178
    Bluestocking Club 195
    divers 165
    A Doll's House 195
    education of women, Jissan
        University 193
    effects of Industrial Revolution 161
    First World War 236
    "good wives, wise mothers" 192, 214
    imperial expansion late nineteenth
        century 212
    industrial development and
        conditions 178
    law forbidding women to speak in
        public 195
    literary tradition 82
    Meiji Restoration 185–7
    nation-building 187
    post-First World War expansion 240
    post-Second World War colleges for
        women 261
    post-Second World War feminist
        roundup 261

post-Second World War revival "good
wives wise mothers" 261
sends student to study worldwide
188
women in Japanese arts 77
women promote contraception 195
Jemison, Mary 149
Jiang Qing 262–3
Jihad, eighteenth century West Africa
150
Jing Pianpian 76–7
Joan of Arc 75
Joshi, Anandi Gopal 201
journalism 202
Judge, Oney "Ona" 97
"Judith Beheading Holofernes" 78

Kalho, Frida 246–7, **247**
Kali 64
Kama Sutra 16
Karim, Abdul 219
Kato Shidzue 247–8
Kaur, Bibi Kaur 267
Kedjou, Sogolon 74
Kemal, Mustafa 245–8
Kennedy, Florynce (Flo) 279–80
Kennedy, John F. 277
Kenya
anti-reformers 244
independence 264–5
Mau Mau 264
Kenyatta Jomo 244
Khadija, as model for Muslims 56–7,
68
Khivi, Mata 68
Kishida Toshiko 195
knowledge, use of Native American
women's by Europeans 91
Knox, Henry 141
Knox, Lucy Flucker 141
Kollontai, Aleksandra 237
Korea
competition for control of, 1890s
209
divers 165
Ewha University demonstrations 241
strikes by factory workers 1970s 293
Korean War, women in 274
Krishna 55, 70–1

Krupp, Bertha 165
Kulthuum, Umm 268

labor, during Black Death 24
Lakshmibai, Rani of Jhansi 209,
212–13
langar (provision for food) 68
Larson, Nella 246
Laske-Schuler, Else 224
Latin America
abolitionism 174
nation-building 187
women reformers 203
Laws of Manu 51–3
learning, love of Sor Juana 124
League of Nations 245
legislation, protective, Britain 178–9
Lei Zu (Empress and goddess of silk
production) 118
Leningrad, Siege of 252–3
Leopold (Belgium) 227
lesbians, white support of Combahee
statement 280
lesbianism, attacks on Marie-Antoinette
142
Liang Qichao 194
liberalism, theory 177–8
Liberia 286
liberty, portrayed as a woman 141
Lien Hanh 64–5
Liliiuokalani (Hawaii, Queen) 217–18
Lincoln, Abraham 192
literacy
Chinese and Japanese women's 156
forbidden to women in South Asia 63
literature, post-colonial 281
little ice age 111
Locke, John 131, 177–8
longevity, late twentieth and twenty-
first centuries 286–7
Louis XVI 142, 146
Louverture, Toussaint 148
Low, Juliette Gordon 223
Lowell Mill girls 162
Loyalists, in American Revolution
139–40
Lucknow, courtesans 211–12
Luther, Martin 72, 82
Lutz, Bertha 270

Luxemburg, Rosa 178
Ly, Hayslip 273–4

Ma Huan 31
Ma Quan 127
Maathai, Wangari 295–6, **296**
Macarthur, Douglas 260
Maghan Kon Fatta (King) 74
Maham Begam (widow of Babur) 79
Malakhova, Vera Ivanova 254–5
Mali, kingdom of 74
Malinche 94
Mandans 21, 89
Manilla 96
Manuela (slave) 106
Mao Zedong 262
Maori
    fertility 227
    women, suffrage 205
Margaret of Valois 46, 48
Marie-Antoinette 128, 142, 151
Marie de l'Incarnation 71, 127
marketing and finance, early modern
    Africa 30–1
markets, early modern Ghana 115
Markandaya, Kamala 277
Markiewicz, Constance 230–1, 236
Maroon community 135
marriage
    Akbar's strategies 46
    bound foot in 100–1
    cassare in West Africa 96
    early modern purpose of 18
    early modern royal women arrange
        45–6
    economic concerns in 22
    Ferdinand and Isabella to build state
        power 46
    Iroquois values in 20
    Native Americans with Europeans 89
    in Protestantism 72–3
    as royal strategy 39
    South Asia 15
    Spanish conquerors to Native peoples
        93
    tool for imperial integration 46
marriage brokers (Aztec, Hindu) 23
martial races 213
Maru 278

Marxism 178
Marxists, in Russian Revolution 237
Mary 55
    desanctified during Reformation 72
    Our Lady of Guadalupe 104–5
    religious syncretism 104–5
    rising Catholic devotion to 68
Mary (England) 131
masculinity
    African "explorer" needs massive
        support to stay alive 220
    Akbar's ever larger harem 41
    autonomy first created in the home
        171
    Cold War 277
    crisis in 225
    effeminacy attributed to Hindu men
        213
    end of nineteenth-century sense of
        male crisis 210
    French Revolution brotherhood motif
        146
    Haitian Constitution empowers
        father 148–9
    Iberian conquerors said to need sex
        95
    nation-building as male event 190
    post-First World War I concern for
        240
    reputation for prowess as imperial
        conquerors 91
    revolutionary brotherhood in
        American Revolution 141
    revolutions against Spain have
        masculine and anti-mother
        motifs 151–2
    reworked in nation 187
    working-class honor 175
Mashinini, Emma 268
mass culture 245
Massachusetts Bay Colony 81
match girls' strike 176
matchmaking, Mughal Empire 79
Mau Mau 264
May Fourth movement 240
Mayo, Katherine 243
Maywa-jan 79
Medicis, Catherine de, as queen mother
    45–6

Meiji Restoration and women's
    resistance 185
Meir, Golda 275, 306
memory, national 204
Menchu, Rigoberta 295
Mendes Pinto, Fernao 49
menstruation as disqualifying in
    religions 67
A Mercy 301
Merian, Maria Sibella 125
Merkel, Angela 303, 306
Mestizo 122–3
Mexican Revolution 231–2
Mexico, Cordoba in Great Depression
    250
Mexico City, UN Conference 1975 297,
    124
microfinancing, late twentieth, early
    twenty-first centuries 300–1
Middle East, women lobby League of
    Nations 245
midwives 30
migration
    early modern 120–1
    ethnicities post-First World War 239
    forced and voluntary early modern
        120–1
    late twentieth and twenty-first
        centuries 288–92
    1920s 239–40
    postwar migration from new states
        aids welfare state 270
    white women's 223
militarization
    of bodies 245
    of history 9–10
    1920s–1930s 235
mining 159, 179
Mirabai 70–1
missionaries
    anti-footbinding 196
    in China 218–19
    Christian 73
    Pacific 227
    spread of religion, nineteenth–
        twentieth centuries 224
Mitra, Suchitra 268
Mizushima Kikuko 185
Mmanthatisi 150

modernity 8
modernization 185–7, 206
Mongols 3
Montagu, Lady Mary Wortley 125–7,
    126
Montessori, Maria 201
Montgomery Bus Boycott 279
Mother India 243
Morrison, Toni 301
motherhood
    duties of Ottoman Sultan's mother 39
    East Africa 287
    imagery in Bolívar's political speeches
        against mothers 151
    imperial motherhood 222, 223
    in Sundiata story 74
    twenty-first century psychological
        287–8
    white motherhood in American
        Revolution 141
"Mothers of the Nation" 198
Mothers of the Plaza de Mayo 276
Mozambique 274–5
Mughal Empire 154
    compared to Western empires 221
    expansion in seventeenth century 113
    grand production of cotton textiles
        116
    state-building 45
Muhammad 56, 61
    as infant 69
Muhammad Ali 190–1
Mulan 73–4
    as model 131
Muller, William 114–15
Murasaki Shikibu 62, 75
Murray, Elizabeth 117
Musgrove, Mary (Coosaponakeesa) 138
Muslims
    Shiia 57
    Sunni 57
    women as teachers and transmitters
        129
mutual aid societies 176
Myeongseon (Empress Korea) 209

Naa Kowa 210–11
Nafisi, Azar 301
Naidu, Sarojini 243

Nanjing, Taiping headquarters 191
Nanny (Queen Nanny) 135
Naomi 245
Napoleonic Code 146–7, 154
nation-building
    Aizu opposition to 188
    characteristics of 185–6
    expands male rights over women 187
National Association for the
        Advancement of Colored People
        199
National Association of Chinese
        Women for Cheering and
        Comforting of the Officers and
        Soldiers of the War of Self-
        Defense and Resistance Against
        Japan 252
National Association of Colored
        Women 199, 278
National Association of Colored
        Women's Clubs 199
National Council of American Indians
        215
National Geographic 217
National Organization of Women
        (NOW) 280
nationalism 227–8
Native Americans
    adopt European attitudes toward sex
        94
    attitudes toward 162
    Cherokee women protest land
        takeovers 189–90
    clothing in Quito 122–4
    conquerors' stereotypes 91
    developing European empires 85–6
    European invasions, eighteenth
        century 138
    housing 3
    lands seized late nineteenth century
        217–18
    Marie de l'Incarnation's dictionaries
        of native languages 127
    political decision-making by early
        modern women 40
    provision European invaders 87
    Ursulines among 71
    viewed as whores by invaders 94
    women as deciders of war 2

Natives Land Act 228
Nectar in a Sieve 277
Nehru, Jawaharlal 268, 277
neo-liberalism 290–1
Neri, Margarita 231
A Nervous Condition 301
Netherlands
    contraception developed in 202
    suffrage 205
"New Life Movement" 246
"A New Society" 162–3
"New" women 200
New Zealand, suffrage 205
Ngo Dinh Diem 273
Ngo Dinh Nhu 273
Nigeria
    Igbo women 242
    revive textile production, 1930s
    writers 277
Nigerian Women's Union 264
Nightingale, Florence 200, 202
Nobel, Alfred 237
Nobel Peace Prize 285, 295, 302
non-governmental organizations
        (NGOs) 204, 297–301
Nongquawuse 227
North Africa 91
nuns
    in Buddhism and Catholicism 68
    needlework and general
        industriousness 120
    Spanish America 105–6
    Ursulines in Canada 71
Nur Jahan 45
nursing 200–1
Nwapa, Flora 277
Nzinga (Queen, Ndongo and Matamba
        Kingdoms) 1–2, 94, 101–3

occult 224–5
Ollague, Maria del Carmen 106
One Thousand and One Nights
        61–2
Orange Free State, resistance to passes
        229–30
Origin of Species 225
Orlando 224
orphans, Portuguese marriages 92
Osu, Koko 96

Ottoman Empire
  changing marriage patterns in 43
  compared to Western imperialism 221
  conquest of Byzantine Empire 86–7
  First World War 236
  harem 125
  investors 117
  literary women's networks 80–1
  persecution of Armenians 240
  seclusion as mark of high status 124
  time modernization 197–8
  women's protest 176
Our Lady of Guadalupe 104–5
outwork 164

Pak Chongae 274
Pakistan 266
Palestine 275
Pan-Africanism 226, 241
Pan-American International Women's
    Committee 204
Park Chung Hee 293
Parks, Rosa 278–9
pass system 228–30
Passing 246
patriarchy 5, 86, 160
Peace of Paris 239
Pequa, Oset 92
Peters, Carl 220, 231
philanthropy 173–4
Philippines 218, 294
photography, of colonized women 217
Pizarro, Francesca 94
Pizarro, Francisco 94
Pizarro, Gonzales 94
Pizarro, Hernando 94
Phule, Jotia 173–4
Phule, Savithribai 173–4
pilgrimages and sacred journeys 33, 67
piracy 136
Pisan, Christine de 75, 80
poetry, in Qing China 128–9, 130
Polgren, Rachel Pringle 97
politics 203–4
Politkovskaya, Anna 304
pollution, female 55–6, 171, 177
Pompadour, Mme de 142
population, early modern rise in 111
Portugal 85, 92, 212

post-feminism 302–4
Precious Record from the Maidens'
    Chambers 155
priestesses 66, 67
Prince, Mary 166–8
professions 200–4
property 23
prostitution
  casual, seasonality of 180
  for cause of Japanese nation-building
      188
  medicalization 198–9
protestantism 73, 82
protests 136, 177, 181
Proudhon, Pierre-Joseph 178
proxy wars 280
Pueblo Indians 63
purges, Soviet 271–2
purity 171
Purple Hibiscus 302
Pussy Riot 298
Putin, Vladimir 304

Qajar Iran 188–9
Qi Lin 149
Qing Empire 111, 191
Qiu Jin 194
Quadafi, Moamar 2
queen mothers 45
queer dressing 41
querelle des femmes 62, 80–1
quinine 13
Quispe Sisa (Inés Huaylas Yupanqui) 94
Quito 122–3
Qu'ran,
  description 56
  literacy to read 62, 130
  phrases on Egyptian factory walls
      293
  Umm Kulthuum and 268
  on women 56–7, 62
  Zebunissa recites entirely 128, 130

racism,
  feminists charged with 238
  hard times and 5
  indigenous women protest 299
  post-colonial novels target 281
  revival of Nazi racism 263

survives fall of empires 277
Radha 55
Raicho Hiratsuke 195
Rama 66
Ramabai, Pandita 203
Ramadan 216
Ramayana 66, 75, 224
Rangi Topaera 227
Ransome-Kuti, Funmilayo 264, 266, 267
rape 93, 94, 260. *See also* "violence"
Rape of Nanjing 251
raw materials 165
reading and literacy 28, 62, 72
Reading Lolita in Teheran 301
reaper 161
Red Lanterns 219, 262
Reformation, Protestant 72
religion
  Aztec syncretism 104
  in early colonial expansion 103
  increased early modern male dominance 64
  Japanese syncretism 104
  leadership 135
  non-Christians as backwards 222
  religious orders 71
Renaissance 72
reproduction
  child-rearing as essential part of 14
  complexities of cross-ethnic reproduction 107
  as concern of shamans 66
  controlled for community well-being 14
  customs of 15
  eugenics and 226
  harems as site of rule as well as 42
  ingredient of rulership 39
  modern conjugal couple and 172
  monitored by early modern community 18
  after Qing takeover 93
  slave reproduction 166
republican motherhood 146, 156
resistance
  African and Pacific women 227
  to empire 226–31
  South African mine workers 226
to state power 136
  varieties of late nineteenth-century South Africa 228–30
revolts
  general contours of, 1750–1830 136
  jihadis in Africa versus non-Muslim slavers 136
  slave revolts in Caribbean 147
  versus Spain, 1740s-1780s 137
revolution, early modern and modern objectification of blacks and women 156
revolutions, against Spain 150–3
Richards, Mary 159, 161
Riefenstahl, Leni 246
rights
  eradicated in French Revolution 147
  vocabulary of in eighteenth-early nineteenth revolutionary period 156
rituals 11, 32–3
Rivera, Diego 247
Robinson, Mary 295–6
Rockefeller, women of family 224
Roosevelt, Eleanor 271
Roosevelt, Theodore 225
Rose, Ernestine 192
Rosenberg, Ethel 271–2
Rousseau, Jean-Jacques 154
rulership 38, 41, 46–7
Rozanova, Olga 246
Russia
  early modern expansion of borders 88
  First World War 236
  literacy 128
  reeducation of Muslim women 214
Russian Revolution 237–38

Sacagawea 136
Sachs, Nelly 277
Saenz, Manuela 152, **153**
St. Pierre Ruffin, Josephine 199
saints 70
Sakamoto Ryoma 187
Salavarrieta, Policarpa 151
salons 142
same-sex relationships 16–17, 42, 48, 226

Samurai 187–8
San Juan, Caterina de 104
San Luis Potosi 173
Sanger, Margaret 247–8
Scheherezade 61–2
school desegregation 279
science 112
Scientific Revolution 125–8
Seacole, Mary 200–1
seclusion 25, 124
Second World War 235, 251–6
    African Americans in 255
    Asian famine inflicted 252
    Allied powers—China, Great Britain,
        France, USSR, United States 251
    Axis powers—Japan, Italy, Germany
        251
    comfort women 255–6
    everyday life 252–3
    guards in extermination camps 255
    Jews 253
    Jews at Stalingrad 255
    resistance, spies, seducers 253, 256
    Soviet aviators 254
    Stalingrad 253–5
    use of women workers 252, 253, 255,
        256
Seito 195–202
Selim I 41
Seneca 149
service sector (white collar) 202–3
Seven Days War 275
sewing machine 161
sex
    assault of slaves 169
    Catholic attitudes towards sex 94
    "floating world" of urban sex
        workers 15–16
    harems not entirely places for sex 48
    invaders attitudes towards sex 94
    Ottoman court and 48
    sex segregation as power system 38
    sexual relations to produce laborers
        18
    Tantric ritual as holy 17
sexual division of labor 176
sexual harassment 164
Sha'arawi, Huda 242–3
Shahryar (King) 61

Shaka 150
shamans 51–2, 66
Shan Xiuzen 259
Shanghai cotton mills 176
Sheppard, Kate 205
Sima Guang 25
Simango, Celina 274–5
Sinn Fein (We Ourselves) 230
Sino-Japanese War 209
Sirleaf, Ellen Johnson 286
Sita 66
Sitt al-Mulk (Fatamid queen) 57
The Slave Girl 278
slave owners 98, 135
    white women as 98
slave trade 107
    Portugal establishes Atlantic trade 92
    seventeenth century expansion
        increases violence in Africa 113
slavery
    abolition of 106
    ads for runaways 166
    African women 2
    Asian slaves in Western Hemisphere
        97
    Atlantic world 155
    botanical and food processing skills
        important 160
    British justification for 136
    captured along Indian Ocean coasts
        96
    late abolition of in United States,
        Cuba, and Brazil 174
    Native American women trade in
        slaves 32
    opportunities to gain cash 169
    perceived need of African workers in
        Western Hemisphere 95
    pirates and 31–2
    raw materials for industry produced
        165–6
    replaced by day and indentured labor
        172
    runaways 97
        Brazil 169
    wars to obtain slaves 136
    wartime captives sold 31–2
    wetnursing 169
Smith, Zadie 301–2

So Long a Letter 278
Social Darwinism 177, 220, 225
sociability
    everyday life 32
    in favelas 235
    footbinding and 101
    Mandan 21
    Mughal court 17
    uninstructed women and 198
Society of St. Vincent de Paul, Mexico
        City 173
soldiers 231, **269**
"Song of Living Corpses," (Japan)
        19–180
Soo Chin-yee 263
Soong, Mai-ling (Mme Chiang-Kaishek)
        246
Soros, George 297
South Africa 228, 267
South Asia 173
Soviet bloc 271
Spain 87, 93, 212
spirit possession 51
Stanton, Elizabeth Cady 192
state, dynastic 42
state-building 43, 281
status 98–9
status of women, UN findings 298
Stowe, Harriet Beecher 192
street sellers 117
Student Non-Violent Coordinating
        Committee (SNCC) 279
Suarez, Ines 88
suffrage 205–6
Sufism 68–70, 71, 128
suicide, mass
    factory workers, twenty-first century
        292
    Japan, Meiji Restoration protest 185
    Ming China, chastity cult 80
    partition of India 267
    Qing takeover 99–101
    South Asia, widows 24, 33
    Taiping Rebellion 191
    White Lotus Rebellion 149
Sukarnoputri, Megawatii 306
Suleyman, Sultan 41, 43
"The Sultana's Dream" 205
sumptuary laws 124

Sundiata 61, 74, 82, 112
support personnel for armies 2
Suriyothi, Thai queen 39
Suttner, Bertha von 237
"Susanna and the Elders" 78
Swing Time 302
Syria, journalists 202

Tagore, Rabindranath 268
Taiping movement 191–2, 194
Tale of Genji 62, 75
Taliban 285, 304–5
Tanizaki Junichiro 245
Tanzania, Maasai women's activism
        300
Taras, The 64
Tatsu'uma Kiyo 165
teapicking, China 27–8
teaching, in European universities 127
technology 159
    reproductive 285
    in "The Sultana's Dream" 205–6
Tecuichpotzin 94
Terrell, Mary Church 199–200
temple dancers 199
textiles
    artisanal craft for home and trade 29
    domestic work of women 34
    early factories 161
    Indian cottons 116
    industrialization 161
    laws prohibiting wearing of Indian
        cottons 141
    trade in Chinese and South Asian
        cottons 87
Thatcher, Margaret 303
Their Eyes Were Watching God 246
Theosophy 224–5
Thirty Years' War 113
Thought Woman (Tsichtinako) 63
time, modernization of 197–8
Tlazolteotl (goddess of sexuality) 51
To Ayo 37–8
trade
    Anishinabe with Europeans 89
    early modern global expansion 111
    Mandan with Native Americans and
        Europeans 89
    networks in Southeast Asia 115

North American, sixteenth–
   eighteenth centuries 89
Siam (Thailand) 31
trafficking,
   post-First World War 240
   Shanghai 180
trans people 309
transgender (Berdache) 40–1
translators 112
transsexuals 288
Trung sisters 73
Truth, Sojourner 192
Tubman, Harriet 192, **193**, 280
Tung Pai 78
Tunisia 47
Tupac Ameru uprising 137, 150
Tuqan Fadwa 275
Turing, Alan 271
Turkey, International Women's Suffrage
   Alliance meeting in 204

Uchtsiti (father god) 63
Ulloa, Antonio de 122
Ulloa, Jorge Juan de 122
Uncle Tom's Cabin 192
Union of Soviet Socialist Republics
   (USSR)
   Cold War 260
   post-Second World War downgrading
      of women's jobs 261
   postwar daily life 271
   postwar push for fertility 261
   women in postwar economy 261
UN Commission on Human
   Rights 270
UN Decade of the Woman 294
United Nations 269–70
   activism at 294
   postwar women's rights 256, 260
United States
   Civil War 192
   civilizing mission 215–16
   Cold War 260
   deposes Liliuokalani and seizes
      Hawaii 223–4
   "A Doll's House" 195
   fails to ratify CEDAW 297
   First World War 236
   hunt for Communists 272

indirect rule of Cuba and Puerto Rico
   218
invades Haiti 244
nation-building 187
seizes Philippines 218
universities, women's colleges
   and 203
urbanization 181
   co-habitation without marriage 172
   Cuba 169
   early modern urbanization brings
      rising literacy 62
   increases need for education 155
   India 180
   live as individuals rather than in
      family 172
   job growth 164–5
   late nineteenth century India and
      Accra, Ghana 210
   more opportunity to buy freedom in
      cities 169
   post-First World War China 240
   prostitution in 180
Utako Shimoda 193, 199

Validivia, Pedro de 88
Vargas, Getulio 251
Victoria, (Queen and Empress, Britain)
   204, 209–10, 219
Vietnam 195
Vietnam War 273–4
Vigée Le Brun, Elisabeth 142
"Vindication of the Liberties of the
   Asiatic Woman" (1801) 154
Vindication of the Rights of Woman
   153
violence 9–10
   against African slaves in the Americas
      97
   by Belgians during rule in Congo
      213–14
   bombings of schoolchildren 285
   against environmentalists 295–6
   by European conquerors on their
      local wives 94
   of European, Mughal, Manchu,
      Ottoman and other imperial
      invaders 88
   general in early modern life 34

by invaders and imperialists during
    sixteenth-century globalization 87
partition of India 266–7
during Qing takeover of China 93
twenty-first century 306
visual arts 246–7
Voltaire 127

Waddadar, Preeti 243
Wafd 242
wages 163–4
Wang Cong'er 149
Wang Qingdi 191
Wang Yun 130–1
Wanyan Yun Zhu 155
warfare, seventeenth century 112
Warren, Mercy Otis 140
warriors and other armed women 39
    ghazis in Ottoman Empire 41
    Mulan as 74
    Nzinga as 101–2
    prowess of Babur, Monteczuma,
        Suleyman 41
    Soviet aviators 254
    Vietcong 273–4
    Western Hemisphere conquest by 88–9
Wartime Child Protection Association
    252
Wartime Child Welfare Protection
    Association 252
Washington, George 97
Washington, Martha 97
welfare state 270
Wells, Ida B. 226
West Africa 92
wetnursing 169–70
Wheatley, Phillis 156
White Lotus Uprising 149
white male superiority, in Darwin 225
White Teeth 301–2
widows 23–4, 101, 119
wife, head 21
Wilson, Woodrow 237
Winslow, Anna Green 139
witchcraft 103
Wollstonecraft, Mary 152–4, 155, 156,
    188
Women in Black 276
"women identified women" 279

women worthies 6
Women's Christian Temperance Union
    205, 223
Women's Directorial Committee of the
    New Life Movement 252
Women's International League for Peace
    and Freedom (WILPF) 237, 244
women's oppression, as excuse for
    invasions and colonization 221
women's rights in Asia and Europe
    compared 154
Women's War of 1929 242, 268
work
    Accra, Ghana, late nineteenth century
        210–11
    Chinese women, early modern 27–8
    First World War 236
    industry 159–65
    Iroquois patterns of 21
    migrants 289
    Second World War 252
    as slaves in African copper mines 32
    slaves produce raw materials for
        industry 165 passim
    tribute work 26
    twenty-first century 285
    wet nursing 169
World's fair, the Hague 223
writers 62, 142, 210, 283–4, 301–2

Xhosa 227
Xi Wangmu (Divine Goddess of the
    West) 65–6
Xochiquetzel (goddess of sexual excess
    and general disorder) 51

Yaa Asantewaa 210
Yousafzai, Malala 285, 305
Yu Gwa-sun 241
Yu Shih 78

Zaire (Democratic Republic of Congo)
    266
Zapata, Emiliano 231
Zebunissa 127–8, 129–30
Zen Flesh, Zen Bones 65
Zero, Joana de Masi 251
Zetkin, Clara 178
Zitkala-Sa 215, 228